Portuguese Immigrants

(The Centennial Story of the Portuguese Union of the State of California)

by

Carlos Almeida

SECOND EDITION
(REVISED AND ENLARGED)

Supreme Council of U.P.E.C.
San Leandro, California

Printing: Offset Lithography; Suburban Press, Hayward, CA.

LIBRARY OF CONGRESS CATALOG NO. 78-111293

Cover: "The Emigrants" (os Emigrantes) by Domingos Rebelo, Carlos Machado Museum, Ponta Delgada, S. Miguel Azores.
                                                              — Photo by Nobrega

To my daughters — Debbie and Patty

CONTENTS

Page

List of Illustrations v

Introduction ix

I Azores — Source of Immigration to the Americas 1

II The Whale Hunters 6

III The Saga of Andrade 8

IV The Hawaiian Paradise 14

V By Way of Canada 19

VI The Cradle of the Portuguese Fraternal Movement 25

VII San Leandro — Home Away From Home 31

VIII Annual Conventions 40

IX Protection 52

X Charity at Home 57

XI Charity Abroad 61

XII The U.P.E.C. Bulletin 68

XIII Why a Hymn? 73

XIV From Uniform Rank to Band 76

XV Home Office 80

XVI Civic Participation 87
Independence Day — 4th Centennial of Vasco da
Gama — The Visit of the Cruiser *San Gabriel* — The
Panama Pacific Exposition — 5th Centennial of the
Discovery of the Azores — Golden Gate International
Exposition — The Monument to the Portuguese Immi-
grant — Portuguese Immigrant Week — U.P.E.C. Day

XVII The League of Portuguese Fraternal Societies 125

XVIII Education Through Teaching of Language and Culture 130

XIX The Cultural Center 135

XX Dreams That Never Came True 137

XXI Giants in Their Time 144

XXII Built on Respect 148

BIOGRAPHIES:

Supreme Presidents:

1. António Fonte 155

2. José Pimentel 157

3. John G. Mattos 158

4. Francisco Ignacio de Lemos 159

5. António Fernandes Cunha 160

6. Victorino Teodóro Braga 161

7. Antonio José Pinheiro 162

8. João Valadão 163

i

9. Firmino José Cunha 164
10. António Maria Martins 165
11. Jesse Henry Woods 165
12. Manuel Fraga 166
13. Louis Alfred Enos 167
14. José Pereira Mendonça 167
15. António Augusto Sarmento 168
16. João Pereira 170
17. José de Vargas Pereira 170
18. José Carlos Jorge Lawrence 171
19. Anthony Wilson 172
20. Guilherme Francisco Pereira 173
21. José Jacinto Pimentel 173
22. Antonio José Homem 174
23. Manuel Gregorio Azevedo 175
24. José Caetano Avelar 176
25. João Dutra 176
26. José Chrysostomo da Silveira 177
27. Francisco Monteiro Silveira 178
28. António Raulino 179
29. Manuel Severino Soares 179
30. Frank Mitchell Junior 180
31. Frank S. Costa 181
32. Joseph Anthony Freitas 181
33. Manuel Gaspar 183
34. Thomas Francis Lopes 184
35. Frank Silveira Roderick 185
36. Lucindo Freitas 185
37. Francisco Eustachio Pinheiro 186
38. Francis Joseph Lazarus 187
39. Joseph J. Cardoso 188
40. Anthony Joseph Silva 188
41. Francisco António Freitas 190
42. Francisco Hipólito da Rosa 191
43. Manuel John Perry 192
44. Joseph Thomas Lopes 192
45. Manuel Vieira Alves 193
46. Angelo Ramos Ignacio 193
47. Manuel Augusto Freitas 194
48. Arthur Silveira Sousa 195
49. Fernando Augusto Silveira 196
50. Manuel Cabral 197
51. Valentim Macedo Garcia 198

ii

52.	Manuel Pereira	199
53.	Francisco Santos Mendonsa	200
54.	Louis Leslie Vieira	201
55.	Albert Carvalhal Silveira	201
56.	John Bettencourt Simas	292
57.	Manuel da Rosa Furtado	203
58.	João Ferreira Nunes	204
59.	Manuel Ignacio Mendonça	204
60.	Vicente Francisco Azevedo	205
61.	Miguel Borba Azevedo	206
62.	Samuel Machado Lino	206
63.	Edward Clement Massa	207
64.	Francisco Machado Linhares	208
65.	Antone Edward Braga	209
66.	Manuel Neves	209
67.	Manuel Barcellos Silva	210
68.	William Augustine Gerevas	211
69.	Joseph Costa Fagundes	211
70.	William Gier	212
71.	Joe Silva Junior	213
72.	Lewis Correia	214
73.	João Herberto Alves	214
74.	Joseph Machado Faria	215
75.	Tony Xavier	216
76.	Manuel Furtado Simas	216
77.	António Pereira Neves	217
78.	George Anthony Azevedo	217
79.	Steve Machado	218
80.	Victor Gomes	218
81.	Mary Mathias	219
82.	John Gonsalves Vieira	220
83.	Edward C. Costa	221
84.	Helio T. Sousa	221
85.	John J. Machado	222
86.	Hubert J. Trindade	222
87.	George L. Teixeira	223
88.	Adelino Santos	223
89.	Manuel R. Medeiros	224
90.	Mary I. Pereira	224
91.	George E. Corvelo	225
92.	Ilidio C. Pereira	225
93.	Joe C. Rosa	226
94.	Joe P. Rosa	226

Medical Examiners:
      Andrew Joseph Dean 227
      José de Sousa Bettencourt 227
      João Sérgio Alvares Cabral 228
      José Leal de Azevedo 229
      Carlos Fernandes 230
      Luiz Julio Madeira 232
Honorary Members:
      Euclides Goulart da Costa 234
      John Musso 234
      Francisco P. Aragão E. Costa 235
      António de Freitas Pimentel, M.D. 235
      Maria F.P.D. Pimentel, M.D. 236
      Jose Luiz Trigueiros de Aragão 236
      Numidico Bessone 237
      Vasco Vieira Garin 237
      António Leal da Costa Lobo 238
      António Duarte Nogueira, M.D. 238
      Dinis A. Pimentel Silva 239
      António Pinto Machado 239
      Tony Coelho 240
      João Bosco Mota Amaral 240
The Causa Portuguesa Award 241
Lucio José Martinho 242
Manuel Elias Amaral 242
Carlos Almeida 243
Lucio da Silva Gonsalves 244
Guilherme Silveira da Glória 255
Manuel Costa Medeiros 257

APPENDICES
    1. Members Who Served in the Supreme Council
        (other than President, Secretary, and Medical Examiner) 260
    2. U.P.E.C. Subordinate Councils 264
    3. Family Names of Early Portuguese Immigrants in California . . 268
    4. Anglicized California Portuguese Family Names 271

BIBLIOGRAPHY 276

INDEX 281

LIST OF ILLUSTRATIONS

Page

Map of the Azores *(Comissão Regional de Turismo, Açores)* 2
Ad published in the *Progresso Californiense,* 1885 3
Oldest U.S. Synagogue, Newport, R.I. 4
Copy of document No. 31 — Annals of Lajes, Flores 6
The mangling of whale *(Author's Collection)* 7
Manuel Silveira d'Andrade *(Mary J. Vargas)* 8
Facsimile of page of Andrade's diary 8
Facsimile of naturalization document 11
Whaling ships at Honolulu *(Makelina Ltd., Hawaii)* 18
The last good-bye for many *(Author's Collection)* 19
Father and son hugging before boarding ship *(Author's Collection)* 20
Examination of hands for callouses 21
Portuguese immigrants — A labor force *(Author's Collection)* 21
Emigrants bound for Canada *(Author's Collection)* 22
Capelinho's volcanic eruption — Faial *(Urbano Melo Lopes)* 23
Facsimile of constitution of Irmandade Portuguesa 28
St. Joseph's Hall 28
Facsimile of front page of constitution, U.P.E.C. 29
San Leandro, Archbishop of Seville *(Museum of Seville, Spain)* 31
Application for membership used in the 1890s 32
Hall of U.P.E.C. Council No. 1 *(Author's Collection)* 35
Hall of U.P.E.C. Council No. 13 35
Ballot Boxes 36
Preamble of U.P.E.C. Constitution (1892) 37
Column of *Progresso Californiense* (1885) Indagações 37
Initiation team, Vasco da Gama *(Berniece Silva)* 38
Sample of U.P.E.C. Badges 38
Facsimile of resolution signed by António Fonte 39
Invitation and program for the dedication of hall of Council No. 1 41
Facsimile of fidelity bond 42
Founders of U.P.E.C. Council No. 81-Santa Cruz 43
Drill team, U.P.E.C. Council No. 66-Santa Maria *(Joe Silva Jr.)* 43
Different designs of U.P.E.C. emblems 44
Fourth U.P.E.C. Annual Convention *(Clementina Vaz)* 45
Delegates and Officers at 19th Annual Convention 45
U.P.E.C. Uniform Rank *(Addie May Silva)* 47
U.P.E.C. Officers in regalia, City Hall, San Leandro *(Andy Galvan)* 47
1903 announcement — Panoramic views 48
Invitations from Subordinate Councils 49

Portuguese farm house — San Leandro *(Andy Galvan)* 50
U.P.E.C. delegation, 15th Annual Convention, San Luis Obispo, 1901 51
U.P.E.C. delegation in session, Oakland, 1972 51
Copy of assessment notice 52
Facsimile of membership certificate — Class "B" 53
House for the aged 54
The most outstanding leaders of U.P.E.C.'s early life *(Clementina Vaz)* 55
Article on Saint Anthony's Hospital *Reporter (Barbara Silveira)* 58
Copy of the report from Faial — Donations 59
Facsimile of a letter — Fund raising drive — Povoação 62
Copy of a letter requesting funds for Horta's hospital 63
Rua da Areia, Horta, Faial, after 1897 earthquake 65
Clothing unloading at São Jorge, 1964 *(U.S. Air Force)* 65
Copy of a check payable to President Woodrow Wilson 66
Front page of U.P.E.C. Bulletin, Issue No. 1 69
Back page of U.P.E.C. Bulletin, Issue No. 1 70
Facsimile of cover of U.P.E.C. Hymn, first edition 74
Reverend Joaquim S. Serrão *(Dr. Fernando R. Costa)* 74
U.P.E.C. Uniform Rank 76
Resolution of thanks to Mário B. Camara 77
U.P.E.C. Band, 1906 78
Minutes of the ceremony of the laying of corner stone 81
Memento of dedication of U.P.E.C. Building 83
U.P.E.C. original Home Office 84
U.P.E.C. Home Office and Cultural Center *(Nello Giannini)* 84
Conference Room 86
U.P.E.C. Home Office dedication ceremonies, 1964 86
Facsimile of front page of U.P.E.C. Bulletin, 1904 88
Circular letter announcing committee reception, *San Gabriel* 89
First Page of visitors book at the Supreme Council 91
Signatures and comments — Commander of the *San Gabriel* 92
Cruiser *San Gabriel (Dr. António Pinto Machado)* 93
Front page of *O Imparcial (Barbara Silveira)* 95
Silveira, Dr. Bettencourt and Lemos, Lisbon *(Ilustração Portuguesa, Lisbon)* .. 96
Portuguese Pavilion 97
Dedication ceremonies of Portuguese Pavilion *(Joe Comelli)* 98
Tower of Jewels 98
Portugalia, March 1932, 5th Centennial of Azores 102
Miss Maria Homem 103
Scene from *Life of Queen Elizabeth* play *(Leopoldina C.R. Alves)* 104
U.P.E.C. folklore group 104
Golden Gate International Expo 105
Stand of Portugal 106

Portuguese Pavilion *(Alberto Correa)* 107

Excursion of the club *Castles of Portugal (Alberto Correa)* 108

Golden Gate Expo — Portuguese Day Committee *(Alberto Correa)* 108

U.P.E.C. Float — Portuguese Day Parade *(Alberto Correa)* 109

Actress Ilda Stichini *(Alberto Correa)* 111

Monument to João Rodrigues Cabrilho *(Alberto Correa)* 111

Sculptor Numidico Bessone, Caxias *(Author's Collection)* 114

Assembly of monument *(Author's Collection)* 116

António Braz, John Silva and Joe Gonsalves 116

Dedication ceremonies — Monument to Portuguese Immigrant 117

Message from Mota de Vasconcelos 118

Judge Manuel "Jesse" Bettencourt 119

Governor Ronald Reagan signing resolution *(Amancio C. Leite)* 120

Assembly rules committee — resolution 121

Portuguese Immigrant Week Banquet *(Amancio C. Leite)* 122

U.P.E.C. civic participation — Sister City 122

U.P.E.C. leaders received by Governor of the Azores
(Foto Rápida San Miguel, Azores) 123

U.P.E.C. soccer team 124

U.P.E.C. baseball team — Orland, California 125

Facsimile of a check issued by League 126

Guns on display at Hotel Oakland *(Alberto Correa)* 126

Luncheon served U.S. Soldiers, World War I 127

J.C. Valim, teacher of Portuguese *(Revista Portuguesa, Hayward, California)* . 131

Chief Justice Earl Warren 131

Lecture Hall, U.P.E.C. Cultural Center 135

João B. Mota Amaral — visitor at *J.A. Freitas* Library 136

Resolution authorizing Board of Directors merger 138

M.T. Freitas *(Revista Portuguesa, Hayward, California)* 144

Full page ad — Portuguese-American Bank 145

J.A. Silveira *(Revista Portuguesa, Hayward, California)* 146

Contents of invitation to King Carlos of Portugal 149

Telegram sent to the President of the United States 150

U.P.E.C. State Youth Council 151

Copy of a telegram sent by President John F. Kennedy 152

Certificate of decoration given by the Portuguese Government 153

Message of Supreme President of U.P.P.E.C. 153

Except where noted, all photographs are from the J.A. Freitas Library collection.

INTRODUCTION

The history of the União Portuguesa do Estado da California has intrigued me since 1959, the time I became involved as its Supreme Secretary-Treasurer. My curiosity grew as I held informal conversations with leaders of the fraternal movement, many of them old-time members who had rubbed shoulders with our pioneers.

In July of 1968 I decided to do research in an attempt to shed light on the beginnings of our fraternal society, its founding and the role it played in the lives of thousands who came to know the inside of the society.

I began my research by first learning about the backgrounds and lives of our early presidents and officers. The more I learned about them the more fascinating my work became. One fact led to another and out of my investigations came the idea of this book. The available newspapers and society records, most of them written in Portuguese, provided the majority of my information.

The history of the U.P.E.C. is indeed part of that of a people who helped make California a better state and a giant in the dairy and agricultural fields. It was here that the Portuguese immigrants, mostly from the Azores, found themselves at their best.

My work could not have been completed without the help of individuals like Dr. Francisco Carreiro da Costa, Azorean folklorist; João Afonso, writer; Lyle A. and Carmen Moya Cox; Peggy Hannigan Collett; José Salgueiro; and Alberto Correa, who helped me many times to find the connection between events he witnessed and experienced as one of the oldest Portuguese newspapermen in California.

My appreciation to my wife Fernanda for her encouragement at all times and to all Portuguese immigrants and their descendants who were always ready to talk with me and give accounts of the experiences they lived through, not only in their home villages, but also after their arrival in the United States. Their initiative and courage are indeed examples for the Portuguese newcomer to follow.

Carlos Almeida

San Leandro, California
July, 1978

x

AZORES
SOURCE OF IMMIGRATION TO THE AMERICAS

To better understand the reasons behind the immigration of Portuguese from the Azores to California, one should try to perceive the nature of their birthplace. The Azores Archipelago, also known as the Western Islands, is situated in the North Atlantic and was the second or third discovery in a series that would make Portuguese seafarers the most intrepid in the world. This boldness and seamanship gained for their tiny country a reputation which persists to this day.

Azores is named after a bird found in this area and is described as being the hawk family, believed later to be the buzzard, *Milhafre.* There are in total nine beautiful islands which legend attributes as being the remains of the Continent of Atlantis (Atlantida), found in the descriptions of *Chrythias* by Plato. The islands are approximately 814 (N.A.) miles west of Portugal and 2,008 (N.A.) miles east of New York. Historians are still not quite in agreement on the question of discovery, but generally point to the year of 1427 as being the date of the finding of the island of Santa Maria, leaving Flores and Corvo undiscovered until 1452.

Santa Maria, the southern most island, and the first discovered, comprises an area of nearly thirty-eight square miles. Here Columbus' crews paused on their return from their first trip of the discovery of America.

San Miguel, the largest and most industrious, has an area of 288 square miles. It contains more than fifty percent of the entire population of the archipelago, approximately 265,000 inhabitants. Terceira, meaning the third in discovery, has an area of 153 square miles and possesses a most important air base, a strategic element in the balance of European powers, dating back to World War II. Graciosa, meaning Gracious, with an area of approximately 24 square miles, is followed in size by São Jorge with ninety-two square miles. The latter is famous for cheeses, said to be made of recipes brought by Flemish settlers.

On the western part of the archipelago lies Faial (Beechgrove), at one time the best known island of the Azores. Faial has an area of sixty-six square miles, and elegantly watches the majestic island of Pico, the second largest covering an area of 168 square miles. On the western most tip is the last discovered jewel: Flores (Flowers) with fifty-five square miles and Corvo (The Crow) totalling nearly seven square miles with a population which has never exceeded eight hundred inhabitants. Of these last two islands, Flores played an important role in navigation and immigration to America.

The Azoreans, excellent agricultural people, courageous fishermen and whale hunters for centuries, came from a mixture of ethnic groups which include Moors, Romans and Anglo-Saxons. The first settlers arrived in 1439 and are said to have come from Algarve and other parts of Portugal. Later the French and Flemish came to the area.

The first Lord Lieutenant of the island of Faial was a Flemish nobleman, Josse de Hurtere, a name from which Horta, capital of that island, is derived. Items existing today such as: the windmills, the solid wheel ox-carts and the costumes can be traced to these early settlers. The popular feast of St. Mark, *Festa dos Cornos,* celebrated on the 25th of April of each year in Faial and other islands, is another of the few testimonies of the Flemish presence, not to mention the blue eyes and blond hair adorning many Azoreans.

The islands' history includes the French and Spanish who engaged in sea battles off their rugged coasts. The French of Breton are said to have touched the island of São Miguel. Constance de Rohan, Princess of Soubise, married the Count of Ribeira Grande in 1684.

The inhabitants of these islands survived throughout centuries of disasters such as earthquakes which, time and again, destroyed their villages, often by complete burial. Additionally, they had to fight pirates who came from England and hid in the coves of the islands awaiting the Portuguese vessels on their way to Lisbon loaded with spices and skins from India. Crops were destroyed by strong winds; vines were attacked by illness, crippling wine production for European markets as well as destroying acres and acres of delicious oranges, abundant at one time in the Azores for export. These factors coupled with the sad fact that Azoreans were vastly ignored by the homeland, left the populace to their sad destiny — ignorant and illiterate, exploited by the self-imposed aristocracy who, with a few exceptions, would worsen those conditions for their own economic and social benefit.

In most cases, land was poorly divided, leaving the working population in a status of forever renting the land. They had to work in order to support their large families and pay fees and royalties. These fees took the form of shares of crops called for in the agreements and leases of the landlords.

The islands, with their exuberant scenery consisting of flora species from all over the world: palm trees, banana bushes, azaleas, camellias, tobacco and tea, were not so appealing to those whom fortune had given these "Black Rocks" as a birthplace. However, one alternative was always available. It laid beyond the vast horizons — emigration to faraway lands. At times the Azoreans wished they could settle in the wealthy Portuguese possessions of Angola and Mozambique in Africa. But, every time they tried, they found their wishes met by so much red tape that they ended up going to the Americas, for it was easier to go there than to their country's overseas provinces.

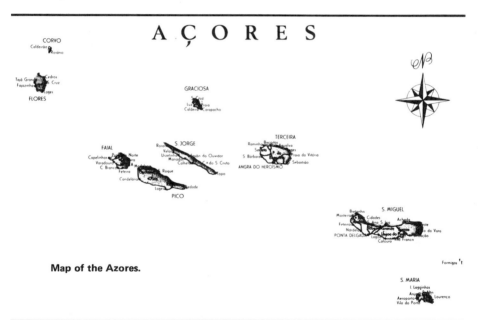

AÇORES

Map of the Azores.

The Azorean had experienced the worst, therefore, he was ready to adapt to any new situation, no matter how difficult. He left by sailing ship, later by steam and most recently by air. He left hoping to come back and enjoy the peace and beauty of those ugly rocks lost in the middle of the Atlantic. He never did return to stay. At least most of them never did. Yet, as strange as it seems, the Azorean has always had a longing for his place of birth — black basalt adobes covered with whitewash in

2

Ad in the "Progresso Californiense" newspaper published in San Francisco, Ca. in 1885.

the middle of the plush green of the islands. That hope for returning home was, in part, a stimulus to endure life in a strange land.

Here they came — by the thousands — poor, timid and very often illiterate. But they possessed a strong will to conquer and better themselves economically so that their descendants would not have to suffer the humiliations they did in the Azores or in the early days of life in the promised land, the U.S.A. They came to California lured by the whaling vessel captains and attracted by the news of the Gold Rush. They arrived by way of Hawaii, Canada and Brazil.

Azoreans were already a product of emigration from European Portugal and other countries. Therefore, their descendants continued a destiny forced upon them by geographic and economic circumstances. Their departure from these islands was at times considered a blessing both for those who ventured to the unknown and for those who stayed behind. Those left behind were relieved of an ever-growing population confined to limited space and resources. Jobs left by those who emigrated were absorbed by the many unemployed. In later years these acquired blessings would have another dimension. Besides decreasing the number of mouths to be fed, emigration represented a source of income. Often times, the immigrant would send to the islands much of his savings, to pay for debts incurred prior to departure, purchase a house and land, or simply to help support family members who could not earn enough to live.

As it turned out, many of these immigrants never achieved their wishes of returning home. As time went by, they became accustomed to the new world that destiny had forced upon them, and their bones were buried here and there, along with those sacrifices and deeds left unsung.

The major emigration movements from the Azores were registered around the sixteenth century towards Africa and India. Later on Azoreans sought Brazil as an escape from their hard life and it was not until the 19th century that they came in large numbers to the United States of America and more recently to Canada. The Portuguese also came from Continental Portugal, Madeira, Cape Verde Islands and other provinces, including Macau in China, but in a percentage much smaller than from the Azores.

Oldest U.S. synagogue dedicated in Newport, R.I., in 1763, where services were conducted in Portuguese for many years.

4

The first Portuguese of record immigrating to the U.S.A. were Jews from Brazil who escaped persecution in that country and came to settle in New Amsterdam (New York) around 1654. In 1763 they built, in Newport, Rhode Island, what is known today as the oldest synagogue in our country. By the time of the Revolutionary War in 1776, there were between two and three thousand Jews in all colonies, most of them merchants and traders known as *Sephardin,* descendants of Portuguese and Spanish. In the Azores the expression *Safardão* is apparently derived from *Sephardin,* which meant a smart dealer, able to persuade.

In later years whaling, one of the major industries of this country, became responsible for most of the Portuguese emigration from the island of Brava, the Cape Verde group, and from the Azores. Azoreans were lured aboard whaling vessels that would touch Azorean (Flores and Faial) and Cape Verdean coastlines. These ships were seeking supplies and laborers able enough to endure the long voyages necessary to reach the hunting ground of the sperm whale in the Pacific Ocean, along Northern California, Alaskan and Russian coasts.

THE WHALE HUNTERS

How did Azoreans make their way to the west coast? For an answer, one must go back more than a century and search in those logs and letters, numbering in the hundreds, written by both the captains and crews of whaling vessels which crossed the oceans. The center of the large whaling industry was located on the east coast of the United States.

These "amphibious factories" produced thousands of barrels of extract of whale oil — not to mention margarine, soaps, artificial wool, meat extracts, flour, fertilizers and even Vitamins A and B. The pancreas of the whale supplied insulin. Later, as mineral oils were discovered, the whale oil lost its market in the U.S.A. decreasing almost to nonexistence. In the words of Barrows, in his book *The Great Comodore,* in the year 1845, the Port of New Bedford registered 685 whaling vessels sailing under the U.S. flag, alone.

These vessels would leave New Bedford and cross the Atlantic in search of whale. A stopover in the Azores was part of the routine. The island of Faial offered conditions to refuel, repair and supply these vessels; for in Horta, capital of the island, there were the Dabneys, an American family who had spent over a century as the only consignees for every ship that touched the island's port.

Their commercial initiatives promoted not only their own wealth, but also that of many others. Their spirit of enterprise made the island better known, more sought by navigation and foreigners, and transformed its port into an important maritime center.

John Pomeroy Dabney was the first of the Dabneys to come to Faial. He was named American Consul in 1808 and died years later leaving a son, Charles William,

DOCUMENTO N.º 31

Mapa dos Navios q. entrarão na Ilha das Flores em fodo o ano de 1811 (a)

Nação	Nome dos navios	Portos donde vem	Portos para onde vam	que carga ou refresco tomaram	Com que pagaram
Escuna portuguesa	N. S. das Angustias	Fayal	Fayal	carregada e veio em lastro	—
Sumaca portuguesa	Fortaleza	navio da terra	Fayal	foi carregada e veio em lastro	—
Sumaca portuguesa	Fortaleza	navio da terra	Madeira	foi carregada e veio em lastro	--
Escuna portuguesa	N. S. das Angustias	Fayal	Fayal	veio em lastro e foi carregada	—
Escuna portuguess	Ligeira	Madeira	Madeira	veio carregada e foi carregada	—
Sumaca portuguea	Fortaleźa	navio da terra	Fayal	foi carregada e veio carregada	—
Escuna portuguesa	Carellote	ilha 3.ª	ilha 3.ª	veio em lastro e foi carregada	—
Barg. Londrista	Jos Mout	Da Terra Nova	irlanda	refrescar, galinhas, porcos, ovos	Dinheiro
Galera amoricana	Leri	Luverpol	Findelfe	refrescar galinhas, porcos, ovos	»
Galera amoricana	indrustia	Antoquete	p.ª as baleias	refrescar, batatas, porcos, ovos	azeite
Galera amoricana	Lião	Antoquete	p.ª as baleias	refrescar batatas, porcos, ovos	»
Galera amoricana	John Jaemes	Antoquete	p.ª as baleias	refrescar batatas, porcos, ovos	»
Galera Londrista	Cabo verde	Londres	Terra Nova	refrescar agua e galinhas	dinheiro
Galera amoricna	Prezeverousa	Antoquete	p.ª as baleias	refrescar batafas, porcos, galinhas	azeite
Galera amoricana	Edeward	Antoquete	p.ª as baleias	refrescar batatas, porcos, ovos	«
Chalupa amoricana	Dov	Antoquete	p.ª as baleias	refrescar bstatas porcos, ovos	»
Nau londrista	Intone	Rlo de Janeiro	Londres	refrescar batatas, porcos, vos	letra
Brigue londrista	Rover	Londres	Cruzar	refrescar bois, agua, galinhas	letra
Um comboio de 13	londristas	indias	Londres	refrescar bois, batatas, galinhas	letra
Galera amoricana	Feme	Antoquete	p.ª as baleias	refrescar bois, batatas porcos	azeite
Galera amoricana	Estrelim	Antoquete	p.ª as baleias	refrescar, batatas, porcos ovos	»
escuna amoricana	Caredonia	Boavista	Fayal	refrescer batatas, porcos, ovos	dinheiro
Galera amoricana	Quitéria	Antoquete	p.ª as baleias	refrescar galinhas, porcos, ovos	»
Galera amoricana	Xasquana	Leuvepol	Boston	refrescar água, galinhas, porcos	»
Galera Londrista	Jupiter	Rio de Jan.º	Londres	refrescar água, galinhas, porcos	»

a) Conservou-se a ortografia

(Biblioteca Pública e Arquivo Distrital
— Angra do Heroismo — Capitania Geral)

Copy of Document No. 31, published in the *Annals of Lajes, Island of Flores*. These data show the nationality, name and destination of vessels which landed at that Island in Azores in 1811. Most of these vessels were headed to hunt the whale.

The mangling of whale caught in Azores waters. This whale is being processed at the Whaling Station in the Island of São Miguel.

a great benefactor to the Island of Faial. The third heir was Samuel Dabney. He left the island with his family on January 12, 1892 for the U.S.A. where he died on December 26, 1893, in San Diego, California.

When New Bedford owned vessels stopped offshore in Faial for supplies, consisting mostly of food stuffs and water, the crew would be sent ashore in small boats. Their return to the ship would bring not only those goods necessary for the long voyage, but also some intrepid young boys, attracted by the meager pay offered by sea captains, in return for many months of hard work on the high seas. Some would stow-away to be discovered or to find themselves in the hands of the officers on board when ships were heading to Cape Verde Islands, and therefore too far to be put ashore in Faial, port of origin for many of these young Azoreans. Later, unable to carry on the hard work required of them in these "amphibious factories," they would run ashore in the islands of Trinidad, south of the West Indies, in San Domingo, St. Thomas and others would desert when they reached the islands in the Pacific, including Hawaii, known then as the Sandwich Islands.

These expeditions would go around the Cape and hunt the sperm whale, wanted mainly for its oil and other extracts. Life aboard these ships, at the command of heartless captains, was considered hideous. Descriptions are found in diaries kept by these poor Azorean souls who found themselves many a time serving the devil rather than a human being, whose promises of a quick travel to American shores would only materialize one or two years later, if at all. In fact, these clandestine departures were watched closely by authorities in these islands, especially Flores where a law was enacted allowing small boats to patrol along the shores. These boats were equipped to shoot, on sight, anyone attempting to escape or to recruit laborers. Once aboard the vessel, these Azoreans would not touch shore until captains had satisfied their egos or the production quota established by the "Lords of New Bedford," owners of these fleets. To escape, many men had to jump and swim ashore either in Hawaii or along the California coast under musket fire from the ferocious captains. These captains disliked seeing their crews depleted of valuable and strong Azoreans of all ages who had traded the quiet village in their islands for the unknown of a new world.

On the voyage through the high seas of the vast Pacific, as whales were caught, they would be processed aboard. the fat of the mammal would be placed in caldrons and melted for its oil. The confined quarters of these ships would provide terrible breathing atmosphere. Poor hygiene and nausea were in abundance aboard ship. The oil would be placed in barrels and stored on ship until it was met by other vessels in the ocean who would take them to the markets — thus preventing the factory ship with all hunters or fishermen aboard from touching shore.

III

THE SAGA OF ANDRADE

Manuel Silveira d'Andrade, born in the village of Castelo Branco, Faial, Azores, was one of many who came to the U.S.A. aboard a whaling vessel. His work, like that of his companions, never became known, never reached the headlines. He came and went unnoticed like many thousands who came to work the hard soil of California.

Manuel, at the age of 18, went to the island of Flores to work as a carpenter. He had received some education in his native island, enough to be considered above the many friends he had left in Castelo Branco. A whaling vessel, *Bark Pacific,* of New Bedford, which had stopped off the coast of Flores soon changed Manuel's destiny. His occupation was one of those much needed aboard the 396 ton vessel and without much convincing he found himself in the hands of Captain Jacob A. Howland, in command of an "amphibious factory" on its way to a hunting trip around the Horn.

There she was sailing off to the nearby island of Faial, Manuel's homeland. Twenty-two hours later, on that 12th day of August, 1859, the vessel had unloaded some 110 barrels of sperm whale oil, extracted from the mammals they had caught in the two months' trip from New Bedford to the island of Flores, Azores.

While the vessel laid offshore, a small boat was dispatched returning aboard immediately. Aboard that boat was Manuel, who had been denied permission to go ashore to his own native land. *"I had the privilege of holding the spyglass in my hand for only a moment to look upon my own dwelling and some others in my neighborhood. How pretty they looked to me,"* wrote Manuel in his diary. Two days later he sailed off towards the south, towards the unknown, never to return to the little island of Faial.

Facsimile of a page of Andrade's diary (August 1859). He later translated into English in his own handwriting.

Manuel Silveira d'Andrade, early Portuguese immigrant from Faial, Azores. (Photo courtesy of his daughter Mary J. Vargas of Oakland, California, alive at age 95, when interviewed by author in 1964.)

The toughness of Captain Howland was not only demonstrated with his refusal to permit Manuel to step ashore and say good-bye to his parents and few friends. He was to follow instructions in a language totally unknown and he was to obey orders, be judged, treated and fed by the man who, aboard ship, was considered Master and "God knows what else" as sailors usually said.

One Sunday, October 23rd, two months and eleven days later, a voice from the mast was heard, "land ahoy." Within ten miles Terra del Fuego began to show its foggy mountain tops. Cold, rain and gale winds fell upon the vessel now moving westward. Cries for all hands were sounded off to help save the anchor hanging from the ring, loosened by the violence of the mountainous seas. A few days later the wind slowed down. The right time to hunt offered itself to the anxious crew. Sunday, November 13, the first whale was seen by Manuel. Here began the adventures of a crew of hunters, consisting of members from different nationalities who had enlisted for the trip way back in New Bedford during mid-summer of 1859. He was the only Portuguese aboard and took his adventure gracefully for he was learning about life on the other side of the world. He registered in his diary all vessels that passed: *Rebecca Sims* of Fair Haven; *Helen Snow; Phoenix; Nile;* and many others.

Around 8:00 p.m. on March 31 they anchored in Maui. The captain reported 1,100 barrels of whale oil and about 7,500 pounds of bone. On April 1st (April Fool's) the tough looking captain ordered all hands ashore except for one boat's crew. Their main purpose was *"to go to church and give God thanks for all mercies He has given us. One of the carpenters on board, along with the blacksmith, was discharged of his duties aboard, due to 'home sickness'; and in his stead a few natives, 'Kanakas,' are taken aboard.* While at Maui, according to Manuel's notes, *"all took a quantity of Irish and sweet potatoes, some firewood, water and a few other things that they were in need of, and unloaded our whale bone so it could be shipped on board the 'South Sims' while on her way home (New Bedford) and signed for the ship's articles there, in the presence of the American Consul, for the remainder of the voyage."*

After a stopover of one day in Honolulu they steered off west by north. May 17th, they found themselves approaching the OKOTSK Sea in the North Pacific Ocean off the coast of Russia. Cold and icy, Manuel recorded the several vessels that passed by telling of their distance from home (New Bedford) in time — *"Bark Callao was 22 months from home carrying 1,100 barrels of whale oil."* Hunting in these northern waters proved profitable. *"One whale turned out 140 barrels of clear oil."* Manuel goes on to explain, *"We took the length of this fellow; according to the length of the ship, it must have measured between 75 and 80 feet from tip to tip and it was not so large around as a cow whale for this was a bull one. The blubber of the bull whale is also different from the cow whale's, the cow whale when she has no calf is always fatter than the bull whale, and another thing, take a cow whale before she calfed and take another one of just same size and weight and her calf; both will make just as much oil as the first one will, not a drop more even if they are two to one, because the calf while sucking, takes the fat of its mother away, more than any other body in the world."*

"On October 15 we anchored at Maui at 6:00 p.m., having a strong wind, and the deck full of water during the whole trip of 22 days. While in Maui we discharged 17,000 (seventeen thousand) pounds of bone to go aboard the 'South Sims' of New Bedford."

They sailed off to Honolulu. This time there was speculation that they would head south and homeward. The vessel was carrying 2,200 barrels of oil and that was considered a good load. They were disappointed when Captain Howland ordered the transfer of 800 barrels to the *Silver Star,* a vessel scheduled homebound, taking with her a few of Manuel's companions who stowed away while the transfer of oil took place. The loss of men enraged the captain to the point that no one was allowed ashore during the remainder of their stay in Honolulu. Everyone, including

Manuel, was getting tired of the hard work and lengthy trip. It had now been over a year since he had left the island of Flores.

A month later, on the trip, they reached land. A small settlement, a few dwellings were soon discovered, Manuel accounts: *"One boat went ashore, with the captain to find out what was the best news there, and with the intention of getting some fresh grub if he could. They came aboard at 9:00 p.m., after being off since 5:00 o'clock. They say that there was a great cultivation of potatoes and corn, but none ripe yet, or in proper state of use, instead of potatoes and green corn they brought aboard a load of fleas, as many as they could get on their clothes. Not finding this out till they got aboard, they were put separate from each other and changed their rags, so they could be among the crowd without suspicion of having fleas. They also let the captain know it, so he could change his clothes and be clear of them. They say that there were some women ashore, but not even one man was seen. The women said that their husbands had gone together back into the mountains to have a fight with the Spaniards or the natives of this coast, about something or other that they would not come to agree with them."*

On December 17, they had been cruising the whole week without seeing a single whale. They were about ten miles north of San Quentin Bay and were exhausted. Captain Howland began to feel unrest among some officers aboard who had already begun to refuse to obey orders. They wanted to rest. This was understood and, for a few days, the ship stayed off the coast to allow her crew to harmonize and continue the hunt without trouble. A few of the members jumped ashore. Captain Howland ordered a musket on deck loaded with three balls as a warning to any other crew members who dared to jump ship and swim ashore. Manuel saw this as a great threat to everyone and began to think that he had better be discharged before he was affected like his fellow crew members, who appeared to be losing their minds.

On October 25, 1861, Manuel decided that two years, two and a half months, was too long at sea and too much for him. He was sad to learn that one of his friends who had jumped ashore a few months back had boarded a vessel named *San Lucas,* homebound, which later caught fire off the coast of California, leaving everyone dead. So he wrote, *"Here (Honolulu) I ended my whaling trip by having my discharge before the American Consul, and paying a man to go in my place, in accordance with the law of the United States, since I had been contracted for the remainder of the voyage. On November 7, and from shore, I waved good-bye to the 'Pacific' when she left for home after a whale hunting trip which netted 52 whales, 3,700 barrels of oil and 24,000 pounds of bones."* On November 12 he boarded the *Bark Phillip I* of N. London, sailing from Honolulu, arriving in San Francisco on December 4, 1861, after a passage of twenty-two days.

The adventure of Manuel S. Andrade exemplified the courage and determination of the Portuguese immigrant who settled in California.

Manuel S. Andrade was later the right arm of Antonio Fonte, for he was the one with a good knowledge of Portuguese who would write the first by-laws of the organization. On October 9, 1870, he married Rosalina Geraldina Fagundes, a native of Flamengos, Faial, Azores, who lived in San Leandro, California. Following the example of his countrymen he became an American citizen receiving his papers, as they commonly referred to citizenship certificate, on June 24, 1874, in the Third Judicial District Court of the State of California in and for the county of Alameda. His naturlization was witnessed by Louis Martin and Antonio Rogers, both early settlers in San Leandro. He died on November 23, 1916.

THEY KEPT COMING . . .

In those days, statistics, if any existed, were kept very poorly both in the U.S.A. and in Portugal, let alone in the Azores, where most clandestine emigration took place. Numbers quoted by different people do not correspond to the true exodus of

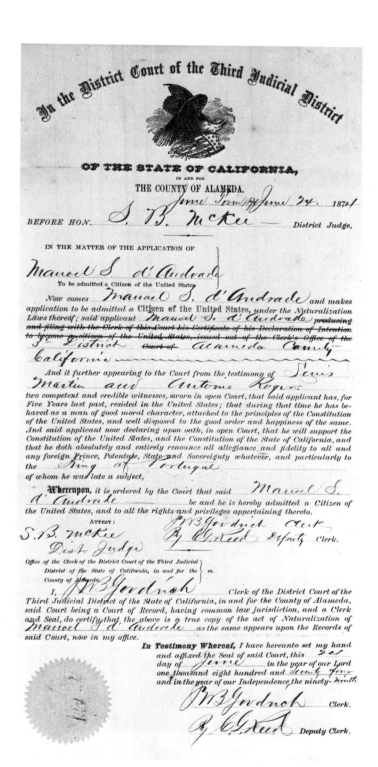

In the District Court of the Third Judicial District

OF THE STATE OF CALIFORNIA,

IN AND FOR

THE COUNTY OF ALAMEDA.

June Term 1874 June 24, 1874

BEFORE HON. *S. B. McKee* District Judge,

IN THE MATTER OF THE APPLICATION OF

Manuel S. d'Andrade

To be admitted a Citizen of the United States

Now comes *Manuel S. d'Andrade* and makes application to be admitted a Citizen of the United States, under the Naturalization Laws thereof; said applicant *Manuel S. d'Andrade* ~~producing and filing with the Clerk of this Court his Certificate of his Declaration of Intention to become a citizen of the United States, issued out of the Clerk's Office of the~~ *District* ~~Court of~~ *Alameda County California*

And it further appearing to the Court from the testimony of *Lewis Martin and Antonio Rogers* two competent and credible witnesses, sworn in open Court, that said applicant has, for Five Years last past, resided in the United States; that during that time he has behaved as a man of good moral character, attached to the principles of the Constitution of the United States, and well disposed to the good order and happiness of the same. And said applicant now declaring upon oath, in open Court, that he will support the Constitution of the United States, and the Constitution of the State of California, and that he doth absolutely and entirely renounce all allegiance and fidelity to all and any foreign Prince, Potentate, State and Sovereignty whatever, and particularly to the *King of Portugal* of whom he was late a subject,

Whereupon, it is ordered by the Court that said *Manuel S. d'Andrade* be and he is hereby admitted a Citizen of the United States, and to all the rights and privileges appertaining thereto.

ATTEST: *W. B. Gordner* Clerk

S. B. McKee   *By C. G. Reed* Deputy Clerk.
Dist Judge

Office of the Clerk of the District Court of the Third Judicial
District of the State of California, in and for the } ss.
County of Alameda.

I, *W. B. Gordner* Clerk of the District Court of the Third Judicial District of the State of California, in and for the County of Alameda, said Court being a Court of Record, having common law jurisdiction, and a Clerk and Seal, do certify that the above is a true copy of the act of Naturalization of *Manuel S. d'Andrade* as the same appears upon the Records of said Court, now in my office.

In Testimony Whereof, I have hereunto set my hand and affixed the Seal of said Court, this *24* day of *June* in the year of our Lord one thousand eight hundred and *seventy four* and in the year of our Independence the ninety-*ninth*

W. B. Gordner Clerk.

C. G. Reed Deputy Clerk.

Facsimile of Naturalization Document issued to
Manuel Silveira d'Andrade in June of 1874.

11

Azoreans which took place until the 1930s when the Portuguese government began watching the immigration movement closer and maintaining some sketchy statistics, compiled at first from town hall tabulation sheets.

William J. Bromwell, in his *History of Immigration to the U.S.A.,* indicates the arrival in 1820 of 139 immigrants (passengers) from Portugal and three from the Azores. Unfortunately, records kept on Portuguese individuals in this country seldom distinguish the native of the Azores from that of Continental Portugal. Consequently, in most cases, the figures quoted for immigrants from Portugal is larger because it includes many of those from the Azores. According to Bromwell's statistics, between 1820 and 1855, out of 4,212,624 immigrant arrivals in this country, 2,049 came from Portugal (?); 1,288 from the Azores; 203 from Madeira and twenty-two from the Cape Verde Islands. A total of 3,562 immigrants of Portuguese background arrived in those thirty-five years.

In that period, the highest number of arrivals, in any one year, was 638 in 1833. Larger numbers were registered after the gold discovery in California, which attracted many Portuguese from the mainland, for a time, in numbers superior to those of the Azores. Bromwell's statistics show eighty-seven arriving in 1848; sixty-seven of whom came from Portugal (?) and twenty from the Azores. In 1850 Bromwell accounts for 366 coming from Portugal and 180 from the Azores. But in the next five years the statistics are reversed. Between 1851 and 1855, this document records 1,099 coming from the Azores, 490 from Continental Portugal and seventy-eight from the Madeira Islands.

At that time some immigrants from Portugal also came to California through the Isthmus of Panama and through Louisiana, of which there are no statistics, other than a mere mention in newspaper accounts published in the Azores at the time.

Most immigration, between 1855 and 1890, was processed through Castle Garden at the foot of Manhattan Island in New York. As the years went by, the United States began to industrialize and the need for labor increased, to cope with the rapid rate of mass production. Immigration was not only open, but encouraged in large numbers. However the United States in 1882 began putting these arrivals through scrutiny in order to avoid undesirables which England was sending over, thus easing the state of their support. This practice continued for all countries even after January 1, 1892 when Ellis Island, off Manhattan, was opened as an immigrant receiving station.

Between 1905 and 1906 the greatest number of immigrants registered. Out of the 3,285,349 who came to this country through the East Coast, 1,280,593 were processed in Ellis, known to many as "Tears Island" — for in the speedy process many homes were broken, as some disqualified family members were shipped back to their homelands. The law then required that these immigrants be examined upon arrival, before they could be allowed entry in this country. Many husbands saw their wives sent back because they suffered from certain illnesses not acceptable by immigration standards, and vice versa, many husbands were refused entry and the wives would be allowed entry alone. There are even accounts of children ten years and younger, considered unfit, being sent back to Europe while their parents were allowed to remain. Reasons cited for deportation, besides sickeness were, among others, prostitution, polygamy, insanity and crime.

As years went by, the experience with the immigrant element caused the government to enact laws to curtail immigration. The first attempt was made in 1917, notwithstanding President Woodrow Wilson's veto. A law was adopted effective February 5 of that year calling for a literacy test of all immigrants age sixteen and over. This law classified people in their own language and considered thirty-three classes which was a disguised legislation to eliminate the southern and eastern Europeans, Portuguese included. No doubt that this measure came to ease the labor market, saturated at the time with high unemployment as a result of the conflict which would threaten to engulf the world in war. This law was repealed in 1952.

The literacy tests were conducted at Ellis Island and other immigrant stations throughout the U.S.A. This test affected, somewhat, immigration from Portugal — especially the Azores, where illiteracy was very high (estimated at eighty per cent). Since these tests did not seem to reduce much of the immigration flow, on June 3, 1921, during President Harding's term, the quota system went into effect (known as the Johnson Act), placing an annual ceiling of 358,000 immigrants a year. The quota system was based on three per cent of each nationality living in the United States, according to the 1910 census. Needless to say, this law had racial overtones for it favored the Nordics.

By 1924 the economy of the country began to decline, and unemployment soared. The quota system was changed, cutting still further the proportion of new immigrants. The percentage in July of that year was reduced from three per cent to two per cent of the different nationalities shown on the 1890 census, thus placing a ceiling of 164,000 immigrants a year.

In 1929 another revision of the law was made by the so-called National Origins System, by which admissions were lowered to 150,000 a year. This time the change greatly affected the immigration from Portugal, since the analysis for the quota was based on the national origin of the numbers of those, both native and foreign, born as disclosed in the census of 1920. The Portuguese would have to wait many years, if not a lifetime, before they could be given visas to immigrate to the U.S.A.

However, the Azores continued to supply some of the immigration on a family basis for many marriages were made between friends, and sometimes relatives, living in this country and those in the islands. In this manner they were assured a faster means of coming here, by-passing the ever growing waiting lists of prospective immigrants, filed in the U.S. Consulate in the Azores.

In fact, it was not until 1958 and 1959 that some Azoreans on waiting lists saw a way of circumventing the system, as a result of an Act of Congress allowing a few thousand victims of the volcanic eruption off the island of Faial (Capelinhos) to immigrate to the U.S.A.

All of the unfairness created by the immigration quota system came to an end, when John F. Kennedy focused attention on its injustice. The bill he fought for was passed, two years after his death, on October 3, 1964, and signed into law by President Lyndon B. Johnson. It called for the elimination of quotas and allowed immigration based on the skills needed in the country. This change resolved, as well, a very humane problem, which was to allow the reuniting of families who had been separated for years as a result of the old quota system.

IV

THE HAWAIIAN PARADISE

Approximately thirty years after Christopher Columbus accidently discovered America the Pacific waters were, so to speak, invaded by Portuguese and Spanish vessels. Juan Gaetano (Caetano), to whom historians refer as the discoverer of the Hawaiian Islands in 1555, was probably Portuguese, who like many others in those days placed himself at the disposal of Spain when no chance of navigation was offered them in their own country, Portugal. Examples of these were found with many discoverers, namely, Fernão de Magalhães (Ferdinand Magellan), and João Rodrigues Cabrilho.

Gaetano, as a pilot of a galleon commanded by a captain cruising under the flag of Spain, is believed to have cartographed the Hawaiian Islands. These charts were kept on file by the Spanish Crown. Scientists however place that discovery of the Hawaiian Islands, by either Spanish or Portuguese navigators, in doubt, claiming that the little group of islands charted and named Los Major, Los Menjes, Los Desgraciadas and others was placed in the wrong latitude. Battles of scientists have raged for decades over this question of discovery, as valiantly waged as battles upon seas. The question of "longitude" has always been the rock upon which their arguments have been wrecked.

Hawaiian traditions tell of the arrival of mysterious foreigners who remained and intermarried, merging into the aboriginal population and to this day several eminent families of Hawaiians claim descent from these early foreigners.

Further consternation occurred when Captain James Cook, Royal Navy of Britain came upon the islands on January 17, 1778, naming them for the Earl of Sandwich, while cruising southward from the South Seas. However, he had the same fate of Magellan when the navigator touched the Philippine Islands. In January of 1779, Cook anchored in Kealakekua Bay, Hawaii, where on February 14, he was slain, presumably due to misunderstandings on the part of both English sailors and the Kanakas.

The call of the seas and the urge to adventure has always been one of the dominant characteristics of the Portuguese. But they have also grown used to seeing much of their deeds of discovery claimed by English and usurped by the Spanish and the Dutch. Therefore it does not matter which one discovered these islands. What is important is that the Portuguese immigrated in large numbers to Hawaii, as early as 1820, as a result of the whaling vessels' stopovers, giving crew members open chances to escape. The never-ending sagas they were put through in the long hunting of the mammal trips commenced in most cases, in the Azores Islands.

Many of these men, upon reaching shore, would retire from maritime life, and began to farm. Later, many of these pioneers took up large tracts of land and became cattle ranchers and dairymen. This situation turned out to be similar to California — not only a lucrative business but also providing work for the less enterprising colonists.

Around 1877, with the arrival of large numbers of Chinese, the Portuguese laborers were the ones who suffered most. They were laid off and forced out of the jobs by unscrupulous bosses and foremen who would impose all kinds of dues and charges against their salaries, leaving those poor and illiterate workers with meager change saved. Things would turn for worse in some instances when salaries were paid in "Kanaka" currency, as it was known then, instead of U.S. gold and silver. The local currency, when used by the workers for payments of goods bought from the bosses, would suffer a reduction of twenty per cent in value (800 reis or 80 centavos — Portuguese). Most contracted immigration, however, began only in 1878 to meet the labor supply demands of the sugar industry, which became evident after the signature of the reciprocity agreement with the United States.

Dr. William Hillebrand, a German botanist, who had returned from Hawaii in 1871 and was residing in Madeira, offered to assist in the recruiting of immigrants from the Azores and the Madeiras, since both areas had a similar climate. Later, in 1877, he was commissioned by the government of Hawaii to carry out the labor contract as set by the Board of Immigration of the islands, which, according to Norris W. Potter, called for a three-year stay in the sugar plantations, from the date of arrival. The working month consisted of twenty-six working days, ten hours per day. Men received $10.00 a month and women $6.50, paid in U.S. gold or silver. The contract also included lodging, daily food rations, medical care and free medicine, as well as a garden ground where Portuguese grew vegetables for their staples, including the *Inhames,* or taro root, part of the Azores culinary still common in Portuguese homes of California. It is usually cooked in salt water, sliced and fried to accompany pork dishes. The daily food rations consisted of: 1 pound of fresh or salt beef; a half pound of salt or dried fish; one and a half pounds of rice; one pound of taro roots or other vegetables and one third ounce of tea.

Hillebrand contracted with Hackfeld and Company of Breman, Germany, for the transportation of these immigrants. The fares were paid by the government of Hawaii at $75.00 for each adult. The first group of these immigrants arrived aboard the *Priscilla* on September 30, 1878, and many followed thereafter originating both in Madeira and San Miguel in the Azores.

In 1881 King Kalakaua went on a tour around the world, and stopped in Portugal where he was well received. As a result of this visit, more immigrant families were to be sent to Hawaii. This agreement, negotiated with Lisbon by Henry A.P. Carter, Minister-Envoy of the Kingdom of Hawaii, was signed on May 5, 1882.

As thousands of Azoreans made preparations to leave for Hawaii, local newspapers questioned the feasibility of such contracts, cautioning them by pointing as an example the fate of some of their predecessors, both from the Azores islands and the Continent who ended up in New Orleans, Louisiana, working in the bayous of the Mississippi River and cotton plantations of Louisiana.

Trips used to take months. The voyage of the *Amana* lasted 155 days from Funchal, Madeira, to Honolulu. They recorded ten births and four deaths aboard the vessel.

Between 1878 and 1899 approximately 11,937 Portuguese immigrants landed in Hawaii. In fourteen shiploads of Portuguese, the percentage had been thirty per cent men, twenty-two per cent women and forty-eight per cent children, which turned out to be very valuable for the population of the island, but expensive as a labor supply.

The population census of Hawaii, taken as of December 31, 1884, showed that out of a population of 80,578, 40,104 were natives; 4,218 Mongrels; 17,939 Chinese; 116 Japanese, 9,377 Portuguese (5,239 men and 4,138 women) and 8,914 other nationalities. The Chinese were the only ones who exceeded the Portuguese in number. The same census showed that in Honolulu there were 580 Portuguese residents (309 males and 271 females) of which 112 were married and only 120 of the total 580 were able to read and write.

It was only in 1882 that Portugal recognized the importance of her subjects in those Pacific islands and decided to commission a qualified Consul by sending A. de Sousa Canavarro, who replaced Jason (Jacinto) Perry, of Faial, Azores, a local resident who acted on diplomatic matters on behalf of the Portuguese government. Jason was the father of Antonio J. Perry, who later became an Associate Justice of the Supreme Court of Hawaii.

Payment on the plantation was based on ethnic origin. Lawrence H. Fuchs, in his *Hawaii Pono: A Social History,* indicates that in 1901, while a Scotch blacksmith averaged $4.16 a day, a Portuguese would average $2.37, followed by the Japanese earning $1.50 for the same job and skill. The same inequity happened to carpenters. Americans would be paid $3.67 a day, Scotch $2.90 and Portuguese

$1.54.

As late as 1915 Scotch and American overseers were being paid seventy-five per cent more than their Portuguese counterparts. As years passed, these immigrants reached better positions on the plantations such as "Lunas" (overseers), mechanics, teamsters and stone cutters. They built houses wherever they were employed. The construction was mostly of lava rock, similar to that found in the home villages of the island of San Miguel, where such rock also abounds. In 1893 and succeeding years many Portuguese left Hawaii as a result of the economic depression affecting those islands and the revolution which followed in the last years of the monarchy, a prelude to the annexation by the United States.

The Portuguese feared political upheaval to the point of requesting protection from Antonio de Souza Canavarro, then Consul of Portugal in Honolulu. They had a petition signed by 171 people requesting the King of Portugal to send a battleship to the island in case the situation deteriorated as it did in 1895 when political turmoil was caused by those trying to restore Princess Liliuokalani to power.

ARRIVALS OF PORTUGUESE IMMIGRANTS IN HAWAII

Date of Arrival	Name of Vessel	Number of Immigrants	Port of Departure
*Sep. 30, 1878	Priscilla	180	Madeira
Aug. 25, 1879	Ravenscrag	419	Maderia
Jan. 21, 1880	High Flyer	332	Madeira
May 2, 1881	High Flyer	362	San Miguel
Aug. 25, 1881	Suffolk	488	San Miguel
Mar. 27, 1882	Earl Dalhausie	322	San Miguel
Jun. 8, 1882	Monarch	857	San Miguel
Sep. 11, 1882	Hansa	1,177	San Miguel
May 4, 1883	Abergeldie	945	San Miguel
Jul. 9, 1883	Hankow	1,462	San Miguel
Nov. 1, 1883	Bell Rock	1,405	San Miguel
Jun. 13, 1884	City of Paris	824	Madeira
Oct. 3, 1884	Bordeaux	708	Madeira
Jan. 19, 1885	Dacca	278	Madeira
Mar. 4, 1886	Sterlingshire	467	Madeira
Sep. 23, 1886	Amana	488	Madeira
1888	Thomas Bell	394	
**1895	Braunfels	720	Oporto & San Miguel
1899	Victoria	109	Madeira
***1906	Suveric	1,326	Azores
1907	Kumeric	1,129	Madeira
1909	Swanley	868	Madeira

* Compiled from *Progresso Californiense* Oct. 28, 1886.

** *Uniao Portuguesa* 1895.

*** *Portuguese in Hawaii (Resource Guide)* Reprint-Thrum's Hawaiian Annual

Many of these immigrants arrived in Oakland in the early part of 1893 causing certain apprehension to the long established Portuguese community. They had sold all of their possessions in Hawaii to pay the fare to California and, upon arrival in Oakland, found certain difficulties in starting a new life, finally having to seek help from the County Board of Supervisors for clothing, food and furniture. This prompted Manuel Stone, Editor of *A Pátria,* to come out publicly denouncing this attitude, going as far as suggesting that the U.S. government, at the time considering annexation of these islands, be encouraged to prohibit the Portuguese immigration from Hawaii to California just as they were considering doing with the Chinese.

Manuel F.M. Trigueiro, Director of *União Portuguesa,* criticized Manuel Stone in an editorial published on March 2, 1893, defending the actions of these Portuguese from Hawaii who had suffered enough in the hands of many cruel bosses found in almost all sugar plantations.

In 1897, once again the Portuguese found themselves in difficulty. This situation was due to the landing of thousands of Japanese, demobilized soldiers of the China-Japan War, who were contracted for the sugar cane fields at much lower salaries than those paid Portuguese workers. This caused some Portuguese to leave for Timor, a Portuguese possession of Indonesia, while others chose California.

They came and settled around San Leandro and Oakland. In San Leandro they sought the most modest and inexpensive housing available on what is known, even today, as Orchard Avenue (between Davis and Williams). The large influx of these immigrants from Hawaii caused, again, certain resentment in the Portuguese community, which at that time was beginning to experience the pleasures of acceptance by their Anglo-American hosts, attained after hard work and economic independence.

So the Portuguese in California went on to label their brothers from Hawaii as the "Kanakas" — a name designating the Hawaiian native. This nickname resulted in Orchard Avenue being referred to as "Kanaka Row," due to the large number of Portuguese immigrants from the Pacific islands who settled there. The name stuck and today is used to tease, jokingly, some of these people and their descendants.

In the census taken in 1910 of the foreign stock which composed the islands, 11.6 per cent were Portuguese (22,301); followed by the Chinese, 11.2 per cent (21,674); topped only by Hawaiians, 13.5 per cent and Japanese, 41.5 per cent.

By 1930 the Portuguese who stayed in Hawaii had emerged from the labor class, and only thirty per cent of all males remained in that class. They numbered 29,117 or 8.6 per cent of the whole population. Out of those, only 2,986 were registered voters.

The Portuguese from Hawaii, most of them descendants of those born in Madeira and San Miguel Island in the Azores, are among the most friendly and warm personalities, perhaps as a product of their exposure to Hawaiian paradisaical life . . . if only a paradise for those who did not have to earn the daily bread in the sugar cane and pineapple fields which made the Spreckels and the Sanfords rich. In later years many of the Portuguese succeeded in reaching better positions in the professional social and political fields. Their sons have honored the fields of legislature, the judicial, finance and industry. They were present when the Hawaiian flag was lowered and the American flag raised over the former Royal Palace on August 12, 1898 and were among those who first aligned themselves with the two dominant political parties of the U.S.A.

Of the Portuguese of Hawaii, one can truly say they were and are proud of their heritage. This is attested to by the simple but important fact that most of them kept their original family names, unlike many of their compatriots in other states of the union who, through the years, had the tendency to anglicize their names. On the other hand, they almost lost their Portuguese language and touch with the homeland.

Today, save the *linguica* sausage and the sweet bread sold in Hawaiian markets, of the few things left by the Portuguese is the Ukelele, produced in Hawaii between

1877 and 1879 by a Portuguese cabinet maker, Manuel Nunes. He patterned it after a small guitar known as *cavaquinho,* a popular string instrument typical of Madeira Island. Nunes died in 1923. However, it was Arthur Godfrey, through television, who re-introduced this instrument and transformed it into the family instrument of America back in the late 1920s.

Whaling ships at Honolulu Harbor, Hawaii

V

BY WAY OF CANADA

Another source of Portuguese immigration to the United States (mostly to the New England states and California) is our neighbor to the north, Canada.

The Portuguese, and again mostly from the Azores, began immigrating to Canada in 1953 when a group of eighteen men from the island of São Miguel, Azores, left for that country on an experimental basis. They were followed in May of the same year by another group from the mainland. In future years, thousands settled mainly in the provinces of Quebec, Ontario and British Columbia. At first they were mostly drawn from the unmarried male labor classes. Later, married men were accepted, even though they had to travel alone for a period of adaptation, ranging from a year to a year and a half. They were contracted for the agricultural fields and the railroads.

The majority were poor and had to borrow funds to pay their fares from the Azores to Montreal, P.Q. of to Toronto, Ontario in addition to having to buy a minimum of one hundred dollars, in Canadian currency, to meet first expenses upon arrival. Money was loaned at interest rates sometimes reaching fifteen per cent and eighteen per cent per annum.

The Canadian government was not allowed by Portuguese authorities to use their Assistance Passage program, which would have taken care of the funds for these fares at no interest. In addition, this program called for repayment to the Canadian government in installment amounts commensurate with each immigrant's earnings in Canada by means of a pay check deduction. The refusal by the Portuguese authorities to allow this assistance is attributed to the fact that they wanted to assure incoming flow of Canadian currency, thus boosting Portugal's economy, where revenues derived from immigrant remittances were always considered one of the main sources of income for the country.

The last good-bye for many as they leave the harbour of Ponta Delgada, San Miguel, Azores, to board chartered planes in neighbor island of Santa Maria, destined for Canadian Provinces, 1956.

19

Of the immigrants who left the Azores between 1954 and 1957, eighty per cent went to work for the Canadian National Railway gangs and were contracted for one year at ninety-eight cents per hour including room in box cars. Most of them fulfilled their contracts to the letter, replacing thousands of wooden ties on the vast railroad lines across towns and forests of Canada, under all kinds of rough conditions including snow-cold weather coupled with a lack of hygiene and comfort. They found themselves not only in a land foreign in language and culture, but also, at first, in far worse working conditions than those they were exposed to in their home villages. They had to learn how to light a coal stove in order to keep their bodies warm inside the old freight box cars, their home for at least a year.

In groups ranging from twenty to sometimes 120, they worked hard, saved some money and later moved to cities of their liking or where the best opportunity was offered to escape from railroad units or "gangas" as they used to call them.

Father and son hugging before boarding ship in the Azores.

While sitting on the edge of his railroad bunkbed, or in the isolated corner of a cold Canadian barn, the immigrant from the Azores, unlike his compatriot from the mainland, dreamt of a possible escape to the United States, thus breaking a promise made to the Canadian Embassy Inspectors. Many feared these inspectors, for they would promptly deny visas to prospective immigrants who either had their names on the quota waiting lists in the U.S. Consulate or would, in the course of the interview, unwarily reveal some close relationships in America. Those who felt life might be better in the United States, took a chance in crossing the borders and stayed, may have at times, found better opportunities had they stayed in Toronto, Montreal or Vancouver, where large communities of Portuguese have prospered.

Unlike early immigration to the United States, the Portuguese arriving in Canada were cared for and placed in jobs compatible with their physical strengths in farming and in construction. There were those who were so eager to leave the islands that they faked their clerical nature professions, obtained false identification cards from labor and trade synidcates. Others misrepresented even the minimum elementary education requirements (third grade) in order to obtain passports and try their

Examination of hands for callouses, during interview of prospective immigrants for Canadian railroad jobs — Ponta Delgada, S. Miguel, Azores.

Portuguese immigrants — a labor force of thousands who took railroad jobs in Canada.

luck in the new foreign land of opportunity in the North American continent — Canada.

Dozens of office clerks, salesmen and even police officers throughout the Azores would work at home shoveling or hammering in order to create calluses on the palms of their hands to pass as laborers before the Canadian inspectors. Most of these never fooled anyone but themselves; for soon, upon arrival, they were unable to endure the hard work they were contracted for on Canadian soil, and a few months later they would be back in the Azores at the old desk or sales counter jobs. Others came across to work in the mills of New Bedford and Fall River, Massachusetts or in the dairies of the San Joaquin Valley in California.

Most Portuguese from Continental Portugal, Azores, Madeira or Cape Verde, wherever they went, would struggle hard, but seldom found themselves confused

21

between the two cultures. They were possessed of a group consciousness and aware of the fact that many times they were barred from participating in activities promoted by the established populace of these lands. Banding together, similar to immigrants from other countries, they developed their own societies which represented communal attempts to meet material needs in times of crisis and, above all, to satisfy the desire for companionship, softening the effects of contact with a strange environment. The function of these societies, as the U.P.E.C. did, was to preserve in America, the familiar cultural pattern of the old country, Portugal.

It was not easy for most of these Portuguese immigrants. The hardest, if not the most urgent problem of adjustment related to their participation in the American way of life, was their lack of knowledge of the English language and of political expediency. The latter was in part, due to the fact that all but a few had been

Local ship transporting emigrants from San Miguel to the airport in Santa Maria, Azores, to board charter planes (below) bound for Canada.

Capelinho's volcanic eruption in Faial, Azores (1957)

Ashes cover houses in Praia do Norte, Faial

Village houses — a total destruction

denied the right of suffrage in the home country. Previous experience in schooling and civic life had done little to prepare them for the experience of political and social power in this country.

Nevertheless, they would go on working hard, saving money and buying land. Unlike other ethnic groups, the Portuguese looked upon the land as a sign of security that they forever sought and seldom achieved, especially in the Azores and the Madeira Islands.

This need fo security represented by land ownership, led many Portuguese throughout the years, even today, to prefer seeing their children work the farms and in the factories than attending school or college. This attitude resulted in the lack of numbers the Portuguese register in the professional fields of medicine, law, engineering and teaching, and in sadness for those who feel proud of their heritage.

These masses of laborers, belittled by nick-names, such as 'green horns,' hyphenated Americans of DP's, as they were known in Canada, who came to work in the New World did, however, contribute to the American scene and its prosperity.

The Jews evidenced themselves in clothing, the Italians in the building trades, the Irish in construction, the Germans as wheat growers while the Portuguese, with their conservative methods, left their marks in farming, dairying and fishing, especially in California and the New England states.

The history of the first century of the União Portuguesa do Estado da California is a tribute to those who, through their hard work and initiative, overcame their handicaps without fanfair and made life in these United States simpler for the Portuguese immigrants who would arrive later in pursuit of happiness, security and freedom.

Dedication Ceremonies of the monument in honor of Antonio Fonte in Prainha Do Galeão, Pico, Azores. The bronze likeness of the Founder of the U.P.E.C. was a gift from the membership of The Fraternal Society.

VI

THE CRADLE OF THE PORTUGUESE FRATERNAL MOVEMENT

According to the notes left by Manuel S. Andrade in a manuscript on file with the U.P.E.C., the first attempt to organize a fraternal society in California dates back to 1867, when Francisco Pimentel, a native of the island of Flores in the Azores, and a resident of San Francisco, received from some friends on the East Coast, a copy of the by-laws and regulations of the *Sociedade de Beneficiencia* of Boston, Massachusetts.

Pimentel was very impressed with the goals of the organization and made copies to be stuided by a few of his friends, who immediately thought of forming an organization patterned after the one in Boston. Pimentel's efforts at first encountered a certain resistance, but he persisted with the idea. On August 2 of the following year, he gathered José Maciel, Manuel Peixoto, Joaquim Peixoto, José Soito, Frank Moniz, António Leal, Alfonso José Toza, José de Freitas, George Netto, João Vieira, Candido Antonio, Manuel Teixeira, Manuel Medeiros and others, numbering over thirty. They formed an organization named *Associação Portuguesa de Beneficiencia da California.* Francisco Pimentel was elected President; António Christiano Cordon, Vice-President; José De Freitas, Secretary and José Maciel, Treasurer.

The community was proud of this accomplishment and immediately began telling others of the new society. Conversation was created in the boarding houses and saloons the Portuguese owned and managed in the city. Memberships were sought for the organization whose main purpose was to assist the Portuguese immigrants with benefits during disability periods caused by serious illnesses.

Among those who first joined was Henrique Rocha Martinho, a barber born in Castelo Branco, Portugal. He later became a dentist and anglicized his name to Henry R. Morton. Everything was going moderately well for the newly formed association until Morton managed to initiate in the order a fellow countryman who had lost a hand. The newcomer was not received with much joy by the rest of the proud membership, who saw in the organization a sort of exclusive group destined to receive none but the best people available. The organization was but three days old and it already began to experience dissention among its few members. The members proclaimed loud and clear their repulsion for the admission of this poor handicapped *O Maneta* (Portuguese nickname for a man without a hand). Morton, considered one of the few Portuguese with a certain amount of education, became indignant and immediately withdrew from the society, taking along some of his friends, who on the 6th day of August, 1868, formed a society named *Associação Protectiva.* As a result, the Portuguese community found itself divided.

For awhile both organizations continued their existence in spite of the strained atmosphere created among the Portuguese. There were two parties. Any friend or relative who was affiliated with one society was considered an outcast in the opinion of his relative or friend belonging to Morton's group. Many times this division led to debates and exchanges of insults wherever members of both societies happened to meet.

Meanwhile Francisco Pimentel, President of *Associação Portuguesa de Beneficiencia,* moved to Hayward and with twenty of his friends, some residing in San Leandro, he opened a subordinate council (No. 2) of his society. Among them were: Manuel Silveira Andrade, Leanço A. Ferreira and Francisco Williams. They elected Joe Silveira as President and José Pimentel as Secretary.

A few months later Francisco Pimentel decided to move his residence to the neighboring village of San Leandro, where there already resided a good number of Portuguese members of the *Associação Portuguesa de Beneficiencia.* Once in San Leandro he met with António Lucio and organized another subordinate council

(No. 3) in July, 1870. The council had as its first officers: António Lucio, President; Leanço A. Ferreira, Vice-President; Manuel Silveira Andrade, Secretary; Frank Williams, Treasurer; Trustees, Francisco E. Correia, António Damino, Francisco José Ignacio, Manuel F. da Cunha, António F. Da Cunha and João Baptista.

They continued to grow in peace and harmony, even while facing great difficulties. The Portuguese community was tired of the idea of having so many divisions. They wished to be united, especially since both groups were striving for the same goal — to uphold the good name and character of Portuguese immigrants and to place them on the same level as people of other civilized nations. On July 4, 1870, both societies were invited to participate in a parade held in San Francisco to celebrate the independence of the United States. This caused great joy for both societies, and rivals as they were, they showed up together and formed one unit in the parade.

Subsequently numerous letters were exchanged between *Associação Portuguesa de Beneficiencia* and *Associação Protectiva* in an attempt to consolidate the two groups. In the early part of 1871, and after a series of meetings between leaders of both groups, they agreed to consolidate and the *Associação Portuguesa Protectiva e Beneficiencia* (A.P.P.B.) was formed. The new group elected Jas. Lloyd of Sacramento as President, Henry R. Morton of San Francisco as Vice-President, and Manuel Silveira Andrade of San Leandro as Secretary.

A few weeks later they chose delegates from the five subordinate councils of the *Associação Portuguesa de Beneficiencia* who were to convene in San Francisco with those of *Associação Protectiva* to decide upon the formation of a Supreme Council. On the day that they were to hold this convention, delegates from the San Leandro Council of the *Associação Portuguesa de Beneficiencia* arrived a little late and stopped at the residence of João Cardoso "O Terceira," owner of a boarding house on Jackson Street, San Francisco. There they learned that nothing had been accomplished during the early hours of the meeting due to some representatives of the *Associação Protectiva* Council having exceeded the instructions they had received. Therefore the assembly had voted against the formation of a Supreme Council, thus revoking any previous arrangements. They did not want anything to do with a Supreme Council. In view of this attitude, there was nothing else for the San Leandro delegation to do but return home.

Even though they were disappointed, they never lost faith and continued to work for the consolidated council named *Açoreano,* after the consolidation as Council No. 5, since it was already becoming well established in San Leandro. They also decided to let the leaders of the extinct *Protectiva* go about their business in San Francisco, operating the *Associação Protuguesa Protectiva* (*Protectora* as corrected name) *e Beneficient* Council No. 1. This group confined its activities to the local San Francisco membership, until July 25, 1915, when they organized Council No. 2 in Crescent City, California. The subordinate councils led a life of their own since they had by-laws and were free to manage them without the consent of anyone but local members.

San Leandro members always maintained good relationships with their fellow members in San Francisco, attending their social functions including the Fourth of July Parade, said to be the first national festivity in which the Portuguese in California took part. At one time, António Lucio, president of the San Leandro council, was chosen the Marshal for the parade, receiving many compliments from the committee for the manner in which he conducted himself — thus bringing prestige to the Portuguese nationals at the time.

The fifty four members who constituted the San Leandro Council, *Açoreano,* No. 5, of the *Associação Portuguesa Protectiva e Beneficient* seemed to enjoy a good standing. At last peace was reigning amongst the Portuguese community and everything was going well for the council until a terrible accident took place on a Sunday afternoon, June 9, 1872. According to William Halley's centennial yearbook, *Alameda County (1876):* "Vincent Cardoz, Frank Cardoz and Minewll (Manuel) Paes, all Portuguese, were at Vincent Cardoz' house on Chicken Lane

(Dutton Avenue) just outside the corporation limits, on the day named, engaged in making firecrackers. They had a keg of powder for that purpose and were seated around it together with the wife and infant child of Vincent Cardoz and the son of Frank Cardoz, all being on the porch or piazza of the house. By some means a spark came in contact with the powder in keg, which contained about fourteen pounds, and the explosion which followed tore the clothes from the bodies of all the parties, burned the hair from their heads, tore the nails off the fingers of one of them, and left them all prostrate. Vincent Cardoz' child, aged about ten months, was so badly injured that it died within four hours. The explosion took place about noon. Medical aid was promptly summoned, but without avail. Those who were present at the scene of the disaster soon after it occurred say the victims presented a most heart-rending appearance. A broken pipe, filled with tobacco, which had evidently been lit and suddenly extinguished, was found near the spot after the explosion; and the only way the accident could be accounted for is that one of the number was trying to light his pipe when a spark from it came in contact with the powder. The firecrackers which they were manufacturing were to be used two or three weeks after, in some religious observances peculiar to the Portuguese."

Some of the Cardoz' family and friends who were victims of this terrible accident were members of the Association, Council No. 5, and as such were entitled to sick benefits at the rate of $10 per week. With just a little over fifty members contributing, the funds of the council suffered a blow which later led to almost complete bankruptcy since expenses were exceeding receipts. At the end of 1873, the funds of the council were exhausted, leaving the members sad and disappointed to the point they did not wish to attend any meetings. Since a Supreme Council had never been formed, they had no one else to turn to for help but their own members who, at the time, were poor. They thought of discontinuing payment of sick benefits, but that would have been disastrous. They decided then to cut expenses. They packed all the paraphernalia and books and left the hall they rented for membership meetings for which they were paying $35.00 every three months and stored the council's property in the house of one of their fellow members who volunteered the space for storage.

Even though the council had no place to hold meetings they continued the Association by respecting each other as members, until they saw that they could no longer continue with such a burden. The few dollars left in the council treasury was given to charity since, according to their by-laws, no individual could claim any portion of the funds. Manuel S. Andrade concludes, "and the council was dissolved and everything returned to the old dark days — going from door to door whenever a Portuguese died, begging for money for a decent burial, a custom used in some villages of the Azores Islands."

This process was not only humiliating, but also tired people of donating since there were weeks with three and more deaths.

In the early part of 1876 the Portuguese residents of San Leandro were restless with this situation. They wanted to be respected like other citizens and so they organized a society to take care of the growing problem of assisting those less fortunate fellow members.

On May 1, 1876, a group of Portuguese gathered in the attic of Smith's Hall, owned by William Dutra, also known as William D. Smith, a merchant in San Leandro, and formed the Independent Order of the Portuguese Patriots *(Ordem Independente dos Patriotas Portugueses)*. The group was composed of the following individuals:

António Fonte, Pico (S. Mateus)
Vitorino Teodoro de Braga, Santa Maria
William Dutra Smith, Faial (Feteira)
José Pereira Laureano, Faial
Angelo Enos, Faial (Feteira)
Manuel Martins da Rosa, Faial (Feteira)

27

CONSTITUIÇÃO,

LEIS E REGULAMENTOS D' ORDEM

DA

Irmandade Portugueza do Estado de California.

INSTITUIDA EM SAN LEANDRO, ALAMEDA COUNTY,
No Primeiro de Maio de 1876.

OAKLAND, CAL.:
IMPRESA DO DIARIO TRIBUNE E DIVERSOS TRABALHOS A VAPOR
1878.

Facsimile of *Constitution of Irmandade Portugueza do Estado de California.*

St. Joseph's Hall, Davis Street, San Leandro. Where U.P.E.C. was organized in 1880.

28

António Vitorino Pacheco, S. Miguel
Caetano José do Sousa, Flores
Manuel Garcia da Rosa, Pico
Manuel Pereira, Belchior, Pico
António Correia, Picanço, Faial (Horta)
Francisco Joaquim Braga, Santa Maria
José Vieira Goularte, Pico (S. Joao)
Vitorino José de Vargas, Pico
Camilo José Betencourt, Pico
Leanço António Ferreira, Santa Maria
José de Vargas Correia, Faial (Feteira)
José Pimental, Flores (Santa Cruz)
José Joaquim Serpa, Pico
José Silveira Dutra Flores, Faial (Flamengos)
António Francisco Noia, Flores (Santa Cruz)
João Gonçalves da Silva, Sr., Faial (Feteira)
Manuel José Cardoso, Faial (Flamengos)
José Martinho, Flores (Santa Cruz)
José Joaquim de Braga, Santa Maria
António de Oliveira, Cunha, S. Jorge
Francisco Pimentel, Flores (Santa Cruz)
José Silveira da Rosa, Faial (Flamengos)

All of these men were immigrants born in various islands of the Azores. It is interesting to note that they all lived in San Leandro with the exceptions of Manuel Martins da Rosa, who gave San Lorenzo as his residence; Manuel Pereira Belchior, residing in Warm Springs; and José Vieira Goularte, José Pimentel and António Francisco Noia, all of Hayward, California.

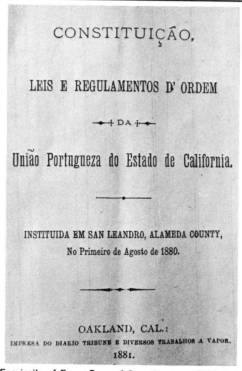

CONSTITUIÇÃO,

LEIS E REGULAMENTOS D' ORDEM

—+ DA +—

União Portugueza do Estado de California.

INSTITUIDA EM SAN LEANDRO, ALAMEDA COUNTY,
No Primeiro de Agosto de 1880.

OAKLAND, CAL.:
IMPRESA DO DIARIO TRIBUNE E DIVERSOS TRABALHOS A VAPOR.
1881.

Facsimile of Front Page of Constitution of U.P.E.C.

The new organization began to take shape, with António Fonte as its leader. In the meantime, a change of name was suggested to *Irmandade Portuguesa do Estado da California* (Portuguese Brotherhood of the State of California). At the end of 1877 a constitution was drafted, approved and ordered to be printed in the early part of 1878. The constitution provided for financial assistance only in case of death (burial insurance), excluding completely any provision for sick benefits, since they had learned from past experience that such coverage could be disastrous for the organization.

On August 1, 1880, at a meeting held in Saint Joseph's Hall, formerly Smith's Hall, on Davis Street, San Leandro, the name of the organization was again discussed and unanimously changed to *União Portuguesa do Estado da California* for in the opinion of its members the word Union would seem more appropriate than brotherhood. A new constitution was approved. It differed slightly from the one of 1877. In addition to rules and regulations, it also contained a list of the thirty men who attended the meeting of August 1, 1880, who approved the change of the society's name. These have since then been referred to as the founders or charter members. They are the same twenty eight credited with founding of the Independent Order of the Portuguese Patriots on May 1, 1876 with the addition of two names: José Maria Telles, a wine manufacturer born in Coimbra, Portugal and Francisco Rodrigues Vieira, a laborer born in Lajes, Flores, Azores.

On August 1, at St. Joseph's Hall (William Dutra Smith's Hall), the constitution is signed by those thirty men having the following preamble:

"We the undersigned declare that we met in assembly and from our own free will unanimously adopted this constitution of the society 'Portuguese Union,' as the first founders. Praise to the Lord so that we progress and serve as an example and memorial for the future of our sons and compatriots; and when we no longer exist, be it known to all men, that the purposes of this society 'Portuguese Union' is for the benefit of our homeland, heritage, honor and glory of our Portuguese nationality."

VII

SAN LEANDRO — HOME AWAY FROM HOME

San Leandro, named after Saint Leandro, Archbishop of Seville, Spain, became a center for Portuguese immigrants, whose importance would grow with time. Struggling against the element of racial descrimination, born of the anglo-saxon ethnocentrism, the Portuguese immigrant now had a crutch to lean on — the *União Portuguesa do Estado da California*. The years to follow would make San Leandro a household name for the Portuguese in California, in faraway Portugal and the Azores.

The motivating force behind these immigrants who came here to settle and raise their families was expressed in their desire to acquire that ever-wanted place under the sun. The soil was rich and somewhat abandoned. The Azoreans seized the hoe to plow the land; they planted the fruits and vegetables which would later also become their fortunes. Excellent agriculturists, they cultivated the fields and carried their produce on horse-drawn carriages to markets as far as Oakland. To the surprise of the natives, they employed techniques which enabled them to get most of the land they bought at higher prices. The soil they tilled was in later years to be undersold to manipulators and opportunists who abounded everywhere, often living high from the easy money they made, either by ingenuity or political expediency.

Saint Leandro, Archbishop of Seville. Born in Cartagena, Iberian Peninsula in 540 A.D. (Painting by Murillo, Museum of Seville, Spain.)

31

The Portuguese were given little credit for their efforts except for a couple of historians who, perhaps due to a slip of the tongue, revealed admiration for their enterprises.

As Lawrence Kinnard wrote in his *History of San Francisco Bay Region,* "The American drove out the Spaniard and now the Portuguese threatens to drive out the Americans . . . The Portuguese, with his industry and close economy in growing vegetables, can get four and five times as much out of the land as the American has succeeded in doing."

Jack London, in his visits to San Leandro, could hardly conceal his surprise at the Portuguese. His feelings are contained in several references made to those hard-working immigrants in the *Valley of the Moon,* one of the most interesting works by the author dealing with the various ethnic groups he met in the Bay Area and Northern California.

According to the *1911 U.S. Congress Senate Report of the U.S. Immigration Commission* (Vol. 24, Part II, *Immigrant Farmers in the Western States,* Chapter XIV), The Portuguese in San Leandro at that time already numbered 2,600, roughly two-thirds of the inhabitants. They were there, not only to stay, but to eventually become a base for the most powerful statewide institution the Portuguese community ever knew in the pioneering years.

Application for membership used in the 1890's.

On Sunday, August 1, 1880, after the ratification of the constitution of the *União Portuguesa do Estado da California,* all thirty charter members paid their dues and proceeded with the election of their first officers as follows: President, Antonio Fonte(s); Vice-President, Victorino Theodoro Braga; Secretary, José Maria Telles; Treasurer, William Dutra Smith; Finance Committee, Victorino José de Braga, M.J. Cardozo, Angelo Ignacio de Mello, José Pimentel, António Vargas, José Ignacio Dutra and António Victorino.

A rule was made that no officer could post any fidelity bond for another officer. José Martinho (Martin) was appointed to select a doctor to examine all candidates seeking admission to the council. This first meeting adjourned at 5:00 P.M. with a motion authorizing both the Secretary and the Treasurer to buy the necessary stationery needed for the work of these officers. The minutes concluded with the following, "and we all went about our way in peace and harmony . . ."

The membership met thereafter every week on Sunday at 2:00 P.M. At these early meetings every effort was made to consolidate opinions and unite all Portuguese immigrants and their descendants, regardless of their political or religious convictions. Birthplace was also disregarded. Continentals, Madeiran or Azoreans put clannish feelings aside and united to assist each other in the conquest of respect in the strange land of America.

Little or no argument was known that would deter the determined leadership from accomplishing the goal they had set to meet. The motivating force behind them was António Fonte(s). Notwithstanding, three months later he threatened to resign the office of president due to gossip in the Portuguese community which came to a climax at one of the meetings when Fonte confronted Leanço A. Ferreira. This was the only altercation of record, and it was soon resolved with Fonte continuing in the presidency. Also, José Maria Telles resigned the secretaryship due to a change in his employment schedule. José Pimentel held the office on a pro-tem basis until Manuel S. Andrade was elected by the assembly to fill the vacancy.

The society was open to all males between ages fifteen and fifty-five. Later the minimum age was changed to sixteen. At first, only those of good health, moral and social character and who could understand the Portuguese language were solicited for membership. The requirement of knowledge of the Portuguese language was changed on July 3, 1887, allowing Dr. Andrew J. Dean to become a member of Council No. 3, Hayward. On October of that year he was elected Supreme Medical Examiner. He was the first non-Portuguese to join the society.

He was followed by Jean Batiste Martin Marce from France; James Stanley, a blacksmith from Canada; and Solomon Ehrman, a merchant from Germany. All of them joined Council No. 5, Centerville, in the year 1888. San Leandro, Council No. 1, only began accepting non-Portuguese in 1892 when admission was granted to G.R. Morgan, undertaker and Joseph Herscher and Louis Borman, merchants. born in Germany. Most of the non-Portuguese joined for business reasons as one may conclude from their occupations.

This characteristic remained unchanged from the first annual convention in October of 1887. They admitted all nationalities of the Caucasian race, as long as they gave consent for their names to be screened by the investigating committee composed of several members of the subordinate council. The committee would endeavor to look into the character of the proposed individuals and would finally make recommendations for admission or rejection. The committee's recommendation would then be voted on by the brotherhood who always had the final say on admissions. The balloting of candidates was secret. A wooden ballot box was placed in the center of the hall. White balls cast meant acceptance, three black balls meant rejection.

They continued for about three years recruiting membership from various localities: Warm Springs, Hayward(s), East Oakland, Alvarado, San Francisco, Antioch, Walnut Creek, Pinole, Mission San Jose, Centerville, Napa, Dublin, San Pablo, Pleasanton and Hollister. On September 5, 1881, the Board of Directors of the council, then composed of five members, adopted a resolution calling for the incorporation of the society for a period of fifty years and they went on to rename it *Conselho Supremo da União Portugueza do Estado da California.* (*Portugueza* spelled with a "z" was changed to Portuguesa with an "s" on November 15, 1931 when the Articles of Incorporation were amended calling for its existence to be perpetual.)

The Board of Directors' resolution also certified that the purposes for which the corporation was formed were "social, charitable, benevolent and especially to protect its members and their families, to provide aid and relief to the members of said corporation, and to the widows and children of the members thereof, by assessments and payment of dues." The Articles of Incorporation also granted the Board of Directors such powers as purchasing and selling bonds, owning, renting, leasing, buying and selling real estate, borrowing and loaning money on real estate. The document fixed the number of members who could serve on the Board of Directors to be five (changed to nine in 1931). The document was executed on September 28, 1881 in the presence of Stephen G. Nye, Notary Public. The charter was granted by the Department of State on November 15 of the same year.

San Leandro, Cal., 28 de Setembro de 1913

State of California,

      Department of State.

I, L.H. Brown, Secretary of State of California, do hereby certify that a copy of the Articles of Incorporation of Conselho San Leandro No. 1, da U.P.E.C., certified by the County Clerk of County of Alameda, as a copy of such Articles filed in his office, was filed in this office on the 8th day of January A.D. 1897, which Articles and the copy thereof contained the required Statement of Facts, to wit: First, the name of the Corporation as aforesaid; Second, the purpose for which it is to exist; Fifth, the number of its directors or trustees, and the names and residences of those who are appointed for the first year.

And I do hereby certify that the Articles of Incorporation set forth the holding of the election for directors, the time and place where the same was held, that a majority of the members of such association were present and voted at such election, and the result thereof, which facts were verified by the officers conducting the election.

Witness my hand and the Great Seal of State at office in Sacramento, California, this the 8th day of January A.D. 1897.

      L. H. Brown,

          Secretary of State.

By W. T. SESNON,

      Deputy

Hall of U.P.E.C. Council No. 1 (demolished in 1970).

Hall of U.P.E.C. Council No. 13, located at the corner of 7th and Henry Streets, West Oakland, California.

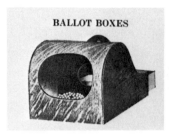

BALLOT BOXES

BALLOTS

Ballot boxes commonly used in U.P.E.C. subordinate councils for admission of new members.

The society had laid its foundation and the members were determined to unite the Portuguese who were scattered throughout the state, not knowing of each other other than through a newspaper published in San Francisco known as *Progresso Californiense* whose front pages would insert weekly an entire column entitled "Indagacões," listing names of Portuguese trying to locate one another in California.

On October 27, 1883, through the efforts of Francisco Pimentel and Leanço A. Ferreira, U.P.E.C. organized its second branch in Hollister with twenty-one members, followed by Council No. 3, *São João,* in Hayward, in June of 1885, with twenty members and Council No. 4, *Santo António de Padua,* Petaluma, on September 26, 1886. The next council, with thirty-one members, was organized on August 12, 1888, almost two years later in Centerville. From then until 1918, and without interruption, they organized branches all over the state of California and Nevada — from Arcata to San Diego and from Fallon, Nevada to Monterey on the California coast.

They named most branches after heros of the history of their homeland, Portugal. For the discoverers and explorers they chose *Serpa Pinto* in Pleasanton; *Infante D. Henrique* in San Francisco; *Mousinho de Albuquerque* in Concord; *Fernão de Magalhaes* in Stockton; *Cabrilho* in Fairfield; *Vasco da Gama* in Elmhurst and *Colombo* in Cayucos. Political figures were represented by *Marquês de Pombal* in Sausalito; *Dom Carlos* in Wilmington; *Rainha D. Amélia* in Novato; *Teófilo Braga* in Ryde; *Bernardim Machado* in Wayne and *Oliveira Salazar* in Artesia. There was a council named for *Luiz de Camões* in Mendocino, foremost figure of the Portuguese letters. Others were named after islands of the Azores and popular saints.

Between 1920 and 1945 only nine councils were organized. The last charter granted by the society was in 1951 to Council No. 173 in Escalon. Throughout the years, many of the councils closed for lack of membership while othere were unable to survive due to competition with nearby very active councils. Councils met regularly and enacted by-laws for their own government, subject to approval by the Supreme Council. They went on practicing charity and providing funds to help sick members. (The first sick benefit fund was organized by Council No. 12, Watsonville, in 1896.) Many councils, at one time, held real estate, such as: Council No. 1, San Leandro; No. 13, West Oakland; No. 18, Benicia; No. 19, San Rafael; No. 47, Rio Vista and No. 55, San Leandro. The properties provided land for meeting halls and other quarters for rental income. Most of the council investments in real estate were from sick benefit funds, excepting Council No. 1, San Leandro, and No. 13, West Oakland.

PREAMBULO

Sepultando no indifferentismo todos os credos politicos e as preferencias a posições distinctas na sociedade, actualmente eivada de preconceitos condemnaveis e prejudiciaes a todos, temos as nossas convicções religiosas, que a cada momento nos demonstram claramente a existencia do Grande Architecto Universal, Creador de todo o'mundo e da humanidade, e os nossos sentimentos patrioticos que nos prescrevem o dever de nos auxiliarmos mutuamente, afim de não irmos cair no terrivel e horroroso abysmo da miseria.

Para este fim, altamente louvavel, no primeiro d'Agosto de 1880, organisou-se em San Leandro, a UNIÃO PORTUGUEZA DO ESTADO DE CALIFORNIA, cujos principios fundamentaes são:—ministrar a mais sincera protecção a seus membros e suas familias, manter entre elles a mais franca amizade e harmonia, crear um cofre para, em caso de morte d'alguns de seus membros, beneficiar quem lhes sobreviver, de modo que estes lhes possam garantir sua ultima morada e fiquem ao abrigo da miseria, que a muitos tem arrastado ao vicio e ao crime.

São já decorridos annos que a União Portugueza do Estado da California segue rigorosamente a sua missão, não conhecendo difficuldades e obstaculos, porque a fraternidade que une os seus membros e os elevados sentimentos patrioticos e caritativos de todos, teem contribuido para que na actualidade esta Sociedade se torne digna do seu nome.

As paginas dos seus annaes, contendo somente actos de verdadeira philantropia e o cumprimento da sua missão, são outros tantos titulos honorificos e que patenteiam·a todos a sua actual florescencia.

Para mais facilmente todos conhecerem as suas leis, o Concelho Supremo houve por bem reformar a sua Constituição, pondo em vigor esta para seu governo e dos Concelhos Subordinados.

Preamble of U.P.E.C. Constitution (1892 edition).

INDAGAÇOES.

Deseja-se saber noticias de Manuel José Trigueiro, (Larangeira) filho de Caetano Furtado Gomes, (Larangeira) e de Anna Ursula, viuva: A ultima noticia que houve d'elle foi ha 5 annos, estando elle então em Los Banos, Merced Co. Cal. Desde então não tem havido noticia d'elle. Qualquer informação á redacção d'este jornal, ou a seu irmão Antonio F. Gomes, (Larangeira) 315 Drumm st., San Francisco, Cal., será muito agradecida.

Deseja-se saber noticias de Manuel J. Borges, natural da freguezia de Santa Luzia do Pico, filho de João Manuel Luiz (fallecido) e Anna Felicia da ilveira. A ultima noticia que se recebeu d'lle foi ha 15 annos, estando então n'uma terra chamada Nozilla. Pede-se encarecidamente a quem souber alguma noticia d'elle a fineza de o partecipar á redacção d'este ou a seu irmão João Manuel Luiz Borges, Milpitas, Santa Clara county, Cal., que será muito agradecida. 329tf

Deseja-se saber qual o destino de José da Costa, filho de Marianno José da Costa, do Pedregulho, da freguezia de Nossa Senhora da Luz da ilha Graciosa. Elle saiu d'esta ilha em Setembro de 1882, e em 1883, Março, embarcou para os estados Unidos. A ultima noticia que houve foi que se tinha ido empregar na lavoura em New Bedford, mas nunca escreveu a seu pae, que muito grato ficará a quem d'elle lhe der noticias, ou melhor á redacção d'este jornal. 364 tf

Column of _Progresso Californiense_ published in 1885, where names of immigrants seeking to reunite with family and friends dispersed all over California.

Initiation team — Vasco da Gama.

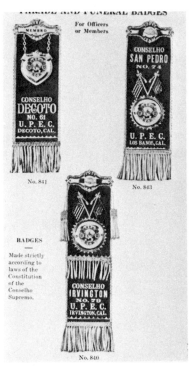

Sample of U.P.E.C. badges still in use by many subordinate councils.

Resolução

Resolve: Que a Junta dos Directores da União Portugueza do Estado de California, uma Corporação
cuja Corporação peça emprestado
a Francisco C. Barrados Sr., a
quantia de $1800.ºº pelo prazo de um
anno com o Juro de 8 por cento por
anno, pago Simi-Annual. e o mesmo ser assigurado com Nota e Hypotheca, e o Presidente e Secretario
por isto são instruidos de fazer
e executar tal nota e Hypotheca
debaixo do nome da acima dita
Corporação sobre a propriedade
recentemente comprada pela a
acima dita Corporação.

Antonio Fonte

San Leandro 15
de Abril de 1884

Facsimile of resolution signed by António Fonte
for a loan secured by the land on which the hall of
Council No. 1 was built.

39

VIII

ANNUAL CONVENTIONS

The true uniting of the membership actually took place during conventions, where those from the north met and still meet their fellow brothers from the south, and those from Nevada met their compatriots of California.

On October 3, 1887, the society held its first state convention in the town of San Leandro with four councils, the only ones then in existence. The society had a total of 354 members. They participated with the following delegates:

Council No. 1-San Leandro: António Fonte, Francisco Pimentel, N.S. Bulcão, F.C. Barradas Sr., F.C. Banadas Jr. and Lucio José Martins.

Council No. 2-Hollister: Manuel Freitas and A.J. Enos.

Council No. 3-Hayward: José Pimentel, José Smith and Manuel Alexandre do Amaral.

Council No. 4-Petaluma: João Joaquim Coelho and António Joaquim da Silveira.

This first convention lasted two days. Jose Pimentel read a draft of the new constitution for the Supreme Council which would superintend the affairs of all subordinate councils in existence and those they would diligently seek to organize throughout the state.

On the last day they held the election of officers for the state organization with the following results:

President: Francisco Pimentel

Secretary: Lucio (Lucindo) José Martins (Martinho)

Treasurer: M. S. Bulcão

Directors: V. T. Braga, José Pimentel, F. C. Barradas Jr., M. A. Amaral and Manuel Mello.

A committee was appointed to prepare a budget for the newly created office of the Supreme Council. After a meeting of a half an hour the committee informed the assembly that it needed $102.00 to defray the expenses of the Supreme Council, including the printing of the new constitution. An assessment of thirty cents was levied against each member for a general fund. Guilherme F. Mariante and Gregório António Almeida posted a one thousand dollar fidelity bond for the Secretary and António Fonte, and M.A. Amaral posted a two thousand dollar bond for the Treasurer. The new constitution permitted officers and members to bond both the Secretary and the Treasurer.

The next twelve months led to the organization of Council No. 5, Centerville, and on the first Monday of October, 1888, the Second Annual Convention was held again in San Leandro. John Garcia de Mattos was the delegate sent to this convention by Council No. 5. Supreme President António Fonte, in his report showed ninety new members initiated and encouraged the organization of new councils in West Oakland and Watsonville. The society then numbered 454 members affiliated with five councils, 283 of them with Council No. 1. It was during this convention that José Pimentel, Manuel T. Freitas and John Garcia de Mattos Jr. formed a committee of three to draft the first ritual to be used at members' funerals.

In the following year the society held the Annual Convention in Hollister. The session opened at 10:00 A.M. with the singing of a hymn composed and written for the U.P.E.C. by Francisco Ignacio Lemos and Father Guilherme Silveira Glória, and based on the works of Reverend Serrão and A.F. Castilho. Also, at this convention some of the Masonic-influenced secret signs were introduced for the first time at the suggestion of Manuel T. Freitas. He argued that these secret signs would enable the identification of members of other societies who would soon begin to infiltrate the society.

John Garcia Mattos, Jr. introduced a resolution calling for the appointment of a

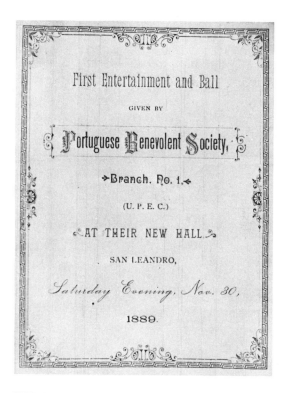

Programme.

1 Music   -   -   -   Silver Cornet Band

2 Introductory Remarks,   -   -

3 Address   -   -   -   Dr. J. S. Bettencourt

4 Song   "Come where the Lillies Bloom"
   C. Reid, W. Reid, W. Foreman, J. Buckholz,
       T. Gill, J. Gill.

5 Piano Solo   "Put Me in my Little Bed—echoes."
      Miss Ella Smith.

6 Vocal Solo,   "Alla Stella Confidente"
    Senhora Maria Da Silveira,
  with cello obligata by Dr. Regensberger.

7 Piano Solo   "Camoens March"
    Miss Gertrude Marrack.

8 Song   "Annie Laurie"   Double Quartette

9 Recitation,   "Camoen's Address to King Sebastian
    Miss Annie Fonte.
   (See opposite page for brief explanation.)

10 Vocal Solo,   (Selected) Miss Marie E. Fonte

11 Specialties,   A. J. Rosborough

12 Selections   Orpheus Mandolin Club
   Will Durant, Chas. Dietz, Will Johnson.

Invitation and program for the dedication of hall of
U.P.E.C. Council No. 1.

committee of three to work on a ritual to initiate new members in the society. The ritual called for new members to be present at initiation ceremonies within three months of approval of their applications. Failure to attend initiation ceremonies resulted in forfeiture of membership rights. Victorino T. Braga suggested that the society adopt an insignia or emblem. José Pimentel, in a beautiful presentation, was able to get the unanimous approval for his concept of the emblem "that should depict two flags, the Portuguese and the American, crossing each other; and a boat facing the sun, symbolizing *Vasco da Gama* in his trip to India."

Facsimile of fidelity bond posted by members of the society in favor of Council Secretary, José Pimentel.

Founders of U.P.E.C. Council No. 31, Santa Cruz, Oct. 1897.

Drill Team — U.P.E.C. Council No. 66, Santa Maria.

The Third Annual Convention closed with a secret session where all delegates received the new secret signs including a password needed to identify themselves wherever they went. The secret signs included a handshake and three taps on the hand with the index finger. In the early fifties the secret signs were discontinued, leaving the password as the only means of identification still in use today. It was not until 1889 that the offices of Marshal, Master of Ceremonies and Guard were created. M. Mitchell was the first member elected to the office of Guard (*Porteiro*). He was assigned to the entrance door of the halls where meetings were held, where he asked individuals for the password before they were allowed admission to the sessions.

DIFFERENT DESIGNS OF U.P.E.C. EMBLEMS ADOPTED IN VARIOUS YEARS

Emblem designed and adopted in 1925. (Note error in year of the independence of U.S.A.)

Emblem adopted in 1889.

Emblem adopted in 1913 and presently in use.

The Fourth Annual Convention was held in the newly constructed hall of Council No. 1, situated on East 14th Street, San Leandro. The sessions lasted three days and adjourned at two o'clock in the morning on October 8, 1890. During that year they admitted 850 new members to the eight councils the organization had in the cities of San Leandro, Hollister, Hayward, Petaluma, Centerville, Mendocino, Oakland and Pleasanton.

Conventions provided, and still provide a forum for memberships, through elected delegates who have a voice in the management of the society's affairs. These sessions provide opportunities to democratically debate issues and render opinions on legislative matters affecting the society's entire structure. It was, and still is, the maximum power and ultimate voice of the membership. It was through the subordinate council meetings and convention sessions that most Portuguese immigrants learned the principles of democracy, parliamentary procedures and political maneuvers. It was through their active participation in these meetings that many of them began to value their fellow members' feelings and learned how to get along and respect others. This achievement was perhaps the most important job performed by the society on behalf of the community.

In their contacts with others they broke away from the shy life they were accustomed to in the villages back in the Azores islands. As their participation increased they became more effective. They learned how to speak in public, and address those of higher ranking office in the lodge, as called for in the rituals they swore to obey. The fraternalist became a better man through the teachings of the society, thus strengthening the bonds of brotherhood so much needed to conquer a position of respect and acceptance to which he aspired in the American community.

Fourth U.P.E.C. Annual Convention (1890). The first convention held at the hall of Council No. 1, San Leandro, California.

Delegates and officers at the 19th Annual Convention held in 1905 in Stockton, California.

The delegates would travel to faraway cities all over the state, when in the month of October, they would gather for a few days, participating not only in the democratic process of the business sessions, but also in the variety of programs usually prepared by host councils for their entertainment. They had pride in their tasks at times trying to outdo the previous convention hosts.

In 1901 delegates were paid $2.00 per day, an expense shared by the Supreme Council for one delegate, while the balance would be paid by their respective subordinate councils. Representation was based on the size of membership — one delegate for each thirty-five members or fraction thereof. In later years the Supreme Council assumed the cost of the entire number of delegates allowed each council. Also the basis was changed to forty members or fraction thereof.

In the 1900s a typical convention consisted of six days of activities. The program for the society's convention held in San Rafael on October 9th through the 14th, 1904 was as follows:

Sunday, October 9

3:15 p.m.   All officers and delegates to board the ferry boat in San Francisco (North Shore R.R. Co.) for San Rafael.

3:30 p.m.   Officers and members of Council No. 19 will meet in the U.P.E.C. Hall to march in the company of the 5th Regiment Band of the California National Guard to the station where officers and delegates will land.

3:45 p.m.   Officers and delegates arrival at the dock in Sausalito where they will be met by members of Council No. 14 and the Richardson's Band, who will escort them to San Rafael.

4:10 p.m.   Arrival of the Supreme Officers and delegates at the north shore station in San Rafael, from where they will be escorted by several bands to the Cochrane-McNear Hall.

4:30 p.m.   Arrival at the Hall for initiation of new members. All Supreme Officers and delegates will be handed out lists containing information on hotels, restaurants and rates.

8:00 p.m.   The city will provide electric illumination for a band concert in front of the court house until 10:00 p.m. In the Cochrane-McNear Hall there will be a showing of slides of historical places of Portugal and the Azores.

Monday, October 10

9:30 a.m.   March of all officers and delegates from the North Shore R.R. Station to the Cochrane-McNear Hall, accompanied by the 5th Regiment Band.

8:00 p.m.   Reception to officers and delegates offered by Council No. 19 (all officers are requested to be inside the hall at 8:00 p.m.; all members are requested to be at the door at 7:00 p.m.).

Tuesday, October 11

All Day   Business Sessions

8:00 p.m.   Stage play at the Opera House

Wednesday, October 12

8:00 a.m.   Business Session

10:00 a.m.   Parade from the Hall at 4th and E Streets, escorted by military and civil organizations of San Rafael.

2:00 p.m.   Picnic at Schuetzen Park, Band Concert (The California Northwestern R.R. furnished a special train to carry members to the part at ten cents round trip.)

8:00 p.m.   Variety Show, Opera House, while there will be band concert in the plaza until 10:00 p.m.

U.P.E.C. uniform rank marching in convention parade held in San Rafael, California.

U.P.E.C. Officers in regalia pose in front of old City Hall, Davis Street, San Leandro, California for July 4, 1888 parade. From left: Carl Iversen, Joseph Bettencourt, Manuel Andrade, Manuel Rodgers, Jesse Woods, Joseph Olympia, Manuel Braga, Joe Barbara and Manuel Avilla.

47

Thursday, October 13

Business Sessions until 3:30 p.m.

3:30 p.m.   Contest (Cavalhadas) amongst members of the society at the Baseball Club Park.

8:30 p.m.   Grand Ball, Armory Hall

8:30 p.m.   Informal dancing (Azorean popular dance - Chamarrita) at the Cochrane-McNear Hall. (All delegates were admitted upon presentation of badges. Guests were given admission by special ticket furnished in advance by the Convention Committee.)

Friday, October 14

Conclusion of convention business

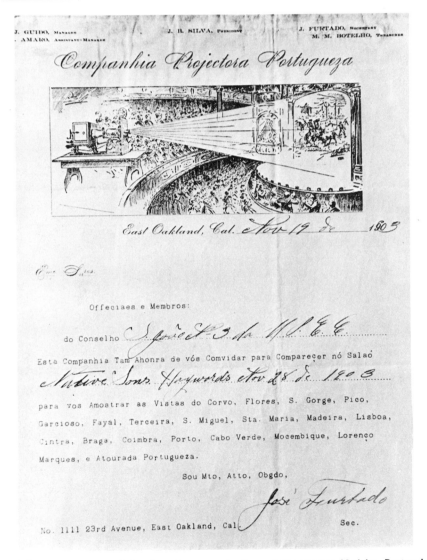

1903 announcement of showing of panoramic views of the Azores, Madeira, Portugal, etc., a typical entertainment offered by subordinate councils at conventions.

Stockton, California, October 17, 1912.

President and Secretary U. P. E. C., Supreme Convention,
Watsonville, California.

To the Officers and Members of the U. P. E. C. Supreme Council now assembled in State Convention in the city of Watsonville.

Gentleman: The city of Stockton sends greetings to you and I as Mayor of the city and in behalf of our citizens extend to you a cordial and sincere invitation to hold your next State Convention for the year 1913 in the city of Stockton. The city of Stockton is one of the most progressive and up-to-date cities of the State and I will assure you all will have a royal good welcome by the citizens and the Mayor. Hoping that I may receive a favorable answer to this invitation is my wish yours respecfully.

R. R. REIBENSTEIN,
Mayor of the City of Stockton.

Stockton, California, October 17, 1912.

The Hon. U. P. E. C. Convention,
Watsonville, California.

Gentlemen: The Stockton Merchants Association offers and wishes to extend to you an earnest invitation to hold your next. State Convetion in the City of Stockton it will be a pleasure for this association to cooperate with our esteemed and honored U. P. E. C. No. 24 in securing special railroad rates and hotel accomodations for the delegates to your convention in making their stay while here most pleasant and agreeable. Our geographical position with three transcontinental railroad lines daily steamer services to and from San Francisco and electric lines make this city easy of access and with the accommodations and many attractions which it affords gives no hesitancy in asking for your next state convention. Gentlemen a cordial welcome awaits you.

Yours respectfully

THE STOCKTON MERCHANTS ASSOCIATION,
By Raymond S. Miller.

Watsonville, California, 14 de Outubro de 1912.

Aos Dignissimos Oficiais e Membros do Conselho Supremo da U. P. E. C. reunidos na sua vigesima-sexta sessão anual.

Nós abaixo assinados propômos que a proxima sessão anual deste Conselho Supremo tenha lugar na cidade de Stockton, séde do Conselho Fernão de Magalhães, No. 24, da U. P. E. C.

LUCINDO FREITAS

LAW T. FREITAS

M. S. LIAL

JOSE RODGERS

Representantes do 24.

Invitations from subordinate councils and other entities inviting U.P.E.C. annual conventions.

49

Conventions would provide the organization and the Portuguese community with a tremendous stimulus. The towns receiving such conventions would roll out the red carpet for the length of the members' stay. Speeches went on for hours inflaming listeners with enthusiasm and pride.

In later years the U.P.E.C. Band and drill teams added to the pageantry of the convention programs. They would escort the Supreme Officers and delegates from the railroad stations to the halls where meetings were held. Mayors and even state officials would turn out to greet the leaders of the first and "most powerful society in the United States," as U.P.E.C. was often referred to by the press.

The parades would incorporate representatives of other Portuguese fraternal societies as well as subordinate councils of the U.P.E.C., carrying their beautiful banners in marching units, followed by horse-drawn carriages where the Supreme Officers would travel. The convention meant business for the host towns. Invitations would pour in from all over in a fierce competition. They would come not only from the hotels, but also from the mayor's office, local newspapers, banks, chambers of commerce and even from subordinate councils of other lodges in those localities.

As the years went by, the duration of conventions was reduced due to the cost of accommodations. Also, population growth in California cities diminished the freedom and safety once offered in the downtown areas. The bands became a thing of the past, as did the parades, whose permits became harder to get due to the transit regulations of certain towns. More difficulties arose when the State Highway Division gained access to quite a few of those main streets once controlled by municipalities.

Notwithstanding the pains of progress, conventions still provided the same opportunities for delegates to voice opinions, elect officers, legislate, make new friends and renew old acquaintances. Reduced to a combined four days of business sessions and entertainment, delegates still meet the spirit which reigned in years past — to unite all from far and near.

Portuguese farm house, San Leandro, California.

U.P.E.C. delegation to the 15th Annual Convention held in 1901, in San Luis Obispo, California. António Fonte (center) stands behind banner.

U.P.E.C. Convention Delegation in session at the Hilton Hotel, Oakland — 1972.

IX

PROTECTION

A cardinal principle of the society was the protection of "those who are near and dear to you" as stated in the initiation ceremonial. The protection offered then was based on assessments of one dollar for each members' death and fifty cents for the wife's. The first death claim was paid on November 15, 1880 to Maria Freitas Gravata in the amount of $59.00 for the death of her husband Manuel. The second claim was settled on June 19, 1881 in the amount of $133.00 for the death of Charles Borges.

The assessment method continued for the next eleven years. Membership kept growing and in 1892 the constitution was changed to introduce a plan called Class A. Members would contribute the amount of $1.50 per death in the subordinate council based on the total membership up to one thousand four hundred persons. Once the society exceeded that number of members, the assessment rate would then drop to one dollar per death. This plan provided an insurance amount of $1,400 for each member. Also, it contained a provision that should the wife of the member predecease him, he would collect a sum of $400 leaving a balance of $1,000 payable upon his death to his beneficiaries. Under this plan members continued to be assessed fifty cents for each death of a member's wife.

Copy of assessment notice — member's death.

Four years later the convention adopted a second plan similar to Class A. The new plan was known as Class B and provided a $700 death benefit, $200 of which was payable upon the death of a member's wife. Also at this time assessments were changed to one dollar for Class A and fifty cents for Class B for each member's death. The assessment for the wife's death was set at twenty-five cents for Class A and twelve and one half cents for those who had selected Class B. Therefore, it was only from 1896 on that members were given a choice of two plans of protection. It is interesting to note that, even though wives of members were given protection, they were never given voice in the management of the society's affairs until 1952, when the constitution and by-laws were amended to allow admission of women.

Around 1912 the society introduced two other plans which became known as Class C in the amount of $1,000 and Class D in the amount of $300. Rates on these plans were calculated without actuarial input and the inevitable result took place. Insolvency would haunt the membership for the next few years. Adjustments on rates by group ages were made by the inexperienced men time and time again until 1935, when the Insurance Commissioner of the State of California stepped in with a strong recommendation for readjustment of all rates for Classes A, B, C and D in order to bring the society to one hundred percent solvency.

Facsimile of membership certificate Class B.

The actuarial firm of Barrett N. Coates of San Francisco was involved in this tremendous task which was dealt with at a special convention held in San Leandro, California, in that year. This was the only special one ever held. As a result of the measures adopted at this convention many feelings were hurt, especially of those members whose advanced age called for a substantial increase in the prevailing rates. These reforms affected other societies as well both in California and in other states.

Deficit over deficit was registered in the Reserve Fund dating back to 1905. Deaths were mounting and the miscalculated rates were insufficient to cover the deficits. The open contract feature, characteristic of the fraternal benefit system, is what saved the society. Otherwise, the organization would have had to be dissolved or taken over by a company appointed by the Insurance Commissioner.

The monthly rates after the adjustment ranged from $1.50 for a sixteen year old to $5.20 for a fifty-five year old with a Class A plan. The American experience, or legal reserve plans, were made available to members and prospective members for the first time in April, 1929, even though they had been adopted on October 13, 1927. There were only two such plans available: the Twenty Payment Life and Endowment at Age Sixty-five for amounts from $500 to $3,000 per life.

House for the aged (today known as a rest home). A dream of Jose Pimentel never realized.

In 1942 U.P.E.C. introduced the Endowment at Age Eighty-five, the Twenty Payment at Age Sixty-five, and the Twenty Year Endowment. They reduced the minimum amount of coverage that any member could buy on the two original plans from $500 to $250. The maximum amount of coverage remained the same, $3,000. It was during this year that the juvenile class was initiated for ages zero to fifteen. The plans available were the same as in the adult class, except for those calling for settlement at age sixty-five. In addition, juveniles were offered two new plans, the Thirty Payment Life and Thirty Year Endowment for a maximum of $1,000 of insurance.

At this time the society was struggling for membership. The question of protection was somewhat overlooked in the process. In 1951 amounts of coverage were increased for ages zero to five, to a maximum of $2,000 per life. One year later the maximum coverage for everyone was raised to $5,000, optional double indemnity coverage. Later, the maximum of $5,000 was changed to $10,000 and finally in 1960 the society lifted this ceiling and made available all of its insurance programs up to one half million dollars per life, reinsuring a portion of the risks with one of the largest companies in the world.

The Reserve Fund, which began in 1895 with a mere sum of $4,098, had grown to $203,219 by 1907 and $1,054,614 by 1925. By 1926 the society's assets had reached $1,178,733 and consisted of four funds: The Reserve, $1,155,428; Special, $18,240; Building, $3,227; and the General Fund, $1,836. Death claims paid had gone from a total of $73,302 in 1893; $222,381 in 1899; $1,675,408 by 1914 and $11,159,464 by 1964, the largest amount of death benefits ever paid by any of the Portuguese fraternal benefit societies organized in the United States of America.

In spite of the problems caused by hard times, premature deaths, poor underwriting practices, coupled with an economic depression and, at times, inadequate investment policies, not to mention the indirect effects of two world wars, the society today boasts a surplus of close to one million dollars for the protection of its members and appearance of any contingency. The present insurance plans offered to members meet a variety of needs, including those for tax sheltered annuities. One can truly say that the Portuguese conservative ways brought from the old country have succeeded in the light of adversity.

The feeling of unity among members at times was not so prevalent as a result of the emotional nature of some of the Portuguese. But it was indeed deep rooted in the hearts of its members who were always determined to succeed, if for nothing else than their own pride and rejection of failure. The Society provided for protection of their brothers. After all the protection they sought under our roof was the true manifestation of love for those who were near and dear to them. They bought,

The most outstanding leaders of U.P.E.C. early history (standing from left): António Fonte, John G. Mattos and José Pimentel; (seated) Francisco I. Lemos and Lucindo J. Martins.

and still buy, that protection insurance not because they had to die, but because others had to live without being put to shame as it happened time and again prior to 1880. The shame or the "dark days" referred to by Manuel Silveira Andrade could well be interpreted by today's language as racial descrimination. How depressing it was for the Portuguese to see their compatriots cremated by the county against their religious convictions.

The protection brought about in 1880 by those thirty men meant more than the dollars and cents that went to soothe the orphans and widows. These funds helped meet the spirit of the letter of the societies burial ceremonial that "there is no man so poor that he shall be denied the repose of a grave." For those taken ill, the society provided living benefits through funds created in several subordinate councils under the management of local memberships. They usually called for weekly benefits for loss of time.

In 1926 Joseph A. Freitas introduced an amendment to the constitution of the society calling for the creation of the Sick Benefit Fund in the Supreme Council. One year later, the rules which would govern this Fund were spelled out in detail. Initially it was open to all males age sixteen through fifty, and contributions were set at seventy-five cents monthly. Benefits derived from this plan would range from $5.00 to $10.00 per week with a ceiling of $150.00 in any one year. The Fund was in competition with those managed by local councils, so throughout the years this program did not go as well as expected. The Supreme Council's recent growth is a result of the consolidations of many of those funds managed by the subordinate councils which have lacked support of local members. In 1974 women were allowed to join the Supreme Council sick benefit.

Conventions brought the memberships together in pride and fraternalism.

X

CHARITY AT HOME

The society's purposes included those of charity to deserving members and causes. However, it was not until 1890 that an attempt was made to organize a charity fund. In that year a resolution was introduced by J.C. Rodrigues calling for five percent of all monies received by the Supreme Council to be set aside to help members "in case of a calamity." The resolution was defeated by the convention delegation.

The calamity alluded to by Rodrigues did not take long to happen. On April 18, 1906 the earth shook and as a result almost destroyed the city of San Francisco. According to the *Arauto* (issue of April 28, 1906), the Portuguese settlements around Jackson Street suffered most. Commercial establishments, hotels and barber shops were all destroyed. The Portuguese-American Bank was condemned and its offices transferred temporarily to 2129 Laguna Street (corner of Clay). Later it was moved to Market and Post Streets and it was the first savings bank to open for business after the earthquake. All typographical material of the *U.P.E.C. Bulletin,* housed at 525 Front Street offices for the *Uniaõ Portuguesa* newspaper, were also destroyed.

Many Portuguese lost their houses and found themselves in the streets like many other victims of that tremendous catastrophy. The horrors of the quake were also felt in many other cities, such as San Jose, Santa Rosa and Oakland. On the morning of the earthquake, many of the Portuguese immigrants living in Oakland who worked and owned businesses in San Francisco found themselves unemployed and destitute.

On April 25 the Board of Directors of the Supreme Council called a special meeting to consider the emergency of the situation and adopted a resolution granting a waiver of payment of dues which would have been payable in the month of April of that year.

A committee was sent to San Francisco to evaluate the needs of the members affiliated with Councils No. 15 and 30 of San Francisco. As a result of the survey the committee recommended to the Board of Directors dispensation of payment of dues for the months of May and June, in addition to a donation in the amount of $300.00 made from the General Fund. Subordinate councils also raised funds for that purpose. Also noted was the noble gesture of the Portuguese from the island of Faial, Azores, who held a drive for funds which netted $220.00, sent directly to the U.P.E.C. for distribution among their countrymen in San Francisco. As the news of the catastrophy became more clear, the U.P.E.C. again drew from its General Fund for donations — this time donating $270.00 to those victims of Portuguese background who were not members of the society.

The years went by and the idea of a fund to assist those in need seemed to find certain opposition. Help was always given, but the General Fund always supported the donations. Many moving scenes are described in detail in the convention minutes. The hat was usually passed around the delegation to collect funds in favor of the less fortunate.

Finally in 1928 a Charity Fund was established which would provide assistance, mostly in the way of dues and premium payments, to aid those members in need who otherwise would have had to let their certificates of burial insurance lapse. The Charity Fund was the result of several years of attempts by U.P.E.C. leaders to build a hospital *(Casa Hospitalar)* for members who could not afford other private facilities.

The suggestion for the hospital was introduced in 1913. A committee was appointed to spearhead a drive for funds. The Supreme Council set aside $1,500 from

The best Portuguese illustrated news paper in the State of Califor nia. Largest circulation in Western States including Hawaiian Territory. The best advertising medium to get the Portuguese trade.
Our Place is Grove 501

O Reporter

ORGAO DA COLONIA PORTUGUEZA NOS ESTADOS UNIDOS

ANNO VIII   OAKLAND, CAL., 18 DE MARÇO DE 1905   No. 388

O Hospital Portuguez de Santo Antonio

Progresso dos Con-dados de California

FOI FUNDADO EM OAKLAND, CAL., A 6 DE JUNHO DE 1904

Estatistica dos ultimos dez annos

Dr. M. M. Enos, Presidente do Hospital de St. Antonio

Edificio do Hospital de Santo Antonio. Esquina das ruas 18 e Grove, Oakland, Cal.

Article on Saint Anthony Hospital as it appeared on the front page of "O Reporter," March 18, 1905.

Relação dos donativos angariados pela Commissão Operaria Fayalense prometora dos festejos do 1o. de maio para soccorrer os portuguezes victimados pela catastrophe de San Francisco da California.

Producto do Bando precatorio .. ..186$000
Subscripçao promovida entre alguns socios da associação de soccorros mutuos "Artista Fayalense 4$000
Anonymo .. ..250 reis
Manuel Emygdio Gonçalves .. ..500 reis
Manuel Nunes da Silva .. ..655 reis
Jose Carlos da Silva .. ..250 reis
Subscripçao promovida pelo parocho da freguezia da
    Ribeirinha, rev. Jose da Rosa Terra .. .. 15$125
Idem de Pedro Miguel, rev. Jose Duarte .. .. 11$850
Idem dos Flamengos, rev. Thomaz Pereira Luiz .. .. 16$000
Idem do Salao, rev. Jose Silveira Goulart .. ..   4$125
Idem de Castello Branco, rev. Francisco Silveira de
    Avila .. .., ...   6$060
Idem dos Cedros, rev. Jose Maria Martins .. ..   2$00
Idem da Payra do Almoxarife, rev. Feliciano A. de
    da Silva Reis .. .. 10$550
Idem da Feiteira, rev. Manuel Moniz Madruga .. ..   8$625
Somma reis moeda açoreana .. ..264$060
    Horta, 11 de junho de 1906.

A Commissao

Manuel Lourenço da Silva,
Joao Meyrelles Antunes,
Joao Garcia Jr.
Manuel de Serpa da Silva,
B. Augusto,
Jose da Silva Cardoso
Henrique Garcia da Silva,
Vicente Cezar Espinola,
Victor de Lemos e Silveira,
Joao Silveira Luiz,
Guilherme Augusto da Rosa,
Manuel Nunes da Silva,
Joao de Deus Teixeira,
Manuel Silveira de Brum **Jr.**,
Manuel de Sousa Wenceslau,
Antonio Joaquim da Silva **Jr.**

Copy of the report from Faial showing the donations collected for Portuguese victims of the San Francisco earthquake. (U.P.E.C. Minutes, page 148, 1906.)

its General Fund to initiate the drive. The idea never came to a fruitful conclusion, in spite of the offer of a ten-acre site made by João Borges, a member of Council No. 18, Benicia. In 1927 a resolution was introduced by John J. DeGlória calling for all monies raised for the hospital to be returned to the donors. One year later, since there were still unclaimed hospital funds, a motion was made that the money on hand be deposited in an account to start a Charity Fund.

In the years to come the fund would grow with donations from individual members and events promoted for such purposes. One of those events was the showing of *Life of Queen Elizabeth,* a stage play organized by the S.P.R.S.I. during the visit to California of Cardinal Cerejeira of Lisbon. The site selected for the stage play was Hanford. The net proceeds were to go to the Charity Fund, but as it turned out the attendance at the show was so poor that the General Fund of the Supreme Council of the U.P.E.C. ended up paying a deficit of $331.93.

Since 1943 the fund has been maintained by a twenty-five cent contribution made annually by each member in addition to individual donations made mostly at conventions and by insurance certificate proceeds willed by some good-hearted members. Disbursements from the fund are authorized to needy members of the society and only upon requests made in writing by subordinate councils after which they are screened by the Board of Directors.

XI

CHARITY ABROAD

Charity was also expressed towards many causes in and out of the United States, especially to countrymen in the Azores. Acts of this nature are reflected in the minutes of the society as well as in accounts made public in the press. This desire of U.P.E.C. members to assist projects in the home country has been traditional. One might even say that it is in their veins. The first of such acts appeared during the administration of President José Pimentel.

On August 28, 1893, a cyclone had caused great damage in some islands leaving hundreds homeless and without means to earn a living, since the storm had destroyed all of their boats. An appeal was made through various councils on October 17 of that year resulting in the collection of $292.50. This sum, even though small, was a gesture of solidarity from the part of a membership that at the time was struggling to meet their own needs in California. A check for $195 was drawn and mailed to Father José Leal Furtado of Horta, Faial, and another in the amount of $97.50 to the Bishop of Angra do Heroismo, Terceira. The following letter of thanks was received explaining how money was spent:

> "Do que sem tem recebido já foram soccorridos os pobres maritimos que haviam perdido as suas embarcações, unico meio de ganharem of pão quotidiano, concertando-se umas, substituindo-as por outras as que de todo haviam ficado inutilisadas — construindo-se um barco de cabotagem entre of porto do Calhau da ilha do Pico e esta ilha, estando dois eguaes no estaleiro para os portos de São Matheus e de São João d'aquella ilha. E tenciona-se edificar as casas dos probres que a enchente de mar n'aquelle dia desastroso arrazou completamente."

San Miguel Island in the Azores is the second place to have benefited from U.P.E.C. members. A flood inundated the villages of Povoação and Ribeira Quente on November 2, 1896, leaving the villagers in deplorable situation. A check for $153.50 (U.S. dollars), equivalent to 275 *Reis Moeda Insulana,* was sent to Francisco Xavier Pinto, treasurer for the committee in Ponta Delgada entrusted with the collection of donations for the relief of those victims.

On the evening of May 4, 1899 a fire gutted the only hospital and asylum for the poor in Horta, Faial, leaving it completely destroyed. An appeal for funds was sent to the U.P.E.C. since, according to the request, "the membership of this benevolent society is known for its great sentiments."

A check for Thirteen British Pounds (around $65.00 in gold) was obtained from the membership of six councils and sent to help the reconstruction of a new hospital building.

But the generosity of those who made up the various councils of the U.P.E.C. knew no nationalities or religious backgrounds. Where there was a need, they were there helping to meet it. On January 2, 1909, a most touching letter was written by João Pereira, then Supreme President, requesting funds to be sent to Sicily and Calabria, where nearly two hundred thousand had been killed in an earthquake which destroyed some twenty cities and villages in one of the greatest catastrophies known to mankind.

COMMISSÃO EXECUTIVA

Angariadora de soccorros para as victimas da catastrophe na villa da Povoaçao, Ilha de S. Miguel, Açores.

SECRETARIA: Donohoe Building, Rooms 6 e 7, Market Street, San Francisco.

DR. I. DA COSTA DUARTE, presidente; DR. J. DE SOUZA BETTENCOURT, vice-presidente;
M. BETTENCOURT DA CAMARA, secretario; CESAR BETTENCOURT, thesoureiro;
F. DA CAMARA, STONE, vogal.

San Francisco, Cal., 3 de janeiro de 1897.

Exm.º Snr.

A commissão executiva angariadora de soccorros para as victimas da recente catastrophe na villa da Povoação, ilha de S. Miguel, Açores, que tenho a honra de secretariar, encarrega-me de ir solicitar de V. Ex.ª o favor de communicar a essa distincta sociedade que esta commissão implora uma esmola para minorar os soffrimentos de tantos infelizes attingidos por essa tremenda desgraça, cujos horrorosos pormenores são do dominio publico.

Esta commissão, sr. secretario, espera dos tradicionaes sentimentos de philanthropia d'essa benemerita sociedade que não se negarà concorrer para suavisar os soffrimentos de tanto desgraçado, e roga a V. Exa. se digne patrocionar perante ella esta causa, que repùta santa, porque é causa de centenas de desventurados sem casa, sem roupa e sem pão.

Outro sim, roga esta Commissão a V. Exa. se digne communicar-lhe, opportunamente, qual a importancia da esmola com que essa sociedade concorre para fim tão humanitario.

Aproveito a occasião, sr. secretario, para apresentar a V. Exa. a affirmação do meu respeito muito profundo.

Deus Guarde a V. Exa.

Exm.º snr. secretario. *da Unno San João*

N.º 3 da U. P. E. C.

Hayward

BETTENCOURT DA CAMARA, Secretario.

Facsimile of a letter addressed by Executive Committee for the fund raising drive for victims of Povoação, presided by Dr. I. da Costa Duarte, then Consul of Portugal in San Francisco.

Copia.—Santa Casa da Misericordia da Horta.—No. 4. Illustrissimo e Exmo. Sr.—Em a noite de 4 de maio proximo findo a população d'esta cidade da Horta, ilha do Fayal, Açores, foi sobresaltada por um pavoroso incendio que em poucas horas destruiu totalmente o edificio onde se achavam installados o hospital e azylo de mendicidade. Se, graças a esforços e dedicação incomparaveis, foi possivel salvar das chamas apenas com excepção de um, tantos desgraçados que alli encontravam abrigo, o mesmo não se pode dizer com respeito ao edificio, mobiliario, roupas, etc., que tudo o fogo devorou. Reconstruir, pois, o hospital e provêl-o do necessario para satisfazer ao seu fim, tornou-se o pensamento dominante d'esta Meza Administrativa; mas como os recursos proprios são insignificantes, resolveu ella recorrer á phylantropia e caridade publica solicitando quaesquer donativos com a alludida applicação. Por isso, e porque conhecemos a grandeza de sentimentos que distinguem os illustres membros da benemerita Sociedade Portugueza, de que V. Exa. é mui digno presidente, vimos respeitosamente implorar a reconhecida generosidade d'essa phylantropica aggremiação a favor da obra de caridade que pretendemos levar a effeito. —Deus Guarde a V. Exa.—Sala das Sessões da Meza da Santa Casa da Misericordia da Horta, 1 de Julho de 1899.—Illustrissimo e Exmo. Sr. V. T. Braga, M.° Presidente Supremo da União P. E. C.—Está conforme— L. J. Martins—Sec. Sup.

(Copy of letter requesting funds for Horta's hospital.)

Floods raged through Indiana and Ohio and the society made its presence known with an offer of funds sent to the Governors of both states to assist victims.

World War I was in progress and Portugal was involved. Victims of the war were numerous and again the society took leadership in obtaining relief funds.

Carlos Rangel de Sampaio, Consul of Portugal in San Francisco, assisted the committee with plans. Groups of ladies organized charity balls to raise funds. One of the balls was given on the evening of October 11, 1916 during the U.P.E.C. convention. The proceeds of this particular event were then divided between the Portuguese war victims and the American Red Cross. During that very same convention the delegates unanimously approved a resolution authored by Francisco I. Lemos for a $500 donation to be given to the Portuguese victims and a like sum to be sent to the American Red Cross.

Appeals continued for war victims in 1917. A committee, under the presidency of Firmino J. Cunha, organized a bazaar and open market to raise more funds. The San Leandro Reporter in its issue of November 3, 1917, calls the attention to the event on a front page article which opened with the following headlines and text:

BAZAAR TO AID WAR VICTIMS IN PORTUGAL
GRAND BAZAAR AND MARKET TO BE HELD IN THE OAKLAND AUDITORIUM NOVEMBER 7 TO 10 BY LOCAL AND OAKLAND PORTUGUESE

Although the Portuguese are fighting in Africa for more than one year and on the French soil for more than six months, they are the only allies of Uncle Sam that, so far, did not come to us for National Loan or applied for help for their Red Cross Society and many other organizations that have been aiding their victims of war, on the front and at home.

Now, however, the resources of those Portuguese patriotic and charitable organizations are sinking, and the Portuguese Red Cross, the Cruzada of the Portuguese women and some other equally meritable institution of Portugal have sent on an appeal of distress.

On November 8, 1917, the Board of Directors authorizes a disbursement of $500 on behalf of its Portuguese victims of the war; and $1,000 in favor of the American Red Cross.

On April 11, 1918, a check for $1,140 was sent to the Portuguese Red Cross, this time from members of Council No. 157 in Lovelock, Nevada, and another from the Supreme Council in the amount of $1,100 payable to the President of the United States, Woodrow Wilson, who was presiding over the American Red Cross.

The hearts of U.P.E.C. members were open and many were the donations they gave and obtained from family and friends to be sent directly to the Consul of Portugal in San Francisco, J. Soares, to the League of the Portuguese Women in Favor of War Victims, and to hundreds of friends and relatives of soldiers living in Continental Portugal and Azores.

IN 1921, funds were raised to assist the *Sé de Angra do Heroismo* in Terceira, Azores. Also in 1921 on April 14, $940.50 was sent to the Consul of Portugal in San Francisco, Euclides Goulart da Costa, to assist in the relief of victims of a famine which had struck the islands of Cape Verde. The proceeds went to pay for a shipment of one thousand sacks of corn, one thousand sacks of flour and two hundred fifty sacks of beans.

In 1923, the poor in the Azores were benefited with $2,942.57 of which $1,419.94 was sent to the island of San Miguel for distribution by Father João Pereira Damaso. The balance was divided amongst seven of the islands with a much smaller population. On February 14, Valentine's Day, 1924, the House of the Poor

Rua da Areia — Horta, Faial, after the 1897 earthquake.

Clothing unloading at São Jorge Island to help victims of São Jorge earthquake — 1964.

in Faial once again received assistance from U.P.E.C., so did the orphanage in Angra, Terceira.

In 1926, it was U.P.E.C.'s turn to help with a donation in favor of Faial inhabitants who were victims of an earthquake, returning their gesture during the San Francisco catastrophy of 1906. Various festivals were held including one in the Oakland Auditorium.

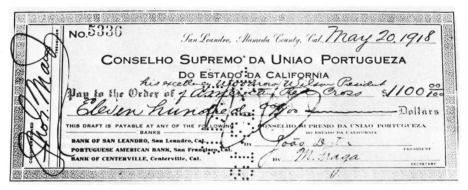

Copy of check payable to the order of President Woodrow Wilson. Donation to the American Red Cross.

THE WHITE HOUSE
WASHINGTON

June 1, 1918

My dear Sir:

The President very deeply appreciates the generous action of your organization in making so substantial a contribution to the war relief work of the American Red Cross, and he asks me to convey to you and to everyone concerned an expression of his cordial thanks.   Your letter of May 25th and the accompanying check for $1100.00 is being turned over to the Treasurer of the general society.

Sincerely yours,

Secretary to the President

In 1924, the island of São Jorge benefited from the generosity of U.P.E.C. members. Lists of those who were recipients were published in the U.P.E.C. bulletin by villages. This type of acknowledgement was later discontinued, since it was somewhat of an invasion of privacy.

In 1943 the island of Corvo, the tiniest of the Azores group, suffered a blow with the loss of a fishing vessel and her crew. U.P.E.C. again extended its charity to the families of the victims. One can truly say that the nine islands of the Azores found friends within U.P.E.C. even to present days, including those of Capelinhos, victims of Faial's volcanic eruption.

The most recent of such assistances took places in 1964 when U.P.E.C. received a telegram requesting clothing for earthquake victims on the island of São Jorge. The project was named "Carpet of Friendship" and involved the various Portuguese societies of the League, some Portuguese radio hours, Kings County Trucking Co., owned by M. Mancebo, and the United States Air Force. Within a span of three weeks, over seventy tons of clothing were collected and airlifted from Travis Air Base for distribution in São Jorge, Azores. Captain John Luque coordinated the project in the Azores.

In 1966, members of San Leandro Council No. 1 bought an ambulance which was flown to Terceira, Azores, an island served at the time by only one of such vehicles.

Charity has been extended abroad to the Azores, Africa and Italy. From far and near, those in sickness always found a place in the hearts of the U.P.E.C. family. But charity did not consist only in alms giving. It "embraced sympathy, compassion and fair mindedness, a consideration for the faults of others, a forgiving disposition, a just judgment for the motives of the fellowman." These were the teachings spelled out in the initiation ceremonies which, when well performed, impressed the newcomer in turn motivating him to restore peace to the troubled hearts of his fellow brothers.

The earthquake, which hit the Island of Terceira, Azores, on January 1, 1980 left many historical sites partially destroyed. The U.P.E.C. raised funds to assist the victims in the early stages of the catastrophe.

XII

THE U.P.E.C. BULLETIN

The appearance of this official publication can very well be attributed to the somewhat unstable relationship between the U.P.E.C. leadership and the Portuguese press.

The first newspaper published by the Portuguese in California dates back to 1880, the year when *Voz Portuguesa,* edited by Manuel Stone, appeared in San Francisco. This four-page newspaper, even though supported by a great number of subscribers in the Bay Area, did not last too long and disappeared in a few years. In 1885 it was replaced by *Progresso Californiense,* edited by Vicente da Virgem Maria, (known among the Portuguese as António Maria Vicente). Maria was in partnership with Manuel F.M. Trigueiros who, in 1887, published *A União Portuguesa,* a newspaper with a wide circulation in California until July 13, 1942, when it ceased publication.

One of the right arms, if not *the* right arm, of Trigueiros was Mário Bettencourt Camara. He worked part-time as editor of the *A União Portuguesa.* He had the command of the Portuguese language and possessed a vast knowledge of Portuguese culture and history. He was highly emotional and disapproved of the Catholic priests whom he considered "leeches" of the Portuguese community.

In turn, some priests were antagonistic towards the fraternal order and began to gather the Portuguese in large numbers to teach them how to work together and be civic minded in order to gain the respect of the American hosts.

This led to Camara's decision to initiate a bulletin for the society in order to combat some of the ill feelings he encountered among some of the newspaper owners. At times these men for their convenience would side with the priests and allow publication of tendencious articles or subjects considered private business of U.P.E.C. and in other instances would refuse or ignore publication of societies' events. In their envious attitudes they could not tolerate the growth and power that the society gradually was attaining. They therefore viewed it as a threat to the Catholic priests and newspapers who were both seeking economic support from the Portuguese immigrants.

In spite of these events Camara went ahead and on March 1, 1898, published for the first time the *U.P.E.C. Bulletin,* using the presses of *A União Portuguesa,* located at 525 Front Street, San Francisco, where he worked parttime. The new publication and the first one of its kind had four 9x12 inch pages. It contained the directory of both the Supreme Council and of the subordinate councils, the President's message, and some advertisements to help defray printing expenses.

The press run numbered 2,500 copies at a cost of $18.30 per month. Subordinate councils were to receive twenty-five percent of proceeds collected for ads they sold. The new monthly publication was sent to each member at a forty cents annual subscription or ten cents if bought in single copy.

After its appearance, the expected events took place. Many opinions were given about its format, quality and kind of subjects to be included, and of course, there was talk that Mario Bettencourt Camara had his name prominently in front as its Director-Owner. Publication of the bulletin gave reason for panic. People feared Camara's pen and knew of his feelings as a Republican and his feelings towards the Catholic priests, something Trigueiros never had allowed him to do in his own paper, *A União Portuguesa.* Everyone was skeptical of the idea, but Camara knew better. He had learned his lesson two years earlier in his fourteen issues of *A Chronica.*

Soon the U.P.E.C. Bulletin had the size of its pages increased to 18x12 inches, confined its contents to news related to U.P.E.C. activities only, and banished all advertisements which could influence its editorials and independence. The Supreme

BOLETIM da U.P.E.C.

PERIODICO MENSAL

Orgão official da "UNIÃO PORTUGUEZA DO ESTADO DA CALIFORNIA"

Sociedade fundada em San Leandro, California, no dia 1 de agosto de 1880.

ANNO 1	San Francisco, Cal., 1 de março de 1898	N.º 1

Entered at San Francisco Post Office as second class matter.

BOLETIM DA U.P.E.C.

Director-proprietario:
M. Bettencourt da Camara.

ESCRIPTORIO: 425 Front street.
OFFICINAS: International Printing House
(M. V. Lacnar. 719 Montgomery street)
SAN FRANCISCO, CAL.

EXPEDIENTE

O primeiro numero do BOLETIM que hoje temos a honra de apresentar aos nossos numerosos e dignos consocios na benemerissima União Portugueza do Estado da California, está longe de nos satisfazer. A morosidade em colher dados e informações dos srs secretarios, de um lado, e o limitadissimo espaço de que dispomos, de outro, concorreram convergentemente para nos inhibir de dar maior expansão á materia.

No proximo numero procuraremos condensar ainda mais, se isso for possivel, essa materia e corrigir o Directorio, procurando corresponder quanto melhor á confiança que em nòs depositou a exma. Direcção Suprema.

A demora da maioria dos srs. secretarios dos conselhos subordinados em enviarem os esclarecimentos solicitados pelo sr. secretario supremo; e, ainda, a forma incompleta e imperfeita como uma grande parte forneceu esses esclarecimentos, deu logar, com profundo pezar d'esta direcção, a elaborar-se um Directorio imperfeitissimo e sobre modo desigual.

Esperamos, porem, que os srs. secretarios dos conselhos cujas infor-

mações vieram incompletas, porão um pouco mais de boa vontade no pedido que de novo se lhes faz agora, a fim de que no proximo numero o Directorio saia completo e uniforme.

Eis as informações que devem ser enviadas a esta direcção pelos srs. secretarios dos conselhos que não teem ainda taes esclarecimentos no Directorio:

Data da organização do conselho.

Dias, *building, hall* e horas das reuniões.

Se dà soccorros em caso de doença, e quanto dà em dinheiro, e se dà medico, ou qualquer outra ajuda.

PARTE OFFICIAL

PRESIDENCIA SUPREMA

Circulares :

N.º 1.

(Em 12 de fevereiro de 1898)

Aos Conselhos Subordinados:
Senhores consocios:

Em virtude dos deveres que me são impostos na Sec. 1 do Art. IV da Const. dos Cons. Sub., na parte em que me manda "superintender em toda a sociedade" faço conhecer aos Conselhos Subordinados, para seu entendimento e fins convenientes, que a admissão de membros honorarios sò pode ter logar quando concorram no candidato positivamente todas as qualidades estatuidas na Sec. I e II e seus numeros 1 a 4 do Art. IV da Const. dos Cons. Sub., particularmente na condição de terem "PRESTADO RELEVANTES SERVICOS" á sociedade; e,

Considerando que a faculdade con-

cedida aos Cons. Sub. de fazerem essa admissão, tem dado logar a abusos;

Considerando que taes abusos constituem damno especial quando, como quasi sempre succede, taes honorarios teem por fim passar à categoria de socios de beneficio, e

Sendo certo que os deveres impostos à Presidencia Suprema de "Superintender em toda a sociedade" importa stricta obrigação de não deixar falsear as disposições da sua lei fundamental,

Faço saber que todas as propostas para membros honorarios apresentadas aos Cons. Sub. serão rejeitadas sempre que os candidatos não tenham prestado os SERVIÇOS RELEVANTES exigidos pela lei.

Mais faço saber, para o mesmo bom entendimento e fins consequentes, que a passagem de membros honorarios à classe de beneficios deve recahir em individuos que tenham adquirido a classificação de honorarios, nos termos expressos na lei, sem o quê, esta Presidencia, depois de obter a PROVA PROVADA de que taes membros não satisfizeram às condições impostas para merecerem a admissão como honorarios, recusará conferir-lhes os certificados de beneficios, submettendo os casos como "questão de lei" ao futuro Conselho Supremo.

N.º 2.

(Em 20 de fevereiro de 1898)

Aos srs. Presidentes e secretarios dos Conselhos Subordinados.

Toda a "Parte Official" do BOLETIM deve ser lida na 1.ª sessão de cada mez dos Conselhos Subordinados, devendo ser submettida à apre-

ANNUNCIOS E AVISOS: Em uma columna de 2 e 3-16 pollegadas.			
Tempo	1 Pollegada	2 Pollegadas	3 Pollegadas
1 mez ou 1 n."	$ 1,00	$ 1,75	$ 2,50
2 " " 2 "	1,75	3,00	4,00
3 " " 3 "	2,50	4,00	5,50

ASSIGNATURAS - por 12 numeros:

	Edição	
	Official	Especial
Estados Unidos :		
Para os membros da U. P. E. C. ...... **Gratis**	30 cents	
Para extranhos.................... 20 cents	50	"
San Francisco e extrangeiro :		
Para os membros da U. P. E. C. ...... **Gratis**	40	"
Para extranhos ....35 cents	60	"

Edição Especial, para os membros da U. P. E. C., 3 mezes ou 3 numeros, 10 cts, numero avulso, 5 cents.

A. B. Woods, 276 9th street, Oakland.

Foi organisado no dia 27 de dezembro de 1896.

Reune-se nas primeiras e terceiras terças feiras, r o Pithyan Hall, esquina das ruas 12 e Franklin, ás 8 horas da noite.

Secção de soccorros: Subsidio semanal de 7 dollars.

Membros no dia 1 do mez ultimo: ... 91

Pinole, n.° 26; Pinole. Pr., Manuel Pedro Maciel; v. p., Manuel Jose Lima; sec., Manuel P. S. Cabelleira; th., João J. Thomaz.

Reune-se nos ultimos domingos no Foresters Hall Tennett Ave., a 1 e mei a hora da tarde.

Membros no dia 1 do mez ultimo:

Da Apolice A

" B ... 29

San Pablo, n.° 27 ; San Pablo. Pr., Antonio P. de Faria; v. p., Antonio Garcia de Soito; sec., J. J. Pimentel; th.,Manuel da Roza Pereira.

Santa Clara, n.° 28; Santa Clara. Pr., Jose C. Soares; v. p., Manuel R. Martins; sec., Geraldo R. Martins; th., Manuel Vargas.

Reune-se nos segundos domingos no Espirito Santo Hall, cor. Louis e Lafayette sts., ás 2 horas da tarde.

Membros no dia 1 do mez ultimo:

Da Apolice A

" B ... 23

Merced, n.° 29; Merced. Pr., J. A. Coelho; v. p., M. F. Cardoso; sec., F. A. da Costa; th., J. A. Silveira.

Foi organisado a 10 de maio de 1897.

Reune se todos os domingos no K. of P. Hall, Front e Hoffman Ave., ás 2 horas da tarde.

Membros no dia 1 do mez ultimo:

Da Apolice A

" B ... 23

Corte Real, n.° 30; San Francisco. Pr., Antonio S. Martinho, 91 Jackson st.; v. p., Antonio C. Saraiva; sec., Jose M. Peregrino, 4 Sacramento st; th., Manuel S. Simas, 427 Davis st.

Reune-se nos primeiros e terceiros domingos no

Washington Hall, no 35 Eddy st., ás 7 horas da noite.

Secção de soccorros: Subsidio mensal de 7 dollars e serviços medicos.

Membros no dia 1 do mez ultimo:

Da Apolice A

" B ... 38

Santa Cruz, n.° 31; Santa Cruz. Pr., Manuel Mitchell; v. p., Jose S. Bento; sec., Jose B. Perry; th., Manuel S. Machado.

Membros no dia 1 do mez ultimo:

Da Apolice A

" B ... 39

San Jose, n.° 32; San Jose. Pr., Manuel F. Rosa; v. p., Guilherme P. Rosa; sec., Francisco P. Gomes; th., John S. Williams.

Danville, n.° 33; Danville. Pr., L. J. Martin; v. p., J. L. Bispo; sec., Jose S. Maciel; th., M. J. Medina.

Numero de membros no dia 1 do mez ultimo ... 16

Council financed the publication and recovered the costs by charging its members for subscriptions. In 1907 Camara was told to discontinue his involvement with the bulletin and every council was instructed to mail all communications for publication in the bulletin directly to the Supreme Secretary, Lucio J. Martins. The Board of Directors determined that all communications addressed to Camara were to be disregarded.

The magazine grew in number of subscriptions and its preparation was sought by various printing shops which began to flourish in the Portuguese community.

In 1908 Joaquim de Menezes, editor of *O Arauto,* located at 4 Folsom Street, San Francisco, was the successful bidder for the bulletin. In 1911 it went to International Printing and Publishing Company at 330 Jackson Street, San Francisco and in 1913 Manuel B. Quaresma of 1411 Twenty-First Street, Sacramento became its publisher. At this time the bulletin page size was reduced to 8½x11 inches.

In 1921 Rev. Guilherme S. Glória had a chance to print it at 1011 Franklin Street, Oakland. Five years later it went to the printing shop of *A Colônia Portuguesa* newspaper at 1927 East 14th Street, Oakland. In 1930 it moved again to Guilherme Glória's shop at 237 East 14th Street, Oakland, and in 1933 it went to J.J. Pimentel, owner of the Signal Press in Atwater where it stayed until 1950.

This constant change of printing shops indicated the politics of the press to gain access to the printing of the bulletin, thus tantalizing their competitors. The holder of the printing contract always played as a favorite for the society working it to his advantage, especially seeking subscriptions for their newspapers provided by the mailing lists of the society. Almost all of the bulletin printers had a newspaper or influence over one.

In 1951 the printing of the bulletin came back to Oakland where it was handled by John M. Brazil and in 1957, moved to San Leandro's Service Press, then owned by Mayor Jack D. Maltester. It was then published every two months instead of monthly.

In 1960 the Board asked for bids for the bulletin, by then reduced to eight pages, and *Jornal Portugues* of Oakland got it but lost it one year later to *Voz de Portugal* of Hayward. In 1967 its publication was interrupted to allow the experiment of a radio program. For the next six months the U.P.E.C. social events were broadcast simultaneously in English and Portuguese, over several morning radio stations programs throughout California.

The voices of Celeste dos Santos Avila (Rosinha) and Carlos Sousa were heard on the radio program entitled "Voice of the Union." Even though it was a well directed program it did not meet the communication needs among the membership of the society. The program, at a cost of $440 monthly, was discontinued and in its place appeared a quarterly publication known as *U.P.E.C. Life,* which is still distributed to all households in the U.P.E.C. family. The bi-colored publication, initiated in January of 1967, contains news of activities of the organization and articles of a Portuguese historical and cultural nature, spread through its twenty-four pages, many of them illustrated. In 1930 the bulletin contained a section entitled "Coluna da Saude" (Health Column), authored by Dr. José Leal de Azevedo, then U.P.E.C. Medical Examiner, in which he gave medical advice to the society members.

The bulletins, at times, contained open columns which encouraged participation of the membership. Of those, we single out "Subordinate Councils Mail" and "Criteria," which became very controversial and led to its discontinuance.

Prior to 1957 the bulletin was entirely written in the Portuguese language. Lack of an editorial staff with the proper knowledge of the language and the fact that a large portion of the membership consisted of second and third generations who could not read Portuguese led to the publishing of the magazine in English. Lately the magazine is becoming more and more bi-lingual to satisfy the needs of a large number of Portuguese members who recently have joined the organization.

Even though the magazine does not accept advertisement, it did however carry ads encouraging the purchase of War Bonds in the forties. In 1942 and 1943 its pages contained slogans such as "That's Right, Keep Buying to Keep Flying for Uncle Sam"; FDR says, "Curtail Spending, Put Your Savings Into War Bonds Every Payday" and "Back the Attack — Buy War Bonds and Stamps." All of these ads were of a patriotic nature, for World War II was under way and U.P.E.C. had many members enlisted in the armed forces.

Articles authored by several members were accepted for publication. They were usually either of an historical nature or oriented towards motivating the society's membership to participate in social and charitable activities. António Conceição Teixeira was one of those who regularly, and for many successive years, contributed such articles.

The bulletin has always abstained from publishing articles of a political nature. However, it did not refrain from touching upon issues of a delicate nature whenever such issues affected the interests of the membership at large. One of those articles in the columns of the U.P.E.C. Bulletin dealt with the attacks on the fraternal societies, especially the I.D.E.S. made in 1924 by Aristides de Sousa Mendes, Consul of Portugal in San Francisco. The protest, signed by leaders of both societies and some members of the Portuguese press, was the only so far ever to find a place in the bulletins of our society.

The issue raised by Consul Mendes intended to offend those who had worked hard to enhance the good name of the Portuguese in California through fraternal activity.

The bulletin has served as a means of communication among the members, bringing them closer to each other. Its present circulation of nearly 5,500 is also extended free of charge to universities and cultural institutes, including some overseas in the islands of the Azores. There families and relatives of immigrants browse through its pages and see relatives, who, through their participation in the promotion of the society, are pictured by our volunteer photographers.

Everyone who misses an issue is always ready to advise the society of the fact, for it is important to them. Sometimes, however, the fault might be with the mailers, the post office, or, as in 1899, the member who used an Americanized name different from the one used in mailing the bulletin.

First newspaper published by the Portuguese in California.

XIII

WHY A HYMN?

It is customary in every organization to have a flag or a banner showing the colors and emblem selected by its membership. But not everyone can offer a hymn. So the question is why U.P.E.C. would choose to have one. Hymns, besides being of great inspiration can also cure evils.

Some of the first members of the society were Masons, a common affiliation at the time among Portuguese. The order accepted anyone regardless of religion or creed, to attain the goal it set out to meet — unity of its members. At first only men were allowed to enter session rooms. Therefore some ladies would be left at home going about domestic affairs while others would stay with friends, gossiping about this new society whose members were forbidden to "discuss any of its workings in public or with anyone not affiliated with the order." This secrecy led women to become suspicious and even scared, for there were rumors that their husbands and boyfriends were "making pacts with Satan." As many Azoreans are superstitious, this thought soon found a nest to grow.

This affair only became really serious when an article about Masonry, written by Father Manuel Francisco Fernandes, appeared in the *Progresso Californiense,* issue of February 5, 1887, published in San Francisco, California.

"I know we have some individuals in the Masonry (Freemasons) who ignore the danger they are in regarding salvation. Therefore we write these lines on their behalf hoping that they will not in them our influence in saving their souls and make them retire from a society headed by Satan, whose meetings consist, in the words of Bergier, in orgies and Bacchanadas and have for their principal aim the destruction of the Church of God."

This article may or may not have been directed to the U.P.E.C. at a time when a Supreme Council was in the process of being organized.

Francisco Ignacio de Lemos, of Council No. 3, Hayward, and Father Guilherme Silveira Gloria, met one day to see if they could think of an idea to combat these rumors intended to destroy the already flourishing society. After some thought they agreed that the best they could do was to write a hymn that would sing both of patriotism and religion. This no doubt proved, especially to the *Damas da Colonia* (ladies of the Portuguese community), that the society was not a Masonic one.

This step was of great importance especially since Father Glória had already joined U.P.E.C. Council No. 1. The idea of a hymn, and of having the priest as a member of the order, would suffice to calm fears — and it did. A few days later, the U.P.E.C. Hymn was being played and sung for the first time at Mesdames Isabel and Ana Glória's residence on Callan Ave., San Leandro.

The music was adapted by Francisco Ignacio Lemos from a composition of Reverend Joaquim Silvestre Serrão, a very famous Portuguese composer of religious music who spent most of his life on the island of San Miguel, Azores. The lyrics of nine syllables, with an accent on the third, sixth and ninth, were written by Fr. Fuilherme S. Glória, patterned after the *Hino do Trabalho* of António Feliciano de Castilho.

In a short time this hymn was sung in every meeting hall, in private houses, at the various festivities promoted by the society and even within Catholic and other churches. Every officer and member learned those very inspiring lyrics and displayed pride and enthusiasm when the occasion called for its singing.

The hymn, in the words of Glória, was "an appeal to religion and to the patriotism of our grandfathers. It was a solemn declaration that the arms of the new society were God and Country — the two strongest and most noble ties that unite the hearts of man, with the intelligence of man to earth and heaven." The hymn made those rumors about satanism disappear, and gradually the Portuguese women began defending the society, encouraging their husbands and friends to join. Today, the hymn is still sung at conventions and played in churches and funeral parlors as a last tribute to U.P.E.C. members.

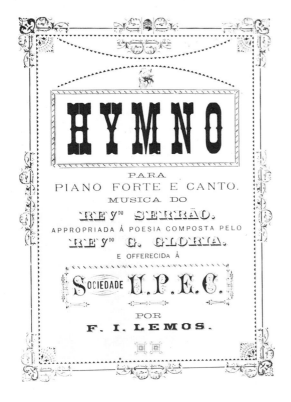

Facsimile of cover of U.P.E.C. Hymn - First Edition

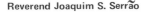

Reverend Joaquim S. Serrão

HYMNO DA SOCIEDADE, U. P. E. C.

Voz.

Meus Irmãos, trabalhemos unidos
Nestes laços tão santos d'amor;
Que seremos do céo protegidos!
Trabalhemos Irmãos, com valor!

Côro.

Gloria, Gloria á União Portugueza,
Que o bom Deus lá do céo nos doou;
Que n'angustia soccorre a pobreza,
Cumpre a lei que Jesus ensinou!

Voz.

Vamos firmes, fieis e constantes
Uns aos outros levar protecção;
Porque, embora da Patria distantes,
Somos filhos da mesma nação!

Côro.

Gloria, Gloria á União Portugueza, **etc.**

Voz.

Quantos pobres da sorte prostrados,
Ante a morte sentiam horror!
Vendo os filhos sem pão desherdados,
E as esposas sem ter protector!

Côro.

Gloria, gloria á União Portugueza, etc.

Voz.

Para esses na ultima hora
Oh! que amarga e cruel afflicção!
Nem uma esperança a fulgir...Mas agora
Vem valer-lhes a nossa União!

Côro.

Gloria, gloria á União Portugueza, etc.

Voz.

A "União Portugueza" é um abrigo,
Que á viuva e ao orphão Deus dá!
E que ao morto offerece um jazigo!
Oh! que esmolla maior haverá!

Côro.

Gloria, gloria á União Portugueza, **etc.**

Voz.

Vamos firmes, fieis e **constantes**
Uns aos outros levar protecção;
Porque, embora da Patria **distantes,**
Somos filhos da mesma nação!

Côro.

Gloria, gloria á União Portugueza, etc.

Voz.

Portugal, Nossa Patria adorada,
Não negamos da gloria o teu brilho!
Foste rica! e, se és pobre, és honrada!
Cada qual d'entre nos é teu filho!

Côro.

Gloria, gloria á União Portugueza, etc.

Voz.

Foste grande no mar e na terra,
O teu nome tornaste immortal!
Foste grande na paz e na guerra,
Nunca escravo serás Portugal!

Côro.

Gloria, gloria á União Portugueza, etc.

Voz.

Um Livro ha, que te canta a historia,
Livro d'Oiro, que o mundo já leu;
Que tornou immortal tua gloria,
Foi Camões que esse Livro escreveu.

Côro.

Gloria, gloria á União Portugueza, **etc.**

Voz.

Quem tua gloria negar, sem brio **mente!**
E'covarde e vilão descortez!
Nunca leu a historia: é demente!
E'mentira! Não é Portuguez!!!

Côro.

Gloria, gloria á União Portugueza, **etc.**

Voz.

Vamos Firmes, fieis e constantes
Uns aos outros levar protecção,
Porque, embora da Patria distantes,
Somos filhos da mesma nação!

Côro.

Gloria, gloria á União Portugueza, etc.

Voz.

Portuguezes, ávante! prostrados,
Invoquemos de Deus a benção;
Que o Senhor nos conserve ligados
N'estes laços de Santa União.

PADRE GUILHERME GLORIA.

XIV

FROM UNIFORM RANK TO BAND

On August 15, 1902 F.J. Mathews (Mateus), then President of Council No. 25, Oakland, in a letter addressed to Supreme President, F.I. Cunha, announced that among the members of his council a troupe had been formed and the twenty-five participants had named it the Uniform Rank Division No. 1. The main purpose of the newly created team was "to make U.P.E.C. better known and to increase the social and recreational activities of the council."

The new idea was presented at the annual convention held in Merced, California, in October, 1902. The delegation immediately reacted favorably to the report of a committee appointed to study the possibility of even having what they called a General Command which would superintend all future Uniform Rank Divisions that any council wished to organize. The members of these divisions were then assessed twenty-five cents per month to help defray expenses incurred with the uniforms and hardware, which consisted of swords inscribed with the U.P.E.C. name — a total of twenty-two dollars for all.

In 1903 the convention delegates authorized the disbursement of $119 to pay for the fares of those members of the Uniform Rank who came to participate in the U.P.E.C. parade of delegates and officers.

In 1905 António Fonte presented a resolution calling for an allocation of $200 for the purchase of instruments for a band that the Uniform Rank proposed to organize. The band, in the words of Fonte, "would not only bring prestige to the society, but also a lot of publicity and no doubt attract the young generation."

U.P.E.C. Uniform Rank. António Fonte (center) and Mário B. Camara (left of Fonte).

Mário Bettencourt da Camara was elected director of the band and soon it was a consumated fact. The Portuguese press applauded the U.P.E.C. for consenting to the organization of the band, which attracted new members to the organization. Everyone wanted to belong to the band, for it gave them an opportunity to travel all over the state and present themselves publicly for the enjoyment of thousands that would come to listen to its concerts. Every convention program called for a parade with the Uniform Rank Drill Team and its band, in addition to public concerts given almost every evening in public squares where bandstands were available.

So the young men who made this band saluted Mayors, Governors and Lieutenant Governors at their residences and escorted them in parades. The morale booster, which emanated from the wind instruments, was enough to uplift the spirit of the Portuguese immigrants everywhere who proudly pointed to the navy blue uniforms sent from Portugal at a cost of $1,200 and which identified with the philharmonic bands of their own villages in the faraway Azores.

Official U. P. E. C. Band
Vallejo, California,
October 12, 1933.
To the Supreme Officers and Delegates,
U. P. E. C. now convened in the
Forty-Seventh Annual Convention
Vallejo, California.

Greetings:

We, the members of the Official U. P. E. C. Band, present, and those who through business ties were unable to attend, wish to extend our appreciation to your most august body for the honor and privilege of being part of your convention, and for the many pleasant and interesting trips you have made possible for us to share with you.

The majority of this band's membership is made up of men whose average participation in your lodge functions has been for twenty years and more.

During these many years, we have grown to love, honor and cherish, with ever increasing respect and devotion, our own loyal and true brother, and director, Pofessor Mario B. da Câmara. At the time he organized the U. P. E. C. Band in 1905, the material he had to choose from, were men whose knowledge of music, if any, was very limited. As a direct result of his inspiration and leadership, his untiring efforts, and many personal sacrifices, both in behalf of the U. P. E. C. and the band, he has, week after week, throughout the years, given his time and priceless experience to the rehearsals of our band so that it might become as we think it is today, an organization of well trained musicians of which any order might well be proud.

We respectfully petition, therefore, the adpotion of the following resolution: Be it resolved: that we, the members of the U. P. E. C. Band, wish to express our sincere appreciation of the constant guidance of Professor Mario B. da Câmara and trust that he may continue directing us as he has in the past, with honor to himself and to the organization he represents. God bless him!

THE U. P. E. C. BAND,
JOS. P. ROSE, Secy.

Resolution of thanks to Mário B. Camara, Director of U.P.E.C. Band.

It was not easy, but Camara, a strong and determined man who never recognized or accepted defeat, made it all happen. It was discipline in action. No one could miss rehearsals, held at his house, nor take hold of an instrument for fun. It was all serious, so serious that Camara was not ashamed to let John Philip Sousa conduct it at the International Exposition.

Stockton, Cal., October 16, 1918.

U. P. E. C. Grand Lodge.

Brother Americans:

Owing to the alarming spread of the Influenza here in Stockton during the last 48 hours the Board of Health have ordered the theatres and all places of public amusement closed; and it is necessary to provide some public amusement. Your magnificent band has in the past few nights provided the finest music heard in Stockton for many years. If they could, without interfering with your program, extend their entertainment for half an hour longer, while they are here, we are sure it will be appreciated.

With the best of wishes for the future of your benevolent association, we remain,

Very respectfully yours,

AMERICAN DENFENSE SOCIETY OF STOCKTON.

Resolution of Thanks.

U.P.E.C. Band, 1906.

A good thing is usually imitated or envied by others. In 1909 Mário Bettencourt Camara was found at odds with the matter of calling it the United Band of U.P.E.C. and I.D.E.S. This idea was argued by Lemos who expressed a strong feeling against such a name. The band went on for a while as the United Band and soon rivalries among the musicians led to naming it the U.P.E.C. Band — a name that lasted for many years to come.

After Camara's death in February of 1936, the band almost went out of existence. The musicians had lost a leader whose respect and interest for them would be hard to replace. On March 12, 1937, the friends of the band, and leaders of the U.P.E.C., during a fish dinner served at the hall of Council No. 13, located at the corner of Seventh and Henry Streets in Oakland, delegated to Manuel C. Medeiros the directorship of the band with Mike King as his assistant. New uniforms were ordered and paid through donations made by various members. The society never funded the band until recent years when musicians were union members and, as such, were paid wages according to scales set out by union rules.

Despite opposition from many members and officers, the Board of Directors for sake of tradition authorized payment for band concerts and participation in parades, a cost which sometimes reached the $2,500 mark.

Unhappiness about the U.P.E.C. Band reached a peak when musicians, without the knowledge of the Board of Directors of the society, contracted with the city of San Leandro and were found giving public concerts under the name of San Leandro Municipal Band. The musicians would trade caps when they were contracted for U.P.E.C. programs.

Upon Medeiros' death on June 20, 1966 his son Walter took the leadership of the band. A year later the Board of Directors, under pressure from the membership, considered the U.P.E.C. Band officially terminated. By that time U.P.E.C. had already given up parades which, year after year, were becoming more difficult because of lack of participation from the delegates, mostly in advanced age. Another factor leading to the demise of parades was the apathy that such parades were receiving from city officials and police departments, which were not about to interrupt traffic and close streets for an event whose significance was no longer of the greatness and brilliance enjoyed in the past. Many were those who mourned the band concerts that had gathered strangers and friends alike to listen to the amateur musicians, numbering sometimes thirty or more who so gallantly displayed their spotless uniforms and interpreted pieces written by the most famous composers.

U.P.E.C. Band posing during a concert given at the Golden Gate Exposition in Treasure Island (1939).

XV

HOME OFFICE

Once the Supreme Council was organized in 1887, the Supreme Directors began seeking space for the state headquarters which for a while functioned in the home of Supreme Secretary Lucindo J. Martins. Two years later members of Council No. 1, San Leandro, dedicated their two story wood frame building consisting of an office and a bar on the ground floor and an assembly hall on the second. Once the building was completed the Supreme Council became its first tenant, occupying the office space on the ground floor for the state headquarters at a monthly rental of five dollars.

The Home Office, consisting of a staff of three, would remain there for the next twenty years. This tenancy did not establish the best of relationships between the Board of Directors of the Supreme Council and the trustees of Council No. 1. The reason was that the hall had been built on land the Supreme Council owned as collateral for the bank loan obtained by trustees of Council No. 1 for the construction of their building.

In the meantime, the members of Council No. 1, in order to exercise freedom from the growing bureaucracy the state organization was bringing about, decided to incorporate. The articles were filed on January 8, 1897 with L.H. Brown, Secretary of State for California.

In 1899 the trustees of the San Leandro Council notified the the Supreme Board of Directors that the Home Office could no longer occupy their building and should seek space elsewhere. The next few years were busy ones for the several committees the Board of Directors appointed to locate a site for their own building. It was not until 1903 that the delegates to the 16th Annual Convention held in Merced, adopted a resolution calling for the creation of a building fund consisting of monies paid to the General Fund at the rate of twenty-five cents per month. The fund continued for as long as necessary in order to accumulate funds needed to pay in cash for the site and construction. Six years later the fund had received $9,721.45 from assessments and investment return.

In February of 1909, the Board proceeded with the purchase of a lot owned by A. Rogers for $4,000.00 which was not too far from Council No. 1. Directors Francisco Ignacio de Lemos and John G. Mattos Jr., both lawyers, were appointed to examine the title and prepare the necessary documents to conclude the transaction. On March 11 the purchase was ratified by the Board. On July 29, 1909 a special Board meeting was called to examine bids for the construction of the two story brick building. The bids were as follows: L.J. Larsen of West Berkeley, $12,372.00; F.J. Williams of Oakland (architectural designer of the building) $12,680.00; G.C. Hilchock of Oakland $12,356; and Knox and Sinnet of Oakland $11,895.00. Even though all bids were over the budget originally stipulated by the Board, the construction was awarded to Knox and Sinnet and was initiated immediately. A contract was drawn between the two parties. Conditions contained in the agreement called for the contractors to put up a bond in the amount of $5,947.50 and completion of the building before November 15, 1909. If the building was not completed before that date, the contractors were to be penalized $20 for each day after November 15 until the construction was completed.

Directors Cunha, Fraga and Pereira were appointed to develop a program for the ceremonies of the cornerstone placement scheduled for September 12 at 8:00 p.m. To preside over this affair they selected Dean John G. Mattos Jr. On the day chosen for the ceremony, San Leandro was adorned to receive officials and representatives of various organizations, and members from various parts of the state. A parade was formed at the site of U.P.E.C. Hall of Council No. 1, half a block east of the loca-

Auto do assentamento da
Pedra Fundamental
do edifício do Conselho Supremo
U. P. E. C.

Aos doze dias do mez de setembro do an_
no do nascimento de Nosso Senhor Jesus Christo
de mile nove centos e nove, no lote da Corpora_
ção Conselho Supremo da União Portugueza do
Estado da California, n'esta cidade de San
Leandro, Condado d'Alameda, Estado da Cali_
fornia, que se tinha vestido de gala, proce_
deu-se á ceremonia do assentamento da
pedra fundamental do edifisio da socieda_
de em conformidade com o approvado pe_
lo Corpo Director, na forma seguinte:
        Pelas duas horas da tarde partiu do
salão do Conselho No. 1 da U.P.E.C., onde se
tinha reunido, o dito Corpo Director do Conse_
lho Supremo, acompanhado de officiaes su_
premos e officiaes e membros de varios Conse_
lhos subordinados, bem como do corpo Uni_
formisado da U.P.E.C. e da sua banda, en_
caminhando-se o cortejo para o lugar da
ceremonia, indo na frente a dita banda,
em seguida o referido Corpo Uniformisado,
e depois em duas alas os membros da so_
ciedade na ordem da sua jerarchia, sen_
do numeroso o concurso de pessoas de to_
das as classes e condições.
        Chegados ahi tocou a banda o Hymno
Nacional Portuguez e depois o Ex.mo Dca_
no e Presidente dos Directores John G. Mattos jr.
dirigiu-se á esquina do norte do edifisio e fez
as ceremonias da collocação da pedra an_
gular auxiliado por alguns officiaes supre_
mos.

Minutes of the ceremony of the laying of the corner stone for U.P.E.C.
Building (1909).

Em seguida fizeram-se breves allocu-
ções com respeito á ceremonia os fins da
sociedade e os benefícios que ella tem espa-
lhado, e em que foram enaltecidos os feitos dos
seus fundadores, e se fizeram honrosas re-
ferencias a todos os que se tem esforçado
para o engrandecimento da associação e
para o alevantamento da colonia portugueza em geral, no estado da California.

Por fim a banda tocou o Hymno Nacional Americano e deu-se por concluida
a ceremonia.

E para constar, eu abaixo assigna-
do F. I. Lemos, Director-Secretario, lavrei e
subscrevi a presente que vae assigna-
da pelos Directores e officiaes Supremos
presentes, tirando d'ella dois traslados, um
para ser archivado na secretaria suprema
e o outro para o archivo da Direcção
do Conselho Supremo da U.P.E.C.

Director Supremo da U.P.E.C.

_____, Director-Secretario.

F. J. Cunha, Director Supremo
J. Mendonça, Director Supremo
Guilherme F. Pereira, Director Supremo
Manuel Fraga, Director Supremo
J. B. Mendonça, Director Supremo
A. A. Sarmento, Director Supremo

João Pereira, Presidente Supremo
_____ V. Pereira, Vice-Presidente Supremo
F. J. Martins, Secretario Supremo
_____, Mestre de Ceremonias Supremo
_____ T. Braga, da Junta Financeira
_____, Ex-Presidente Supremo
F. L. de Freitas, da Junta Financeira
_____ Cunha, Ex-Presidente Supremo
_____

Conclusion of minutes of laying of the corner stone of U.P.E.C. Building (1909).

tion of the ceremony. U.P.E.C. Band led the procession, and the Portuguese National Anthem was heard. Dean John G. Mattos, Jr. stepped out of the procession and placed the cornerstone. Speeches were heard stressing the importance of the event, which was no doubt a step forward in the progress of the society, and also in the engrandizement of the Portuguese name in general. The ceremonies concluded with the playing of the Star Spangled Banner by the U.P.E.C. Band.

Memento of dedication of U.P.E.C. Home Office Building - 1909.

The following items were placed in the cornerstone: five kings (Portuguese currency) coined in 1880 (year of organization of U.P.E.C.); a five and a ten cent piece coined in 1909 (year building was constructed); a copy of the Constitution of U.P.E.C. 1881 and 1907 editions, offered by V.T. Braga; a copy of the minutes of the Annual Convention of 1908; a copy of weekly newspaper *San Leandro Reporter*; a copy of the *União Portuguesa, Arauto* and *Reporter,* Portuguese newspapers published in California; first pages of three largest dailies of San Francisco, the *Chronicle, Call* and *Examiner,* dated September 12, 1909 (day of ceremonies); an American Silver Dollar coined in 1880, and a picture of António Fonte, first Supreme President of U.P.E.C.

On September 29, 1909, at the request of Director J.B. Mendonça, the Board of Directors called a special meeting. The purpose of the meeting was to discuss Mendonça's charges that the contractor was trying to use cheaper materials than those called for in the specifications. Mendonça wanted to have the contractor dismissed. Arguments were settled and Mendonça was instructed to continue to watch closely the movements of workers and the quality of materials used in the construction of the proposed headquarters of U.P.E.C.

On February 10, 1910, the building was examined and declared complete. An American Flag was purchased to fly on the new building.

U.P.E.C. original Home Office (from left) Lucindo J. Martins, Mário B. Camara, and João Silveira Bettencourt.

U.P.E.C. Home Office and Cultural Center Buildings.

Some of the expenses incurred with this tremendous project (which some members at the time thought of as a foolish venture which no doubt would be completely catastrophic to the organization) were of this magnitude: search of title made by Joseph Lyson, $25; plans and specifications, $50 paid to F.J. Williams; survey of the land, $12.50 paid to R.H. Goodwin; cornerstone, $34.50; property taxes for one year in the amount of $36.96 paid to James B. Barber, Tax Collector of the City of San Leandro, $23.28; bronze medallion, $250 paid to Thomas Booth Co.; sewage, $75.00 paid to Agrella; 252 feet of sidewalk, $30.24 paid to Terrazo and Mosaic Co. of Oakland; plus a few hundred dollars for furniture and fixtures. An extra employee was added to the staff, Antônio Gomes, janitor, at a monthly salary of five dollars.

A color print of the front of the new building was ordered surrounded by faces of all Supreme Presidents and Supreme Secretaries who had served the society since its organization. This beautiful memento was then offered to anyone who proposed five new members for the society.

This building which once housed departments of San Leandro City Hall and also the city's Post Office withstood the years for its construction was as solid as the character of the men who conceived it except for a little incident in September of 1913. A five passenger Reo, driven by John Goldstone of Alameda, struck a slippery spot on the railroad track running along East 14th Street and skidded clear across the street onto the sidewalk and collided with the U.P.E.C. Building. Several bricks were loosened and fell. The front end of the machine just barely missed the plate glass window.

On August 1, 1900 the Supreme Council deeded back to Council No. 1 the site where their hall stood. However, the quit claim deed was not recorded until October 1913. In 1960 the Board of Directors appointed a committee comprised of Joseph A. Freitas, Carlos Almeida and Arthur Gonçalves (Neto) to look into the remodeling of the nearly obsolete building. The report, given on January 14, 1961, called for its demolition and for the construction of a new one.

A committee of five Board members was appointed to either sell the present site and relocate the Home Office or buy additional land adjacent to the present site. Edward C. Massa, a realtor and Past Supreme President of the society, recommended the purchase of additional land and proceeded with its acquisition.

On December 8, 1961, architect Morgan Howell of Hayward was contracted for the drawing of plans. However, it was not until July 13, 1963 that the final plan was accepted. A bid for demolishing the existing building was accepted in the amount of $5,760.00 and in January of 1964 the structure which once had been the pride of the Portuguese fell to the claws of progress.

During construction the U.P.E.C. Home Office was relocated on the second floor of the Wells Fargo Bank on the corner of East 14th Street and Estudillo Avenue for nine months until the new building was completed.

On March 14, 1964 the contract for the construction of what became the first office building in the downtown redevelopment area of the city of San Leandro was awarded to Anthony Morsilli, Inc. at a cost of $160,275.00. New furniture was purchased and a completely new look was given to the face of the society which then began to realize that time was of the essence if they were to meet the challenges of the future.

History repeated itself for there were the same human elements at play. There was the concern from many that such a big investment would not be profitable since it was located in the oldest section of town. The Portuguese may have missed having their names in large print in the many written historical accounts of the State of California, but the fact remains that they seldom missed in the investments they made in real estate. Their names are found in small print all over the State of California in books of a different nature — those that can be found in the real estate assessors office in every county in our state.

Therefore, the leadership of the society knew from instinct and experience that the U.P.E.C. Home Office soon would find itself in what was becoming the new downtown. Today this area is near completion with its shopping areas, the U.P.E.C. Cultural Center and financial institutions which the affluence of many, including Portuguese, helped to build.

On December 12, 1964 the newly constructed building was dedicated with the

Conference Room — U.P.E.C. Home Office.

U.P.E.C. Home Office dedication ceremonies, 1964.

presence of Mayor Jack D. Maltester, Dr. Manuel Pedro Ribeiro da Silva, then Consul General of Portugal, and hundreds of guests who came to visit the different suites now exhibiting the new and fresh look of U.P.E.C. leadership and determination to modernize.

In the words of Josephine Roberts, then writer for the *San Leandro Morning News:*

> Because buildings are conceived and brought into existence by humans with all their hopes, dreams, successes and failures, the story of the two U.P.E.C. buildings (old and new) is not a simple tale of steel, glass and stone or about mortar, brick and wood. It is a narrative about mankind's eternal quest for beauty and achievement for capture of that elusive mystery which the poet calls 'the light that was never on land or sea.'

XVI

CIVIC PARTICIPATION

INDEPENDENCE DAY

Throughout the years U.P.E.C. either initiated or promoted most of the Portuguese related civic activities held in the state. For other activities U.P.E.C. officers were usually found in committee positions of leadership.

One of the oldest such events ever held in the Portuguese community dealt with the independence of Portugal from Spanish rule. The celebration was held on December 1, 1894 when U.P.E.C. Council No. 15, of San Francisco, offered the Portuguese and American communities an evening filled with drama, music, and dance which received the best references from the local press. This date was celebrated for many years by the U.P.E.C., not only in San Francisco, but in many other cities.

4TH CENTENNIAL OF VASCO DA GAMA

In February 1898, Dr. Ignacio Costa Duarte, Consul General of Portugal in San Francisco, called a special meeting of representatives from all fraternal societies at the U.P.E.C. Hall in San Leandro to discuss ways and means of celebrating the fourth centennial of the return of Vasco da Gama from his famous voyage of discovery of the sea route to India.

Supreme President A.F. Cunha presided over the committee with António Fonte as Vice-President.

The festivities, scheduled for May of that year, did not take place since there was concern over the war that was going on between the United States and Spain which could create problems which might impede the celebration.

The Portuguese community's first attempt to come out publicly in a show of strength and pride had received a setback — this one understandable. However another occasion would not be long in coming.

THE VISIT OF THE CRUISER *SAN GABRIEL*

At the end of 1909 the news that a cruiser from the Portuguese Royal Navy was coming to San Francisco, was like a spark that ignited the flame in the hearts of the Portuguese immigrants in the state. The ship, *San Gabriel,* was like a messenger from the distant homeland that would bring prestige. The visit was a chance for all Portuguese to unite and show their patriotism.

Less than two years earlier, King Carlos had been assassinated, and Portugal at the time was engulfed in political strife between the monarchists and those advocating the Republic. The voyage of the *San Gabriel,* ordered by King Manuel II, was seeking support and understanding from the Portuguese communities wherever she touched shore. The leaders of the Portuguese community in California immediately began to exchange views about the reception.

One of the leaders of the movement was José Vargas Pereira, then Supreme President of the U.P.E.C., who decided to have a special meeting of the four largest Portuguese fraternal societies, in spite of an editorial of *O Arauto,* printed on January 1, 1910, which suggested tht the initiative for the reception should come from the Portuguese Consulate rather than from the fraternal societies — for according to the paper they "should not get involved in manifestations of this kind." The Consul of Portugal at the time was Dr. Ignacio Costa Duarte, and the Vice-Consul was Dr. José Sousa Bettencourt.

The meeting called by Pereira took place on January 28 at the Home Office of the I.D.E.S. where the Supreme Presidents of only three societies met and discussed preliminaries for the reception to be given the officers and crew of the visiting ship.

BOLETIM  DA U.P.E.C.

PERIODICO MENSAL

SEGUNDO LUSTRO

ORGÃO OFFICIAL DA UNIÃO PORTUGUEZA DO ESTADO DA CALIFORNIA

Sociedade portugueza fundada em San Leandro, Cal., no dia 1 de agosto de 1880.

ANNO III.   SAN FRANCISCO, CAL., 1 DE MARÇO DE 1904.   No. 8

"BOLETIM DA U. P. E. C."

Entered at San Francisco Post Office as Second Class Matter.

BOLETIM da U. P. E. C.

Director: BETTENCOURT DA CAMARA Ex-**Director Supremo da U. P. E. C.**
Escriptorio: 525 Front St. — Telephone Black 5694
San Francisco

PARTE OFFICIAL

THESOIRARIA SUPREMA

Importancias recebidas n'esta thesoiraria suprema durante o mez de dez. de 1903:

Conselho	Cofre Geral	Cofre Especial	Total
1$	9 50$	577 15$	586 65$
2	4 15	99 45	103 60
3	4 15	430 10	444 25
4	1 45	136 00	137 45
5	8 80	593 50	
6	4 05	139 85	140 86
7	7 58	573 75	581 33
8	3 05	237 15	240 20
9	1 20	124 95	126 15
10	1 77	192 95	194 72
11	6 75	328 95	335 70
12	1 45	160 65	162 39
13	10 55	606 45	616 60
14	2 95	191 25	194 05
15	84 50	217 60	
16	1 47	157 95	158 72
17	5 00	205 70	210 99
18	7 31	275 40	282 91
19	85	65 45	60 30
20	1 10	63 75	64 85
21	88	255 00	343 68
22	50 80	138 55	195 35
23	7 20	186 15	193 45
24	16 55	181 90	198 45
25	1 75	107 50	109 25
26	41 80	183 60	225 40
27	7 50	224 40	231 90
28	36 66	96 65	137 71
29	5 20	175 95	181 05
30	6 18	192 25	198 43
31	4 40	50 15	50 64
32	4 10	75 65	79 75
33	7 20	70 50	77 72
34	85	68 00	68 05
35	58	48 45	49 03
36	47	50 40	50 40
37	4 30	92 00	96 30
38	5 00	107 95	112 87
39	68	95 40	95 40
40	4 50	139 15	139 15
41	1 25	94 35	95 40
42	4 00	135 15	139 15
43	3 85	37 40	41 25
44	22 69	69 70	92 39
45	23 84	61 20	85 04
46	25 60	36 25	61 85
47	75	90 25	93 55
48	75	79 15	79 90
49	45	45 90	46 35
50			
51	6 29	36 10	62 39
52	60	56 70	56 70
53	14 58	32 30	46 88
54	60	60 35	60 95
55	1 00	64 60	65 60
56	4 36	77 35	81 71
57	40	27 20	27 60
58	4 22	46 75	47 97
59			
60	10 00	26 35	36 35
61	4 09	72 25	76 34
62	51 85	51 85	53 20
63	4 15	93 50	97 65
64	12 05	26 35	38 40
65			
66	60	26 35	26 95
67	30	38 85	39 24
68	5 05	59 05	64 10
69	39 10	25 50	64 60

$845 47 $9,655 05 $10,102 11

Centerville, Cal. 1 de jan. de 1904:
João G. de Mattos Jr.
Thes. Sup. da U. P. E. C.

PRESIDENCIA SUPREMA

18.° Exercicio Presidencial 1903-1904

Aos srs. officiaes supremos, officiaes

JOAO RODRIGUES CABRILHO

Retrato do descobridor da California, ao qual o dignissimo presidente supremo J. H. Woods iniciou a idéa de erigir um monumento na cidade de San Diego.

e membros dos Conselhos Subordinados da U. P. E. C.

Carta Presidencial No. 4

Aos devidos effeitos e fins convenientes, faço saber o seguinte:

1° —Que visto que existem n'este Estado sociedades e clubes organizados para o fim de trazer perante o povo todas as "land marks" antigas e factos dos pioneers de 1849, ao mesmo tempo que se deixa para traz o mais importante facto da historia da California, a descoberta do mesmo estado pelo navegador portuguez Cabrilho, tomei a iniciativa de recordar ao mundo e ao povo do estado da California que a honra maior devida a qualquer dos antepassados pertence aos portuguezes.

A minha idéa para que tal demonstração nunca seja olvidada, é a seguinte:

Erigir em San Diego, em commemoração do feito do navegador portuguez Cabrilho, um monumento que fique para sempre affirmando aos vindiros que foi dos portuguezes a honra da descoberta da California e que aos portuguezes membros da U. P. E. C. coube a honra de commemorar o facto d'uma maneira que ha de immortalizar toda a colonia da California, ao mesmo tempo que a descoberta da California por Cabrilho.

Antes de fazer publico o meu plano, escrevi ao governador Geo. mia e ao senador George C. Perkins, do estado da California, e ao mesmo tempo quando estive na cidade de San Diego consultei com a camara do Commercio d'alli para ter a opinião dos tres corpos mais importantes da California

---

As respostas foram as seguintes:

"Sacramento, Jan. 14th, 1904—
Jesse H. Woods, Esq.—Supreme President of U. P. E. C., Haywards, Cal.—Dear Sir:—I am in receipt of your favor of Jan. 14th, directing my attention to the movement which has been inaugurated by some of our citizens of Portuguese birth or descent for the erection of a monument at San Diego to commemorate the discovery of that bay and of the coast of California by the great Portuguese explorer Cabrilho.

Permit me to say that it gives me very great pleasure that the first explorer of the California coast should be honored with a monument and that there is no place more fitting for its erection than the splendid bay where white man first set foot on California's soil. I hope the movement which has been started may be entirely successful, and if there is any way in which I can contribute to such success, please be assured that you can command my services at any time.

Very truly yours,
Geo. C. Pardee.
Washington, D. C., Jan. 14, 1904.
Jessie H. Woods, Esq.,
Haywards, Cal.

Dear Sir:—I am in receipt of yours of the 14th relative to the desire of the Portuguese Union to perpetuate the discovery of California by Cabrilho, and can say to the Association, that I am in hearty sympathy with its desire, and shall be glad to co-operate in any way I can to this end.

Yours very truly,
Geo. C. Perkins.

Alem d'estas duas cartas tam-

AVISO IMPORTANTE.

Faz-se saber a todos os membros da União Portugueza do Estado da California que devem pagar até ao dia ultimo d'este mez, às 12 horas da noite, a importancia que lhe cumprir para o Cofre Especial do Conselho Supremo, a saber:

Os membros que possuem a Apolice A............$1 70
Os membros que possuem a Apolice B............ 85

Todo o membro que até à referida hora de meia noite do dia ultimo do presente mez não effectuar o pagamento da referida Contribuição, ficará ipso facto suspenso e a sua Apolice sem effeito ou valor algum, pois que todos os privilegios, direitos e regalias ficam suspensos desde aquelle momento.

(Veja-se Constituição dos Conselhos Subordinados, Artigo X, Sec. II.)

L. J. MARTINS, Secretario Supremo.

bem tive a promessa do auxilio da Camara do Commercio de San Diego e da cidade em geral, devendo o sitio para o monumento ser no centro do City Plaza, o qual não ia custar nada á sociedade.

No meu parecer, com o auxilio d'estes tres corpos mais importantes do estado e dos membros da U. P. E. C. e dos portuguezes em geral, devia ser um dos actos mais recommendaveis na historia da sociedade e para o bom nome da mesma e para o povo portuguez do Estado da California.

Já fui criticado n'um dos jornaes portuguezes porque nada d'isto tinha passado no ultimo Conselho Supremo e que eu ainda nada tinha dito aos directores e premos e que não se podia usar dos dinheiros dos cofres da sociedade.

Esto tudo é verdade. Porem, deve haver tempo e remedio para tudo.

A primeira ez que fallei n'este assumpto para ser uma realidade foi a 14 de janeiro de 1904, quando estive em San Diego.

Era impossivel estar ao mesmo tempo presente na ultima sessão dos directores.

Estou certo que esta idéa vae ser approvada por aquelle corpo e por toda a pessoa que pretende ser um bom portuguez e um bom cidadão.

Nào só das sociedades dos homens espero receber auxilio, mas tambem das sociedades de mulheres, e das creanças que attendem as nossas eschólas.

Esta exposição no BOLETIM é só para annunciar o inicio da idéa, ficando à espera de resposta de qualquer a favor ou contra a mesma, de conscio ou de pessoa portugueza no estado da California.

Não podemos bem n'este estado, sem usar dos cofres da sociedade, realizar dinheiro bastante para tal fim. Os differentes conselhos podem dar bailes e entretenimentos e o seu resultado ir para um cofre especial para aquelle fim, e estou certo que em pouco tempo, não obstante haver quem diga que isto é impossivel, vae ser fallado um tudo a casa portugueza e o interesse nenhum dará uma allegria para todos, e aos poucos mil dollars necessarios vão ser realizados se os jornaes americanos não publicar e nosso bom trabalho nas suas folhas.

Peço a todos os secretarios que estas linhas sejam lidas nas suas sessões, e que os conselhos tomem interesse a valer para ver se podemos ir avante com este bom trabalho.

2°—Que visitei o Coss. Decoto, achando-o em desordem, em razão de a maioria ter transferido as sessões para o domingo de tarde, o que era contrario aos desejos dos officiaes.

Depois de fazer sentir àquelles officiaes que era obrigação sua attender as seus deveres até que os seus successores tomassem os seus logares, e que elles deviam ser os primeiros a respeitar a opinião da maioria, d'isto ficou satisfeito, menos o digno secretario, que resignou, sendo eleito e installado no seu logar o consocio A. Ferreira.

Dignou-se acompanhar-me n'esta visita o digno thesoireiro do 3, Jose Bernardo, que me foi de bastante auxilio n'aquella occasião.

Presidencia Suprema da U. P. E. C., Haywards, 20 de jan. de 1904. 23.° exercicio social e 18.° periodo presidencial.

Jesse H. Woods,
11. Presidente Supremo.

SECRETARIA SUPREMA

O numero 6 do BOLETIM do mez passado, custou aos diversos Conselhos o seguinte:

1 $5 24 18	2 04 35	73 52	60
2 60 19	3 36	60 33	36
3 4 12 70	62 37	58 34	90
4 1 45 21	48 38	75 55	1 00
5 4 32 22	2 43 39	93 56	11
6 1 31 23	1 54 40	1 02 57	40
7 5 83 24	1 98 41	1 06 58	42
8 3 05 25	2 01 42	1 89 59	30
9 1 38 26	1 47 43	70 60	49
10 1 77 27	87 44	69 61	82
11 3 36 28	1 17 45	62 62	49
12 1 60 29	2 94 46	57 63	91
13 2 41 30	1 47 47	1 06 64	99
14 1 78 31	1 71 48	67 65	19
15 74 32	1 93 49	44 66	65
16 1 38 33	40 50	33 67	25
17 1 47 34	82 51	46 68	19

Observações para os dignos secretarios dos Conselhos Subordinados:

Todo o membro que passar de casado e morte, tem direito ao beneficio por morte se sua esposa, conformar-se com a Sec. XIII, Artigo IX da Const. do Conselho Supremo, e para que ella tenha direito a receber a importancia da Apolice por morte de sua esposa, é necessario que elle transfira immediatamente a Apolice para o nome de el-

COMMISSÃO CENTRAL DA COLONIA PORTUGUEZA DA CALIFORNIA

PARA

RECEPÇÃO DO CRUZADOR "SAN GABRIEL"

SEDE: PORTUGUESE-AMERICAN BANK BUILDING, FRONT AND CLAY STREETS, SAN FRANCISCO, CAL.

PRESIDENTE HONORARIO—O Illmo. e Exmo. Ministro Plenipotenciario e Enviado Extraordinario de Portugal em Washington, D. C.

VICE-PRESIDENTES HONORARIOS—Os Exmos. Consul e Vice-Consul de Portugal em San Francisco, Cal.

PRESIDENTE—M. T. Freitas, presidente do Portuguese American Bank of San Francisco e presidente dos directores supremos da I. D. E. S.

VICE-PRESIDENTES—Dr. J. Leal d'Azevedo, medico supremo da U. P. E. C.; J. de Vargas Pereira, presidente supremo da U. P. E. C.; Mrs. A. C. Costa, presidente suprema da S. P. R. S. I.; Mrs. A. D. Fonseca, presidente suprema da U. P. E. C.; F. I. de Lemos, advogado e director supremo da U. P. E. C.

SECRETARIO—M. Bettencourt da Camara, redactor d'**A União Portugueza** e Commandante do Corpo Uniformizado da U. P. E. C.

THESOUREIRO—J. G. de Mattos, Jr., presidente do Bank of Centerville, e decano e thesoureiro supremo da U. P. E. C.

VOGAES—Mrs. A. B. d'Azevedo, ex-directora suprema da S. P. R. S. I., Oakland; rev. padre J. L. d'Azevedo, Sacramento; Jose Baptista, vice-presidente do Portuguese American Bank, Oakland; J. S. Bello, vice-presidente do Portuguese American Bank e presidente da Portuguese Hotel Co., San Francisco; commendador dr. Jose de Sousa Bettencourt, vice-consul de Portugal, San Francisco; Mrs. M. S. Brazil, directora suprema da S. P. R. S. I. Oakland; Edward A. Cunha, advogado, San Francisco; F. J. Cunha, director supremo da U. P. E. C., Oakland; R. A. S. Encarnação, inspector supremo da R. A. B. A. Michaelense, Oakland; John Enos, capitalista e director do Portuguese American Bank, Bakersfield; dr. M. M. Enos, medico supremo da I. D. E. S. e director do Hospital de Santo Antonio, Oakland; dr. J. B. de Faria, ex-medico supremo da I. D. E. S., Oakland; V. L. de Figueiredo, thesoureiro do Portuguese American Bank of San Francisco, San Francisco; F. L. de Freitas, advogado, Oakland; rev. padre Galli, parocho da egreja portugueza de São Jose, Oakland; Mrs. M. C. Lemos, presidente das directoras da S. P. R. S. I.; A. M. Martins, director supremo da I. D. E. S.; J. C. Mendonça, thesoureiro supremo da I. D. E. S., Pleasanton; J. P. Mendonça, director supremo da U. P. E. C., Oakland; J. de Menezes, redactor d'**O Arauto**, Oakland; J. Oliveira, presidente da Portuguese Mercantile Co., San Francisco; G. F. Pereira, director supremo da U. P. E. C., Oakland; João Pereira, director da U. P. E. C., San Leandro; A. J. Pinheiro, director supremo da U. P. E. C., Benicia; Mrs. Belle Pimentel, directora suprema da U. P. E. C., Oakland; J. I. Rafael, director supremo da I. D. E. S. e director-gerente da Portuguese Mercantile Co., Oakland; Miss T. R. Rodrigues, secretaria suprema da U. P. E. C., Oakland; J. Chrysostomo da Silveira, agricultor e ex-thesoureiro supremo da I. D. E. S. San Leandro; Joaquim A. Silveira, director do Portuguese American Bank e presidente da American Creamery Co., Oakland; M. C. Simas, redactor d'**O Amigo dos Portuguezes**, Oakland; M. F. M. Triguciro, proprietario d'**A União Portugueza**, Oakland.

Commissão Executiva

Sede: Portuguese-American Bank Building, San Francisco, Cal.

PRESIDENTE. M. T. Freitas;

SECRETARIO. M. Bettencourt da Camara;

THESOUREIRO. J. G. Mattos, Jr.

VOGAES: V. L. de Figueiredo, dr. J. B. de Faria, F. J. Cunha, Joaquim A. Silveira, dr. J. L. d'Azevedo, G. F. Pereira, Mrs. A. C. Martins, Mrs. A. D. Fonseca, F. L. de Freitas, J. I. Rafael, F. I. de Lemos, R. A. S. Encarnação, A. M. Martins, rev. padre Galli e José Baptista.

Circular letter announcing the composition of the reception committee for the *San Gabriel*, cruiser which visited the San Francisco Bay in 1910.

Mrs. Anna C. Martins of the S.P.R.S.I. and Adelaide D. Fonseca of the U.P.P.E.C. were present at this meeting. It was agreed among those three presidents that the press, clergy, other Portuguese associations and merchants should be invited to a meeting to take place at the Rectory of Saint Joseph's Church in Oakland on February 5.

As a result of this gathering, another meeting was set for the 14th of February, during which Manuel T. Freitas, at the time President of the Portuguese-American Bank, was elected President of the committee for the reception program. Others elected were Dr. José Sousa Bettencourt, Vice-President; Mário Bettencourt da Camara, Secretary and John Garcia de Mattos Jr., Treasurer. One of the matters discussed at this meeting was a drive for funds to help pay for the expenses of the festivities. The first donation was received from U.P.E.C. Council No. 5 (Amor da Patria) in Centerville, in the amount of $25.00.

By the time the San Gabriel arrived in April the committee had raised, amongst the Portuguese in California, close to five thousand dollars, mostly from subordinate councils of U.P.E.C. which alone contributed a total of $1,248.20. That gesture showed the enthusiasm the Portuguese had at that time by raising that sum in two months' time. This feat was even more admirable considering that communications consisted only of mail and notices inserted in the weekly Portuguese newspapers published in San Francisco and Oakland.

The O Arauto, a weekly Portuguese newspaper published in Oakland, printed on the front page an account of the receptions that were being given the cruiser as she touched the different ports in Brasil and Argentina until she rounded the Cape and headed up the Pacific towards San Francisco. She finally docked on the afternoon of April 21, 1910 under the command of Antonio Jervis d'Athouguia Ferreira Pinto Basto.

The most impressive scene was when the steamer George W. Elder left the San Francisco harbor carrying the reception committee, numerous members of the Portuguese community, and the U.P.E.C. Band to greet the San Gabriel already half way inside the bay.

The Elder was escorted by many small power boats owned by the Portuguese who lived in the San Francisco Bay Area. All these boats were decorated with Portuguese and American flags. As the Elder approached the visiting ship, the U.P.E.C. Band proudly executed the Portuguese National Anthem followed by several musical numbers. After the cruiser docked, the reception committee, the Consul of Portugal, Mr. McCarthy, Mayor of San Francisco, and other officials went aboard to welcome the officers and crew, offering them their hospitality.

At this time the San Gabriel was giving a twenty-one gun salute to the Presidio, followed by another of eleven guns to the Governor of Yerba Buena Island and then a nine gun salvo to the Consul of Portugal, Ignacio C. Duarte. In all the excitement, off one of the rug boats loaded with Portuguese, a man named Domingos fell into the ocean and was saved by sailors of the San Gabriel. The San Francisco Examiner referred to the reception as being one of the largest ever given any foreign ship.

A vast program of festivities followed for the next eight days which included a show at the Columbia Theater, tours of San Francisco, Sacramento, Vallejo, Mare Island, Marin County, Mt. Tamalpais, the University of California at Berkeley, and San Leandro where they visited the U.P.E.C. Building in the company of the Viscount of Alte, then Ambassador of Portugal in Washington, D.C.

On April 26 the S.P.R.S.I. offered a dinner in honor of the officers at the Key Route Inn in Oakland. A parade which included the sailors was formed at Broadway and marched down Seventh Street to the Portuguese National Church of Saint Joseph where they attended Mass. Two days later the San Gabriel left port.

On October 5, 1910, the Monarchy was overthrown and Portugal became a Republic. The Portuguese sentiment here in California was evidently in favor of the deposed King and this feeling lasted for many years. In fact the Monarchy symbols

Este Livro de Registo de Visitantes da Secretaria do Conselho Supremo da União Portugueza do Estado da California, foi inaugurado no dia 28 de abril de mil novecentos e dez, pelo Illmo. e Exmo. Sr. Visconde d'Alte, Enviado Extraordinario e Ministro Plenipotenciario do Governo de Sua Magestade Fidelissima, em visita expressamente fixada por S. Exa., por occasião da visita á bahia de San Francisco do cruzador da Armada, S. Gabriel, a cuja recepção S. Exa. o sr. Visconde d'Alte veiu assistir, a convite da Colonia portugueza da California, assignando tambem o exmo. sr. Antonio J. Ferreira Pinto Basto, capitão commandante do São Gabriel, que acompanhou o illustre diplomata na visita, bem como os briosos officiaes, dá Ferreira e Martins, que tambem assignaram.

San Leandro, Cal. 28 d'abril de 1910.

José de Vargas Freire
Presidente Supremo

L. J. Martins
Secretario Supremo

M. Bettencourt
Ajudante do Secretario Supremo

150

First page of the visitors book at the Supreme Council commemorating the visit of the cruiser *San Gabriel*.

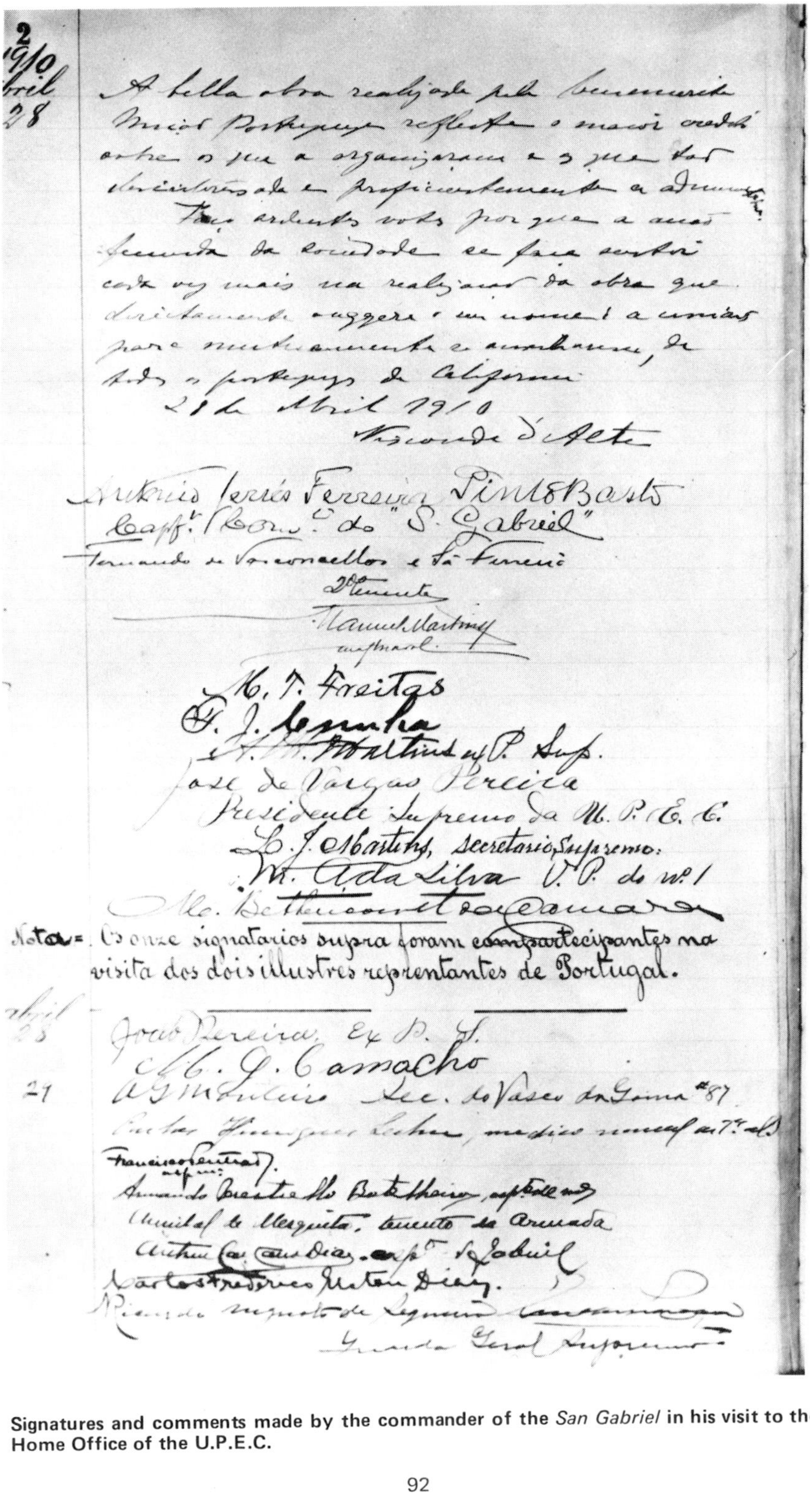

A bella obra realisada pela benemerita
União Portugueza reflecte a maior credito
sobre o seu a organisaram e o que dos
directores ella e proficientemente a administra

Tão ardentes votos por que a acção
benefica da sociedade se faça sentir
cada vez mais na realisação da obra que
directamente auggere e em nome a commum
para muito ..... e acabamos, de
todos os portuguezes da California

21 de Abril 1910

Visconde d'Alte

Antonio Ferrão Ferreira Pinto Basto
Capp.te Comm.te do "S. Gabriel"

Fernando de Vasconcellos e Sá Ferreira
2.º Tenente

Manuel Martins
...

M. P. Freitas
F. J. Serra
... Martins ... P. Sup.
José de Vargas Pereira
Presidente Supremo da U. P. E. C.
C. J. Martins, Secretario Supremo
M. A. da Silva V.P. do n.º 1
M. Bettencourt ....

Nota = Os onze signatarios supra foram comparticipantes na
visita dos dois illustres representantes de Portugal.

Abril
28
João Pereira, Ex P. S.
M. J. Camacho

21
A. J. Monteiro, Sec. do Vasco da Gama n.º 87
Carlos Henriques Lebre, medico ..... a 7.ª ...
Francisco Pereira ?
Armando Castelo Batalharia, ...
.... de Mesquita, tenente da Armada
Arthur .... Dias, ...p.te S. Gabriel
Carlos Trevores ..... Dias,
Ricardo .... de Segurar ....
Guarda Geral Supremo

Signatures and comments made by the commander of the *San Gabriel* in his visit to the Home Office of the U.P.E.C.

remained unchanged on the banner of the Supreme Council of U.P.E.C. for a long time. A few years later the community found itself again involved in work and festivities. This time they were involved in one of the greatest events they ever participated — The Panama-Pacific Exposition.

Cruiser *San Gabriel*

THE PANAMA PACIFIC EXPOSITION

One of the most fascinating civic activities in which Portuguese-Americans of California participated was without question the one which took them to San Francisco's Panama Pacific Exposition to commemorate the outstanding event of the opening of the canal. The waterway was a feat for mankind to celebrate, and it spoke of American tenacity and determination, which after work beyond man's comprehension, united the two blue giants — the Atlantic and Pacific oceans.

The canal was an occurrence that challenged every engineering manual, for it consisted of removing a mountain which separated the two bodies of salt water. This lofty elevation of earth and rock was removed inch by inch, shovel by shovel, under a feverish tropical climate. The canal also meant a billion dollars lost to the French, who for ten years fought against nature in hopes of accomplishing the feat which destiny would reserve for the audacity of the Americans. The clamor of victory was heard the world over and the Portuguese in California did not wish to be left out, for they were in America and therefore wanted a share in the rejoicing of the accomplishment of man over nature.

It was with this pride and desire of identification that John G. Mattos Jr., on October 13, 1910, during the U.P.E.C. Convention held in Vallejo, introduced a resolution seeking support for a senate constitutional amendment No. 52 before the California legislature calling for the levy of a tax to raise five million dollars to help the exposition which would be held in 1915 to commemorate the opening of the canal. The resolution was adopted and printed in the *U.P.E.C. Bulletin.* Copies were sent also for insertion in the daily newspapers of San Francisco and Oakland, as well as in all Portuguese publications within the State of California.

The following months and years would place the Portuguese of California in a unique showing of unity, for they formed an executive committee to make sure that Portugal participated in the fair along with other nationalities. Now and then people find fault with the manner in which the project should have been accomplished. The Consul of Portugal was attached in the press and emotions ran high. J.C. Valim called for certain groups to come to terms and stop spending energies in offensive remarks aimed at discrediting the Portuguese community leaders, who in the end, would be called to take the leadership and carry out the question of Portugal's participation in the fair.

John da Cunha Valim's words echoed in the hearts of the Portuguese after he turned public his concern in an article published in the *O Arauto,* August 26, 1911. On November 26, 1912, J. Batalha de Freitas, a Portuguese Minister to China, on his way to his post from Lisbon, stopped in San Francisco where he was received with military honors. At the request of the Portuguese government he signed an agreement which accepted the invitation of the U.S.A. to participate in the fair after he had personally selected the site where a pavilion would be built. On December 11, Minister Freitas was honored at a reception held at the Masonic Hall in San Leandro under the auspices of Council No. 13 of the R.A.B.A.M.I., headed by Antonio R. Mattos.

The months went by, and the Portuguese Executive Committee, consisting of community leaders, went to the fairgrounds almost daily and watched other countries' pavilions being built. As to Portugal's, no sign of construction — just a bare site growing weeds. So pressure was put to the Portuguese government to accept the invitation that President Taft extended to Portugal to participate in the International Fair.

On January 11, 1914, the community elected a Central Committee to prepare the Portuguese exhibit. The committee was presided by John G. Mattos Jr. and included Mrs. Maria A.B. Encarnação, First Vice-President; F.I. Lemos, Second Vice-President; João Enos, Third Vice-President; J.C. Valim, First Secretary; Mário B. da Camara, Second Secretary; Joaquim A. da Silveira, Treasurer; J.C. Jorge; F.J. Cunha; Mrs. Isabel G. Luiz; Dr. J.S. Bettencourt; Mrs. Maria Enos Freitas; F.L. Freitas; V.L. Figueiredo; G.F. Pereira; A.C. Martins; Mrs. Maria Jerónimo; L. Goncalves; George Oliveira; Mrs. Rosa Sarmento; Dr. M.M. Enos; M. Fraga; A.F. Nunes; Mrs. Maria da Glória and J.P. Mendonça. They decided to call upon the Consul in San Francisco, Dr. Simão Lopes Ferreira, who indicated that the matter of Portugal's participation in the fair was being debated in the assembly and finding strong opposition due to political comments.

In view of what they heard from Consul Ferreira, the committee held a meeting and decided to send a delegation to Lisbon in order to save the prestige of the many thousands of Portuguese in California who faced the possibility of seeing the Portuguese government fail to honor their commitments. The three representatives were Joaquim A. Silveira, then President of the Portuguese-American Bank of San Francisco and of the American Creamery of Oakland; Francisco Inacio de Lemos, Attorney from Hayward; and Dr. José Sousa Bettencourt, a distinguished physician with offices in San Francisco. They were chosen to be sent to Portugal not only to obtain the country's participation at the fair, but also to seek funding for a pavilion to attest to the Portuguese presence in a manner to be remembered with pride.

Dr. Bettencourt and F.I. Lemos, in the words of J.C. Valim, Secretary for the Executive Committee, published in *O Imparcial,* announcing the selection of these delegates, "represented the intellectual and associative segment of the Portuguese community while Silveira represented the industrial, commercial and financial side."

On April 22, 1914, hundreds of Portuguese, along with the U.P.E.C. band, saw these outstanding individuals leave their professions for the next few months and take the Overland Limited of the Southern Pacific from San Francisco to New York where they went to Lisbon via Paris. On May 11, they arrived in Lisbon where they met with industrial and commercial firms to obtain support in the building of the Portuguese pavilion in the fairgrounds in San Francisco.

"It is noted that the accent and timbre of their voices was something close to that of North Americans. But through their words, their enthusiasm, we discover a Portuguese soul well alive and vibrating, which they had never lost. It is their high patriotism that brought them to Lisbon, so that our country is not of the last ones

O Imparcial
SEMANARIO INDEPENDENTE E NOTICIOSO

ANO I — SACRAMENTO, CALIFORNIA, 22 DE ABRIL DE 1914 — NUMERO 29

Portugal na Exposição de 1915
A Colonia Portuguesa da California Envia Tres Delegados a Lisboa

F. I. LEMOS

DR. J. S. BETTENCOURT

J. A. SILVEIRA

Continúa na pagina 2

Front Page of *O Imparcial,* **announcing the selection of three representatives of the Portuguese Community that would go to Lisbon, Portugal.**

95

to enter the exposition in San Francisco and in this manner honor the country they never forgot." That was the local paper's account of the first impressions of these Azoreans. The article goes on to state that "the Portuguese throughout the world, even today, 1914, in every corner of the globe are the best defenders of the prestige of our country."

The mission in Portugal for the three delegates from California was not an easy one. They had to convince the Portuguese government of the importance of their participation in the Exhibition and at the same time make industry and commerce aware of the potential markets for their products if they were displayed at the fair.

So the Portuguese Parliament agreed to finance a pavilion and spread the cost over the next three years. This resolution was obtained through the efforts of Dr. Caetano Rego, then delegate for the Union of Agriculture, Commerce and Industry, who was able to show the advantages of such participation. The budget was studied by a committee of members from the Portuguese Geographic Society, the Fine Arts College, Department of Foreign Affairs and others whom the government appointed, to see that the country would be represented with dignity.

Telegrams were sent by the Supreme President of the U.P.E.C. in May of 1914 to the Minister of Foreign Affairs in Lisbon, asking for the approval of the California delegation's request. Other Portuguese organizations and newspapers followed, partially causing the government to react more favorably. Meanwhile invitations were extended to the U.P.E.C. by Charles C. Moore and Rudolph J. Taussig, President and Secretary of the Panama-Pacific Universal Exposition, for the organization to hold the 29th Annual Convention in San Francisco in 1915. The city had been selected by Congress with the approval of the President of the United States as the official site for celebrating the uniting of the waters of the Pacific and Atlantic, the greatest physical accomplishment achieved by man to that time.

Silveira, Dr. Bettencourt and Lemos upon their arrival in Lisbon, Portugal (Ilustração Portuguesa, Lisbon, June 15, 1914).

Portuguese Pavilion.

As the date for the dedication neared, the committee·initiated a drive for funds to help defray some of the expenses and projects, which included the publication of an album. The appeal was spread on all seven columns of *Arauto* on January 23, 1915: "Portuguese cast aside differences of opinion, hard feelings and many other of lesser importance, and let's take care of the essential — and that is to uphold the pride of our Portuguese community." This appeal of J.C. Valim, Secretary of the committee went on, calling for the Portuguese to unite and raise the funds needed. One of the largest donors was Joaquim A. da Silveira, who alone donated $1,000.

The exposition opened on February 20, 1915, but it was not until Friday, March 5, that the fifty thousand dollar Portuguese pavilion was officially dedicated, even though construction had only begun on November 17, 1914, under the direction of the Consul of Portugal, Simão Lopes Ferreira. The visitors from Portugal, who included Roldan Y. Pegas, Commissary of Portugal, were met at Scott Street by the executive committee. All were presented with medallions bearing a picture of the pavilion and red and green ribbons, colors of the Portuguese flag.

The U.P.E.C. band, under the direction of Mário Bettencourt da Camara, led the parade to the pavilion, followed by the U.S. Navy, under the command of Major J.T. Myers, a choir of one hundred ladies, dressed in white and wearing scarves of red and green, Directors of the exposition, Hon. Hiram W. Johnson, Governor of the State of California, Mayor James Ralph Jr. of San Francisco and many others. A hymn was composed for the fair, with music by Rev. Candido Ribeiro of Oakland and lyrics by J.C. Valim.

A description of the Portuguese pavilion, which was designed by architect Antonio Couto d'Abreu, assisted by sculptor Costa Motta and styled after Portuguese renaissance (Manuelino), is given by Frank Morton Todd in his *History of the Exposition:*

> In many of its architectural details, the Pavilion of Portugal followed

Dedication ceremonies of Portuguese Pavilion.

Tower of Jewels.

those of old Portuguese convents and cathedrals: the Jeronimos, at Lisbon, built on order of King Manuel I to commemorate the discovery of the seaway to India by Vasco de Gama; the Batalha, near Leiria, commemorating the battle of Aljubarrota, in which the Portuguese, under the Holy Constable and aided by 500 English archers, defeated the Castilians; and the Convent of Christ, an ancient see of the Knightly Order of Christ of Portugal, near the city of Tomar. The lavish ornament in Gothic mode, the frieze of shields about the upper walls, and the statues of Prince Henry the Navigator and Pedro Alvares Cabral, discoverer of Brazil, which flanked the entrance, suggested the great days of Portuguese chivalry in the Moorish wars, and the Golden Age of Discovery in which Portuguese rulers and navigators played so grand a part. The style was what is designated as the Manuelino, Manoeline or Manoellian, in which Hindu and African decoration, introduced into Europe through the expansion of the Portuguese empire southward and eastward, was superimposed on Gothic forms; and the somewhat crowded beauties of which are relieved in Portuguese construction by the gigantic scale of the operations. This was Portugal's main contribution to the noble art of building. The architect and designer of the Portuguese pavilion was António Couto d'Abreu. The local architect was W.C. Coulter of San Francisco. The building was just north of the Cuban pavilion and faced the Avenue of Nations.

The pavilion itself was not especially large, but the grandeurs of the colossal architecture it represented were most effectively exhibited on the walls of its octagonal interior, in framed photographs several feet square, showing facades and portals and selected studies of convents, monasteries and castles in this romantic land of Visigoth and Moor. It was an architectural feast and not unlike a journey to the little country that was once the greatest maritime, commercial, and colonial power in Europe, and divided with Spain the title to the new world.

Here was a fine view of the richly ornamented interior of the Convent of Jeronimos, near Lisbon, rather florid, but very beautiful, with heavily carved columns supporting a well-ribbed and vaulted roof. Another picture showed the Castle of Pena, its domes and towers rising from a rocky height once occupied by the Jeronimos monks. The castle was built here by Ferdinand II in 1838.

Near it was the Cathedral of Coimbra, dating from the 12th century — built by order of King Alfonso Henriques. Here, too, was the convent of the Order of Christ, in the city of Tomar. Apparently they had worked along on it from about 1160 to 1551. It was richly and profusely decorated in what appeared to be Roman, Byzantine, Gothic, Moorish, Renaissance, and Manuelino, and so it was a great stone book of history. Besides, it suggested Portugal's part in the Crusades, and in the long wars against the Infidel on her own soil, for it had once belonged to the Templars. The intricate, lace-like stone carving was shown in detail in a separate picture of a window of the convent. And there was also a photograph of a portal and two windows of the Convent of Jeronimos at Lisbon. Here, too, was the very baroque church of Estrella at Lisbon, said to have been built on order of Queen Mary I at a cost of about $6,400.000.

The bold square donjon and rounded towers of the Castle of Almourol rise from an island in the Tagus, where Guadim Paes, Master of the Templars, built it on a site once occupied by a stronghold of the Moors. The castle dates from 1160, and the picture of it, with its views of the river, was very interesting.

Among all this romance was a scene of classic interest — the only temple of Diana on the Iberian peninsula, the one at Evora. It looked quite severe by contrast with the other. Eleven fine Corinthian columns still stand, with lintels in place, and part of a second course. Borrow, who visited it in 1835, says of it: Part of it was evidently of Roman architecture, for there was no mistaking the beautiful light pillars which supported a dome, under which the sacrifices to the most captivating and poetical divinity of heathen theocracy had probably been made; the original space between the pillars had been filled up with rubbish of a modern date, and the rest of the building was apparently of the architecture of the latter end of the middle ages.

Over the register desk was a very fine photographic study of the main portal of the Convent of Batalha, rich in Gothic ornament, with touches of the Manuelino. Finally there was an interior view of the library of the University of Coimbra, ornate and sumptuous with the heavy carven ornament of grand Renaissance interiors. In alcoves all about were dioramas of scenes in Portuguese ports, such as Oporto, Lisbon, and Funchal.

Altogether these pictures were interesting and delightful, and formed one of the most effective methods of display. In addition, there were cases of fine lace and needlework that were much admired. Well printed, beautifully illustrated literature, calculated to promote travel to the places of romantic and historic interest depicted, received a large distribution, for the pavilion was most attractive and had hundreds of thousands of visitors.

The Portuguese were represented in the Palace of Fine Arts and Food Products. However, the representation in the field of Fine Arts, under the direction of A. de Sousa Lopes, was indeed outstanding. It included paintings of Columbano, Veloso, Salgado, Malhoa (the *Nightingale's Veranda*), João Vaz, Cardoso, D. Zoe Batalha Reis, Campas, Saude, David de Melo, Arthur Prat and Bonvalot. The field of architecture introduced Costa Mota, Tomaz Costa, Simões de Almeida, Julio Vaz Junior and Rodrigo de Castro. Also, Maria Augusta Bordalo Pinheiro displayed some of her embroideries.

In the months ahead the fair was visited by people from all over. Meanwhile, The Executive Committee of the Portuguese community decided to promote the Portuguese Day at the fair. They selected October 5, a date with political connotations, for it celebrated the day of the overthrow of the Monarchy and the beginning of the Republic.

All Portuguese girls over twelve were invited to participate in a choir, under the leadership of Mário Bettencourt da Camara. The rehearsals were held beginning September 8 at the U.P.E.C. Hall, San Leandro, every Wednesday and at Phillip's Hall located at the corner of East 14th Street and 23rd Avenue in Oakland every Sunday. The Portuguese Fraternal Societies were requested to cooperate, especially the U.P.E.C., I.D.E.S. and U.P.P.E.C. who were having their conventions around that time.

The program was publicized and called for a parade to be formed at Market Street at 10:00 A.M. with floats depicting the most important Portuguese industries in California and four bands including the U.P.E.C. In the Court of Abundance there were speeches and recitals in the presence of city and county officials, Directors of the fair, the Governor of the State of California and Archbishop P. Hanna. At 6:00 P.M. in the Old Faithful Inn in Yellowstone Park a banquet costing $3.00 per plate was held followed by a Ball and theatrical show.

Admission tickets to the fair were 50¢ each and were sold in advance along with a ticket allowing a ride in any of the 400 cars in the parade.

Prizes from $50 to $100 were offered for the float categories excluding any floats entered by subordinate councils of fraternal societies or the eight ordered built by the Portuguese Executive Committee and paid for with donations received from the community.

All Portuguese who owned automobiles were invited to enter the parade. Prizes were also available for the best decorated cars in addition to free admission to the fairgrounds. Deadline for entries was October 1.

These were the plans. But in the Portuguese community emotions always ran high and the plans of the Executive Committee reflects just that problem. The Portuguese Ambassador, Viscount of Alte; the Consul of Portugal in San Francisco, S.L. Ferreira; and Vice Consul, Manuel T. Freitas were not invited to partake in the program, which was held in the Court of Abundance.

They, however, had their own program by the Portuguese Pavilion. This unfortunate circumstance, according to the press at the time, was due to someone in the Executive Committee who disliked the Consul or the Vice Consul of Portugal. This incident caused certain distress in the Portugese community and immediately made front page news in the *San Francisco Chronicle,* which referred to it with certain irony, including it in its comic section.

The *O Arauto,* in its issue of October 16, 1915, concluded its coverage of the event in the following manner: "We never expected that the only occasion we had to show ourselves with certain dignity in the eyes of the Americans residing or visiting here, would end as bad as it did."

This editorial was then followed by an article "Quem Torto Nasce . . . ," (he who is born crooked . . .) revealing, as always, that the Portuguese community was a victim of personality clashes and animosities between the Portuguese press, the Consul of Portugal and certain individuals of rival factions, this time between Clay and Jackson Streets interests.

The article disclosed that the real cause for the two celebrations on October 5 was due to disrespect towards the Consul of Portugal in San Francisco, who had been ignored by the Portuguese community of San Francisco due to misunderstandings between he and the Vice Consul, Manuel T. Freitas, also an officer of the Portuguese Bank of Clay Street.

The Portuguese participation in the International Fair could have been an opportunity to bring the people together instead of driving them apart in the years to follow.

Not all was as bad as the Portuguese press tried to make it. There were, especially amongst the fraternal societies, gestures that became historic.

The U.P.E.C. and U.P.P.E.C., for instance, held their conventions in Oakland on the week of October 5. A first took place in the history of fraternalism when the U.P.P.E.C. delegation passed a resolution making U.P.E.C. Supreme President, A.J. Homem, an honorary delegate to the U.P.P.E.C. convention, then a ladies organization. In turn, U.P.E.C. delegation conferred the title of honorary Past Supreme President on Mrs. M. Cardozo, Supreme President of U.P.P.E.C., in addition to purchasing admission tickets to the fair for all the delegates of U.P.P.E.C. in order to attend the U.P.E.C. Day festivities at the fair.

The exposition lasted through December 4, 1915. One of the phrases which denoted the enthusiasm of U.P.E.C. leadership was in a speech delivered at the Court of Abundance on October 5, by Hon. John G. Mattos, stressing the fact that U.P.E.C. had donated $500 to the fair for Portuguese Day and "that in every occasion in which the Portuguese patriotism is put to a test, to honor Portugal, the U.P.E.C. is always there in the front, giving an effective and benevolent example to the other institutions, which, generally they follow."

In years ahead, U.P.E.C. participated in other events: the celebrations in honor of Gago Coutinho and Sacadura Cabral, two Portuguese pilots who first crossed the South Atlantic by air, connecting Lisbon to Rio de Janeiro, Brasil, in 1922. Ten years later the fifth centennial of the discovery of the Azores was remembered in California, as was the seventh centennial of the death of Saint Anthony.

The first of these events directly tied to most Portuguese in California, for the majority came from the islands of the Azores, while the other, of a religious nature, honored a popular Saint, born in Lisbon, Portugal, on August 15, 1195, and whom the society adopted as its patron Saint by a resolution introduced by Francisco I. Lemos and approved by the delegation assembled in Turlock, California in 1921.

The two significant historic events were jointly celebrated on April 3 and 4, 1932, by the society in the city of Oakland, with Manuel S. Soares presiding over

A Festa de 3 de Abril

Comemorando o 5o. Centenário da Descoberta dos Açores e o 7o. Centenário da Morte de Santo António de Lisboa.

HINO A' TERRA DOS AÇORES

F. I. LEMOS.
Presidente Honorário da Comissão da
Festa do dia 3 de Abril

No Sacrário da nossa aliança
Nós depômos a terra em penhor,
Invocando um hino de Esperança,
Numa vénia de crença e louvor.

Irmãos, filhos da Pátria querida,
Embalados nas ondas do mar;
Se dispersos andamos na vida,
Nem por isso a deixamos de amar.

Terras santas nos coube em partilha
Património de graça e de amor,
Cada qual aceitou sua Ilha
Sem ciumes de sorte e valor.

NOVE ESTRELAS de vária grandeza,
Mas, do brilho invejas não têm;
Cada uma tem sua beleza
No regaço bendito da mãe.

"S. MIGUEL" que pesou na balança,
Com riquezas e adorno sem par,
Tem colinas, jardins, abastança
E crateras de sonho e pasmar.

Primogénita, "SANTA MARIA"
Veneranda de antigo solar,
Uma concha que, em branda harmonia
Reproduz os bramidos do mar.

A "TERCEIRA," primaz do Heroísmo,
Orgulhosa de nobres brazões,
Tem herois nos anais do civísmo,
E na Praia, inauditas acções.

Eis "S. JORGE" de verdes pastagens,
Estendida num manto de azul,
Tem ao norte belezas selvagens
Iriais quédas de água no sul.

"GRACIOSA," altaneira, escarpada,
Atalaia do grupo central,
Terra grata, cultura esmerada,
Podução dum labor sem rival.

O "FAIAL" a gentil, primorosa,
Esmeralda de brilho e de luz,
E a baía tão bela e formosa
Que ao entrar nos encanta e seduz.

Vêde o "PICO," disforme, alteroso,
Que, das nuvens, domina em redor;
Quém não viu o colosso espantoso
Não realiza um assombro maior.

Mais além surge a ILHA das FLORES
Cujo brilho das mais não desdiz,
Saudemos os nossos maiores;
Vai no rumo da rota feliz...

Eis o "CORVO," o fanal do cruzeiro,
Onde a lenda augurando o porvir,
Numa estatua poz um cavaleiro
Apontando o caminho a seguir.

Portugalia, March, 1932 dedicated to the 5th Centennial of the Discovery of the Azores.

the committee in charge of the program. Other members included F. I. Lemos, Joseph J. Cardoso, Jose C. Jorge, Anthony Silva, Frank E. Pine, Frank Roderick and Alberto Moura. It is estimated that over forty thousand people, mostly Portuguese, from all over California took part in these festivities which began at nine o'clock in the morning with a three-mile parade headed by Serra Assembly and St. Francis Assembly of the Fourth Degree, Knights of Columbus. This parade included fifteen bands and forty-five uniformed drill corps of various Portuguese and Catholic societies who marched through the streets of downtown Oakland and dispersed at the Civic Auditorium where Bishop Robert J. Armstrong of Sacramento presided at the solemn high mass which was celebrated by Father Joseph Galli, a salesian priest from Oakland.

In the afternoon a barbeque was served to thousands of guests, followed by a drama-literary program which recalled the discovery of the Azores by Goncalo Velho Cabral. The celebrations concluded on Monday with a Grand Ball in the Civic Auditorium during which the Honorable James G. Rolph, then governor of the State of California, crowned Miss Marie Homem queen of the festival.

Miss Maria Homem
Queen of the Celebration

In 1936 the U.P.E.C. leaders took part in the celebrations of the sixth centennial of the death of Queen Elizabeth, which were promoted by the S.P.R.S.I. These celebrations, held in Oakland, gathered thousands of Portuguese from all over California and were considered some of the most outstanding in recent years. These festivities accounted for the visit of Cardinal Goncalves Cerejeira of Lisbon. There was a play about the life of Queen Elizabeth which were presented in several stages in communities where Portuguese lived.

The Portuguese fraternal societies, and other community organizations, soon joined forces and once again, publicly, showed their pride in the heritage a large number of their members claim today. The occasion was the Golden Gate Exposition in 1939 and 1940, held at Treasure Island in the middle of the bay between Oakland and San Francisco, cities which, by that time were already linked by the Bay Bridge.

GOLDEN GATE INTERNATIONAL EXPOSITION

In 1939 another International Exposition was held in California. One purpose of

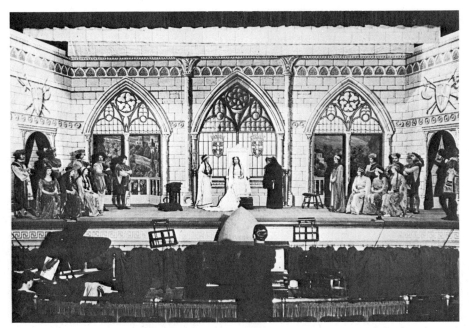

Scene from *Life of Queen Elizabeth* commemorating the fifth centennial of the Saint's death in 1936. The play toured California.

U.P.E.C. folklore group, directed by Mr. and Mrs. Nelson Gomes.

the Exposition was to expose visitors the world over to another extraordinary American fete — the link to the San Francisco Peninsula by the way of two bridges — the Golden Gate and the San Francisco-Oakland Bay Bridge. Many Portuguese immigrants had labored in construction of these bridges.

The Golden Gate Bridge, the longest, highest, single steel suspension span, single deck bridge in the world at that time is seven miles long and was built at a total cost of thirty-five million dollars. Its towers stand 746 feet tall, or 191 feet higher than the Washington Monument. The length of the main span is 4,200 feet. Its clearance over high water is 220 feet and the height of the deck above water at center is 266 feet. It has two sidewalks. One of them is available to pedestrians, and has attracted millions of visitors since it was open to the public in May of 1937. Sad as it may seem, the Golden Gate Bridge has claimed over 500 suicide victims.

The San Francisco-Oakland Bay Bridge, commonly known as the Bay Bridge, is double decked, eight and one-quarter miles long, of which four and hone-half miles are over navigable water. It was built at a cost of eighty million dollars. Construction began on July 9, 1933 and opened to automobile traffic on November 12, 1936, while train service on the lower deck began on January 15, 1939. Trains were eliminated recently to accommodate the ever increasing commuter traffic. The upper deck is now open to traffic bound towards San Francisco, while the lower deck takes in traffic towards Oakland. Each pier supporting the bridge has a depth of 242 feet, considered at the time a new engineering record for depth below water. The west crossing comprises twin suspension spans, and the east crossing has 1400 foot cantilever spans and nineteen truss spans.

The Golden Gate Exposition was conceived in 1931 by the Junior Chamber of Commerce of San Francisco, and the site they selected for the event was adjacent to Yerba Buena Island and became known as Treasure Island, named after a novel by Robert Louis Stevenson, a famous American writer. According to information contained in the *Portuguese Day Souvenir Program,* the island has a seawall of 287,000 tons of rock, thirteen feet higher than mean low water, and is more than three miles long, enclosing twenty million cubic feet of sand raised by eleven dredges from sections of the bay, and is considered the world's largest artificial island. It took eighteen and one-half months to build and sits on ten thousand piles driven to rock bottom. Total cost was $3,710,800 in W.P.A. funds.

The Portuguese again were represented at the exposition, even though more modestly than before. The Pavilion was thirty-five feet wide, by seventy five feet long and thirty feet high, covering 2,280 square feet. The design was made by

Golden Gate International Exposition, Treasurer Island, San Francisco, California.

Stand of Portugal - 1939

Portuguese architects Jorge Segurado, Bernardo Marques and Carlos Botelho. Tomaz de Melo was responsible for the interior decorating. It was financed both by Portugal and the Portuguese in California.

Funds were raised amongst radio, press, clubs and other community people, but only reached the sum of $2,664.12. The committee had to come up with the difference of $4,165.52 to make the total of $6,829.64, which represented the community's share of the cost of the pavilion, a commitment assumed before by the Portuguese government. The funds were handed to Antonio Ferro, the Portuguese High Commissioner for the World's Fair held simultaneously in New York, during his visit to California on July 3, 1939. The Portuguese Pavilion was late in opening due to delays at the San Francisco Custom's Office in clearing the many articles which were sent for display.

At the entrance of the pavilion was a twelve foot model of the monument to Joao Rodrigues Cabrilho, created by Portuguese Sculptor Alvaro de Bree. The monument, made after this model was on display at the World's Fair in New York, and was later offered to the State of California and today stands at Cabrilho National Monument Park in Point Loma, California. However, its arrival in San Diego was only possible after several months of arguments amongst Portuguese community leaders who took so long to agree on a location. Oakland and Monterey were among several suggested for its location, but it took some action from a legislator in Sacramento and a crew of able movers to take it from a garage in San Francisco all the way to San Diego. The monument situation is referred to as a sort of an overnight kidnapping by some old timers who are still around to tell of the monument to Cabrilho's discovery.

There was another Portuguese Day at the Exposition. History was made again,

Portuguese Pavilion, Golden Gate Exposition, 1940.

for this time five fraternal societies held a joint convention in the city of Oakland from September 2 through September 7, 1939 (U.P.E.C. presided by Angelo R. Ingnacio; I.D.E.S., Cipriano Cardoso; S.P.R.S.I., Cecilia de Figueiredo; U.P.P.E.C., Isabel Medina and U.P.C.E.C. by Antonio Marques). To give an idea of the spirit which reigned at the time amongst those fraternals, they put aside petty differences and banded their efforts for a showing of unity. The Hotel Oakland, located at 13th and Harrison Streets, was selected for the headquarters for the five societies.

On Sunday, September 3, the program consisted of a parade of all Supreme Officers, delegates, bands, drill teams and an enormous crowd of visitors who gathered at the convention headquarters and marched to the Civic Auditorium, where in the arena, a mass was said by Most Rev. John J. Mitty, Archbishop of San Francisco, with a sermon by Right Rev. Alfredo M. de Sousa. After mass, a variety show was held in the theater adjacent to the arena. In included a drama entitled *The Mysterious Woman* by J.W. McConaughy (original of A. Bisson). Admission tickets were seventy-five cents for orchestra seats and fifty cents for the balcony.

On Monday, September 4, a joint Grand Ball, held in the Civic Auditorium was attended by six thousand people. On Tuesday, all officers and guests gathered for a banquet served in the Scottish Rite Temple on Oak Street. On Wednesday the convention recessed to attend Portuguese Day at the Fair. After the business sessions were concluded on Thursday, the societies found themselves back at the Civic Auditorium, where they held a joint installation, the only one of its kind ever held by these organizations who then formed the League of the Portuguese Fraternal Societies. João de Bianchi, Ambassador of Portugal in Washington, D.C., in his message of greetings, referred to it as "a significant event which made history in the Portuguese communities of the United States."

Portuguese Day at the Fair was held on the 6th of September under the auspices of all fraternals in addition to the Cabrillo Civic Club, Portuguese-American Civic Club, Queen Elizabeth Dramatic Club, Inc., Portuguese-American Athletic Club, Castle of Portugal Club (Castlemont High School), Portuguese newspapers *A União Portuguesa, Jornal Portugues, O Progresso*, and several radio programs. The person selected to lead the community in this important event was Manuel Severino

Excursion of the Club "Castle of Portugal," Castlemont High School, Oakland, California, to the Golden Gate International Exposition on May 29, 1939, Oakland Day.

Soares, Past Supreme President of U.P.E.C. and President of the League. Soares, a very distinguished gentleman, was elected Chairman of the General and Executive Committees who handled both the Portuguese Day at the Exposition as well as the joint conventions of the five fraternal societies. The Executive Committee included John C. Valim, Secretary; António Barroca, Treasurer; Leopoldina C. Rodrigues Alves; Mae S. Pimentel; Dr. J. C. Lopes and António R. Mattos.

Golden Gate Exposition, Portuguese Day Executive Committee: (from left) John C. Valim, Secretary; Manuel S. Soares, Chairman; and António Barroca, Treasurer.

U.P.E.C. Float — Portuguese Day, Parade.

The day at the Fair began around 12:30 P.M. with a parade formed at the Athletic Field, Treasure Island, and included, besides marching units, several beautifully decorated floats. In the evening there was a variety show, featuring Portuguese actress Ilda Stichini. The Portuguese Day queen was Mary Simas of San Luis Obispo, who received 200,650 votes, and was assisted by Maids of Honor: Frances Fortuna of Tracy, Marie June Silveira of Oakland, and Genevieve Gomes of San Jose. Portuguese attendance was put at twenty-five thousand people.

It was estimated then that the total number of California citizens of Portuguese birth or descent numbered a little over one hundred thousand — most of them engaged in dairying, diversified farming and sheep raising in the valleys of California, except in San Diego, where Portuguese always played an important role in the fishing industry. In the pavilion there was a giant sign showing seventy-five percent of the Portuguese in the dairy industry, twenty percent in agriculture, fifteen percent in housework, ten percent in commerce, nine percent in various industries, two percent in fishing, one percent in professional and one percent as longshoremen.

About forty percent of the total estimated Portuguese population were affiliated with one or another of the eight fraternal societies then in existence, three of which had not joined the League (A.P.P.B., Portuguese Protective and Benevolent Society Association of San Francisco; A.P.U.M.E.C., Madeirense Union Protective Association of the State of California, of Oakland; and the S.E.S., Holy Ghost Association of Santa Clara).

The Portuguese Pavilion, far from the opulence displayed in the Panama Pacific Exposition of 1915, was described by Jack Burroughs of the Oakland Tribune as follows:

So we went into the Portuguese Pavilion and International Hall, and there is a split globe over the Portuguese Pavilion . . . . Portugal and California are the two bright spots on this globe, with a line running from each to a conventionalized sun above. The sun consists of a thin wooden ring with wooden rays running out from it, which probably does not sound very exciting or decorative unless you happen to have seen what those gifted Portuguese artists and interior decorators can do with a few simple things like that.

The walls of the Portuguese Pavilion are eloquent, and I don't mean with the assistance of concealed loudspeakers, either. They are eloquent with epigrams, quotations, and statistics too, in raised wooden letters.

I shall give the walls the floor, and lest I convey the impression that the pavilion is collapsible, I hasten to add that I am merely going to let the walls speak for themselves. The split globe display is given significance by the following legend: 'When you are in Europe and long California, pay a visit to Portugal.'

In smaller wooden letters, various reasons backing up this suggestion are set forth. One of these reads as follows: 'For the shores of California and Portugal are the sun's favorites.' The halved globe shows clearly that Portugal and California occupy practically the same position in relation to the sun. The list of 'fors' includes this one: 'For the stars of Portugal's sky are as lovely as the stars of Hollywood.'

If you don't think there is anything artistic about sardines, drop in at the Portuguese Pavilion some day and see what Portuguese decorators can do with the sardine theme when they really go to town.

The keynote of all those wall decorations seems to be expressed in an epigram captioning a group of photographs showing phases of life in Portugal. 'Portugal, the land of imagery, in its own legend, its own film.'

In the past I have thought of statistics, when I thought of them at all, as long rows of figures laid end to end. On the walls of the Portuguese Pavilion the statistics are there, laid end to end, but they are accompanied by fascinating streamlined designs. In this remarkable set-up, figures do not lie, but they recline, stand, sit and otherwise pose in a manner at once appealing and unforgettable. They illustrate the story of Portugal's government, industry, recreational life, colonization, fraternal organizations and other manifold activities.

I grew enthusiastic.

'The work of these artists represents the very last word in the decorative scheme of things,' I exclaimed.

I could tell by my all-knowing friend's expression that I had stuck my chin out again.

'You're wrong, my friend,' he said. To prove his point he introduced me to the pavilion's hostess, Miss Mary Santos, who was clad in a colorful Madeira peasant costume. Verily, there is no wisdom like unto the wisdom of this all-knowing friend of mine.

Miss Santos showed us a remarkable collection of peasant costumes on figurines which were themselves works of art. Even the jewelry worn by these small and extremely artistic models is done to scale. The group includes a peasant of Ribatejo; a vendor from Minho; a fisherman from Monte Gordo; seaweed gatherers from Praia da Praia da Apulia; a peasant and a peasant woman from Madeira; a woman plougher; a trap bearer; a shepherd from Serra da Estrela and a vintager from Douro. I thought I might scare up a few vagrant words to make you see these figurines as I saw them, but the thought perished as I caught sight of that 'you are wrong-my-friend' look in the eyes of my all-knowing friend.

The Fair closed in December of 1939, but on May 24, 1940 reopened. The Portuguese Pavilion occupied the building, which in 1939 had housed the display from Guatemala. Most of its refurbishing was done through the cooperation

Actress Ilda Stachini and Dr. R. Gaspar Henriques.

Monument to João Rodrigues Cabrilho at Naval Station, San Diego. Later the monument was moved to the Point Loma Promontory where it now stands.

of James Sousa, President of *Casa de Portugal* in San Francisco. It was wartime in Europe which made it difficult to import rare art objects from Portugal that could have been made available to visitors to the Fair on a second exhibit.

On June 16, 1940, once again, Day of Portugal was celebrated and attended by some five thousand Portuguese. The U.P.E.C. Band gave a concert on that afternoon in the International Court.

It is interesting to note that in 1940 Portugal celebrated its empire and world achievements with a Fair *(Mundo Portugues)*. The double centennials (1140-1640-1940) echoed in all parts of the world, including California.

The five societies composing the League, alone spent over fifteen thousand dollars with the joint conventions and the maintenance of the Portuguese section at the Exposition. This event was one of the many contributions the League made for the good name of the Portuguese community of California.

The years after the exposition were quiet ones. The Portuguese families were mourning many of their close relatives who lost their lives in combat. World War II was under way and many Portuguese-Americans enlisted in the Armed Forces.

Public celebrations quited down but reappeared in 1960 when the Portuguese, world over, celebrated the fifth centennial of the death of Prince Henry. Several organizations gathered to form a committee to honor the Prince of Navigation and contributor to world discovery. The U.P.E.C. and San Leandro Chamber of Commerce joined in the tribute with Mayor Jack D. Maltester, John Deadrich II and Portuguese Consular officials.

Two years later, on June 10 in San Jose, for the first time in many years, the U.P.E.C. and the Portuguese-Americans in California celebrate the Day of Portugal in honor of the greatest of Portuguese poets — Camões. Over six hundred people participated in the festivities which began with a solemn high mass at the Five Wounds Church, one of the only two Portuguese national churches still in existence in California.

After mass the hall of the *Irmandade do Espirito Santo* (I.E.S.) opened its doors to serve a free luncheon to members of the organization and guests, followed by a variety show with Alvaro Marcella as the Master of Ceremonies. The afternoon was filled with speeches, recitations, Portuguese music and songs by local artists.

The event concluded with a dance open to the public, especially the recent arrivals from the island of Faial who had emigrated from that Azorean island. The committee composed of members of U.P.E.C. Council No. 32, Alum Rock, was presided over by Gil Alves. The "Day of Portugal" since 1966 has been celebrated by the Luso-American Education Foundation of Oakland as part of their cultural program.

THE MONUMENT TO THE PORTUGUESE IMMIGRANT

In 1964 the U.P.E.C. once again promoted another event, this time to pay tribute to the early Portuguese pioneers of California.

It started with a visit made to Maria Ascenção Carvalho Rogers by Carlos Almeida on June 15, 1961 in answer to a call to pick up some books she was selling for J. Mota Vasconcelos, a newspaperman from the island of Madeira. Mrs. Rogers expressed her sorrow for the cold reception several people in the Portuguese community of New England had given Vasconcelos' idea to build a monument honoring the islander immigrants. She confessed that, likewise, her hopes for the project had met with the same fate — at least with those contacts she had established in California.

On June 17 Mayor Jack D. Maltester was contacted by Carlos Almeida about the possibility of accepting the statue, should U.P.E.C.'s Board of Directors concur with the idea of raising the necessary funds for its purchase from sculptor Numidico Bessone of Caxias, Portugal. The total cost of the statue was $5,500, in addition to transportation and assembly costs. Mayor Maltester immediately contacted the City Council and secured their approval to accept the monument should it be a gift from

IN THE CITY COUNCIL OF THE CITY OF SAN LEANDRO
RESOLUTION NO. 4751 C.M.S.
RESOLUTION OF THANKS
(U.P.E.C.)

Whereas, the U.P.E.C., the Portuguese Union of California, is presenting a white marble statue to the City of San Leandro to be dedicated to early pioneer emigrants who settled and developed this State; and

Whereas, San Leandro is proud to be the home of this great and beneficial Portuguese association; and

Whereas, San Leandro is pleased to be chosen as the recipient of this artistic monument, which is symbolic of the early pioneer emigrant spirit; and

Whereas, this Council has unanimously approved location of the statue on that historic landmark of San Leandro, Root Park;

Now, therefore, the City Council of the City of San Leandro does RESOLVE as follows:

That this City Council wishes to extend their gratitude and thanks to the Uniao Portugueza do Estado da California for the artistic monument so generously offered by the descendants of these same early founders of our State.

Introduced by Councilman Gill and passed and adopted this 29th day of January, 1962, by the following called vote:

Ayes:	*Councilmen: Cheatham, Gill, Kant, Suerstedt, Swift, Taylor, Maltester*	*(7)*
Noes:	*Councilmen: None*	*(0)*
Absent:	*Councilmen: None*	*(0)*

Jack D. Maltester
Mayor of the City of San Leandro

Attest:
Richard H. West, City Clerk

1/26/62/nf

the U.P.E.C. The location for the monument was left open. Later, two sites were suggested — the downtown plaza and the newly built Marina Park. It was agreed to place the monument at Root Park, where it now stands, across from the Home Office of the U.P.E.C.

From July 15, 1961, when the Board appointed a committee to spearhead the

Sculptor Numidico Bessone carving the Monument to the Portuguese Immigrant, Caxias, Portugal.

project and raise the necessary funds for the purchase of the monument, to March 15, 1964, when the monument was unveiled, there were many obstacles which had to be overcome. The committee appointed by the U.P.E.C. Board of Directors consisted of Joseph A. Freitas, Chairman; Antone E. Braga, Vice-Chairman; Carlos Almeida, Secretary; Joseph A. Furtado; Manuel E. Mendonsa; António J. Frade; Louis A. Silva; Manuel Cabral; John Gulart and Manuel M. Frizado.

All of these men sought financial support only among U.P.E.C. members. The first donation was received from the San Leandro-Oakland U.P.E.C. Convention Committee, followed by individual contributions from officers and from drives made by subordinate councils of the society. Money was slow coming in. The situation really improved when the *Jornal Portugues,* of Oakland, came out with an editorial criticizing the idea. This attitude was indeed what was needed to encourage the balance of the money to flow in at a faster pace. The relationship with Albert Lemos, editor of that newspaper, was not the most harmonious — for his loyalties lay with another Portuguese fraternal society, a competitor of the U.P.E.C. which no doubt was anxiously awaiting the project of the monument to the Portuguese immigrant to fail.

In the meantime, efforts were being made by sculptor Bessone and Mrs. Rogers to secure free transportation of the monument from the Carregadores Acoreanos an Azorean based steamship line, whose President, Jose H. Gago da Camara Medeiros, known as the Viscount of Botelho, was a close friend of Bessone. While Almeida was trying for a commitment from Mayor Maltester to pay for transportation from New York to San Leandro, the committee decided to have the names of any donor who gave one hundred dollars or more engraved on the monument, thus encouraging donations which were still short of the amount needed. Finally, on August 18, 1963, the drive closed. The amount of $5,544.87 was solely collected from U.P.E.C. members, except for $200.00 from the Cabrilho Civic Club No. 11 of Alameda County and the *Voz de Portugal,* a newspaper recently founded in Hayward, California, by Gilberto Lopes Aguiar.

On September 1, 1963 the forty-one crates of carved white marble left the studio of sculptor Bessone to board the *S.S. Azores* on its way to Brooklyn, New York, where it arrived on September 22. At this time the East Coast Overseas Corp. in New York was contacted by the U.P.E.C. for an offer of free storage for the crates. The San Leandro City Council authorized disbursement of over two thousand dollars to the Sea-Land Co. for freight charges to the Port of Oakland and from there to the City Corporation Yard located on Washington Avenue where the monument awaited its assembly from November 14 to December 4, 1963.

Meanwhile, a slight problem arose. The Municipal Public Works Department was at odds regarding the assembly of the monument and ended up by seeking help from the Vermont Marble Company of San Francisco, who were also puzzled with the manner in which those forty-one pieces of white marble were to be assembled to form the twenty-foot monument to the Portuguese pioneers. Strange as it may seem, the U.P.E.C. committee was already looking for financial support to pay for the fare of sculptor Bessone who probably would have to be summoned to direct the assembly of the stones.

But when there is a will, there is a way. A last chance was considered before inviting Bessone, who was already alerted of the problems by a telegram which was sent as soon as the Vermont Marble Company had shown reluctance about assembly.

The last opportunity for local assembly was Bras and Silva Monuments of Hayward. Antonio Gomes Bras was called upon by committee members. The problem was explained to him and after two days of study, he decided to take a chance. With his workers and partner, John Silva, and a crew assigned by the San Leandro Public Works, they began assembly of the monument on December 4. They successfully completed work on December 27, 1963 with hardly any incident, except for the breakage of one foot of the *Immigrant* when a crane slacked and hit the base.

115

Assembly of monument to the Portuguese Immigrant - Root Park, San Leandro

(from left) Joe Gonsalves; John Silva and Antonio Braz, responsible for assembly of the forty one marble sections which make the monument

The repair was made by a sculptor from San Francisco, California, at a cost of $250. The defect is hardly noticed.

All the fund raising and coordination of the project to that date was done solely by the U.P.E.C. committee and spearheaded by Joseph A. Freitas, who many times pledged his own money just in case the committee ever ran short.

Mrs. Rogers limited herself in the beginning of the project to communicate with sculptor Bessone in Lisbon and to pray for the project to end up well . . . while Freitas and his committee went throughout the state and tried to raise funds, employing political influence to gain acceptance for the project which was already becoming the envy of the other Portuguese fraternal societies, our competitors.

U.P.E.C., in the drive was trying hard to gain the respect of the community, support they once had and which, in the last seven years had lessened due to the pains born of the failure of merger attempts by four other fraternals.

On January 29 community leaders met in the Conference Room of the San Leandro Chamber of Commerce to decide on the program for the unveiling of the monument covered with sheets of black plastic. George Pimentel, then chairman of the special events committee for the Chamber, appointed a group of leaders, both from U.P.E.C. and the Chamber to work out the program for the dedication ceremonies.

On March 15, 1964 over one thousand five hundred persons assembled around the park. Hays Street was blocked to traffic to accommodate the crowd of guests who came from all over California. The monument, the first and only art work of its kind in the city of San Leandro, was unveiled by both the Supreme President of U.P.E.C., Manuel Neves and Mayor Maltester.

Over one thousand five hundred witnessed unveiling at Root Park, San Leandro, California.

The ceremony included a concert by the U.P.E.C. Band, speeches by several city and county officials, as well as Dr. José Luiz Trigueiro de Aragão, Consul General of Portugal. Aragão, for reasons still unknown, had decided at the last minute not to attend the unveiling ceremonies, a decision he reversed after receiving from the Ambassador of Portugal in Washington, D.C., Vasco Vieira Garin, instructions to represent the government of the country whose sons, pioneer immigrants, were being paid homage for their untiring and honest work in California soil.

The main speaker for the afternoon was Judge Manuel Jesse Bettencourt, and the Master of Ceremonies was Hal Peary, noted radio and television personality of Portuguese descent and a native of San Leandro. In the evening, at the Boys Club, a crowd of over five hundred guests attended a banquet whose keynote address was delivered by Edward C. Massa, thus concluding the full day's ceremony, and almost three and a half years of hard work. In the end, the project proved rewarding to the organization for it attracted wide publicity and made U.P.E.C. better known, not only in the United States, but also in the Azores, Madeira and Portugal itself.

A MINHA MENSAGEM - MINHA SAUDAÇÃO

Senhor Governador do Estado da California
Senhor Presidente da Camara Municipal de San Leandro
Senhor Embaixador de Portugal em Washington
Senhores Directores da U.P.E.C.
Amigos e Irmaos Portugueses

Neste momento de historica solenidade em que duas Patrias -
Os Estados Unidos da America do Norte e Portugal - estao a teste
munhar e a exaltar o elo antigo e forte da cooperacao luso-ame
ricana simbolizado no Monumento que se ergue ao honrado e labor
ioso Imigrante Portugues, eu quero, em espirito ardente e comov
ido, a todos vos estreitar no meu abraco de amor e gratidao por
ter sido possivel pela vossa solidaria compreensao, pelo vossa
dedicadissima ajuda, erguer nas terras uberes e abencoadas da Ca
lifornia, agricultadas, em grande parte, com os suores e as lag
rimas e as saudades de gente boa de Portugal, um monumento que
eternamente ha-de memorar a grandiosa fraternidade de duas Na
coes, do dois Povos que secularmente andam empenhados ao servico
do Progresso e da Civilizacao.
Eu vos saudo a todos, jubilosamente, cordialmente, elevando
a Deus, elevando ao Ceu os meus votos para que deste extraordin
ario evento possa renascer, possa apertar-se, mais e sempre mais,
os elos da cadeia de uma solidariedade largamente fraterna que sir
va e bafeje legitimas e sas aspiracoes comuns.
As pedras vivas do Monumento que os bons e genuinos portu
gueses da California doaram, em gratissima oferenda, a hospital
eira Nacao que os acolhe e onde eles sao a expressao fiel da ar
dorosa e missionaria colonizacao lusitana, ha-de ser pelos temp
os fora, pelos tempos alem, um sinal de admiravel e constante fra
ternidade, uma fraternidade tao cara e tao desejada a irmandade e
duas Patrias que agora mais do que jamais unidas devem estar para
melhor vencerem os obstaculos e os desaires de uma terrivel ad
versidade que as quer ferir e matar.
Portugal vive mais na America do Norte do que a America do
Norte vive em Portugal.
Mas e preciso que a amizade, que a solidariedade seja igual
e aos Portugueses da America do Norte, que sao ja mais de um mil
hao de sangue luso-americano caldeado nas Familias, a esses bons
Portugueses cabe vez mais as fraternas relacoes entre os dois
grandes Povos e dessas relacoes amigas se fazer um entendimento
franco, um entendimen to cordial e sempre presente.
A' prestigiosa e prestantissima U.P.E.C., que e bastiao de
forca e de amor a servir a grande America do Norte; aos seus li
dimos associados que deram magnifica realidade a ideia de uma es
tatua que deve selar e chancelar no enaltecimento uma confratern
al amizade secular; ao Excelentissimo Senhor Jack D. Maltester,
honrado e brioso "Mayor" da ridente e prospera cidade de San Le
andro, que valiosamente e amorosamente patrocinou o grande acon
tecimento que agora se concretisa; a Excelentissima Senhora Dona
Maria da Ascencao Carvalho Rogers, que foi a Madrinha carinhosa

*e dedicada de uma iniciativa vitoriosa; ao Excelentissimo Senhor
Carlos Almeida, Secretario-Tesoureiro Supremo da benemerita U.P.
E.C., que foi o braco direito de tao belo, patriotico e confrater
nal proposito; aos muitissimos e dadivosos subscritores que com
o seu compreensivo e generoso obulo fizeram o milagre do extraor
dinario evento, a todos eu saudo, a todos eu agradeco com o mais
radiante, o mais jubiloso e portuguesissimo reconhecimento por
terem bem compreendido e sentido sa finalidade luso-americana de
um empreendimento que ficara no "amor" e na "historia" de dois
Povos que um imperativo categorico de salvacao comum manda e ob
riga a estarem francamente unidos e prontamente solidarios na de
fesa de seu patrios destinos, que sao os destinos espirituais da
Liberdade, da Justica e da Civilizacao do Ocidente.*

Gloria aos Estados Unidos da America do Norte.

Gloria a Portugal.

                                          JOAQUIM MOTA DE VASCONCELLOS

(Funchal, Marco de 1974)

Judge Manuel "Jesse" Bettencourt Author resolution calling for "Portuguese Immigrant Week" celebration.

119

PORTUGUESE IMMIGRANT WEEK

On the afternoon of March 13, 1965, the first anniversary of the dedication of the monument was observed at Root Park. A wreath of flowers was placed at the foot of the monument by Supreme President, Manuel B. Silva, while Judge Bettencourt recalled the contributions of the Portuguese to the State of California.

In the following year a resolution calling for a proclamation of Portuguese Immigrant Week was introduced by Judge Bettencourt at the U.P.E.C. convention held in Modesto.

The delegation, upon approving the spirit of the resolution, instructed the Board of Directors to ask for the support of every subordinate council in writing letters to their representatives at the State Legislature to have the governor of the state to proclaim the second week of March of each year as Portuguese Immigrant Week.

On February 23, 1967, Assemblyman Joe A. Gonsalves, then Chairman of the Assembly Rules Committee, and Gordon W. Duffy, Assemblyman of the Twenty-first District (Visalia, California), introduced the resolution which embodied the language of the one drafted by Judge Bettencourt. The resolution passed the Assembly, and Governor Ronald Reagan signed the first proclamation in March of that year. The first proclamation was actually given to Mrs. Tillie Perry, U.P.E.C. Council Secretary of Visalia, by Duffy, who called her to the State Capitol and handed it to her for presentation to the U.P.E.C.

Governor Ronald Reagan signing proclamation calling for the Portuguese Immigrant Week.

However, it was not until 1968 that the Board of Directors decided to invite all fraternal societies, clubs and press to form a committee to celebrate the second week of March with appropriate programs designed to involve all the people. The committee was formed during a meeting held in the San Leandro Public Library and became a steering committee whose purposes were to promote and encourage other communities to commemorate the contributions of Portuguese Immigrant Week in California. Carlos Almeida was elected chairman for the celebration.

The festivities in 1968 were spread throughout several communities in California and, in 1969, their importance gained the respect of many Portuguese-Americans who began identifying themselves with the celebration to the point where the

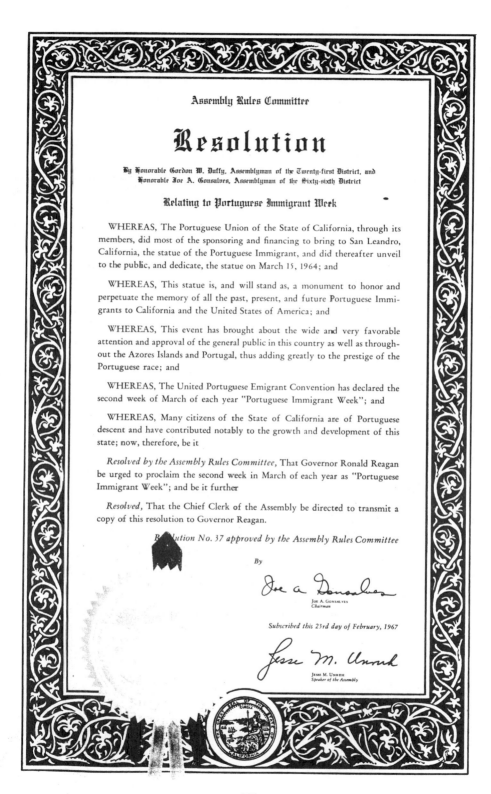

Assembly Rules Committee

Resolution

By Honorable Gordon W. Duffy, Assemblyman of the Twenty-first District, and
Honorable Joe A. Gonsalves, Assemblyman of the Sixty-sixth District

Relating to Portuguese Immigrant Week

WHEREAS, The Portuguese Union of the State of California, through its
members, did most of the sponsoring and financing to bring to San Leandro,
California, the statue of the Portuguese Immigrant, and did thereafter unveil
to the public, and dedicate, the statue on March 15, 1964; and

WHEREAS, This statue is, and will stand as, a monument to honor and
perpetuate the memory of all the past, present, and future Portuguese Immigrants to California and the United States of America; and

WHEREAS, This event has brought about the wide and very favorable
attention and approval of the general public in this country as well as throughout the Azores Islands and Portugal, thus adding greatly to the prestige of the
Portuguese race; and

WHEREAS, The United Portuguese Emigrant Convention has declared the
second week of March of each year "Portuguese Immigrant Week"; and

WHEREAS, Many citizens of the State of California are of Portuguese
descent and have contributed notably to the growth and development of this
state; now, therefore, be it

Resolved by the Assembly Rules Committee, That Governor Ronald Reagan
be urged to proclaim the second week in March of each year as "Portuguese
Immigrant Week"; and be it further

Resolved, That the Chief Clerk of the Assembly be directed to transmit a
copy of this resolution to Governor Reagan.

Resolution No. 37 approved by the Assembly Rules Committee

By

Joe A. Gonsalves
Chairman

Subscribed this 23rd day of February, 1967

Jesse M. Unruh
Speaker of the Assembly

121

Portuguese Immigrant Week banquet held in San Leandro attended by His Excellency Vasco Vieira Garin, Ambassador of Portugal.

Ambassador of Portugal in Washington, Dr. Vasco Vieira Garin, accepted an invitation to come to San Leandro to participate in the event.

In recent years, lack of direction and selfishness on the part of some of the committee members deviated from the original intentions of the resolution of Judge Bettencourt, leading to the withdrawal of the U.P.E.C. from the celebration. Also, failure of the committee to act resulted in the fact that the governor's proclamation was no longer signed. Therefore, it lost all the impact it once had.

Notwithstanding the turmoil and high emotions, characteristic of the new wave of Portuguese immigrants which, in many cases, led to their ineffectiveness to work as a group and rally for a common cause, the *Monument to the Portuguese Immigrant* stands in Root Park attesting to the hard work of their ancestors who were proud of their heritage and, contrary to the attitudes of recent immigrants, were seldom led by emotions.

Therefore, the credit for this accomplishment goes to the old immigrant and to a few of those recent ones who have always shown their capabilities of realization by building morale and seeking the respect and admiration any developed people can offer.

U.P.E.C. civic participation included the Sister City Program (San Leandro—Ponta Delgada). From left: Congressman George P. Miller; Mayor Jack D. Maltester; Carlos Almeida, Supreme Secretary-Treasurer, U.P.E.C.; and Dr. Antônio Costa Lobo, Consul General of Portugal.

U.P.E.C. leaders received by governor of the Azores in 1964 — P. Delgada.

U.P.E.C. DAY

The anniversary of the society was first publicly observed on August 1, 1894 with a picnic held at the San Lorenzo Grove (known today as Halcyon Drive, San Leandro). The expenses for the celebration amounted to $54.00 for the music and $19.25 for the printing of tickets and flyers. The receipts reached $88.00, of which $75.00 was from admissions and $13.00 from beer sales.

The second celebration took place in 1899 at the same place and commemorations continued for a few years, until 1903 when President A. Martins suggested that the anniversary of the society be celebrated in a more dignified manner, and he suggested an evening of a musical-literary nature. As years went by the event became more popular and, in 1921 it was celebrated in Oakland with a certain degree of pride. Eloquent speakers were always invited, and their inflamatory speeches would touch sparks of enthusiasm. In the words of Judge Frank Mitchell Jr., "it was an occasion to recall that, before the existence of the U.P.E.C., the Portuguese of this vast state had no mutual protection and that they were looked upon with indifference by the other ethnic groups."

U.P.E.C. Day is still celebrated although in different ways. It serves as a reason for the membership to get together and promote the society's aims even though it has lost its original purpose, that of singing the "glories of the union and of those who made it great."

YOUTH AND SPORTS

U.P.E.C. Soccer Team - San Leandro, CA

U.P.E.C. Baseball Team - Orland, CA

XVII

THE LEAGUE OF PORTUGUESE FRATERNAL SOCIETIES

On October 13, 1936, during the U.P.E.C. 50th Annual Convention held in Oakland, California, a resolution was introduced calling for its Board of Directors to invite other Portuguese fraternal societies to jointly study a plan to organize a Federation of the Portuguese Societies for the purpose of promoting their welfare and that of the community in general, as long as it did not interfere with the by-laws of the U.P.E.C.

On March 21 of the following year, and at the invitation of the U.P.E.C., representatives of Portuguese fraternal societies met at the Hotel Oakland, then the largest site favored by the Portuguese community for their social events. Thomas F. Lopes, Dr. Joaquim C. Lopes, Frank S. Roderick and Manuel S. Soares represented the U.P.E.C. on this historic occasion. Manuel R. Marcos, Antonio R. Matos and John C. Valim represented the I.D.E.S.; Mesdames Maria T.S. Silva and Ana S. Vieira represented the S.P.R.S.I.; Mesdames Mae A. Thomas, Mae S. Pimentel, Maria C. Fenn and M. Nicholas represented the U.P.P.E.C. Jose Pires, Jose Guardanapo and Manuel Reis represented the A.P.P.B.; Antonio Nunes, Antonio M. da Silva and Antonio Barroca represented the U.P.E.C.; while Arnaldo C.R. Sousa and Manuel S. Lucas represented the A.P.U.M.E.C. The only society not represented was the S.E.S. of Santa Clara.

The meeting was opened by Thomas F. Lopes who explained the purpose for the reunion, centering his remarks around the necessity to constitute a body which would represent the different societies to amicably discuss matters concerning their promotion as well as the protection of their respective interests. The group then delineated a simple set of rules for their guidance. It was also agreed to name this body The League of Portuguese Fraternal Societies of California. Temporary officers were elected: Manuel S. Soares, President; Maria T.S. Silva, Mae S. Pimentel, Manuel Reis and Manuel J. Machado, Vice-Presidents; J.C. Valim and Arnaldo C.R. Sousa, Secretaries and Antonio Barroca, Treasurer.

They met again on May 9 to discuss an invitation to be sent to the Portuguese government for their participation in the Golden Gate International Exposition, perhaps by sending a Portuguese ship to San Francisco Bay. They also considered the possibility of holding a joint convention of all societies which would coincide with the proposed Day of Portugal or Portuguese Day at the exposition.

The League had been formed. One of the first public events it sponsored was a banquet welcoming Dr. Jordão M. Henriques, Consul of Portugal, who had recently arrived in San Francisco.

The banquet was held on January 8, 1938 with a wide representation of all fraternal societies, radio, press and members of the Diplomatic Corps of Brasil.

The Golden Gate Exposition was held and the fraternal societies worked together, giving an outstanding example of unity, especially when Portuguese radio fan clubs were beginning to flourish all over the states. These clubs competed, not only for the social life of each subordinate council of those societies, but also for the youth who appeared to be following the more attractive functions promoted by the two most popular Portuguese radio personalities in the Bay Area: Arthur V. Avila and Lionel Soares de Azevedo.

The League financed most of the expenses incurred with the 1939 Golden Gate Exposition, including the acquisition of the monument to Cabrilho which now stands at Point Loma in San Diego. In 1941 an appeal for funds was made by the League to purchase a weapon to be given to the United States Armed Forces as a sign of Portuguese-American solidarity with this country, then fighting World War II. On August 31, 1942 a check for $10,680.24 for the purchase of two 77mm anti-aircraft guns were presented to Brigadier General Donald B. Robinson on behalf of the Portuguese people of California. These funds were raised mostly through the efforts fo the subordinate councils of all fraternal societies who comprised the League.

The gift was later acknowledged by Henry L. Stimson, Secretary of War, in a letter addressed to Manuel Vieira Alves, President.

Facsimile of check issued by The League of the Portuguese Fraternal Societies for the purchase of two anti-aircraft guns for the U.S. Army.

Guns on display at Hotel Oakland.

RESOLUTION

WHEREAS, *it has been suggested by people living in the southern part of the State, that essentials for courses in Portuguese should be worked out in order that at the earliest possible time said language might be taught in the high schools of California;* and

WHEREAS, *for cultural as well as for practical purposes it seems advisable that at least a minimum knowledge of said language which is spoken by sixty million people all over the world and is the official tongue of Portugal and Brazil, should be provided for the benefit of the young generation of the State, - now, therefore,* be it

RESOLVED *by the League of Portuguese Fraternal Societies, in regular session assembled and representing over thirty thousand men and women in this State, that the Sub-Committee on Foreign Languages of the California Committee for the Study of Education be hereby respectfully and earnestly requested to recommend that the Portuguese language be placed on the approved list of languages for entrance to the Colleges and Universities of California and that courses in said language be provided in the high schools of the State.*

(Adopted April 18, 1947)

Luncheon served U.S. soldiers returning from World War I, U.P.E.C. — Oakland Councils.

At that time the League had succeeded in the promotion of a joint convention of the four largest Portuguese societies: U.P.E.C., S.P.R.S.I., I.D.E.S. and U.P.P.E.C. The three-day convention was held from Sunday, August 31 through September 1, 1942 in the Hotel Oakland, during which they also celebrated the fourth centennial of the discovery of California by João Rodrigues Cabrilho.

These four societies would constitute the League in the years ahead, giving their best efforts to uphold the good name of the Portuguese participating in civic affairs and paying tribute to different community leaders whose advanced age placed them in the "alley of the forgotten." Manuel F.M. Trigueiros, director of the *União Portuguesa,* a newspaper he published for over fifty years, and Joaquim de Menezes, another Portuguese journalist were paid a testimonial. Through the League, these men received public homage for the part they played in the community.

On April 25, 1947 the League, then presided by John C. Valim, circulated a resolution adopted by that body calling for courses of Portuguese to be initiated so that the language would be taught in the high schools of California. The League also promoted receptions to welcome a myriad of dignitaries who visited the Portuguese communities in Northern California.

By 1953 the advocates for the consolidation movement lessened the enthusiasm which reigned in the League. The negotiations for the merger failed, leading to mistrust amongst fraternal leaders, and from 1957 to the middle of 1960 the League merely existed. It was then revised to attract, not only all fraternal benefit societies, but also the *Irmandade de Santo Antonio de Socorros Mutuos, Irmandade do Santo Cristo* and *Irmandade de Santa Maria Madalena* — all societies with small memberships and not licensed by the State of California Commissioner of Insurance.

The U.N.L.I.S. and its State Council, Luso-American Fraternal Federation, at their request, were left out of the re-organization.

The League, as usual, promoted receptions to visitors — many of them of a political nature who sought the Portuguese population's support for Portugal's troubles with her overseas possessions in India and Africa. At a certain point, the political nature of these visits began to affect the Portuguese immigrants and their descendants, causing some division and uneasiness.

The League was soon the target of discredit for its ineffectiveness — a political maneuver of sympathizers to the Portuguese Regime, often activated through their diplomatic representatives in California and Washington, D.C.

The last major activity of the League was staged in 1964 when it launched a drive for clothing to help the victims of an earthquake which destroyed many homes in San Jorge, Azores. The drive culminated with the collection of seventy tons of clothing which were flown to the Atlantic islands by the U.S. Air Force.

The drive was accomplished in less than three weeks and was spearheaded by Joseph A. Freitas, then President of the League, in answer to an appeal from Major John Luque, his son-in-law and political-affairs officer stationed at Lajes Field, Terceira, Azores.

In more recent years the League lost support from some of the fraternal societies. In an attempt to survive, and yielding to pressure from some community people, the League made an all out effort to conquer public support by trying to form a new organization that would encompass all factions of Portuguese civic and professional life in California — a kind of impossible dream. The plan failed because the quality of the leadership of the League at the time was far from matching that of the size of the project.

Recently the League was reorganized confining its membership to Portuguese fraternal benefit societies whose aims are common. There is no question that the League's attempts were the only civic efforts to speak of in the Portuguese community of California. On February 12, 1911, in the city of San Francisco, Luis Gonsalves, a Portuguese lawyer, and Dr. J.B. Nento, a dentist, organized the *Liga Portuguesa-Americana* in an effort to motivate the Portuguese to gather and make themselves heard in the California political scene. On February 24, 1912, also in San Francisco, Manuel T. Freitas, the first president of the Portuguese-American Bank, along with J.A. Silveira, Jose C. Jorge and Francisco Ignacio Lemos, formed the Portuguese Chamber of Commerce. Both of these organizations were short lived leaving the League of the Portuguese Fraternal Societies as the only one that still commands and mobilizes any gathering of the Portuguese and their descendants whenever their presence is required to endow prestige to any meaningful event.

Representatives of the League Fraternals share presentation of check to officials of the Statue of Liberty Foundation. The Fraternals raised over 32 thousand dollars for the project. (From Left) Rod Alvernaz, President of the League; Carlos Almeida, Secty-Tres. UPEC; Jose Azevedo, Pres. of Luso-American Fraternal Federation; John Zoilo, Statue of Liberty Foundation; Jean Fitch, Supreme Vice-Pres. APUMEC; Barney Prenda, Sup. Pres. SES; Tony C. Avila, Sup. Pres. IDES; Cheryl Davis, Grand Pres. SPRSI; Mary Rogers, Sup. Vice-Pres. UPPEC; Joan W. Anderson, Statue of Liberty Foundation, Calif. Region; and John Avila, Sup. Scty-Tres. IDES.

The League of the Portuguese Fraternal Societies as a tradition, honored distinguished visitors to California. Dr. Mário Soares, President of the Republic of Portugal (second from left), when he visited the City of San Leandro.

129

XVIII

EDUCATION THROUGH TEACHING
OF LANGUAGE AND CULTURE

Many portuguese immigrants in California were experiencing certain difficulties, for they had come from rural areas in the Azores where, at that time, few or no elementary schools existed. Coming to a strange land without a basic education was rather hard on them, and especially on their children.

This matter was of great concern to the leaders of the U.P.E.C. who, needless to say, counted in their midst some self-made intellectuals whose leadership was evident in the Portuguese-American community movements. At times they felt embarrassed by this situation which was tending to worsen. Something had to be done to curtail a disgrace that could damage not only their relationships and status in the American society but those of their children as they grew older.

It seemed an unsolvable problem until October 1906 when Joaquim de Menezes, a member of U.P.E.C. Council No. 25 in Oakland, during a convention session proposed that the Board of Directors of the society study the possibility of forming a school for the Portuguese.

This school was to be a mobile one to allow teaching in different communities throughout the state. He even suggested each member contribute "the cost of a beer" (five cents a month) to finance the school and a teacher.

At the time this idea was not received too well by the delegation and some leaders who saw in the school an instrument that would tend to threaten their positions within the society as people became educated and more knowledgeable of its affairs. The idea, therefore, was forgotten. The problem of illiteracy remained to the shame of a few proud Portuguese leaders.

IN 1910 John G. Mattos Jr. proposed the establishment of a scholarship to be awarded any student who was the son of a Portuguese, who in a public contest would prove to have the best knowledge of the Portuguese language. Mário Bettencourt Camara was inclined to have the award offered those students who evidenced themselves in the knowledge of Portuguese culture in general. Both ideas were defeated and in their place Francisco I. Lemos proposed the spending of $600 to establish a school of Portuguese and to leave, to the discretion of the Directors, the locality where such a school was to function as well as the selection of teachers.

Present at this convention was a delegate from Council No. 64, Chico, by the name of John da Cunha Valim, a native of Calheta, São Jorge Island, Azores (died October 9, 1948) who possessed a teacher's credential from the Normal School of Angra, Terceira, Azores. The delegation rallied around him even though he lived faraway from Oakland. He accepted the idea of becoming the teacher and traveled three times a week from Chico to Oakland to teach Portuguese, receiving for his services a salary of twenty-five dollars per month.

Immediately thereafter several movements centered around the school idea began to flourish in the Portuguese communities of the East Bay, to the point of organizing a league for the advertisement of Portugal headed by J.B. Faria. This league also proposed the opening of a school which they named Antonio Fonte, a man whom the Portuguese-American community considered to be the Portuguese of highest prestige and stature at the time.

The U.P.E.C. again financed the teacher as long as the school maintained a minimum attendance of ten students daily. It was formally opened on November 1, 1911 in the city of Oakland, and the average daily attendance was thirty students. Classes were rotated between East and West Oakland.

In 1912, Antonio Maria Martins, President of the U.P.E.C., in his annual report to the delegates, did not exaggerate when he stated that some of the illiterate adults who enrolled, after attending forty classes, were able to write and read correctly and do simple arithmetic. However, it was noted that the children of these immigrants, some born here, were the ones who profited most. Festivals were held around the school and prizes awarded to children who had attended these classes. They would display their achievements by reading Portuguese books and reciting passages of the history of Portugal and the Azores.

According to Martins, the school was "a necessity amongst us, to reduce the percentage of illiterates in our community (Portuguese-American) which is the strongest cause for the retardness in an intellectual and social life."

Later, John da Cunha Valim was elected Supreme Secretary of the I.D.E.S. *(Irmandade de Divino Espirito Santo).* This position excluded him from teaching. The Board of Directors of U.P.E.C. was faced with the selection of a new school teacher. A committee was appointed to meet with other fraternal organizations to agree on a replacement for Valim. A Portuguese society for teaching was then organized, with Alberto Moura as its secretary. This society took on the responsibility of continuing the school.

On April 18, 1920 the Portuguese school was reopened at the U.P.E.C. Hall located in West Oakland. The dedication ceremonies included a cultural program with the participation of Dr. José Sousa Bettencourt, Miss Leopoldina C. Rodrigues, Maria J. Glória, Mário Bettencourt Camara, Dr. J.B. de Faria and Guilherme J. Glória. The society selected Mrs. Adelaide Mendonça to teach Portuguese and Mr. J.B. De Las Casas, a prominent attorney in Oakland, to teach English to the Portuguese immigrants, who were new arrivals in the area. A few years later the school lacked attendance and closed.

In future years the teaching of Portuguese became the prime project of several organizations and individuals. One of these persons who devoted a number of years to the teaching of Portuguese in several high schools, mostly in the Bay Area, was Dr. Joaquim Rodrigues da Silva Leite, a native of Nazare, Portugal, and a member of U.P.E.C. Council No. 1 who, at one time, had served as Vice-Consul of Portugal in San Leandro.

Movements to teach the language of Camões are growing stronger even though many times they do not encounter among community leaders the sense of unity needed to implement the programs both at the elementary and high school levels.

The Department of Education of the State of California, through the efforts of Mrs. Julia Gonsalves, Foreign Language Coordinator, initiated surveys in several

John C. Valim
Teacher of Portuguese at "António Fonte" School

Chief Justice Earl Warren
Member of U.P.E.C. Council No. 55

RESOLUTION

WHEREAS, *in this same building, the Oakland Auditorium, the Teachers' Institute of the Counties of Alameda, Contra Costa, Marin, San Joaquim, and Solano, are in convention assembled to consider educational matters; and*

WHEREAS, *this Supreme Council of the Portuguese Union of the State of California is interested in, and appreciates all things tending to elevate humanity and develop the human mind; and*

WHEREAS, *the Portuguese Union of the State of California, believes that without education the children of its members cannot properly carry out the duties of citizenship, and the aims for which said Portuguese Union of the State of California was organized; and*

WHEREAS, *this Supreme Council is mindful of the work and difficulties that school teachers and educators have and encounter in the discharge of their duties, and that they are the foremost moulders of character;*

BE IT FURTHER RESOLVED, *that this Supreme Council places its offices at the disposal of the said convention, and is in favor of all bonds that are to be voted for, that tend to the health and comfort of school children and those concerned with their education.*

BE IT RESOLVED, *that this Supreme Council places its offices at the disposal of the said convention, and is in favor of all bonds that are to be voted for, that to the health and comfort of school children and those concerned with their education.*

Be IT FURTHER RESOLVED: *that these resolutions be spread upon the minutes of this session, and that a copy thereof be sent to said Teachers' Institutes Convention.*

(Oakland, October 17, 1919)

communities as to the possibilities of adopting programs to enable Americans of Portuguese descent and others to learn the language and culture of a people who gave worlds to the world.

Portuguese is the fifth most frequently spoken language in the world today and is considered one of the critical ones in the country. It has a tremendous potential, not only in Portugal, but in Africa and Brasil where, likewise, economic opportunities are beginning to unveil. The teaching of Portuguese language and culture is for the benefit of this nation of immigrants. The role of the United States is now and always will be paramount in commerce, diplomatic corps and world affairs. As this need becomes more evident, the pressure for the teaching of language and culture will be felt at educational levels.

In recent years the University of California at Los Angeles and Santa Barbara initiated such courses under the directorship of Professors Eduardo Mayone Dias and Jorge de Sena, the latter a very distinguished poet and writer of Portuguese modern literature, who passed away on June 4, 1978 in Santa Barbara, California.

The controversial bilingual classes funded by the Federal Government may not be the answer, but they have in some cases awakened in the minds of community leaders the fact that more attention is to be paid to the education of Portuguese immigrant children if they are later to compete in today's advanced world.

Portuguese-English bilingual programs were first tried at the A.B.C. School District in Artesia, followed by Hayward and San Leandro, the latter through the efforts and persistence of U.P.E.C. leaders. There was great concern that the Portuguese children many times by ignorance or on purpose, would be included in the Spanish surname classification by less knowledgeable principals and administrators in many school districts, thus exposing the Portuguese children to the Spanish-American culture, rather than to their own.

The education in many school districts is being shaken by its foundation from a lack of enrollment which tends to lead to a financial catastrophy. Portuguese leaders are behooved to motivate the community of Portuguese immigrants to take more interest in school affairs to safeguard the future of their children if they are to honor the medical, legal and education professions which count few Portuguese among their numbers.

The lack of proper education is in many cases caused by poor knowledge of the English language in early years. While preservation of the Portuguese language and culture is of importance in the shaping of character and self-esteem of the Portuguese, people should not lose sight of the cultivation of proper English needed for success at higher levels of education.

There is no doubt that education has always been one of the philosophies of the U.P.E.C. and has been expressed in many actions throughout the years through scholarships, grants and by supporting movements in school districts designed to help develop the knowledge of the Portuguese students and their teachers. In 1935 Dr. Joaquim C. Lopes, a member of the Board of Directors of U.P.E.C., requested the continued support for the granting of scholarships for students who had distinguished themselves in the Portuguese classes offered, at the time, at Castlemont High School in Oakland. In later years the U.P.E.C. supported the idea of establishing a scholarship at Saint Mary's College in Moraga, California, as evidenced from the contents of a resolution introduced by José Carlos Jorge in October of 1941.

In 1962 the U.P.E.C. initiated one scholarship in the amount of $300. In more recent years this fund has increased, not only in amount, but also in the number of scholarships awarded annually to qualified student members of the society. In addition, the society offers stipends to students and/or non-members, for postgraduate and graduate studies in accredited institutions in California and Nevada offering courses in Portuguese language and culture. In order to carry out this program of assistance to education, the society in 1974 created a cultural fund maintained by allocations made annually by the Board of Directors and donations by individuals.

The scholarship program was enhanced as a result of legislation adopted by the State of California in 1975 calling for an amendment to the Abandoned Property Act of 1959 which now precludes the escheat of unclaimed proceeds to the state. Instead this money is deposited in the society's cultural fund, exclusive of administration costs, for disbursement in scholarships for the benefit of its members. This law was initiated by Assemblyman William Lockyer of San Leandro at the request of the U.P.E.C. who coordinated the lobbying along with other societies. Their work culminated with passage of the bill under Governor Ronald Reagan's signature.

As part of its cultural programs, the U.P.E.C. co-sponsored several symposiums about Portugal and the Portuguese. The one pictured above was held in the J.A. Freitas Library in conjunction with the University of California at Berkeley.

134

XIX

THE CULTURAL CENTER

The teaching of Portuguese language in schools has always been supported by a twin movement — the creation of a library. The first Portuguese library was founded in Oakland on February 24, 1918 by Maria Josefina Glória, niece of Guilherme S. Glória and one of the organizers of the *Clube Recreativo Portugues,* a club established on April 30, 1916 for the recreation of Portuguese ladies. It was located at the Sousa's Hall and later moved to Mrs. Glória's residence at 3423 East 10th Street, where it closed after nearly thirty years of existence.

It was open to the public and received the support of Euclides Goulart da Costa, then Consul of Portugal, who endeavored, more than once, to obtain books from Portugal. The library, named after Luis de Camões, the greatest Portuguese poet and author of *The Lusiads,* was the showplace for the intellectuals of the Portuguese community who would show it to distinguished visitors from Portugal such as the Bishop of Angra, Azores; D. Antonio Meireles; Antonio Ferro, writer; and many others. When the library closed, many of its books were given to individuals and some universities and knowledge of their whereabouts became unknown.

In the early sixties, interest in the Portuguese culture and its contributions to California began to be felt again. Students from colleges seeking information and literature needed for theses they proposed to present on this little-known ethnic group, led some concerned citizens to attempt creation of a Portuguese books section in the San Leandro City Library.

A few books were gathered and donated by Alberto Correa, Carlos Almeida, and Dr. Fausto Lage, a physician and writer who came from Lowell, Massachusetts and settled in San Leandro. The books were well received and placed in a visible section of the library headquarters. As months went by there were moved to shelves in less prominent areas and finally out of sight for lack of circulation. This move caused the U.P.E.C. Board of Directors in 1964 to consider giving space to begin a library at the headquarters, at the time under construction.

An appeal was made throughout the state for books, newspapers and photographs. Soon thereafter the quarters reserved for the library proved to be insufficient to accommodate the growing collection which had to be moved in 1967 to a new suite and finally to the U.P.E.C. Cultural Center Building, where it is presently housed.

Lecture Hall, U.P.E.C. Cultural Center.

In 1965 the library was named in memory of Joseph A. Freitas, a very active member and former officer of the society who felt regret about the lack of a place where people could learn about the Portuguese and their contributions throughout the world.

João B. Mota Amaral, First President of the Azores Regional Government visits the J.A. Freitas Library, U.P.E.C. Cultural Center.

The library has over four thousand volumes dealing almost exclusively with Portuguese subjects including a section on the Azores which has been classified as a special one by the California State Library, as well as the most complete collection of newspapers and other publications (many of them in microfilm) by the Portuguese in California dating back to 1885. In addition there are a variety of memorabilia and photographs depicting Portuguese fraternal and civic life in the state. Most of the contents of the library were donated by immigrants and their descendants, the Gulbenkian Foundation of Lisbon, and cultural institutes of Ponta Delgada, Angra do Heroismo and Horta in the Azores. Ninety percent of the books are written in the Portuguese language.

The Cultural Center, located at 1120-24 East 14th Street, San Leandro, California, is a joint venture between Council No. 1, San Leandro, and the Supreme Council. The Center also houses a lecture hall adjoining the library with a seating capacity of two hundred people, where the organization has hosted many receptions for distinguished visitors from Portugal. Through its doors passed Dr. Francisco Carreiro da Costa, Azorean folklorist; Francis M. Rogers, writer and professor at Harvard University; João Afonso, writer from Terceira, Azores; Hall Themido, Ambassador of Portugal in Washington, D.C.; Dr. José De Azeredo Perdigão, President of Gulbenkian Foundation; João Bosco Mota Amaral, President of the Azores; Alvaro Monjardino, President of the Azores Regional Government Assembly; Congressmen of the United States, Portugal and Brazil and hundreds of illustrious guests from different parts of the world.

The library is open to the public and available for group tours by appointment and is considered by college students and college professors as a haven for researchers. The center is solely sponsored by the society and volunteer services.

XX

DREAMS THAT NEVER CAME TRUE

Not all of the ideas and projects brought up for discussion by U.P.E.C. members and other community leaders materialized. A mention of some of these is made simply to show that not everything was possible, especially when a persistent effort was not applied.

On the matter of mergers with other societies, the first of such requests came from the *Sociedade Rainha Santa Isabel* (S.P.R.S.I.) in a letter dated October 12, 1901 and signed by their Supreme Secretary, Anna L. Costa, and presented during the U.P.E.C. convention held in San Luis Obispo. A committee of five composed of António Fonte, Firmino J. Cunha, Francisco I. Lemos, John G. Mattos Jr. and J.G. Tavares was appointed to look into this matter.

They concluded that even though such a merger of the two most important fraternal societies in California would have been a great step, it was not a practical one, aside from not being contemplated in the constitution of the society.

The S.P.R.S.I.'s aims at the time differed from the U.P.E.C. for they were strictly a fraternal for women of the Catholic faith, and U.P.E.C. was established for men of mixed creeds which included the Freemasons.

A communication declining the request for merger was sent to the S.P.R.S.I. under the signature of John G. Mattos Jr., Secretary for the special committee.

The S.P.R.S.I. leadership had conceived the idea of a merger with U.P.E.C. at a time when they were seeking support from the Portuguese community to build a hospital where Portuguese people could be treated. Since the community had not reacted favorably to the project, support was then sought from the fraternal organizations. Apparently the ultimate move to accomplish hospital project was the invitation for the merger with the U.P.E.C. The merger idea came to light again in October of 1927. This time the invitation was formulated by the *Associação Portuguesa Protectora e Beneficiente* (A.P.P.B.) of San Francisco. The request was tabled and the idea never reached fruition.

In the next years the U.P.E.C. engaged in all sorts of attempts seeking the unification of all fraternal societies, through a Federation or League concept. Negotiations and meetings on mergers were really intensified beginning in 1936, reaching a climax in 1944, as a result of an accumulation of factors. Among many was the blow of the economic depression and the effects of World War II.

The drain of young people added provisions inserted in membership certificates restraining admission of members and payment of benefits caused by acts of war. The added fact that immigration of Portuguese was practically at a standstill, led the Board of Directors of the U.P.E.C., for the first time, to invite all major Portuguese fraternal societies to a meeting to initiate talks of a possible mutual cooperation amongst all, which could lead to a future merger.

The meeting was held on March 12, 1944 at the A.P.U.M.E.C. Hall near the corner of Fruitvale and East 14th Streets in Oakland. The societies invited included the *Irmandade do Divino Espirito Santo* (I.D.E.S.), *The Sociedade Portuguesa Rainha Santa Isabel* (S.P.R.S.I.), *Associação Portuguesa União Madeirense do Estado da California* (A.P.U.M.E.C.) all of Oakland, California; The A.P.P.B. of San Francisco and the *Sociedade do Espirito Santo* S.E.S.) of Santa Clara, California. The meeting resulted in the call of another one for more clarification. Eventually it was sensed that some of the societies had no interest in a merger and would rather maintain their cooperative efforts at the level of the League which was already in existence for civic projects.

In other words, they would get together only for social events and let the business aspects of each one follow whatever destiny their respective leadership felt proper.

RESOLUÇÃO No. 1

CONSIDERANDO, que as sociedades fraternais portuguesas da California não oferecem oportunidade para futura expanção nas bases em que estão funcionando;

CONSIDERANDO, que seria de interesse para todas as sociedades fraternais portuguesas e para a colónia portuguesa da California que se tomassem as medidas necessárias para evitar a sua decadencia;

RESOLVE-SE que por este Conselho Supremo da U.P.E.C. sejam conferidos á Directoria Suprema do exercicio de 1945-1946 plenos poderes para entabolar negociações com as sociedades fraternais portuguesas da California colectivamente ou com qualquer delas individualmente, com o fim de promover uma fusão de tais sociedades, e

RESOLVE-SE mais que se a referida Directoria chegar a algum acordo satisfactório com uma ou mais sociedades portuguesas para promover a sua fusão, que a mesma fique investida de toda a autoridade e poderes necessários para promover a fusão da U.P.E.C. com uma ou mais sociedades fraternais portuguesas da California, adoptar o nome da nova organização, adoptar a sua constituição provisóra e nomear os seus oficiais provisórios para a gerir e administrar até que a sua primeira convenção se realize e os oficiais permanentes sejam devidamente eleitos e instalados; e

RESOLVE-SE mais ainda, que a referida Directoria fique investida de todos os poderes que são conferidos a este Conselho Supremo para fixar os salários dos oficiais provisórios assalariados, empregar o pessoal assalariado que for necessário e fixar os seus salários, outorgar e assinar acordos e contractos com outras sociedades fraternais para promover a fusão do negócio de seguros da U.P.E.C. com o negócio de seguros dessas sociedades, submeter tais acordos e contractos e relatórios da sua condição financeira á aprovação do Comissário de Seguros do Estado da California, e fazer, praticar e assinar em nome da U.P.E.C. tudo o que para tais fins for necessário sem excepção nem limitação alguma.

Pelos Directores

J. C. JORGE, Secretário

Recomendamos que esta resolução seja aprovada:

Pela Junta de Jurisprudencia

J. J. PIMENTEL, Secretário

Outubro 10, 1945.

Resolution authorizing the Board of Directors to proceed with merger of all fraternal societies (1945).

But not all was lost. On October 10, 1945 the U.P.E.C. delegation adopted a resolution giving the Board of Directors full power to negotiate a merger with one or more fraternal societies, and to adopt a new name, a new constitution and obtain approval from the State Insurance Commissioner for such or any other acts necessary to effect a merger.

The resolution was signed on behalf of the Board by José Carlos Jorge, Secretary and adopted by the delegation in session. With its passage a committee of five was appointed, composed of Thomas F. Lopez, Frank C. Roderick, Manuel Pereira, Manuel Cabral and José C. Jorge. They were to meet with a similar committee already in existence, which had been named by the A.P.P.B. for the merger of the two societies.

Several meetings were held in the months ahead. An agreement was reached and presented at the U.P.E.C. Convention on October 16, 1946. The debate over the merger agreement continued for two days and was finally voted down by the delegation, 117 against, thirty-six for and eight abstaining. Somehow the Supreme Secretary of the U.P.E.C. failed to notify the A.P.P.B. of the result obtained at the convention. This unfortunate incident was rectified by the delegation assembled in the following year when they instructed the Supreme Secretary to officially notify the A.P.P.B. of the result obtained the year before.

The enthusiasm centered around a merger died down, to surface again on June 15, 1953 when António Simas, Vice-President of the *União Portuguesa Continental* (U.P.C.) of Oakland, invited all Portuguese fraternal benefit societies to discuss the matter at a dinner meeting at the Hotel Leamington in Oakland. After a few meetings it was again clear that the S.P.R.S.I., U.P.P.E.C., I.D.E.S. and A.P.U.M.E.C. felt they could go on about their business alone, therefore relieving themselves from participation in any future negotiations. The initiative of António Simas is still alive but can only count with the remainder of the societies. The negotiations go on and the more they are prolonged, the less enthusiasm is aroused.

The views expressed by Andrew Manha, a member of the U.P.E.C. Finance Committee, in the following article published in the *U.P.E.C. Bulletin* of March 1954 are indicative of the feelings of the society's leadership, at the time, towards the proposed new organization:

I attended what was for me a first meeting of the committees of the various Portuguese Lodges where actual work was being done toward preparation for a possible consolidation.

The U.P.E.C., S.E.S., U.P.C. and the A.P.P.B. were represented with a total of sixteen representatives. I was impressed with the sincerity of these men. The text of the skeleton preparation showed a good try at honest agreement between all concerned.

No doubt is in my mind, but what there is a hard task ahead for this committee. Every representative is there because he has particular interest of his Society at heart as well as having foremost in mind the general strengthening of Portuguese Fraternalism.

The first order of business was about deciding a name for this proposed society. From several suggestions, this narrowed to two names that have a familiar ring. Two we have, who will make it more?

Next on the agenda was the specific aims of this new society. What was tentatively adopted had a much larger scope area than what any specific society has operated under thus far. No doubt about the purposeful ideas being idealic, but altogether too altruistic aims may be subject to rejection of those who have made payments for many years in the belief that they were for the benefit of their families when needed. Direct infirmity aid that is, and it may be just a little further than the average member is willing to pay for at this time.

Third matter brought forward was the providing of pecuniary aid and to provide such funds for that purpose. I, as layman am willing to skip this, until the chips are down. I am willing to abide my cautious time to digest this issue.

The fourth matter mentioned was the gathering and coordination of historical data of interest to the Portuguese of California. Our libraries are full of this data for those who would seek it so why spend money on it where so solid comfort or improvement is derived from such expenditures. This will probably get some revising.

Fifth on the list of matters to be discussed was a program of social and civic activity programs to be encouraged in the membership. To my mind the U.P.E.C. has weathered a lot of trouble in its past, but none of it was of a political or religious aspect. Again this is an ambitious program that could be well set aside until such time as our proposed new organization can well attend to it without any loss to the carriers who would maybe unwillingly create such ostentatious activities for those so inclined.

The sixth matter was deleted as having little consequence in the bearing of principles. The next was the classification for membership. Nothing new was arrived at. A member of the caucasion race of good character who never has been expelled from the societies involved will be considered eligible for membership.

Further discussed was the limiting of the number of what for the want of a better word we shall call councils. That was argued on from a census standpoint. The population of the area or city was agreed on as a barometer for the license to operate as a subordinate council.

Of course, the future organization would operate as one and be consolidated as such. Moneys or funds would also naturally consolidate into one fund except the sick benefit fund of each respective council.

The disposition of the sick benefit funds or real estate holdings belonging to the individual councils present problems that are earmarked as something of great proportion. It is expected that the age old struggle of the poor trying to latch onto the wealth of the rich and the rich as always holding on for dear life to what it has, with one eye peeled for whatever else they can add to their fortunes can very well be a stumbler, if not viewed with fairness.

This my fellow members is my view of the first meeting with a group of men that I have reason to believe are doing their utmost toward a solidarity of Portuguese Fraternalism.

To me it seems a bit pathetic how some of our very finest members can be persuaded to think or act contrary to their own welfare.

I have been taken to task for a passage in an article in a recent issue of the Boletim, wherein I stated that as a member of the committee from the U.P.E.C., I would try to safeguard the interest of our members.

First I want to say that if there is anything wrong with such a stand, I believe that I will be wasting time. If my colleagues on this committee do not have the same thought in mind, they too, are wasting their time. I am sure that nothing will come of this attempted merger if all of the societies are not benefited by this change. The U.P.E.C. has been around too long and has enough prestige as well as other very substantial assets to have its heritage snuffed out.

The pros and cons of this controversy, I will not discuss with you, but the fellow who disputes the wisdom of a person resisting intrusion of guaranteed rights of the members of the U.P.E.C. has an argument with this writer. I will even go further than that and say that if I find that any of my colleagues are sacrificing the U.P.E.C. for the sake of harmony, I will take a definite stand against them.

Please do not get the impression that I am attending these meetings as a heckler or pop off artist. To the contrary, I will only be a sideline observer with only one thought in mind. That thought is that a strong and wholesome fraternal organization with size and ambitions to do a much greater good shall come into being.

I leave you in preparation for that fellow who would seek any small advantage of you with this homely: "If life's journey, wherever you may stroll, always keep your eye on the doughnut and never mind the hole."

A little over seventy-three years ago, thirty men with the help of God formed what is today the U.P.E.C. Today it is the leading Portuguese Fraternal Society in California and Nevada.

Seven years after the founding of our great society the first convention was held in San Leandro and from then on, God left the administration of affairs strictly in the hands of those delegated to office.

Therein lies the tale of trials and errors that have beset the U.P.E.C. these many years since.

By October of 1887, the society had grown to the extent that it became necessary to elect a small group to do for them what the members could not do for themselves. A Supreme Council was formed. Officers were elected and legislation enacted. The human factor present then and that, has since always remained with us is, that no matter how wise we tried to legislate, we still never could legislate air tight efficiency.

The reason is simple. Our members seemed always to be interested only in the results and never watched the action that brought the results into being. Those were the days when society was not ripe in wisdom. Instead of occupying the grandstand seat that they paid for, our members were satisfied to just read the score as posted for them. Had they watched the action more closely, they could have plugged the weak spots and thus insure a team that would make fewer errors.

In October 1954, the agreement reached by the U.P.E.C., A.P.P.B., S.E.S. and U.P.C. committees was introduced at the convention and after discussion it was referred for further study to all subordinate councils holding their own sick benefit funds. In the words of Anthony Marques, a native of Aveiro, Portugal, and Supreme Secretary of the U.P.E.C., "The matter was so complicated . . ."

Marques, a former Supreme President of the *União Portuguesa Continental* (U.P.C.) who had managed also to serve in the Presidency of the U.P.E.C. for a short period in 1953, was definitely against the consolidation and did his share to stall the matter to his advantage. Later he was convicted on embezzlement charges and divested of all his titles and membership rights in the society. The agreement, one of the simplest ones after all, was not that complicated nor perfect. The new society was to be known as Consolidated Fraternal Society. Needless to say, the new title was far from appealing.

The aims as spelled out in the agreement, called for the conducting of a fraternal business for the mutual benefit of members and respective families for sponsoring a scholarship program, for providing pecuniary aid to needy members, for sponsoring social activities and encouraging members to participate in civic affairs.

In addition, the proposed organization would try to coordinate historical data pertaining to the Portuguese in California and, last but not least, it would seek involvement of youth in fraternal affairs.

Under the agreement, Oakland would have been selected as the principal place of business and its Board of Directors was set at a minimum of fifteen members and a maximum of twenty-five with the exact number to be fixed annually by resolution.

The entire agreement was well delineated, but contained one unresolved point:

the sick benefit assets owned and managed by the U.P.E.C. subordinate councils. It was around this subject that the U.P.E.C. delegation built their opposition to the merger refusing to go along with it for fear of losing benefits over which they always had control, including several buildings in which sick benefit fund monies were invested.

But that problem was not the only difficulty. The sentiments attached to the name of the U.P.E.C. and its history were too deep. This attachment came to light on October 12, 1955 during the U.P.E.C. convention held in Modesto, when the agreement was finally rejected after Past Supreme President John F. Nunes and John V. Pimentel of Council No. 25, in an outstanding address to the delegation, pointed out the "disgusting" name the committee had selected for the new organization which, if adopted, would tend to erase any affinity with the Portuguese people in California.

In the words of Nunes, "the most logical name to perpetuate the Portuguese traditions in the state was the *União Portuguesa do Estado da California,"* for its outstanding past was without question, a tribute to the Portuguese immigrant's efforts in this state and that the "loss of our name was too great to bear." The delegation, possessed of the emotion of the occasion, went on to defeat the agreement without engaging in further discussions.

This action was followed by a similar one from delegates to the S.E.S. convention and as a result the U.P.C. and A.P.P.B. found themselves alone and proceeded to merge into the *Sociedade União Nacional* in July of 1957. The name was referred to in English as United National Life Insurance Society since many of its members otherwise would associate it with Portugal's national and only political party at the time.

In 1960, thirteen years later, the membership of the U.P.E.C. was confronted with the possibility of a merger with the I.D.E.S. However, it was not until November 9, 1963 that the Board of Directors officially acted upon a formal invitation which came from the I.D.E.S. calling for appointment of a committee to initiate merger negotiations.

Both organizations went through the same experiences they had had with other societies in 1953. After agreements were reached and circulated amongst members, the proposed consolidation was rejected by the I.D.E.S. delegation in 1964 during their convention held in Salinas, California.

Several attempts at the merger and/or consolidation have failed, with the exception of the U.P.C. and A.P.P.B., whose form of government is a centralized one. This philosophy of the original founders of the A.P.P.B., very evident back in 1868 contributed in part to the forming of the U.P.E.C. The dissident group believed that management should be vested in a wide representation of membership who in turn should have direct voice in the management of the society's affairs. This basic philosophy, in fact, has been the major obstacle in getting U.P.E.C. leaders to agree on a merger. Needless to say, everyone is attached to his beliefs and traditions along with a bit of selfishness.

The times have changed as have the aims of the various Portuguese societies. There is no longer the wide separation found in membership based on religion, sex or geographical origins of the Portuguese immigrants. There was a time when the R.A.B.A.M. was founded for the natives of the island of San Miguel, the A.P.U.M.E.C. for those who had come from Madeira and the U.P.C. was geared towards immigrants from Continental Portugal.

These uncalled for divisions no longer exist, including those based on religion which led to the founding of the I.D.E.S. and S.P.R.S.I. who only admitted members of the Catholic faith.

The dream of a merger still lingers on, awaiting a common cause which will drive the Portuguese fraternals to the table for negotiations since the concepts above mentioned no longer stand. That common cause may very well be one based on economics rather than on philosophy for historically economics have many times proven stronger than the heart.

The list of dreams which never came true is long. Among those, a few could have been viable; such as the savings and loan association concept introduced in 1899 by Dr. Alvares Cabral, U.P.E.C. Supreme Medical Examiner, and that of a bank dreamt by Firmino J. Cunha on October 7, 1908. The latter proposal was debated for a few years. The U.P.E.C. Bank, as it would have been called, had already a site granted to João Borges of Council No, 18, Benicia, who in 1911, offered ten acres of land in Solano County for its construction. The society had a surplus of $300,000 then and John G. Mattos Jr., a banker, encouraged the idea, but, eventually it was discarded and instead they build their own Home Office.

In 1929 the Consul General of Portugal in San Francisco suggested that the society nominate three members to a committee to build a monument to the unknown soldier who had died in World War I. The project never materialized.

On November 1, 1912 the idea of building a Rest Home for disabled U.P.E.C. members was entertained. The Supreme Council initiated a drive for funds with $1,500; and even though it was an idea which engaged the minds of the membership for seventeen years, it was never fulfilled. The monies collected ended up in a charity fund created to assist members in need. Those and other ideas showed the interest of U.P.E.C. membership in solving the Portuguese immigrant's needs in California. But those efforts were not always understood by all.

XXI

GIANTS IN THEIR TIME

M.T. Freitas

Many were the immigrants who succeeded in business. Even though they were never elected to the presidency of the society their input was felt, for they served the U.P.E.C. in one capacity or another.

Some of these men are examples of the true Portuguese entrepreneurs, young and old, who came from the Azores islands, committed to make something of themselves. The opportunities were present and they held on to them with all their might.

The names most quoted in recent years include those connected with the fishing industry in San Diego where Lawrence Oliver, Manuel G. Rosa and Manuel Oliveira Medina, all born in Pico, made their fortunes in the fishing of tuna and derivative products. Such was the case of Oliver with his ingenious plant which produced fertilizer for the fields of California out of fish bones.

In the early years of California life there were other distinguished individuals. A good example is found in Manuel Teixeira de Freitas, known as M.T. Freitas, a native of Urzelina, San Jorge, Azores, who came to California in 1871 at the age of eighteen to work as a busboy in the Portuguese restaurants (then abundant in San Francisco on the lower Market Street area) where he learned cooking and later opened a restaurant of his own.

In 1881 he formed a partnership with João Soares Dias and began a general merchandising store, a business he continued thourgh a succession of partnerships with different individuals founding the Portuguese Commission Company and The Azores Mercantile Company with A. does Reis, J.T. Freitas, Edward A. Cunha and F.D. Rodrigues. In later years he founded the Portuguese Mercantile Company at 33 Clay Street in San Francisco. In 1912 he retired from commerce and sold his interests to Bernard Sherry.

Freitas realized the dream of the immigrant of the Azores. All his profits from commerce were applied to the purchase of land. He owned the Home Ranch near San Rafael, California, with 1,210 acres, and the C Ranch (now San Marin), some two thousand acres in Novato and other small acreage in Marin and Solano counties.

His knowledge and initiative led to the founding of the Portuguese American Bank of San Francisco in 1905 of which he became its first president until 1912. By 1915 the bank's assets had reached $2,942,877 and had a branch in Oakland (Franklin and 11th Streets) opened at the suggestion of Joaquim A. Silveira, another native of San Jorge, who succeeded Freitas in the presidency of the Portuguese Bank.

Besides M.T. Freitas and Joaquim S. Silveira, the bank had as its officers and directors the following individuals: John Enas, V.L. Figueiredo, A.A. Silveira, Dr. M.M. Enos, A.F. Nunes, J.M. Santana, A. Avila, M.S. Freitas, B. Sherry and J.B. Mendonça. The latter had vast real estate holdings in San Leandro close to the Marina. Felix F. Trigueiro was in charge of the safe deposit boxes which would rent for $2.50 per year.

Full page ad published in "Revista Portuguesa" (Sept. 1921).

Six years later the bank had extended its services by opening branches in Los Banos (Birch Building) and Newman (O and Fresno Streets). By that time, assets amounted to over four million dollars. In February 1942 the Portuguese-American Bank, the only banking institution of significance ever owned and controlled by Portuguese in the United States merged with the Mercantile Trust Company which was later consolidated with the American Trust Company and in 1960 became the Wells Fargo Bank.

M.T. Freitas also build the Bank of San Rafael and served it in several capacities, including that of president. He was the major stockholder and director of other banks, namely: the Bank of Novato and Bank of Redwood City. He also served in the State Dairy Bureau. In 1896 he married Maria Betencourt Freitas and had eight children. One son, Carlos, became a prominent attorney and judge of the Marin County Superior Court.

Freitas died in 1923 and in tribute to his memory the Marin County Board of Supervisors and the California State Highway Department named both the Freitas Parkway and the area of Terra Linda (beautiful land) where the Freitas Home Ranch once stood after him. Drivers can see both signs when going north on Highway 101, across the lands once bought and owned by one of the many examples of Portuguese contributors to the economy of the state.

The Azoreans, especially from the western group, were good at agricultural and dairy tasks. It was in those areas that their contribution to California economy was most important. Their knowledge of the land and its cultivation as well as the fact that dairying was a difficult enterprise but not one foreign to them, was applied to managing their farms. They worked hard for themselves and their families who, in the end, would profit from the ever-growing value of the large ranches these Azoreans bought little by little.

On March 16, 1916 some men formed one of the most important organizations geared to coordinate the efforts of the Portuguese dairyman in obtaining better prices for the milk they got by working night and day assisted, in many cases, by their wives and children. The Associated Milk Producers, as the organization came to be known, was located in San Francisco (53 Clay Street) and had an initial capital of one hundred thousand dollars.

J.A. Silveira

By the end of 1923 the corporation had a capital stock of one million dollars and operated plants in San Francisco, Holt, Los Banos, Manteca, Oakland and Newman. Francisco I. Lemos was then the president of the association, succeeding George E. Abel. Other officers included: M.J. Lewis of San Francisco, Frank M. Machado of Sunnyvale, M. Silva of Stockton, Antonio Homem and Jorge Oliveira of San Francisco. All of them represented millions of dollars they personally had invested in dairies throughout California.

Other Cooperatives were later organized in different cities throughout the state, many of them in the Bay Area. The American Creamery Company of Oakland (formerly known as the New Jersey Farm Creamery) was a good example of the solidarity which existed amongst the Portuguese. It was founded in 1899 by Joaquim A. Silveira when Oakland had a population of 60,000. Silveira was a native of Ribeira d'Areia, San Jorge, Azores, who immigrated to California in 1891 at the age of seventeen. In 1929 the American Creamery Company, which had served the East Bay Cities,

146

was sold so the Carnation Corporation.

Silveira was married to Edna Fay Silveira and had a son named Joaquim W. Silveira. He lived at 4800 Park Boulevard in Oakland, a large house (which still stands today) and incorporated in its architectural design and structure some of the elements that were part of the Portuguese Pavilion built for the Panama Pacific Exposition of 1915 and to which Silveira contributed a large sum. This outstanding immigrant of the Azores served later as Vice-President of the America Trust Company, and was involved in many of the major initiatives of the Portuguese in California, including that of Secretary of the Saint Anthony's Hospital located in Oakland. He died on May 2, 1947.

Freitas, Silveira and Lemos are only a few of many whose contributions were of great importantce in their time.

The Portuguese immigrants were more than the producers of *linguica,* a typical Portuguese sausage found in almost every supermarket in California, or the adepts of the Holy Ghost, a celebration held in the Portuguese tradition and still deep rooted in the Azores, or the interpreters of the *Chamarrita,* a popular folk dance they and their descendants enjoy in California.

XXII

BUILT ON RESPECT

The U.P.E.C., throughout its history, always distinguished itself for the respect it received from the common man, including the Portuguese immigrant, who had left his native shore for a new one of the Pacific Coast.

That respect was hard to achieve, but once it was, it would leave an impression in the minds of all those who, in one way or another, had come in contact with the fraternal society and her most outstanding leaders.

The respect it demanded and received from its members is noted in the thousands of printed pages containing minutes and reports of conventions, Boards and Committees, in written messages of individuals from here and faraway Portugal and the Azores, expressing admiration for the working of the immigrant on behalf of his fellow brother working in California.

It surfaces in the language of the invitation and acceptance of His Majesty, King Carlos I or Portugal, in 1903, to become the only Honorary Supreme President the U.P.E.C. ever had, and in the spirit of the decorations received from the Portuguese Government in 1935 and again in 1966 for benevolent work.

That respect is expressed in the message from a mayor of the town where U.P.E.C. held an event, in the telegram sent by President John F. Kennedy in 1961 from his residence in Hyannis Port, Massachusetts, greeting the society for having in its ranks Earl Warren, Chief Justice of the Supreme Court, then affiliated with U.P.E.C. Council No. 55; as it is expressed in the rigor with which the law applied when members used improper language or willfully attempted to take advantage of the society.

Through these and other expressions, respect was made the law of the society, for it would be the only foundation for a democracy to exist, enabling the molding of the destituted Portuguese immigrant to proceed, thus assisting him to attain a place rightfully owed to those more advanced ethnic groups already moving in large numbers to the beautiful land of California.

It was within the confines and under the ceilings of the many halls built by the bare hands of the Portuguese throughout the state that this respect was made possible. The initiation rituals of the society containing lessons in unity and the speeches sprung from the hearts of those who had succeeded in their efforts to attain the upper strata of life led the immigrant to a better life in this State of California, then and now.

The eye of the modern newcomer, who today lands at the most advanced airports in the world in the midst of all comforts and conveniences, will never perceive the difficulties their forefathers went through from the minute they jumped ashore from the whaling ships or sailing vessels.

The centennial history of the U.P.E.C. is a very humble account of the Portuguese scene in California and far from complete. It is only a glimpse of what went on, and still goes on, in our state where the descendants of the land of *Luso* worked hard for what they are and own.

BOLETIM  DA U.P.E.C.

PERIODICO MENSAL · Jos. Pereira · SEGUNDO LUSTRO

ORGÃO OFFICIAL DA UNIÃO PORTUGUEZA DO ESTADO DA CALIFORNIA

Sociedade portugueza fundada em San Leandro, Cal., no dia 1 de agosto de 1880.

ANNO I.   SAN FRANCISCO, CAL., 1 DE OUTUBRO DE 1902.   No. 3.

EL-REI

E'CONVIDADO A ACCEITAR A PRESIDENCIA SUPREMA HONORARIA

COPIA

DO CONVITE QUE FOI ENVIADO A S. M. FIDELISSIMA

EL-REI

SENHOR:

Na 15.ª Sessão Annual do Conselho Supremo da União Portugueza do Estado da California, effectuada nos dias 14 a 19 de outubro ultimo, foi apresentada á assembléa uma proposta para que de SUA MAGESTA EL-REI D. CARLOS I, que tão gloriosamente occupa o throno portuguez, fosse implorada a graça de conferir a esta sociedade portugueza a sublime honra de acceitar o titulo de PRESIDENTE SUPREMO HONORARIO d'este Conselho Supremo, titulo unico na nossa sociedade, creado expressamente por aquella proposta e que constituirá a Secção V do Artigo III da Constituição do mesmo Conselho Supremo, apenas VOSSA MAGESTADE haja por bem agraciar-nos com a annuencia de imperecivel honra para que o nome augusto de Vossa Magestade figure no registo da nossa sociedade como seu PRESIDENTE HONORARIO.

Releve-me a ousadia de accrescentar que a leitura de tal proposta, para a immediata consideração da qual foram dispensadas todas as formalidades, foi recebida entre as maiores demonstrações de enthusiasmo por todos os membros do Conselho Supremo e votada por acclamação com ruidosos vivas á SUA MAGESTADE FIDELISSIMA unanime e calorosamente correspondidos por todos os membros do Conselho Supremo e socios presentes á mesma, associando-se áquellas manifestações todos os cidadãos americanos mas de origem portugueza que em grande numero faziam parte d'aquella assembléa, prestando assim alta e sincera manifestação do respeito que mantem pelo nobilissimo soberano que tão sabia e liberalmente tem reivindicado para a gloriosissima nação portugueza, patria amada de seus paes, a fama d'um passado sem egual.

Opulenta como é, SENHOR, esta sociedade não conta no seu periodo inicial, genios nas sciencias, nas artes ou na literatura portugueza. Nem conta, ao menos, do mesmo periodo, um grupo de representantes d'um vasto commercio portuguez n'este estado pois que os membros da nossa colonia, na sua quasi totalidade composta de immigrantes que para aqui vieram attrahidos pela prospectiva de um futuro

mais prospero, não receberam na patria educação que lhes permittisse passar além do marco delimitando na estrada da vida o fim do termo das aspirações aos viajores que caminham sem outra orientação que a utilisada intelligentemente pela observação.

Nem conta ainda hoje, SENHOR, luminares d'aquellas mais alevantadas manifestações da intellectualidade humana, pois que a immigração continuou sempre a fazer-se das mesmas camadas menos instruidas, excepção de uma meia duzia de portuguezes accidentalmente exados aqui. Não obstante, SENHOR, esta pesarosa condição intellectual da nossa colonia ao tempo do movimento inicial d'esta sociedade, conta ella hoje membros que se elevam acima do nivel dos communs, tendo, mesmo entre os que lá nasceram e aqui se educaram e os filhos d'estes, homens proeminentes na politica, no foro, na medicina, nas industrias, no commercio e na agricultura.

Assim reforçada, valiosa e progressivamente nos seus primitivos elementos, poude esta sociedade chegar ao ponto de occupar entre as suas congeneres invejavel e invejada reputação.

SENHOR:

A União Portugueza do Estado da California enche de justo orgulho todos os filhos de Portugal e seus descendentes n'esta região de gente abastada destinada gião. Ella não é uma aggremia-a dispensar-se o prazer de reuniões para distribuição do superfluo da sua abastança entre os mil requisitos da vida luxuosa. Ella é, apenas, uma associação de homens laboriosos, os quaes se auxiliam e amparam reciprocamente nas vicissitudes da vida, amparando egualmente suas familias quando a foice da morte vae ceifal-os impiedosamente ao affecto e á protecção dos que com elles jornadearam na estrada da existencia.

Fundada no dia 1 de agosto de 1880, com 50 membros apenas para o fim de proverem ao seu tratamento em caso de doença e ao seu funeral em caso de morte, por isso que áquelle tempo corriam subscripções quotidianamente pelas ruas implorando a caridade publica, não sómente da nossa colonia, mas, ainda, dos estrangeiros e naturaes, o que nos enchia de vergonha, já está

Contents of invitation sent to Dom Carlos, King of Portugal, who later became the only Honorary Supreme President U.P.E.C. ever had.

RESOLUTION

WHEREAS, the death of the much loved President of the United States, Wm. McKinley, perpetrated by the hand of a miserable assassin, is profoundly felt by every American citizen and by the whole civilized world; and,

WHEREAS, The Supreme Council of the Portuguese Union of the State of California, assembled in this city of San Luis Obispo, in its Fifteenth Annual Session, desires to manifest its great respect and veneration for the civic and moral virtues possessed by our illustrious and revered President; and,

WHEREAS, The loss of the noble President, Wm. McKinley, has created in the office of Chief Executive of the United States a vacancy which it will be very difficult to fill, inasmuch as it has deprived this great nation of a famous statesman, a brave soldier, an exemplary husband and a faithful public servant, whose aim was to elevate the prestige of the American name at home and abroad, thereby securing the gratitude, love and respect of every American citizen without regard to political creed, and also the respect and admiration of all civilized nations; and,

WHEREAS, This Society, composed almost entirely of American citizens whose interests are centered in this country which they have adopted as their home, partakes of the national sorrow; and,

WHEREAS, The Portuguese Union of the State of California is composed of patriotic citizens, faithful observers of the law and respecters of those in authority and of the institutions of this country, - Therefore, be it

RESOLVED: That in the name of this Society represented by this Supreme Council, a vote of profound condolence be spread upon the minutes of this session, because of the tremendous catastrophe which has wounded so deeply every American citizen, at the same time expressing great horror of such barbarous and abominable crime whereby this nation was deprived of the valuable services of its loved President and the whole civilized world of his powerful aid; and be it

RESOLVED: That every subordinate Council, for the same sorrowful reason, drape with crape its respective charter during the period of thirty days, and that this Resolution be inserted in the first number of the Official Bulletin of this Society; and be it further

RESOLVED: That copies of this Resolution, under the seal of this Supreme Council, be sent to the Hon. John Hay, Secretary of State, Washington, D.C., and to the Hon. C.F. Curry, Secretary of State of California.

Adopted unanimously by a rising vote this 17th day of Octo-

ber, A.D. 1901, at the city of San Luis Obispo, California.

L.J. Martins, Sec. Supremo.

The President of the United States,

Washington, D. C.

The Supreme Council of the Portuguese Union of California assembled in its thirty-second annual Session at Stockton, California, resolved to pledge its unqualified loyalty and to tender its resources and membership to the national causes by you so nobly championed and defended.

There are upwards of three hundred of its members wearing Uncle Sam's military uniform and we have invested nearly two hundred thousand dollars, one-fourth of its assets, in securities of the United States Government, besides the amounts donated to the Red Cross and similar organizations.

JOHN G. MATTOS, JR., Treasurer

(Telegram sent to the President of the United States in October 1918)

U.P.E.C. State Youth Council visiting home office.

151

Whereas, the Hon. W. H. Lamb, Mayor of the City of Santa Cruz, California, as the official representative thereof, extended to this Supreme Council of the Portuguese Union of the State of California a most cordial welcome; and

Whereas, this Supreme Council has received many kindnesses at the hands of the people of Santa Cruz during its stay therein; and

Whereas, this session is about to be closed and this Supreme Council desires to show its appreciation of such welcome and so many kindnesses;

Now, be it resolved, that a vote of thanks be given to said Hon. W. H. Lamb, Mayor of Santa Cruz, and through him to the people of said City for said welcome and kindnesses; and be it further

Resolved, that this resolution be spread upon the minutes and a copy thereof sent to said Mayor.

(Signed) F. I. Lemos.

J. G. Mattos Jr.

Duly adopted by unanimous vote this 5th day of October, A. D. 1899.

L. J. Martins,

Supreme Secretary.

WESTERN UNION TELEGRAM

```
DSD051 (OYH003) GOVT  PD YH HYANNIS MASS JUL 7 1961 850P EDT

CARLOS ALMEDIA

   1120 EAST 14 ST SAN LEANDRO CALIF

I WANT TO EXTEND MY GREETINGS TO THE PORTUGUESE  UNION OF THE

STATE OF CALIFORNIA AND TO ALL ATTENDING ITS 75TH ANNIVERSARY

CELEBRATION AUGUST 5TH IN OAKLAND. I COMMEND  THE UPEC FOR ITS

SEVEN AND HALF DECADES OF WORK AND CONGRATULATE IT ON HAVING

CHIEF JUSTICE EARL WARREN AS A MEMBER

MY VERY BEST WISHES

   JOHN F KENNEDY


(622P)
```

Copy of telegram sent by President John F. Kennedy.

República Portuguesa

O Presidente da República
Grão-Mestre das Ordens Portuguesas

Confere á *União Portuguesa do Estado da California*

o Título de *Membro Honorário* da Ordem de Benemerência.

Nos termos do Regulamento da mesma Ordem são-lhe concedidos as honras e o direito ao uso das insígnias que lhe correspondem.

Dado em Lisboa e Paços do Governo da República, aos *17* de *Novembro* de 19*66* .

O Chanceler da Ordem,

Francisco de Paula ......

Certificate of Decoration given by the Portuguese Government, 1966.

Presidencia do Conselho Supremo da U. P. P. E. C.
San Jose, Cal., 20 de Novembro de 1918.

Exmo. Sr. José Chrysostomo da Silveira,
Digmo. Presidente Supremo da U. P. E. C.

Acusando a recepção do oficio de V. Exa., com data de 6 do corrente, cumpre-me agradecer-lhe muito reconhecido os desejos que V. Exa. manifesta àcêrca dos progressos da sociedade a que tenho a honra de presidir. Fazendo votos para que os laços de amizade se estreitem cada vez mais entre as sociedades portuguesas da California, creio que V. Exa. pela sua ilustração ha de no termo da sua presidência manter no mais elevado grau os créditos da U. P. E. C., como a primeira e maior sociedade portuguesa deste Estado.

De V. Exa. Mto. Veneradora,

GEORGINA D. GOMES,
Presidente Suprema da U. P. P. E. C.

Message of Supreme President of U.P.P.E.C.

SUPREME OFFICERS
Administration 1978-1979

BOARD OF DIRECTORS, 1978-1979 — (Standing L to R), Antonio P. Neves, George Azevedo, John H. Alves, Frank Souza. (Seated) Tony Codina, Everett Swayze (Secretary), Victor Gomes (Chairman), Steve Machado (Vice-Chairman) and Manuel Simas.

Supreme Officers: (L to R-Standing) Ernest Nunes, Inside Guard; Dr. Luis J. Madeira, Medical Examiner; Adelino Santos, Outside Guard; John Machado, Master of Ceremonies; Hubert J. Trindade, Marshal; (Seated) Helio Souza, Third Vice-President; Carlos Almeida, Secretary-Treasurer; Mary Mathias, Supreme President; John G. Vieira, First Vice President and Eddie Costa, Second Vice-President. Standing behind Supreme President is Frances Simas, Pianist.

ANTÓNIO FONTE

(1826–1906)

Born on February 25, 1826 at Prainha do Galeão (São Mateus), Pico, Azores. His father came from an agricultural community and his mother from a seafaring class. António was reared to farm life, with no formal schooling, but he was nobly repaid for that misfortune by a self education. In 1845 he changed to a seafaring life, and soon afterward spent about two years sailing from English ports, and still later was engaged in the East India trade for some three years. He immigrated to California in 1851 from Manila, Philippine Islands. His first employment was in a warehouse at Clark's Point, San Francisco, where until October he conveyed milk by whale-boat from San Antonio (East Oakland) to San Francisco. A month later he became assistant to James B. Larue of Oakland in his hotel and store, remaining with him for two and a half years. In 1854 he went into business of his own by opening a boarding house which he operated until 1861. In that year Antonio built a store on the site of his boarding house at 800-802 East 12th Street, Oakland, operating it very successfully for over 40 years. He was a person of integrity, thrift, strong character and highly respected in his community. He was frequently invited to accept nominations to official positions and was once induced to join a forlorn hope by accepting the Democratic Party nomination for Treasurer of Alameda County. With no reasonable prospect and no expectation of success in a county at the time so overwhelmingly Republican, his personal popularity was demonstrated by his receiving 500 votes more than his predecessor on the same ticket. He married Miss Rosanna

Lyons, a native of Ireland, on January 20, 1858, in St. Patrick's Church in San Francisco, California. He had five children from his marriage, all born in Oakland: Henry, Joseph, James, Annie and Maria. Henry died in 1883 when he was 27 years of age; Joseph, a graduate of Saint Mary's College, became a member of the dry goods firm of J.P. O'Toole & Company of Oakland, and later a reporter for the Oakland Times. In 1891 Joseph began the publication of *Independent,* a weekly in East Oakland. James, Fonte's third son died at the age of nineteen. Annie married W.J. McHugh, Manager of the Whitney, Oakland and Standard Express Company.

António Fonte, number one in the Membership Register of the União Portuguesa do Estado da California (U.P.E.C.), along with 29 other members, organized the Society on August 1, 1880. in San Leandro, California, during a meeting held at Saint Joseph's Hall on Davis Street.

In 1887 he formed the Supreme Council of the Society and became the first State President, a position he held through 1893. He presided at Conventions held in several cities: San Leandro (1887, 1888 and 1890), Hollister (1889), Petaluma (1891), East Oakland (1892) and Hayward (1893). He was elected Supreme Director of the U.P.E.C. in 1893 and served in that capacity through April 3, 1906, the time of his death.

During his several years as President he initiated 1,346 members in Councils 1 through 14, which he founded. The assets of the Society, in his last term as President, reached the total amount of $6,465.20. He is remembered in the order as the Founder of the Portuguese Union of the State of California. He was also the second President of the Catholic Mutual Benefit Association of the Pacific Coast and for two years its Grand Treasurer.

San Leandro, Cal., April 4th, 1906.

To the Officers and Members of Conselho, No. . . .,
da U. P. E. C.:

Brothers: You are hereby notified that **Past** Supreme President Antonio Fonte died yesterday. High Mass will take place at half past 9 A. M. at St. Anthony's Church, East Oakland, Saturday, April 7, 1906, and the funeral will take place from Maccabees' Hall, Eleventh and Clay Streets, Oakland, at 1 o'clock P. M. Sunday, April 8, 1906.

All are cordially invited.

By order of the Directors.

Fraternally yours,

L. J. MARTINS,
Supreme Secretary.

N. B.—Please notify members of your Council.

JOSÉ PIMENTEL

(1835—1900)

Born on January 2, 1835 at Ribeira do Barqueiro, Island of Flores, Azores. Pimentel immigrated to the U.S. in 1848 landing in Boston, Mass., where he learned the barber trade. He moved to California in 1861 shortly after his marriage to Miss Rose Freitas. He was attracted by the gold rush and engaged in gold mining for a few years. After acquiring a sum of money, the fruit of his hard work around Nevada County, he decided to move to San Francisco, and opened a hotel and restaurant, which he operated on Jackson Street for four years. Later he came to Hayward where he opened a barber shop in the Hayward Hotel, the first one in this Southern Alameda County city. When Hayward was incorporated in 1876 he became a member of the first Board of Trustees, and thereafter held several offices in that municipality. He served simultaneously as Justice of the Peace and Town Clerk for several years. He was first appointed Justice of the Peace in 1892. After this office became elective he resigned as Town Clerk but held this same office as an elected official for the next eight years, serving until his death on December 7, 1900. He joined the U.P.E.C. on August 1, 1880 and was one of the 30 charter members of the Society together with Antonio Fonte credited with the organization of Council No. 3 in Hayward.

He was elected Supreme President of the U.P.E.C. in 1893 and presided at the Convention of the Society held in Watsonville in October of 1894. During his term of office he initiated 202 members and organized Council No. 15. Assets of the U.P.E.C. when he left the Presidency amounted to $7,826.81 with a membership of 1,353. He served as Director from 1887 through 1889, 1895 through 1898, Master of Ceremonies (1890) and Vice-President for two years (1891-1892). He was responsible for a large portion of the legislation introduced in the beginnings of the U.P.E.C. "The life of José Pimentel," according to an editorial of the *Hayward Review* (December 14, 1900), "has served to show what determination combined with the gentler attributes will accomplish. He was born humbly in a foreign land and came to the U.S. to try his fortune. Hampered by no education he manfully set to overcome this deficiency and his spare moments, after hours in that little Boston shop, were spent in study. In him, to a certain degree, was the spirit of the great unrest which move men to great deeds. He was a born leader in many ways and in his last years his word was law to many. Lured by the golden mystery of the West, he came to California and became a part of the State."

Pimentel, a Freemason, was a member of the Odd Fellows, of the A.O.U.W. of Alameda Encampment. From his marriage there were seven children: Will, Alfred O., Charles, Louis H., Ada, Edward and Mrs. John G. Dassell.

Third President

JOHN G. MATTOS

(1864–1933)

Born on August 1, 1864 at Angustias, Faial, Azores, immigrated to California with his parents in 1879. He attended elementary schools in Horta, Faial, and continued his education in Centerville, California where he settled and practiced law. He became an American citizen on July 31, 1886 and became very active in the Republican Party. In 1888 he was elected road overseer of the Centerville District and was reelected in 1890. In 1891 he was appointed as deputy county assessor for Washington Township, a position he held for four years. In 1889 he was commissioned a notary public, and in 1900 he was elected as a member of the State Assembly for the forty sixth district, which at that time comprised all that portion of Alameda County south of San Leandro creek, (townships of Washington, Eden and Murray) and was reelected to the same position in 1902. While in the State Assembly, he was a member of the code commission and chairman of the roads and highways committee and the committee on education. In 1901 he was appointed by Governor Gage as a member of the board of trustees of the deaf, dumb and blind children at Berkeley. He resigned after five years of service. In 1907 he was appointed by President Roosevelt appraiser of merchandise at the port of San Francisco and served for seven consecutive years. In 1918 he was appointed by Gover-

Elementary School dedicated to the memory of John G. Mattos, in Fremont, California.

nor Stephens a member of the board of prison directors serving for eight years. He was admitted to law practice in August 1897. His office was located in Centerville and in the Bank of Italy, in San Francisco. He was instrumental in organizing the Bank of Centerville of which he was chosen to serve as its President until 1919, the time when the bank was sold to Bank of Italy (today Bank of America). He served the latter as Vice-President and director for many years. In 1893 was elected to the School Board of Centerville, serving continuously for 35 years. He held the office of Justice of the Peace for the Washington Township for eight years and in that time, assessed fines of over thirty-five thousand dollars for violations of the motor vehicle code. He was an alert and vigorous person. His sterling character and progressive ideas deserved the respect of his compatriots as well as of all those who came in contact with him.

He married Ana E. Mattos, but there were no children. He joined U.P.E.C. Council No. 5 in Centerville on August 12, 1888. He was elected Marshal in 1891, Vice-President in 1893 and President in 1894 and 1895. He presided at two State Conventions: Sacramento, 1895 and Pleasanton, 1896; served as Director in 1892, 1896 and 1897, and as Supreme Treasurer from 1898 through 1929. During his administration as President he initiated 430 new members and organized Councils 16 to 23. U.P.E.C. assets at the time he left the presidency amounted to $5,522.01 and membership numbered 1,605. Mattos died on June 26, 1933 and was buried at Holy Sepulchre Cemetery in Hayward, California. A new school was named after Mattos in Centerville in testimonial to his long services to education and his community.

Mattos was the only Portuguese immigrant ever elected to the State Legislature.

Fourth President

FRANCISCO IGNÁCIO DE LEMOS

(1865—1935)

Born on March 10, 1865 at Vila Nova, Terceira, Azores. Son of José and Francisca Ignacia Menezes de Lemos. Lemos studied for the priesthood, entering the seminary of Angra do Heroismo, Terceira, in 1879. He completed his course in 1888 but was never ordained. Lemos came to the United States landing at New Bedford, Mass., on September 20, 1888. After obtaining a loan of one hundred dollars from a friend, he used the money to continue his journey to the village of Mission San Jose, California where he secured employment with *O Amigo dos Católicos* (a Portuguese newspaper founded in Irvington on May 26, 1888 by two Catholic priests, Fathers Manuel Francisco Fernandes and João Francisco Tavares). Printing shops were later moved to Pleasanton and Hayward. Lemos and Quaresma acquired the paper and in 1894 hired Father Guilherme S. Glória to work for the newspaper. In 1896 he was replaced by Joaquim Borges de Menezes. This newspaper was last published on June 6, 1896, appearing under the title of *O Arauto* on July 13 of the same year. It was in circulation under the sole proprietorship of Joaquim Borges Menezes until it was sold in January 1917 to Pedro L.C. Silveira.

Lemos moved to San Leandro, where he remained until February 18, 1889, when he moved to Hayward. Here he entered the office of attorney G.S. Langan, who was anxious to learn the Portuguese language, while Mr. Lemos was equally desirous of learning and improving his English. Lemos remained with Langan for ten years, practicing law following his admission to the California bar on April 25, 1895. He was a Director of the Association of Milk Producers (1916); Director of Bank of Centerville; Director of Bank of Hayward (1919) and Director of the First National Bank of Centerville (1921).

On September 1, 1898 he went to the Azores and married Miss Adelaide Leontina Cotta de Menezes in Vila Nova, Terceira, Azores, and returned with his bride to Hayward. They had a son, Frank Clemente, who was killed in an automobile accident at the age of 18 on February 16, 1919. He served on the School Board of Trustees as chairman for nine years. He loved music and poetry. He joined U.P.E.C. Council No. 3, Hayward on April 20, 1890. Elected Vice-President in 1895 and President in 1896. He presided at the U.P.E.C. Convention held in San Leandro in 1897. During his term as President, he initiated 485 new members and organized Council Nos. 24-30. Assets of the U.P.E.C. at that time amounted to $11,961.56 and membership numbered 2,148. He served as a member of the Board of Directors in 1891, 1892, 1897 and 1899 through August 2, 1935, the time of his death. He was also a member of the I.D.E.S., Fraternal Society founded in July, 1889 in Mission San Jose, serving as Secretary of the Board of Directors (1917) and Chairman (1932). He belonged to the Benevolent and Protective Order of Elks; the Fraternal Order of Eagles; the Foresters of America; the Knights of Columbus; the A.P.P.B. (consolidated with U.P.C. in July 1957). His unfeigned cordiality and friendly manner gained him many friends. He was proud of his Portuguese heritage. He was decorated by the Portuguese Government with the Military Order of Christ on September 29, 1934, however he refused to accept it. Notwithstanding his refusal, the Portuguese Government proceeded with the granting of such honor forwarding the respective insignia and certificate which arrived after Lemos' death.

Fifth President

ANTÓNIO FERNANDES CUNHA

(1853–1925)

Born on October 20, 1853 in Piedade, Pico, Azores. Cunha immigrated to Nevada in 1868 where he engaged in mining for two years. He became a superintendent of a mine at Gold Hill, where he married Miss Margaret Buckley, a school teacher born in Grass Valley, California. In 1870 he moved to San Leandro where he lived for quite some time. From there he went to San Lorenzo and in 1882 settled in Milpitas. In that area he acquired a seventy-five acre fruit ranch and a general merchandise store. In 1885 he was appointed postmaster of Milpitas village. He was the second Portuguese to serve as postmaster in California.

He joined U.P.E.C. Council No. 1 on April 17, 1881 and was elected Vice-President of the Supreme Council in 1896. He presided at the Convention held in

Benicia in 1898. During his term as President he initiated 675 new members, and organized Councils 31-37. At the time he left the presidency of the U.P.E.C. the assets of the organization amounted to $23,435.11 with a membership totalling 2,664. He served as Supreme Director in 1892, 1894, 1895 and 1898 through 1905. He was the father of eleven children, seven sons and four daughters. Three of the sons became lawyers, one became a dentist and the four daughters took up teaching. One of his sons, Edward A. Cunha, was a prominent attorney in San Francisco with an office located at the Flood Building, a graduate of Stanford University (1907) and admitted to the State Bar in 1908. Later he moved to Oakland and became associated with the law firm of Redd, Black and Reed. He served also as Assistant District Attorney before becoming associated with Harry Stanford.

António Fernandes Cunha is a good example of immigrants who settled in California and worked their way up in society. He died on June 27, 1925 in San Francisco, California.

Sixth President

VICTORINO TEODORO BRAGA

(1854—1915)

Born on November 30, 1854 at Vila de Santa Cruz, Santa Maria, Azores. Braga settled in San Leandro early in life, becoming associated with L.A. Ferreira in farming. He married Georgina and had two children, Carlos and Carolina. He joined U.P.E.C. Council No. 1, San Leandro on August 1, 1880 and was elected Master of Ceremonies in 1889, Vice-President in 1897 and President in 1898. He presided at the U.P.E.C. Convention held in 1899 in Santa Cruz, California.

During his term of office 377 new members were admitted to the organization which counted at the time 2,851 members. He organized Councils 38-40 and served as Director in 1887, 1891, 1893 and 1904. Died on April 12, 1915 in San Leandro and was buried at Saint Mary's Cemetery in Oakland, California.

ANTÓNIO JOSÉ PINHEIRO
(Anthony J. Pine)

(1855–1930)

Born on August 9, 1855, in São Mateus, Pico, Azores. Pine immigrated to California in 1874 to engage in mining in Sierra County. In 1888 he established himself in Benicia, California, where he opened a grocery store that he operated for fifty years. He married Mary Thereza Fonte, a native of Sao Mateus, Pico, Azores on August 30, 1886 in Oakland, California. Miss Fonte was a niece of Antonio Fonte, First Supreme President of U.P.E.C. He had eight children born from this marriage: August, Leland, Alfred, William, Eva, Ana, Lillian and Marjorie. He served as a representative for the Associacao Portugueza Protectora e Beneficente, a fraternal society founded in San Francisco, August 6, 1868. He was for many years a member of the Board of Directors of the Old Peoples Bank of Benicia, and when that institution was sold to the Central Commercial and Savings Bank of Vallejo, he was made a Director, a position held until his resignation. Pinheiro also served on the Benicia School Board of Trustees.

He was affiliated with I.D.E.S. and A.P.P.B. He joined U.P.E.C. Council No. 7, Oakland on September 29, 1889. He was elected to the Board of Directors of Supreme Council of U.P.E.C. in 1894 and 1895, Marshal 1887, Vice-President 1898 and President in 1899. He presided over the U.P.E.C. Convention held in 1900 in San Jose and was elected to the Board of Directors in 1900 through 1905. During his term as President he is credited with the initiation of 822 new members, and with the organization of Councils 41-50. U.P.E.C. membership at the time he left the presidency numbered 3,666 with assets amounting to $55,676.17.

Pine was stricken with a cerebral hemorrhage at his place of business in November, 1930, and passed away on December 31, 1930.

Eighth President

JOÃO VALLADÃO

(1848—1924)

Born on March 18, 1848 at Santa Cruz, Flores, Azores. Valladão was employed at Figueiredo Merchandise Store in Horta Faial, Azores before immigrating to the United States. In Flores he occupied several public offices. While in California. he was involved in several businesses and occupations. Prior to his death he owned and operated a saloon in West Oakland. He was well known among the Portuguese community and became of great value to his fellow countrymen. On June 6, 1904 he was one of the founders of the Portuguese Association of the Portuguese Hospital of Saint Anthony, in Oakland, California, the only Portuguese establishment at the time in the entire United States. The Association was headed by Dr. M.M. Enos, a native of Hayward of Azorean parentage, born on July 26, 1875 and a graduate of the San Francisco Medical College (1896) and of the University of Chicago. Dr. Enos also taught surgery at the National Medical School of Chicago. While in California he was a Director of the Portuguese American Bank, with headquarters

Saint Anthony Hospital, corner of 18th and Grove Streets in Oakland, California.

in San Francisco.

The Portuguese Association of the Portuguese Hospital was formed by Joaquim A. Silveira, a native of São Jorge, Azores, and well known industrialist; J.J. Bettencourt, a well-to-do merchant of Oakland, who served as treasurer of the Association; Alexandre P. Borges, a farmer from Contra Costa County; João Balra, an industrialist from Berkeley; José Domingos Oliveira, a merchant of Hayward; and a non-Portuguese, David Williams, who was a school teacher. It is interesting to note that the work and accounting of the Hospital Association was all done in Portuguese.

João Valladão joined U.P.E.C. Council No. 13, West Oakland, on July 7, 1895 and was elected Outside Guard in 1898, Vice-President in 1899 and President in 1900. He presided at the U.P.E.C. Convention held in San Luis Obispo in 1901. During his term of office he initiated 762 new members and organized Councils 51-56. Membership of the various councils amounted to 4,433 and assets had reached $72,597.08. Valladão served on the Board of Directors from 1901 through 1903. He also served on the Board of Directors of the I.D.E.S. He died on January 23, 1924.

Ninth President

FIRMINO JOSÉ CUNHA

(1855–1935)

Born on October 18, 1855 at Lagoa, Praia, Graciosa, Azores. He was a merchant marine who immigrated to California in November 1877. He worked in mines around Gold Hill, Nevada before he opened a clothing store in San Francisco. In that city he operated a hotel and served as state wharfinger (guard) at the San Francisco Harbor for four years. Later in 1888 he moved his clothing and shoe store to 1522 7th Street, West Oakland. Shortly thereafter he sold his business to form a partnership with Virgil Caporgno to venture in the mortuary business under the name of Cunha & Caporgno Mortuary in Oakland, with a branch in San Leandro. He married Emma and had three children, Catherine (Delamothe); Gertrude (Silva) and Fred Cunha. He became a member of U.P.E.C. Council No. 7, of Oakland on September 29, 1889, later transferring to Council No. 25. He was elected Director from 1891 through 1894 (the time when he was elected Vice-President for one year). In 1898 he was elected to the Board of Directors, serving until 1900 when he was again nominated to the Vice-Presidency, this time reaching the Presidency one year later in 1901. He presided at the U.P.E.C. Convention held in 1902 in Merced, California. During his term of President he initiated 1,325 new members, the largest initiation in one year, since the founding of the order. He also organized Councils 57-64. U.P.E.C. membership at the time Cunha left the presidency numbered 5,536 and assets amounted to $101,806.72. He was elected to the Board of Directors in 1902 through 1914 and 1916 through 1919 and again in 1923. He held memberships in the Druids (Vasco da Gama Grove), A.P.P.B. (consolidated with U.P.C. in 1957 to form United National Life Insurance society, headquarters in San Francisco, until 1973, when the Society moved to Oakland) and I.D.E.S. serving on the Board of Directors for a few years. He died on May 31, 1935.

Tenth President

ANTÓNIO MARIA MARTINS

(1858—1912)

Born on November 25, 1858 in Madalena, Pico, Azores. He came to California in the late 1880s, settling around Watsonville. He joined U.P.E.C. Council No. 12 in that locality on October 21, 1894 and a year later was elected Outside Guard. In 1896 he served as Master of Ceremonies, in 1901 as Vice-President and as President in 1902, presiding at U.P.E.C. Convention in 1903 at Hanford, California. During his term of office, he initiated 1,087 new members and organized Councils 65-68. Assets at the time he left office amounted to $132,728.45, while membership was set at 6,172. He served on the Board of Directors in 1903, 1904 and 1907. Later, he moved to Oakland where he died by committing suicide on February 11, 1912. He was married to Anna C. Martins, Supreme Secretary of S.P.R.S.I., Sociedade Portuguesa Rainha Santa Isabel, a fraternal society founded for women on March 15, 1898, in Oakland.

Eleventh President

JESSE HENRY WOODS

(1872—1932)

Born on May 3, 1872 in San Leandro, California. He was one of the best known and most successful businessmen in the area. He was the son of Mr. and Mrs. Joseph Woods who resided in the southern part of San Leandro near the Prince Canning Company. Early in life he entered the Joyce Department Store in Oakland where he worked for several years. In 1900 he started a dry goods store in Hayward. In 1906 he purchased the property of Daniel Luce at the corner of B and Main Streets. He then moved to larger quarters and became a principal businessman of Hayward, known all over the county. In 1915 he retired and shortly after moved with his family to Piedmont. In December 1895 he married Miss Giorgiana (Giorgie) Rogers, a well known San Leandran, daughter of Mr. and Mrs. António Rogers of Dutton Avenue. From this marriage a son and daughter were born, Mrs. Norma (Woods) Reinhardt and LeRoy Woods who was in the commission business in Oakland. While residing in Hayward he organized and served as one of the first officers of the Farmers and Merchants Bank, which later merged with Bank of America. Interested in politics,

Woods was active in the Republican Party and was a close personal friend and advisor of the late Congressman . Arthur Elston. He was a charter worker in the Roosevelt Bull Moose party. While living in Oakland he became a Real Estate Broker and Director (1918) of the National Guaranty and Mortgage Co., serving as its Secretary and in 1924 became one of the Directors of the Prudential Mortgage Securities Company of Oakland. He joined U.P.E.C. Council No. 25 in Oakland (later transferred to Council No. 3, Hayward) on December 27, 1896. He was elected Outside Guard in 1897, Vice-President in 1902 and President in 1903. He presided over the U.P.E.C. Convention held in San Rafael in 1904. During his administration he initiated 834 new members and organized Councils 69-71. The Order then owned assets amounting to $155,284.57 with a membership of 6,373. He served as Supreme Director during 1900-1901. He was very instrumental in obtaining recognition for the Portuguese Nationality of João Rodrigues Cabrilho, discoverer of California. He also advocated the erection of a monument honoring the discoverer in Point Loma, San Diego, California. He was a member of the Lusitanian Club, Native Sons of the Golden West, Piedmont Parlor, I.D.E.S. and Knights of Columbus. Woods died on May 14, 1932 in Oakland and was entombed at Holy Sepulchre Mausoleum in Hayward, California. Woods (an anglicized name for Madeira) was the first California native to be elected Supreme President of the U.P.E.C.

Twelfth President

MANUEL FRAGA

(1865—1949)

Born on December 4, 1865 at Ponta Ruiva, Flores, Azores. Fraga immigrated to California in 1879, first settling on a farm in Merced County. Later he moved to Pleasanton and from there to Benicia where in 1894 he opened a successful hotel and grocery store. In 1898 he went to Berkeley to work for Renas Warehouse Company leaving that company on November 1, 1914 to accept the office of Supreme Secretary of the U.P.E.C. a position he filled with great zeal until October 1943, when he decided to retire. In 1892 he married Adelaide Hattie, a native of San Pablo, and from this marriage he had a son, Arthur Fraga. He joined U.P.E.C. Council No. 8 (Pleasanton) on July 16, 1893, transferring later to Council No. 18 in Benicia. He was elected Master of Ceremonies in 1900; Vice-President in 1903 and President in 1904. He presided over the U.P.E.C. Convention held in Stockton, California in 1905. During his term as President he initiated 625 new members and organized U.P.E.C. Councils 72-75. The assets of the order at the time he left the presidency were $203,311.73. He was appointed to the Board of Directors to fill the vacancy caused by the death of Antonio Fonte in April 1906. He also served on the Board of Directors from 1910 through 1912. He was a man of his convictions, always respecting the opinions of others. He was held in high esteem all through his career within the U.P.E.C. including his term of office of Secretary. He died on May 9, 1949 in Ukiah and was buried at the Mountain View Cemetery in Oakland on May 11, 1949.

LOUIS ALFRED ENOS

(1877–1946)

Born on June 28, 1877 in San Luis Obispo, California. Son of Louis Enos, a native of Pico Island and Maria Glória, of Faial, Azores. Enos studied law under Fred Dorn and Ephian Green and was admitted to the Bar in October 1901. He practiced law in San Luis Obispo until 1942, when ill health forced his retirement.

He first married Miss Florence Lawrence, daughter of Manuel Lawrence and granddaughter of Joaquin Estrada. Of Louis' three marriages there were three sons; Lawrence (Larry) Enos, son from his first marriage, and Louis and Milton Enos from his second marriage. He was married last to Mary Diehl of Morro Bay.

In 1912 Louis Alfred Enos, the son of an Azorean immigrant family, was elected Assistant District Attorney, an office he held for a number of years.

He was a member of the B.P.O. Elks, I.D.E.S., A.P.P.B. and joined U.P.E.C. Council No. 42, San Luis Obispo on February 11, 1900. He was elected Master of Ceremonies in 1903; Vice-President in 1904 and President in 1905. He presided over the U.P.E.C. Convention held in the city of Salinas. During his administration he initiated 601 new members and organized Councils 75, 76 and 77. Total membership at the time he left the presidency was 6,987, with assets that amounted to $243,620.86. He was elected to the Board of Directors of U.P.E.C. in 1906 and 1907.

He died on January 26, 1946 and was entombed in the Catholic Cemetery in San Luis Obispo, California.

JOSÉ PEREIRA MENDONÇA

(1873–1932)

Born on December 8, 1873 in Cedros, Flores, Azores. He immigrated to Boston, Massachusetts at age 13 with his brother, and moved to California where he went into sheep herding in the Hanford area. Around 1909 he moved to the Bay Area to take a job as a wholesale distributor for Joseph Usher, a liquor concern. In 1928 he went to Stockton and became a Field Representative for New York Life Insurance Company, an occupation he held continuously until his last days. He married Maria Marta Pedro, a native of Brown's Flat, near Columbia, Tuolumne County, California. From this marriage he had three children: Maria Amelia (Fraga), Lenora

Louise and Joseph Pereira Mendonça.

He was a member of the I.D.E.S., Magellan Council of the Knights of Columbus; B.P.O.E. and the Order of Red Men, Stockton branch. Mendonça joined U.P.E.C. Council No. 24 on November 1, 1896, transferring later to Council No. 56 of Oakland. He was elected Marshal in 1903, Vice-President in 1905 and President in 1906. He presided over the U.P.E.C. Convention held in the city of Watsonville in 1907. He served as Director from 1907 through 1911 and 1914 through 1918. During his presidential term of office he initiated 1,198 new members and organized Councils 78 through 81. Total membership at the time numbered 7,930 with assets amounting to $295,078.20.

He died on July 24, 1932 and was buried at Holy Sepulchre Cemetery in Hayward on July 28, 1932.

Fifteenth President

ANTÓNIO AUGUSTO SARMENTO

(1860–1946)

Born on December 18, 1860 at São Mateus, Pico, Azores. Sarmento was the son of José Francisco Sarmento and Rosa Jacinto, both of São Mateus. He came to California around 1881 to join his brother, José Pedro Sarmento, in Fresno. He raised cattle for a while but since there was not much profit in this business he went into hotel ventures. He opened the Azorean House and Açores Hotel, both in Fresno and nearby Caruthers. He held title to a gold mine in joint tenancy with his brother Pedro. In 1894 he came to Oakland and opened a clothing store on 23rd Avenue and then moved to San Francisco where he also had the Lisbon Clothing House at 319 Drumm Street in partnership with Cunha until 1897. With the discovery of gold in Alaska he went to that territory and returned to Oakland three years later.

He joined the Fire Department from which he retired in 1919. At age 59 he moved to Turlock where he had large real estate holdings. He was a very charitable person and loved his countrymen with sincerity. He made two trips to the Azores, his native land, and while there contributed financially to some projects improving his village of birth, São Mateus. In California he acquired a sizeable fortune with land holdings located in Turlock, Oakland, San Rafael, San Francisco and Cazadero. On July 13, 1891 he founded and financed *A Pátria,* the first Portuguese newspaper published in the city of Oakland, with Manuel Stone, a Brazilian who directed this weekly periodical until late 1897. (*A Pátria* was a partnership between Manuel Henas, Firmino J. Cunha, José M. da Rosa, Francisco I. Lemos and João Garcia de Mattos Jr.).

Sarmento joined U.P.E.C. Council No. 7 of Oakland on June 4, 1893. He was elected Vice-President in 1906 and President in 1907. He presided at the U.P.E.C. Convention held in Sacramento in 1908. During his administration he initiated 806 new members and organized Councils 82-86. At that time, assets of the society amounted to $343,186.93 with a membership of 8,305. He served on the Board of Directors from 1908 to 1909.

He married Laura Bettencourt, a Californian of Portuguese descent (São Jorge, Azores) and raised three children from this marriage, Rosa S. (Orchard), Laura (Rose) and António J. Sarmento. While in Stanislaus County he served as President of the Merced Stanislaus Sweet Potato Growers Association (Home Office in Livingston, California). He was a member of the Druids. He died on November 10, 1946.

Sixteenth President

JOÃO PEREIRA

(1866—1940)

Born on May 29, 1866 at Feteira, Faial, Azores. He came to San Leandro in 1881, at the age of 15, by working his way to this country on a whaling vessel. He went to work as a farmhand on the huge ranch holdings of Vicente Cardoso (Vincent Kardoza), father of J.R. Kardoza, a San Leandro clothing store owner. In 1895 he first went to work for local schools, securing a job as custodian of the Old Union School (now Lincoln School). Later when the San Leandro school system grew, he was promoted to the position of superintendent of buildings and grounds, a position he held until retirement in 1936. He married Mary Vargas and had one son, Manuel Jesse Perry, who later became Supreme President of U.P.E.C. João Pereira joined U.P.E.C. Council No. 1, San Leandro, on January 31, 1892. He was elected Inside Guard in 1901, Master of Ceremonies in 1902, Vice-President in 1907 and Supreme President in 1908 presiding at the U.P.E.C. Convention held in Fresno in 1909. During his term of office he initiated 801 new members and organized Councils 87-87-89. When he left the presidency, U.P.E.C. assets had reached $358,951.25 with 8,610 members.

He served on the Board of Directors during 1909-1910. He died on December 31, 1940 and was buried at the Holy Sepulchre Cemetery in Hayward, California.

Seventeenth President

JOSÉ DE VARGAS PEREIRA

(1864—1952)

Born on February 25, 1864 at Castelo Branco, Faial, Azores. Pereira was the son of João Pereira and Clara Pereira, both natives of Faial. He immigrated to California in 1890 to join his cousin, Manuel V. Pereira, who owned a farm in Irvington. Two years later he went to work for the Stanford Winery in Warm Springs and remained there for seven years. After saving some money, he bought a ranch in Pleasanton in partnership with José S. Soito. Five years later he bought out his partner and operated the ranch until 1950, when he sold his real estate holdings to retire. He was married to Maria Madalena Gomes, a native of Faial. From this marriage he had 6 children: Joseph, Manuel, Antonio, Olimpia (Lawrence), Beatrice (Cardoso) and Maria

(Garibaldi). He was a member of the I.D.E.S., I.O.O.F. and served for several years in the trusteeship for the Amador Valley High School District in Pleasanton, California. He joined U.P.E.C. Council No. 8, Pleasanton, on May 19, 1895. He was elected Marshal in 1902, Master of Ceremonies in 1907, Vice-President in 1908 and President in 1909. During his administration he initiated 921 new members and organized Councils 90, 91 and 92. Membership at the time numbered 9,026 with assets totalling $392,116.84. He presided at the U.P.E.C. Convention held in the city of Vallejo in 1910. He was elected to the Board of Directors in 1910. He died on February 25, 1952 in Walnut Creek, California, and was buried at Saint Augustine Cemetery in Pleasanton, California.

Eighteenth President

JOSÉ CARLOS JORGE LAWRENCE

(1877—1952)

Born on February 16, 1877 in Corvo, Azores. Lawrence immigrated to California at an early age and became engaged in a variety of businesses. He served as Treasurer of the Portuguese Mercantile Company Inc., located at Clay Street, San Francisco and Secretary of the Portuguese Hotel Co., in the same city. In later years he was active in the dairy industry and occupied several positions: manager of Cooperative Dairyman's League, Inc., manager of the United Milk Producers in Oakland and director and manager of Plant No. 13 in Los Banos. He married Francisca (Frances) G., and from this marriage there were three sons: George, Alfred and Eugene. He held memberships in the I.D.E.S. and Druids. He joined U.P.E.C. Council No. 32 on December 8, 1901 and later transferred his membership to Council No. 29, Merced, California. He was elected Master of Ceremonies in 1908, Vice-President in 1909 and President in 1910. He presided at the U.P.E.C. Convention held in 1911 at Petaluma. During his term of office he initiated 1,100 new members and organized Councils 93-104. Total membership was 9,695 and assets amounted to $426,727.58. He served on the Board of Directors in 1907, 1911 through 1921, 1927 through 1929 and 1934 through January 20, 1952, the time of his death. He was one of the longest serving members on the Board of Directors of the U.P.E.C.

ANTHONY WILSON

(1876–1976)

Born on August 8, 1876 at Gold Hill (two miles south of Virginia City), Nevada. Wilson was the son of Manuel Joaquim Bettencourt, a native of Graciosa, Azores, and Maria Cunha Azevedo, born in Calheta, São Jorge, Azores. The name Wilson was given to his father when he became an American citizen. Anthony narrated the event as his father being somewhat nervous in the presence of the Justice of the Peace. When asked his name, he began mumbling and the witness he had brought to court for the naturalization ceremony called out loud that his name was Wilson in order to speed up the proceedings so that he could return to the mine for his job. From then on he became known as Wilson and, of course, his son was baptized as such. Anthony moved to San Leandro at the age of five with his parents and attended elementary schools there. Later he went to Heald's Business College in San Francisco where he graduated in Business Administration. In 1896 he moved to Stockton and went to work for Potter R. Fire Insurance Agency until 1900. He operated a saloon at 300 West Webster Street in Stockton, known as the Wilson Brothers Bar. But, in 1918 prohibition came along and he had to give it up. He returned to Potter R. Agency and sold casualty insurance until retirement.

He joined U.P.E.C. Council No. 24, Stockton, on January 2, 1898. He was elected Marshal in 1908, Master of Ceremonies in 1909, Vice-President in 1910 and President in 1911. He presided over the U.P.E.C. Convention held in Watsonville in 1912. During his term of office he initiated 1,217 new members in the organization, and founded Councils 105-108; Council 105 in Hanford had the largest number of charter members — 89, 68 of whom were present the night of organization. This council was composed entirely of persons born in Terceira. When Wilson left the presidency, assets of the U.P.E.C. amouned to $478,015.28 with a membership of 10,267.

He served the Supreme Council of U.P.E.C. Board of Directors in 1912, 1914, 1915, 1917 through 1920, 1922 through 1925 and 1930 through 1932. He was a member of the I.D.E.S., Improved Order of Red Man, serving on the Champion Degree Team, Degree of Pocahontas, Holy Name Society and Knights of Columbus. He spoke, read and wrote fluent Portuguese and served on the Grand Jury and Superior Courts of California, acting as an interpreter for Portuguese immigrants.

He was married to the late Lucy Clara on September 30, 1911. Miss Clara was a native of Sonora, California. Anthony Wilson was Dean of the Past Supreme Presidents of the Society for many years, and recalled with pride his association with António Fonte, the first President and founding member of the Portuguese Union of the State of California.

He died on May 7, 1976 — months short of festivities prepared by the Supreme Council to celebrate his centennial.

GUILHERME FRANCISCO PEREIRA

(1864—1942)

Born on October 16, 1864 at Senhora das Dores, Pico, Azores. Pereira was the son of José Rodrigues Pereira, a native of Faial, and of Catarina Pereira, a native of Pico, Azores. In 1883, after attending elementary school in the Azores, he immigrated to California. Upon his arrival, he obtained employment on a ranch. Six years later he married Miss Mary Agnes Silva, a native of Buffalo, New York. From this marriage he had a daughter, Catherine (Vargas). Shortly after his marriage he went to work for the Southern Pacific Railway, quitting in the middle of a big strike to go to work for Mr. Ryder in a lumber camp in Santa Cruz. Here he became a victim of an accident which resulted in the loss of one leg. He later returned to Oakland to operate a grocery store. Before his death on February 14, 1942, he had held a Real Estate Broker's license working out of an office in Oakland. He was affiliated with the I.D.E.S., F.O.E. and Druids.

He joined U.P.E.C. Council No. 13, West Oakland, on October 9, 1893 and was elected Master of Ceremonies in 1910, Vice-President in 1911 and President in 1912. During his term of office there were 1,301 new members initiated, and Councils 109-117 were organized. U.P.E.C. membership then was 10,905, with assets amounting to $530,248.77. He presided at the U.P.E.C. Convention held in Santa Maria in 1913 and was elected to the Board of Directors in 1914, 1915, 1921, 1922 and 1924 through 1927.

JOSÉ JACINTO PIMENTEL

(1876—1947)

Born on January 26, 1876 at Fajãzinha, Flores, Azores. Pimentel immigrated to California when he was a year old. He settled around Merced and operated a grocery store for 21 years, before becoming engaged in farming operations in the Jordan-Atwater and Arena districts. He was one of the major figures in the organization of the Merced-Stanislaus Sweet Potato Growers Association with headquarters in Livingston, serving as sales manager. This association opened a new and important branch in commerce which helped the farmers in that part of the state. The association was organized jointly by Frank S. Sousa, Frank Dutra, J.M. Trindade and João Bettencourt Avila. Avila was a native of Norte Grande, São Jorge, Azores, who immigrated to California around 1883 and farmed around Mission San Jose before settling in Buhach, Merced, California. Avila, at one time, served as Outside Guard of the U.P.E.C.

Pimentel was elected Mayor of Atwater from 1938 to 1940, and City Clerk from 1946 until his death. He was, at one time, the owner of the *Atwater Signal,* a weekly newspaper published in Atwater. He served on the Advisory Board of Merced Bank and later on the same Board with Bank of America, Atwater Branch. In December 1898 he married Maria da Glória Luiz, a native of California and had ten children: Marie (Blandford), Ann (Spafford), Helen (Adcock), Fred, Joseph, John, Frank, Robert, Richard and Jesse.

He joined U.P.E.C. Council No. 29 on November 5, 1899 and was appointed Marshal on August 10, 1911 to fill the vacancy left by the death of R.A.S. Encarnação. He was elected Vice-President in 1912 and President in 1913. He presided at the U.P.E.C. Convention held in 1914 in Sonora, California. During his term as President he initiated 1,282 new members and organized Councils 118-125. Total membership had then reached 11,408 with assets amounting to $573,572.16.

He died on July 23, 1947 and was entombed at Evergreen Mausoleum in Winton, California.

Twenty-Second President

ANTÓNIO JOSÉ HOMEM

(1868–1948)

Born on June 26, 1868 at Urzelina, São Jorge, Azores. Homem immigrated to California in 1880. Around 1902 he opened a general merchandise store on Clay Street in San Francisco, then moved to Oakland in 1925, continuing his store at 5116 E. 14th Street under the name of Melrose Mercantile Store. Around 1918 he served as Secretary and Director of the Associated Milk Producers (53 Clay Street, San Francisco) and Secretary of the San Francisco Dairy Company (1553 Turk Street, San Francisco). Married Helena Fonseca and, from their marriage, had two children: Maria Helena and George Homem. He was a member of the I.D.E.S. and served on this fraternal society's Finance Committee.

He joined U.P.E.C. Council No. 15, San Francisco, on June 25, 1899. He was elected Vice-President in 1913 and President in 1914 and presided over the U.P.E.C. Convention held in 1915 in the city of Oakland. During his administration he initiated 1,518 new members and organized Councils 126-148. U.P.E.C. total membership at the time was 11,979 with assets of $652,974.85. He was also elected to the Board of Directors in 1912, 1915 through 1917 and 1920 through 1924. He died on February 5, 1948 and was buried at the Holy Sepulchre Cemetery in Hayward, California.

MANUEL GREGÓRIO AZEVEDO

(1877–1965)

Born on February 12, 1877 at Portal São Jorge, Azores. Azevedo was the son of Joao and Isabel Azevedo of São Jorge. He immigrated to California in 1891 and went to Delano, Kern County, to join his aunt, Miss Bárbara Albert, with whom he lived for two years. There he attended school to learn the English language. From Delano he went to Marin County and thence to San Francisco, finishing his schooling at the Lincoln School at Fifth and Mission Streets. He spent eight years in that city and one year and four months in Oakland, where he learned the barber's trade. In 1903 he came to Antioch to start a shop for himself. He then built a popular and successful business in the First National Bank Building where he had his three-chair shop. In 1921 he became an agent for the New York Life Insurance Company with an office at his residence (505 Sixth Street) in Antioch. He continued to operate his shop until 1922, when he sold the business to his son, Henry, to solicit life insurance full time.

In 1953 he retired from his position with the water and park departments of the City of Antioch. Azevedo served on the City Council for four years and was also assistant chief of the Volunteer Fire Department of that community. He married Miss Emily Renas of Antioch on November 26, 1900 and from this marriage there were two children: Henry and Maria.

He joined U.P.E.C. Council No. 15, San Francisco, on September 9, 1900 and transferred to Council No. 51, Antioch, in 1905. He was elected Outside Guard in 1910 and was the first member to occupy all chairs in succession from Outside Guard through the Presidency (with the exception of Secretary or Treasurer). He was elected President in 1915 and presided over the U.P.E.C. Convention held in Santa Cruz in 1916. During this convention the host council served a banquet to a delegation of nearly 600 on the beach of Santa Cruz. In his term of office he initiated 1,190 new members and organized Councils 149-153. Assets of the U.P.E.C. at the time amounted to $710,594.37 with a membership of 11,892. He also served on the Board of Directors in 1916 and 1919. He was a member of the Pittsburg Elks, The Order of Red Men, I.D.E.S., a charter member of the Antioch Fraternal Order of Eagles and a longtime member of the East Contra Costa County Chamber of Commerce (1926). He died on January 13, 1965 and was buried at the Holy Cross Cemetery in Antioch, California.

Twenty-Fourth President

JOSÉ CAETANO AVELAR

(1865—1935)

Born on March 14, 1865 in Boston, Mass. At the age of 7 he went to the Island of Flores, Azores with his parents. Around 1884 he returned to the United States, settling in Watsonville until 1904. He then moved to Newman, California and from there of Oakland where he stayed from 1911 until his death on January 29, 1935. In 1887 he married Luiza C., a native of Watsonville, and they had a son named Albert.

He joined U.P.E.C. Council No. 12, Watsonville, August 12, 1895 and transferred his membership to Council No. 7, Oakland, a few years prior to his election to the presidency of the U.P.E.C. Avelar was elected Marshal in 1913, Master of Ceremonies in 1914, Vice-President in 1915 and President in 1916. He presided at the U.P.E.C. Convention held in 1917 in the city of Modesto, California. During his term of office he organized Councils 154-158 (three in Nevada), and initiated 1,686 new members. Total membership during his administration was 12,266, with assets of $745,035.03. He served on the Board of Directors from 1917 through 1920.

Twenty-Fifth President

JOÃO DUTRA

(1878—1952)

Born on August 31, 1878 in Ribeirinha, Terceira Island, Azores. Dutra immigrated to California in 1903. His early life in the Golden State was like that of any alien who left his home country to start a new life in a completely new world foreign to customs and language. He tilled the soil and sheep-herded in the mountains surrounding Hanford until 1906 when he decided to return to the Azores. Later in 1906 he returned to the U.S.A., bringing his family. He worked for Ontario Packing House for a while. Eager to better himself he accepted a job in a men's clothing store, also in Hanford, where he acquired a certain knowledge in merchandising and sales. In 1920 he went to Riverdale and opened his own grocery store, Dutra's Grocery. He retired from the business in later years due to his health. Dutra was known for his kind heart in helping his fellow patriots who used to see in him a counsellor and peacemaker. Often his store was crowded with immigrants seeking his advice in business and family

176

matters. Others would look him up to write a letter to families left behind in the Azores.

He was married to Maria Eugenia, a native of Brasil, in 1896 in Ribeirinha, Terceira. From this marriage there were five children: Tony, Mathew, Mary (Sousa), Elvira (Nunes) and Lena (Simas). In 1914 he married Maria da Rocha Vaz. He was the stepfather of Mary (Alves). He was a member of the I.D.E.S., S.E.S., and A.P.P.B., an organization he served as Supreme President, administration of 1926-27. He was the second Supreme President of that organization.

He joined U.P.E.C. Council No. 105, Hanford, on April 7, 1912. He served as Outside Guard in 1912, Inside Guard in 1913, Marshal in 1914, Master of Ceremonies in 1915, First Vice-President in 1916 and was elected President in 1917. He presided over the U.P.E.C. Convention in 1918 held in the City of Stockton. He served as Director during 1918-1919. During his term as President, he initiated 1,266 new members and organized Councils 159-163. U.P.E.C. membership at the time was 12,491, the highest number recorded in the lifetime of the organization. Assets amounted to $810,508.90.

He died on January 15, 1952 in Riverdale and was buried in the Lemoore Cemetery.

Twenty-Sixth President

JOSÉ CHRYSOSTOMO DA SILVEIRA

(1858—1925)

Born on October 5, 1858 at Flamengos, Faial, Azores. Prior to his coming to California, he served as Mayor of Horta, Faial and was the Chairman of the Board of Directors of Santa Casa da Misercordia, a hospital located on that island. He was one of the early settlers and pioneers of San Leandro. He married Marie and had five children: António, Marie, Helen (Lawrence) who served as Mayor of the city of San Leandro and the first woman to serve as Mayor in California, Joseph and Joaquin. He was possessed of a good heart and was always ready to assist any of his countrymen both here and on his home island. He promoted several music and theatrical shows to raise funds in order to assist charities in the Azores. One of the most important of such fund raising activities was held at the Oakland Auditorium on May 18, 1924.

He joined U.P.E.C. Council No. 1, San Leandro, on September 22, 1895 and was elected Vice-President in 1917. One year later he took the presidency. During his term of office there were 805 members initiated in the society, which numbered at the time 12,178 members with assets of $762,934.81. He presided at the U.P.E.C. Convention held in Oakland in 1919. In 1919 and 1920 he was elected to the Board of Directors. He was a member of the I.D.E.S., serving this organization in the capacity of Director and also as its Treasurer. He was affiliated with Cypress Camp and Woodmen of the World.

He died on October 31, 1925 and was buried at Holy Sepulchre Cemetery in Hayward on November 3, 1925.

177

FRANCISCO MONTEIRO SILVEIRA

(1881–1926)

Born on April 4, 1881 at Manadas, São Jorge, Azores. Silveira was the son of Manuel Machado Silveira and Maria Isabel Monteiro, both natives of Terreiros, Manadas, São Jorge. After attending elementary schools in Urzelina, São Jorge in 1903, he came to California and settled in the San Joaquin Valley. He was the principal owner and partner in a number of dairies, of which the most important was the Stevinson Home Ranch of 510 acres. There he opened a casein factory which brought him quite sizeable wealth. In 1918 he became the manager of a creamery in Newman, with a well-equipped shipping station from where milk and dairy products were distributed to a number of cities in the northern part of San Joaquin Valley. A few years later he ventured in banking in Newman, and as a result he lost most of his real estate holdings and money he had accumulated through the years. He then went to work for the Mutual Creamery in Patterson until his untimely death on January 22, 1926. He married Maria Ferreira, a native of São Jorge, and from this marriage there was a daughter named Evarista (Petropolis).

He joined U.P.E.C. Council No. 8, Pleasanton, on April 21, 1907 and transferred to Council No. 68, Newman, California. He was elected Marshal in 1916, Master of Ceremonies in 1917, Vice-President in 1918 and to the Presidency in 1919. He presided at the U.P.E.C. Convention held in Sacramento in 1920. During his administration he initiated 685 new members and organized Council No. 164, Ripon and 165, Byron. U.P.E.C. membership was then 11,615, with assets amounting to $800,277.15. He was elected to the Board of Directors in 1920 and served for one term only. He was affiliated with I.D.E.S., and the Holy Ghost Association of Newman, California.

He was buried at the Holy Sepulchre Cemetery in Hayward.

Twenty-Eighth President

ANTÓNIO RAULINO

(1873–1934)

Born on January 17, 1873 at Praia do Almoxarife, Faial, Azores. Raulino was the son of José Raulino and Maria Luis, both of Faial. António arrived in New Bedford, Mass. in 1891 aboard a whaling vessel. His work upon arrival was loading coal on the docks for shipment. In 1892 he came to Mono County to work in the mines, a job he held only one year. He then moved to Oakland where he opened a barber shop located on the corner of 17th and San Pablo Avenue. In 1910 he had already acquired a considerable amount of money and decided to go into the grocery business. He owned and operated Raulino's Grocery Store at 32nd and Linden Avenue in Oakland for quite a number of years, then sold it to become the President of the U.P.E.C. After his term of office as President he went to work for Breuner's of Oakland and became their field representative until retirement. He was married to Julia Castro, a native of Oakland, California, and from this marriage he had two sons: Dr. Fred Raulino and Dr. Clarence Raulino, both prominent optometrists in the San Leandro-Oakland areas.

He joined U.P.E.C. Council No. 25 of Oakland on December 27, 1896. He was elected Outside Guard of the Supreme Council in 1915, Inside Guard in 1916, Marshal in 1917, Master of Ceremonies in 1918, Vice-President in 1919 and President in 1920. He presided at the U.P.E.C. Convention held in Turlock in 1921. During his term of office he initiated 1,025 new members in the U.P.E.C. whose assets at the time amounted to $868,396.93 with a membership of 11,589. Raulino served on the Board of Directors in 1921-1922. He died on July 29, 1934.

Twenty-Ninth President

MANUEL SEVERINO SOARES

(1890–1948)

Born on December 26, 1890 in Urzelina, São Jorge, Azores. Soares was the son of João Severino Soares and Adelaide da Glória. At age 15 he immigrated to California and went to work as a farmhand on several ranches in the county. In 1930 he became the General Manager for Darigold Milk Co., Lted., at 1909 E. 14th Street, Oakland, and later formed the Daryglen Creameries Ltd., (later sold to Borden's) of Oakland, which he also managed for many years.

He was married to Amélia Luz Soares and from this union there were four children: Adelaide (Rogers), Dorothy (Botelho),

Rosalina (Morando) and Alfred.

Prior to his death on February 21, 1948 he retired from the dairy industry and was employed by Jackson's Furniture Co. of Oakland. He also presided over the Alameda County Milk Dealer's Association.

He joined U.P.E.C. Council No. 102, Melrose, on May 13, 1912. Soares was elected Outside Guard in 1916, Inside Guard in 1917, Marshal in 1918, Master of Ceremonies in 1919, Vice-President in 1920 and President in 1921. During his term of office there were 1,281 new members initiated in the order which at the time brought the total number of members to 11,617. Assets amounted to $937,326.17. He presided at the U.P.E.C. Convention held in Visalia in 1922. His affiliations other than U.P.E.C. included I.D.E.S. and Knights of Columbus. He was one of the organizers of the Magellan Council No. 2730 of the K.C. and later became its first Grand Knight. He was elected President of the Executive Committee for Portuguese Day at the Golden Gate Fair held in September 1939 at Treasure Island. Soares was buried at Holy Sepulchre Cemetery in Hayward, California.

Thirtieth President

FRANK MITCHELL JUNIOR

(1886—1932)

Born on November 24, 1886 in Portland, Maine. Mitchell was the son of Frank and Rosa (Amaral) Mitchell, natives of the Azores. In 1856 Frank came to Hayward, California, when he was eighteen months old. His parents upon arrival engaged in the retail shoe business until March 1927. One of his uncles came to California in 1856 and served in the Union Army during the Civil War. After Frank attended grammar schools in Hayward, and graduated from high school in 1906, he entered the University of California. Later he completed his studies at Hastings College of Law in San Francisco, receiving a Bachelor's Degree in June 1910.

During the 1907 session of the State Legislature he served as clerk.

In September 1910 he entered the law offices of Gibson & Woolner, remaining with that firm until 1915. In the previous year he had been elected Justice of the Peace for Eden Township defeating Judge D.V. Toffelmier of San Leandro. He served in the San Leandro Court, at the time housed in the Masonic Building, E. 14th and Juana Streets, where he worked daily between 10 A.M. and Noon, while keeping his law offices in the First National Bank Building in downtown Hayward. In 1912 he was appointed City Attorney for Hayward, an office he held through 1916 when he resigned.

From 1917 until 1922 he was associated with J.A. Kennedy and J.J. McDonald. On January 1, 1922 he was appointed chief deputy in the office of the prosecuting attorney of Alameda County under Ezra Decoto but later resigned that poistion in order to take up private practice.

He joined U.P.E.C. Council No. 3, Hayward, on April 21, 1907. He was elected Master of Ceremonies in 1920, Vice-President in 1921 and President in 1922, presiding over the U.P.E.C. Convention held in Arcata in 1923. During his term of office he initiated 587 new members in the society which at the time owned assets in the amount of $1,002,724,32 and had a state wide membership of 11,118. He was a member of the I.D.E.S., Cypress Camp, Woodmen of the World, Benevolent Protective Order of Elks, Young Men's Institute and the Knights of Columbus. His professional connections included the Alameda County Bar Association, of which he was Vice-President for ten years, and the California Bar Association.

He died on March 6, 1932 and was buried at Holy Sepulchre Cemetery in Hayward, California.

Thirty-First President

FRANK S. COSTA

(1880–1947)

Born on November 8, 1880 at Candelaria, Pico, Azores. Costa immigrated to California and settled in Lincoln. Married to Mary F. Costa.

He joined U.P.E.C. Council No. 76, Lincoln, on February 18, 1906. He was elected Outside Guard in 1917, Inside Guard in 1918, Marshal in 1919-1920, Master of Ceremonies in 1921, Vice-President in 1922 and President in 1923. Costa presided at the U.P.E.C. Convention held in San Luis Obispo in 1924. During his term of office there were 609 new members initiated in the U.P.E.C. Membership at the time numbered 10,702 with assets of $1,077,710.06. Costa never served on the Board of Directors. He died on October 17, 1947.

Thirty-Second President

JOSEPH ANTHONY FREITAS

(1889–1965)

Born on October 16, 1889 at Redwood Canyon, California. Freitas was the son of Jose Ricardo Freitas and Maria da Conceição King, both natives of the Island of Flores, Azores. Both parents were brought to California as children. The father came in 1857 when he was 15 years of age and the mother when she was six. His father engaged in farming in Monroe Valley, Alameda County, and also behind Lake Merritt in Oakland. Freitas' father died in Oakland in 1914. Joseph received his schooling in Olinda, Redwood Canyon, and at Garfield School. At the age of fifteen he was apprenticed to the plumbing trade and served for four years. He then bought a shop located in a basement on Fruitvale Avenue in Oakland. As his business steadily increased, he needed to find other quarters. He built a large shop at 2815 East 10th Street in Oakland, where he remained until 1955 when he sold his business and retired.

He was united in marriage to Florence King, a native of California. They had one daughter, Laverne, married to U.S. Air Force Colonel John Luque, a native of San Leandro, California, and of Spanish parentage. Florence died on April 1, 1942 and in 1945 Joseph married Louise Bauer, a native of Lavenworth, Kansas.

He joined U.P.E.C. Council No. 7, Oakland, on March 18, 1906. Freitas was elected Outside Guard in 1919, Inside Guard in 1920, Marshal in 1921, Master of Ceremonies in 1922, Vice-President in 1923 and President in 1924. During his term of office there were 1,627 new members initiated to the U.P.E.C. Membership at that time was 10,905 and assets amounted to $1,164,873.24. He presided at the U.P.E.C. Convention held in San Jose in 1925. He was one of the most popular figures within U.P.E.C. circles and in the Portuguese communities throughout the state. He learned to speak Portuguese within the Society he served since boyhood. In 1959 he was elected President for another term. During his last administration as President he initiated 874 new members. During his second administration he presided at the 1960 U.P.E.C. Convention held in Santa Maria, California. He served on the Board of Directors from 1925 through 1928, again in 1929, 1930, 1932 through 1934 and 1948. He was appointed to the Board to fill a vacancy left by the death of José Carlos Jorge in 1952 until 1959. He returned to the Board in 1960 through 1964. He was nicknamed "Fat Freitas" and "Mr. U.P.E.C." The latter name was a result of his great enthusiasm for the society, something he could never conceal. He presided over the League of Portuguese Fraternal Societies and many other committees including the one who brought over the Monument to the Portuguese Immigrant, which now stands in Root Park in downtown San Leandro. He held memberships in several organizations: the knights of the Maccabees, the Fraternal Order of Eagles, Loyal Order of Moose, the Druids, Native Sons of the Golden West, I.D.E.S., Knights of Columbus, Kiwanis Club, Young Men's Institute, Merchants Exchange, Oakland Chamber of Commerce, the National Plumbers Association, Saint Anthony Society, Cabrillo Civic Club of Alameda County, S.E.S., Santa Maria Magdalena and many others. At one time he presided over *Colonia Portuguesa,* a newspaper published in Oakland.

He died during a banquet held at the G.P.S. Hall, Gustine on March 23, 1965. He was buried at the Holy Sepulchre Cemetery in Hayward. A library of Portuguese works, located in the U.P.E.C. Cultural Center in San Leandro was named in his memory.

MANUEL GASPAR

(1884—1957)

Born on May 9, 1884 at São Mateus, Pico, Azores. He immigrated to Oakland, California in 1903 where, shortly after his arrival he opened a grocery store at 1923 E. 14th Street, which he operated for quite a number of years. Later he opened a similar market in Hayward. Gaspar's Market carried a good stock of Portuguese goods imported for the needs of the large Portuguese clientele in the area. He had interests in other companies such as the Prudential Mortgage Securities of Oakland where he served as Director. In later years he became President of the Dariglen Creameries Ltd. also of Oakland. He served as chairman of the Board of Directors for the *Colonia Portuguesa,* a bi-weekly Portuguese newspaper published in Oakland from March 18, 1924 through June 24, 1932 when merged with *Jornal de Noticias* and *O Imparcial,* both Portuguese papers. The *Noticias* was published in San Francisco on February 8, 1917 by Joaquin B. Menezes and *O Imparcial* published in Sacramento in Sacramento in 1903 by Manuel S. Quaresma, later sold to *Colónia Portuguesa,* until publication ceased in June 1932. The merger of the three newspapers resulted in the appearance of a new newspaper known as *Jornal Portugues,"* published from July 1, 1932, under different ownerships, namely P. L. Silveira and Albert S. Lemos. The *Colónia Portuguesa* was the successor to *Lavrador Portugues,* published by Arthur V. Avila and had some of the most hard working and popular Portuguese community leaders, such as António Martins da Silva as Manager, Dr. Abilio Reis, Alberto Moura, M.P. Silva, M.R. Homem, Adriano Moniz, serving as directors along with Eduardo Nascimento, José Afonso, Francisco Andrade, Silvano J. Pereira, M. Simões was secretary of the corporation, A Fernandes was Treasurer, A.D. Silva, A.M. Carvalho, Fernando Ferreira, António A. Amaral, Frank V. Fontes and Arthur Vieira Avila, as its Director and Editor.

In 1907 Gaspar married Miss Louisa Henas and they had one son, Alfred Gaspar, a real estate broker in Patterson. He joined U.P.E.C. Council No. 63, Oakland, on March 16, 1906 and was elected Vice-President in 1924. A year later he was elected to the presidency initiating 1,735 new members in the society, the largest initiation of membership. Gaspar presided at the U.P.E.C. Convention held in Merced in 1926. At that time U.P.E.C. membership was 11,304 and the organization had assets of $1,231,961.41. He was elected to the Board of Directors in 1926, 1927, 1932, and again on August 10, 1935 to fill the vacancy left as a result of the sudden death of Francisco I. Lemos.

He died on March 10, 1957 in Patterson, California, and was buried at Santa Maria Cemetery in Patterson.

THOMAS FRANCIS LOPES

(1888–1972)

Born on October 12, 1888 at San Luis Obispo. Lopes was the son of Manuel Joseph Lopes and Ann Lewis, both of Pico Island, Azores. He married Miss Marguerite Winant, a native of Newport, Oregon on January 3, 1914. Thomas attended elementary and secondary schools in San Luis Obispo and was a graduate of the University of California, Berkeley, where he received a degree in law in May of 1912. For a great number of years his office was located in the Helm Building, downtown Fresno, California. A son of Azorean immigrants, Tom was indeed a credit to the Portuguese in the state. He served for 13 years as President of the Democratic Party in the Fresno district, and director of the Fresno Fair Board, District 1, for approximately eight years.

In 1920 Dr. Abilio Reis, acting Vice-Consul of Portugal in the San Joaquin Valley, in Hanford, moved to Oakland and requested the Portuguese Government to appoint Thomas as his successor. As a result of Dr. Reis' recommendation, Tom was named Vice-Consul of Portugal, an office he held until 1929. Among his numerous affiliations were the I.D.E.S., the Commonwealth Club of San Francisco, Center Lodge No. 465 of the Masonic Order, the State and County Bar Association and the Boys Club of Fresno, Inc., which he presided for many years. As well as being a world traveller, Thomas accumulated a large fortune with real estate holdings in several California counties and Mexico. He changed the spelling of his name Lopez, leading some people to think he was of Spanish descent.

He joined U.P.E.C. Council No. 23, Fresno, on February 1, 1914. He was elected Inside Guard in 1922, Marshal in 1923, Master of Ceremonies in 1924, Vice-President in 1925 and President in 1926. During his term of office he initiated 1,132 new members and organized Council No. 166, French Camp. Membership numbered 11,901, and assets amounted to $1,299,348. He presided at the U.P.E.C. Convention held in Santa Maria in 1927 and was elected to the Board of Directors in 1927, serving in that capacity through 1948, and from 1951 through 1961. He acted as legal advisor to the U.P.E.C. for several years, a position created by the Board of Directors. He died on March 5, 1972.

FRANK SILVEIRA RODERICK

(1888—1952)

Born on August 16, 1888 at Feteira, Faial, Azores. Roderick immigrated to California, worked at different jobs and became a barber while studying law. He received a degree allowing him to practice in the Supreme Court of the United States. In 1920 he served as deputy clerk for Alameda County. He was director of the First Agricultural Association which promoted the California Garden Show. He married Christine Viveiros and had one son, Frank E. Roderick. His affiliations included the Alameda County Bar Association, I.D.E.S., Knights of Columbus, Elks, and Cabrillo Club No. 11 of Alameda County.

He joined U.P.E.C. Council No. 56 of Oakland on May 14, 1909 and was elected Vice-President in 1926 and President in 1927. During his term of office he initiated 990 new members. U.P.E.C. membership was 10,846 with assets amounting to $1,356,813.28.

He presided at the U.P.E.C. Convention held in Stockton in October of 1928. He served as Treasurer from 1929 through October 1948, Secretary-Treasurer until October 19, 1952, when he died. The office of Secretary-Treasurer was an elective one until October 15, 1952 when it became appointive by the Board of Directors. Roderick was buried at the Holy Sepulchre Cemetery in Hayward, California.

LUCINDO FREITAS

(1889—1934)

Born on January 30, 1889 at Fajã Grande, Flores, Azores. He immigrated to California in the early 1900s. He settled around Stockton where he operated the Nickolodium Theatre on Main Street. He married Vivian Almeida Santos and they had a daughter. He joined U.P.E.C. Council No. 23, Fresno, on September 4, 1909 and transferred to Council No. 24, Stockton, where he served as secretary for a few years. He was elected to the Supreme Council in 1914 as Outside Guard and Inside Guard in 1915, an office he declined in October 1916. In 1927 he was elected Vice-President and President in 1928. He presided over the U.P.E.C. Convention held in Oakland in 1929. During his term of office there were 588 new members initiated to the society, whose membership was 10,451, with assets amounting to $1,412,606.39.

He died in St. Joseph, Missouri after a visit to his home island in Flores in the Azores.

FRANCISCO EUSTACHIO PINHEIRO
(Frank E. Pine)

(1889–1961)

Born on September 20, 1889 at Ribeirin-ha, Faial, Azores. Pinheiro was the son of Francisco I. Pinheiro, a school teacher in Pedro Miguel, Azores, and of Luiza Carolina, also of the same island. Frank attended grammar school in Faial and completed his education at Horta High School. From there he enrolled in the Seminary at Angra do Heroismo, Terceira Island. In 1906 he came to Boston, Mass., where he worked as a barber until 1909. He opened a cleaners in Oakland which he operated for quite a number of years. In 1932 he became manager of Mission Chapel on Fruitvale Avenue, a mortuary owned by Freeman Cox, Roach and Kenney of Oakland. In 1934 he became a partner of Chris J. Borba and went into business under Hanrahan, Wadsworth, Pine and Borba Mortuary at the corner of E. 14th and 5th Avenue in Oakland, later known as East Lawn Chapel. At the time of his death he was associated with Robison Bros.

He joined U.P.E.C. Council No. 25 on February 14, 1909. He was elected Master of Ceremonies in 1927, Vice-President in 1928 and President in 1929. He presided at the U.P.E.C. Convention held in San Leandro in 1930. During his term of office he initiated 573 new members. Assets of the U.P.E.C. at the time he left the presidency amounted to $1,436,291.50 with 10,020 members. He served on the Board of Directors in 1930 through 1932, 1936, 1941 through 1943, 1945 and 1946. He was married to Anna R. Pinheiro, a native of Santa Cruz, California, and from this marriage they had a son. Later Francisco married Thelma Simaria, a native of Matriz, Horta, Faial, Azores. He was a member of the I.D.E.S., one of the founders and President of Cabrilho Club No. 11 of Alameda County, Holy Ghost Association Flor da Mocidade in West Oakland, Knights of Columbus and a charter member of the Lusitania Club. He was a musician and loved the theater. In his early years he took part in many theatrical groups.

He died on December 29, 1961 in Oakland and was buried at the Holy Sepulchre Cemetery in Hayward, California.

Thirty-Eighth President

FRANCIS JOSEPH LAZARUS

(1887–1966)

Born on October 6, 1887 in Mendocino, California. He was the son of Charles F. and Anna J. Lazarus. He came as a young man to San Jose where he attended school and graduated from the San Jose Normal School, now San Jose State College. He became a teacher in Warm Springs where he taught for eleven years. In 1920 he went to work for the old Growers Bank and moved two years later to the Bank of Italy, now Bank of America. He was assistant chief teller at the San Jose Main Branch until his retirement in 1952. He was married first to Margaret H., a native of Decoto, on April 30, 1919 and many years later became the husband of Mary. He was the father of Leonard and the step-father of Velma H. Silva. He was active in fraternal circles such as the I.D.E.S. and S.E.S., whom he served at one time as Treasurer, Columbos Grove, U.A.O.D. and the I.E.S., a Holy Ghost Society in San Jose.

He joined U.P.E.C. Council No. 32 San Jose, on April 25, 1909, transferred later to Council No. 67, Warm Springs in 1910 and readmitted to Council No. 32 in 1923 where he stayed until his death on December 22, 1966. He was elected Outside Guard in 1925, Inside Gaurd in 1926, Marshal in 1927, Master of Ceremonies in 1928, First Vice-President in 1929 and President in 1930. During his term of office he initiated 555 new members. U.P.E.C. membership at the time was 9,651 and the organization had assets in the amount of $1,461,425.94. Lazarus presided at the U.P.E.C. Convention held in Hollister in 1931. He was elected to the Board of Directors in 1931, 1932 and 1952, a position he resigned in February of 1953. He died on December 22, 1966 and was buried at the Calvary Cemetery in San Jose.

JOSEPH J. CARDOSO

(1888–1946)

Born on December 27, 1888 in Terceira, Azores. After attending elementary school, Cardoso enrolled in Angra do Heroismo Seminary. He immigrated to California and settled in Atwater around 1913 and married Mary G. He was employed by Capolino Cannery as a warehouse superintendent for a number of years before going to Planada to take over the job as superintendent of the Lawrence Warehouse Company. He was a Noble Arch of Merced Grove No. 36, Ancient Order of Druids. He joined U.P.E.C. Council No. 29, Merced, on November 9, 1913 and was elected Outside Guard in 1926, Inside Guard in 1927, Marshal in 1928, Master of Ceremonies in 1929, Vice-President in 1930 and President in 1931. He presided over the U.P.E.C. Convention held in Santa Maria in 1932. During his term of office there were 475 new members initiated in the U.P.E.C. Membership at the time was 8,952 and the organization possessed assets in the amount of $1,487,755. He served on the Board of Directors in 1932. He died on January 15, 1946 and was buried at the Calvary Cemetery in Merced.

ANTHONY JOSEPH SILVA

(1883–1955)

Born on November 21, 1883 at Mission San Jose, California. Silva was the son of Francisco José da Silva and Henriqueta, both native of Pico, Azores who settled in California around 1851. He attended Garfield School in Oakland. His first job was the cotton mill in Oakland. A few years later he became a molder for MacCaully Phoenix Iron Works. After leaving this company he opened a dry cleaning establishment, operating it under the name of Ideal Laundry in Oakland. He sold his business and became an insurance agent for five years. In 1921 he tried another venture, hardwood floor polishing, and opened an establishment at 3014 55th Avenue, Oakland, where he went into a business named New Method Floor Polishing. In 1947 he became Supreme Treasurer of the I.D.E.S., a position he held until 1953. He married Berniece Clementsen from Bluffs, Iowa, on October 15, 1937. From his former marriage he had four children: Elizabeth (Castellano), Thelma (Shearer), Beulah

Anthony Joseph Silva (in center).

(Baber) and Henry Silva.

He joined U.P.E.C. Council No. 56, Oakland, on May 5, 1901. He was elected Outside Guard in 1927, Inside Guard in 1928, Marshal in 1929, Master of Ceremonies in 1930, Vice-President in 1931 and President in 1932. He presided at the U.P.E.C. Convention held in 1933 at Vallejo, California. During his term of office he initiated 440 new members. Assets of the organization at the time were $1,438,405.51 with a membership of 8,186. He served as Supreme Director during 1933-34. He was active in many fraternal organizations, including the I.D.E.S., Sociedade Santo Cristo, Império de Santo António (Holy Ghost Association), Cabrillo Civic Club No. 11 of Alameda County, Native Sons of the Golden West, F.O.E., Moose, International Institute of Oakland, the Portuguese American Civic Club and Capitain of the League Cross Cadets (World War I Veterans). Anthony died on November 15, 1955.

Forty-First President

FRANCISCO ANTÓNIO FREITAS

(1882–1942)

Born on April 22, 1882 at Fazenda, Lajes, Flores, Azores. Freitas was the son of Filomeno J. Freitas and Francisca Mendonsa, both natives of Flores Island. After attending elementary school in the Azores he immigrated to the United States of America, settling in California around 1895. An orchardist in the West Side of Santa Clara Valley until 1939, he sold his business to operate a grocery store he owned in Santa Clara until his death on May 24, 1942. He was married to Mrs. Mabel I. Vierra, a native of New Bedford, Mass. Francisco, like many other immigrants, took exceptional pride in seeing, under very difficult financial circumstances, that his children received an education above average. He raised six children, three of whom became school teachers, one a banker, and the other a legal secretary: Eva G. (Maffey), Dillis M. Freitas, Adele C. (McLashan), William Earl Freitas, Vice-President Manager of Bank of America, Willow Glen Branch in San Jose for over twenty years, Louise (Van Dusen) and Lucille F. (Rubino). Francisco was a member of the S.E.S., I.D.E.S. Liberty Grove of the U.A.O.D., an organization he served as secretary. He was also very active in the California Prune and Apricot Growers Association and the original Santa Clara Water Conservation District Organization. He joined U.P.E.C. Council No. 28, Santa Clara, on August 5, 1906, transferred to Council No. 70, San Juan Bautista and then the U.P.E.C. Council No. 32, San Jose on November 10, 1912. He was elected Master of Ceremonies in 1931, Vice-President in 1932 and President in 1933. During his term of office he organized Council No. 167, Artesia, and initiated 578 new members in the U.P.E.C. whose total membership at the time was 7,960 with $1,429,639.17 in assets. He presided at the U.P.E.C. Convention held in 1934 in Santa Cruz, California. He served on the Board of Directors from 1929 through 1931 and 1934 through 1937.

Forty-Second President

FRANCISCO HIPÓLITO DA ROSA

(1886—1976)

Born on June 8, 1886 at Feteira, Faial, Azores. Rosa was the son of Manuel Francisco Rosa, a native of Feteira, Faial, and Maria (Garcia) da Rosa, a native of Candelaria Pico, Azores. He attended both private and public schools in Feteira, Faial, continuing his studies with Father Goulart. He immigrated to the United States, arriving on July 17, 1904 in New Bedford, Mass., aboard S/S Pátria of Brazil Lines. He then came to San Pablo and worked in the Pullman shops until 1907, when he went to work for the Standard Oil Company of Richmond until he retired in 1950. He became a citizen of the United States in 1918. As he prospered, he invested his savings in property in San Pablo and Richmond. He operated an apartment house of 52 rooms in San Francisco from 1920 through 1924. He was elected to the Sanitary Board of the City of San Pablo, a position he held from 1920 through 1942. He was married to the last Miss Josephine Fraga of Oakland. From this marriage there were three children, two died in infancy and one is still living, Genevieve Traverso.

He joined U.P.E.C. Council No. 27, San Pablo, on July 25, 1909. He was elected Outside Guard in 1929, Inside Gaurd in 1930, Marshal in 1931, Master of Ceremonies in 1932, Vice-President in 1933 and President in 1934. He presided at the Convention held in Hanford in 1935 and the only Special Session ever held in the history of the Supreme Council of U.P.E.C., which took place in 1935 in San Leandro. During his term of office he initiated 390 new members. Assets of U.P.E.C. amounted to $1,388,073.37 with a membership of 7,636. He was a member of the I.D.E.S., Benevolent Protective Order of Elks, Santa Maria Magdalena and the San Juan Baptista Holy Ghost Association. He died on December 28, 1976.

Forth-Third President

MANUEL JOHN PERRY

(1894—1958)

Born on November 9, 1894 in San Leandro, California. Perry was the son of João Pereira, a native of Feteira, Faial and Maria Vargas. His father served U.P.E.C. as sixteenth Supreme President. Manuel was better known as Manuel Jesse, a custodian in the San Leandro School District for many years. Before his death he was employed by Eastern Airlines as a stock clerk at the Oakland Airport.

He joined U.P.E.C. Council No. 1, San Leandro, on August 29, 1909 and was elected Outside Guard in 1930, Inside Guard in 1931, Marshal in 1932, Master of Ceremonies in 1933, Vice-President in 1934 and President in 1935. During his term of office there were 776 new members initiated in the society whose assets at the time amounted to $1,395,637. The total membership of the society was 7,452, the lowest since 1907. He presided at the U.P.E.C. Convention held in Oakland in 1936. He was elected to the Board of Directors in 1936 and served through 1938, 1942 and 1944. He died on December 28, 1958 in Fresno and was buried at Liberty Cemetery in that city.

Forty-Fourth President

JOSEPH THOMAS LOPES

Born on April 2, 1909 at Placerville, California. Lopes is the son of Joseph T. Lopes and Anna P. Lopes, both natives of Pico, Azores. He married Alma M., a native of San Francisco, California, on November 29, 1931. He is the father of Albert J. Lopes. Lopes was self-employed in diversified farming all of his life. He served as a member and chairman of the Board of Education in Winton, California for over sixteen years. He was chairman of the local Fire District and Director of the Soil Conservation District, Sacramento County. He is affiliated with I.D.E.S. and S.E.S. fraternal societies.

He joined the U.P.E.C. Council No. 11, Sacramento on August 24, 1924. He was elected Outside Guard in 1931, Inside Guard in 1932, Marshal in 1933, Master of Ceremonies in 1934, Vice-President in 1935 and President in 1936. During his term of office there were 762 new members admitted in the various councils of U.P.E.C. Total membership at the time numbered 7,516 and assets amounted to $1,396,833. He presided at the U.P.E.C. Convention held in 1937 in Sacramento, California. He was also elected to the Board of Directors from 1937-1939.

MANUEL VIEIRA ALVES

(1894—1969)

Born on December 21, 1894 at Santa Cruz sas Ribeiras, Pico, Azores. Alves was the son of José Vieira Alves and Maria Simas Gaspar, both natives of Pico Island. He immigrated to California in 1911 to join his uncles in Sausalito. He was first employed at Mare Island, and in 1920 moved to Oakland. Here he was employed by Hogan Lumber Co. for a number of years. He retired from Western Sash and Door Company in 1963. In 1942 he married Miss Leopoldina Carmen Rodrigues, a native of São Mateus, Pico, Azores, and former President of S.P.R.S.I. and Treasurer from 1927-1945. Leopoldina also served as Secretary from 1945 through 1967. His affiliations included the Knights of Columbus, I.D.E.S., Eagles and Holy Ghost Association.

He joined U.P.E.C. Council No. 25, Oakland, on December 3, 1928. Alves was elected Outside Guard in 1932, Inside Guard in 1933, Marshal in 1934, Master of Ceremonies in 1935, Fice-President in 1936 and President in 1937. During his term of office he initiated 972 new members and organized Council No. 170, Snelling. Assets of the U.P.E.C. amounted to $1,431,031 with a total membership of 7,744. He presided at the U.P.E.C. Convention held in Chico in 1938. He also served on the Board of Directors from 1938 through 1940.

He died on June 28, 1969 and was buried at Holy Sepulchre Cemetery in Hayward.

ANGELO RAMOS IGNACIO

(1902—1966)

Born on January 3, 1902 at Lages, Flores, Azores. Son of Jose Ignacio and Maria, both natives of Flores Island. He immigrated to the United States in 1924 and came to California to join his sister Maria Luisa Mendonca, owner of a grocery store in Vallejo. Angelo worked in the grocery store until 1953 when he moved to San Jose with his family to work for the Santa Clara County Hospital. He was married to Mary and had two children, Jerome and Irene (Chaney). He was a member of the I.D.E.S. and Y.M.I.

He joined U.P.E.C. Council No. 73, Vallejo, on September 18, 1927. In 1955 he transferred to Council No. 32, San Jose. Ignacio was elected Outside Guard in 1933, Inside Guard in 1934, Marshal in 1935, Master of Ceremonies in 1936, Vice-President in 1937 and President in 1938. He presided at the U.P.E.C. Convention in Oakland in 1939. During his term of office there were 751 new members initiated. He organized Council No. 171, King City, California. Total membership at the time he left office was 7,720, with $1,440,230 in assets. He was elected to the Board of Directors in 1939 and 1940.

He died on October 30, 1966 in San Jose and was buried at the Golden Gate National Cemetery in San Bruno, California.

Forty-Seventh President

MANUEL AUGUSTO FREITAS

(1883–1954)

Born on August 19, 1883 at Vila de Santo Espirito, Santa Maria, Azores. He was son of José Maria de Freitas and Maria Jacinta de Chaves. He immigrated on September 23, 1904 to San Leandro. He was employed by Western Pacific Railway in the construction of railroad lines in the Livermore mountains (Altamont Pass). Later in 1913, he purchased agricultural land in San Leandro, including a farm on 143rd Avenue, between E. 14th Street and Washington Avenue. He grew cherries, apricots, pears, corn, cucumbers and other fruits and vegetables for East Bay Markets. On December 15, 1913 he married Miss Mamir Rosely, a native of San Leandro. From this marriage he had two sons, Frank and George Freitas. He was a member of the I.D.E.S.

He joined U.P.E.C. Council No. 55 of San Leandro on May 10, 1908 and was elected Outside Guard in 1934, Inside Guard in 1935, Marshal in 1936, Master of Ceremonies in 1937, Vice-President in 1938 and President in 1939. He presided at the U.P.E.C. Convention held in Turlock in 1940. During his administration he initiated 669 new members. At the time U.P.E.C.'s total membership was 7,631, with assets amounting to $1,488,506. He served on the Board of Directors during 1940-1941.

He died on December 18, 1954 and was entombed at Holy Sepulchre Cemetery in Hayward, California.

ARTHUR SILVEIRA SOUSA

(1893–1971)

Born on March 20, 1893 in Boston, Mass. Sousa was the son of Andrew Silveira Sousa of Terceira, Azores and Ana Sousa, a native of Boston, Mass. Arthur's father was a merchant marine labor contractor and for a number of years he travelled between Boston and Horta, Faial, Azores. In 1900 he took his son Arthur to the Azores, where as a young boy he remained until 1910 when he returned to the United States to San Francisco, California. He remained a few years in that city as a clerk at one of the many Portuguese-owned hotels in the downtown area. In 1913 he moved to Hanford where he was employed on a ranch for the next nine years. In the middle of 1922 he went to work as a store clerk for the Farmer's Hardware where he remained until 1936, when he went into business for himself and opened a grocery store called the Golden State Market, at the corner of Tenth Avenue and 7th Street in Hanford.

On November 18, 1913 he married Maria Dutra Sousa, the daughter of João Dutra, who served as Supreme President of the U.P.E.C. in 1918. Miss Dutra was born in Ribeirinha, Terceira, Azores. In California she was active in fraternal circles, serving as President of the U.P.P.E.C. (União Portuguesa Protectora do Estado da California). From their marriage they had three sons: Arthur, Alberto and Edward.

He was a member of the I.D.E.S., S.E.S., United National Life Insurance Society and I.S.A.S.M. (Irmandade de Santo António de Socorros Mutuos). Arthur and his wife Maria were active in Radio Broadcasting beginning in 1952, when they started a Portuguese Hour, Ecos dos Açores. The program continued under the directorship of Mrs. Sousa until October 1969.

He joined U.P.E.C. Council No. 119, Riverdale and transferred in 1921 to Council No. 195, Hanford. He was elected Outside Guard in 1935, Inside Guard in 1936, Marshal in 1937, Master of Ceremonies in 1938, Vice-President in 1939 and President in 1940. He presided at the U.P.E.C. Convention in Los Banos, California in 1941. During his term of office he initiated 741 new members. U.P.E.C. membership then was 7,730 with assets totaling $1,524,490. He was elected to the Board of Directors in 1941 and served one term. He died on January 17, 1971 in Hanford, California.

FERNANDO AUGUSTO SILVEIRA
(Fred A. Silveira)
(1907—1989)

Born on March 21, 1907 at Merced, California. Silveira is the son of José Augusto Silveira, a native of Fajã Grande, Flores, Azores and Ana Escobar Silveira, a native of Providence, Rhose Island. He attended elementary and high schools in Merced and the University of California at Berkeley and graduated in 1932. One year later he received his degree in law and was admitted to the California State Bar. As a young man he spent some years in the Bay Area delivering the *San Francisco Call* and *Post, San Francisco Examiner* and the *Chronicle.* Later he moved to Merced where he worked as a janitor in the *Merced Sun* and Western Union Buildings. In 1921 he worked as a linotypist for the *Merced Sun,* and later was promoted to the advertising department as a reporter for that newspaper.

His Berkeley campus activities covered a variety of fields, from waiter to band leader. From 1925 through 1929 he waited tables at the *Alpha Ipslon Phi* Sorority, Berkeley Country Club and in 1929 managed a famous marching band. His love for journalism led him to write for the *Daily California* in 1927. On July 15, 1942, nine years after his graduation, he joined the Armed Forces. His skills in communications led him to be in command of radio counter-intelligence forces (O.S.S., Office of Strategic Services) in Africa and Western Europe. He joined as a private in the Army and was discharged with high honors as a Lieutenant-Colonel and received two battle stars for the Italian and Southern France campaigns.

He served as District Attorney for Merced County from 1934 through 1939. In 1941 he was hired as a special prosecutor for two years to handle a kidnapping case and the enforcement of bovine tuberculosis tests in Merced County, the last one to be cleared in the United States. In 1946 he returned to private practice. He was named Assistant City Attorney for Merced in 1947 and later District Attorney. In 1950 he became Chief Radio Officer for Merced County Civil Defense (Emergency Communications). He was named Man of the Year by the citizens of Merced in 1961.

He loves youth and to them he has given his best. Activities among the Boy Scouts range from photography to Morse Code. He taught this international code to over 1,200 boys. He often refers to Thomas Burr, a youngster he helped with his Electronic Engineering Degree, and who at the present is with the Polaris Submarine Service.

He joined U.P.E.C. Council No. 29, Merced on March 19, 1933 and was elected Outside Guard in 1936, Inside Guard in 1937, Marshal in 1938, Master of Ceremonies in 1939, Vice-President in 1940 and President in 1941-1942. However, due to his draft into the Army he was unable to preside at the Convention held in 1942 in the City of Oakland. During his term of office there were 518 members initiated. Assets of the U.P.E.C. amounted to $1,581,428 with a membership of 7,665. He is in part responsible for the youth movement in the U.P.E.C. During his term of office, and through his suggestions and efforts, they organized what was known, for many years, as the Juvenile Class, of which John Alfred, his son who died in 1948, became the first youth member in the Ist of 500 needed to create the youth branch within the U.P.E.C. He married Helen Marie, a native of Merced on January

4, 1937 and has two children: Fred Brooks Silveira and Helen Ann (Thompson). He is a member of the I.D.E.S., S.E.S., Holy Ghost Association (Buhach Pentecost), Knights of Columbus, Fraternal Order of Eagles, Elks, Rotary Club, Merced Chamber of Commerce and the American Bar Association.

He died on December 7, 1989 and was buried at the Evergreen Mausoleum in Merced, California.

Fiftieth President

MANUEL CABRAL

(1903—1966)

Born on August 16, 1903 at Ribeirinha, Pico, Azores. Cabral was the son of Manuel Cabral and Maria Glória (Silva) Cabral, both natives of Ribeirinha, Pico. He immigrated to California at the age of eight, settling around Sacramento where he attended Lincoln School. In 1925 he married Mary. At this time he was working as a haypress laborer. In 1933 he obtained employment with Swift Meat Packing Company, becoming a Plant Superintendent in 1944. Later he went into the grocery retail business operating three markets: Freeport, Manor and Delmar Markets until 1960 when he retired. While in the grocery business he was associated with Manuel Neves, a good friend of his. From his marriage there were five children: Richard, Madeline (Cardoso), Dorothy (Netto), Mary Jane (Neto) and Joseph Cabral.

He joined U.P.E.C. Council No. 40 (consolidated in 1933 with Council No. 11) of Sacramento. He was elected Outside Guard in 1937, Inside Guard in 1938, Marshal in 1939, Master of Ceremonies in 1940, Vice-President in 1941 and President in 1942. He presided over the U.P.E.C. Convention held in Sacramento in 1942 and 1943. During his term of office he initiated 455 new members. Assets of the U.P.E.C. at the time amounted to $1,633,549 with a membership of 8,268. He served on the Board of Directors in 1943, 1945 through 1949, 1952 and 1958 through 1963.

He never forgot his homeland and made a few trips to renew acquaintances and help the people of his village, always contributing some financial aid towards projects improving the lives of his friends and relations in faraway Ribeirinha, Pico. On his last trip he suffered a heart attack and died suddenly at his birthplace on June 4, 1966. He was buried later in Sacramento, California.

VALENTIM MACEDO GARCIA

(1905—1982)

Born on January 22, 1905 at Prainha do Galeão (São Caetano), Pico, Azores. Garcia is the son of Manuel Joaquim Garcia and Maria Delfina, both of São Caetano, Pico. He attended elementary school if Pico and the Horta High School is Faial, Azores. He immigrated to the United States in 1920, aboard *Roma,* Faber Line, landing in Providence, Rhode Island. He worked as a weaver at Coshnet Mill in New Bedford until 1922, when he came to Walnut Grove, California to work in a dairy. A month later he moved to Manteca as a farmhand. Not happy with job, he decided to seek employment with the California Transportation Steam Boat Company as a deckhand aboard Isleton Steamboat and Patch, travelling the Sacramento River between San Francisco and the State Capitol until May 7, 1925. Later he tried his hand as backtender at Fiber Board Paper Mill and remained with it until 1941 when he moved to San Francisco to work as an orderly at Franklin Hospital. In 1947 he went to work for the Southern Pacific Hospital at the corner of Fallon and Bacon Streets, San Francisco until 1954 when he took to the painting trade and went to Pacific Grove as a decorator until late 1957. A few months later he decided to settle in Gustine, where he worked for the West Side Hospital in 1962 and the San Luis Convalescent Hospital in Newman until December 1968. He left that job to become a Field Representative for the U.P.E.C., whose duties consisted of assisting the President in Official Visits throughout the state.

He joined U.P.E.C. Council No. 51, Antioch, on October 4, 1925, transferring to Council No. 37, Monterey in 1950 and then to Council No. 68, Newman. He is now a member of U.P.E.C. Council No. 12 in Watsonville.

He was elected Outside Guard in 1938, Inside Guard in 1939, Marshal in 1940, Master of Ceremonies in 1941, Vice-President in 1942 and President in 1943. During his administration he initiated 364 new members in the organization whose assets at the time amounted to $1,696,201 with a membership of 8,180. Upon medical advice he did not preside at the convention held in 1944 in San Jose, California.

He died on March 23, 1982 and was buried at the Holy Cross Cemetery in Antioch, California.

MANUEL PEREIRA

(1892–1973)

Born on March 4, 1892 at Lages, Pico, Azores. Pereira was the son of Manuel Pereira Bagaço and Francisca de Brum Macedo, both natives of Pico. He immigrated to the United States in 1911. Upon his arrival in California he began working on a dairy farm, buying one for himself four years later. In 1916, during World War I, he sold his farm and enlisted in the C.A.C. Corps and was sent overseas. After three years in the Armed Forces he was discharged and resumed civil life with Union Iron Works in San Francisco, a job he held for a few months. He moved later in 1919 to Hanford where he settled, operating a dairy farm again.

He served on the Board of Directors of the Danish Creamery for 25 years and one year as Chairman. He also served for several years on the Board of Directors of Challenge Creameries of California. He worked for eight years as a Field Representative for the A.P.P.B. He served for several years as a trustee of the Excelsior School. On November 16, 1919 he was married to Modesta, a lady of Italian descent.

He joined U.P.E.C. Council No. 22, Hanford, on December 2, 1917. He was elected President in 1944 and 1945 and presided at the U.P.E.C. Conventions held in San Jose in 1945 and Tulare in 1946. In his two successive administrations he initiated 1,143 new members. He organized Council No. 172 in Orland. Membership of the society numbered 8,403 in the year 1945 and 8,646 in 1946, with assets of $1,766.211 and $1,821,790. He was elected to the Board of Directors from 1937 through 1943, and again in 1946. He died on November 9, 1973 and was buried at the Calvary Cemetery in Hanford, California.

FRANCISCO SANTOS MENDONSA

(1895—1983)

Born on September 19, 1895 at Bandeiras Pico, Azores. Mendonsa is the son of José Francisco dos Santos Mendonsa and Rita de Lourdes Andrade, both natives of Bandeiras, Pico. He immigrated to California on September 1, 1921 and went to work for the Continental Salts Work Co. in Alvarado until 1924. On July 25, 1925 he moved to Hughson to work for the Hughson Condensed Milk Co. until October 1929 when he purchased some farmland to operate a dairy in Turlock until 1953, when he retired.

He was appointed to the Board of Directors of Stanislaus County Fair by Governor Edmund G. Brown in 1961 and served as its Chairman in 1968 and 1969. His activities in support of the vast numbers of Portuguese, who for years have settled around Turlock, covered a variety of fields, from translator and notary public to a to a teacher of night classes at Turlock High School from 1962 through 1965. He helped many Portuguese immigrants attain United States citizenship. In October 1949 he began his own radio broadcast show with KTUR radio station (now KCEY) where his commentary and Portuguese music could be heard seven days a week. His show was called Frankly Speaking.

On January 26, 1920 he married Miss Maria de Lourdes Andrade, a native of Feteira, Faial, Azores. He has three sons and one daughter: Frank M. Mendonsa, Deputy Sheriff in Los Banos, California; Gilbert, Vice-President of the Commonwealth Bank in San Francisco; Caton Lawrence, Chief Examiner for the First Western Bank and Maria Dolores (Azevedo).

He joined U.P.E.C. Council No. 75 on January 19, 1936 and was elected Outside Guard in 1940, Inside Guard in 1941, Marshal in 1942, Master of Ceremonies in 1943 and 1944, Vice-President in 1945 and President in 1946. He presided at the U.P.E.C. Convention held in San Diego jointly with S.P.R.S.I. in 1947. During his term of office he initiated 561 new members in the U.P.E.C., which then had a total membership of 8,832 with assets amounting to $1,903,520. He was elected to the Board of Directors in 1947 through 1949 and appointed to the Board on February 14, 1953 to fill the vacancy caused by Manuel R. Furtado's resignation.

He died on July 19, 1983 and was buried at the Turlock Memorial Park Cemetery in Turlock, California.

Fifty-Fourth President

LOUIS LESLIE VIEIRA

Born on July 9, 1915 in Modesto, California. He is the son of Antonio J. and Maria Soares, both of Azores, Portugal. He attended Hughson High School, Modesto Junior College, Golden Gate Law School, Cal-State and Los Angeles City College. He was employed as a Field Representative by the California State Auto Association for four years. Later he became a Branch Manager with Zurick Insurance Company, a position he held for four years. In 1971 he became the Operations Manager for Wilshire Insurance Company, with headquarters in Los Angeles. Later he moved to Grants Pass, Oregon.

He married Miss Patricia Marie, a native of Turlock, on September 10, 1939. From this marriage there were two sons and one daughter: António J., Louis Leslie Jr. and Kathleen Marie.

He joined U.P.E.C. Council No. 116, Hughson, on March 4, 1936, later transferred to Council No. 95, Bakersfield, and in 1951 to Council No. 167, Artesia. He was elected Outside Guard in 1941, Inside Guard in 1942, Marshal in 1943 and 1944, Master of Ceremonies in 1945, Vice-President in 1946 and President in 1947. He presided over the U.P.E.C. Convention in 1948 held in the City of Oakland, California. He was elected to the Board of Directors in 1948, 1959 and 1969 through 1971. During his term of office he initiated 603 new members in the U.P.E.C. whose assets at the time amounted to $1,896,593.

Fifty-Fifth President

ALBERTO CARVALHAL SILVEIRA

(1902–1967)

Born on July 26, 1902 at Fajã Grande, Calheta, São Jorge, Azores. Silveira was the son of José Machado de Borba and Maria Serafina Carvalhal Silveira, both natives of the Azores. He immigrated to the United States in 1919 after attending grammar school in Calheta, São Jorge. He first worked in a dairy in Crows Landing and later formed a partnership with his brother-in-law, Frank Couto, in a dairy until 1932 when he became self-employed. He served as Field Organizer and later as Director of Public Relations for the U.P.E.C. He led an interesting life in California and was very active in theatrical groups and singing on various Portuguese radio programs, one of them in Modesto, California, jointly broadcasted over KTRB with Arthur V. Avila.

He joined U.P.E.C. Council No. 130, Patterson on August 23, 1931. He was elected Outside Guard in 1942, Inside Guard in 1943 and 1944, Marshal in 1945, Master of Ceremonies in 1946, Vice-President in 1947 and President for two consecutive terms 1948 and 1949. He presided at the U.P.E.C. Conventions held in Sacramento and Merced. During both terms he initiated 1,053 members. He served as Director from 1950 through 1953. While Field Organizer he was named again to the Vice-Presidency of the Supreme Council but declined that nomination a few years later. He was married to the late Margarida and at the time of his death was the husband of Emily Silveira, a native of Concord, California. From his first marriage he had three children: Guilherme, Carmen and Albert Delwyn. Albert died in Fresno during a reception held in honor of the President of the U.P.E.C. On June 18, 1967. He was buried at the Patterson District Cemetery.

Fifty-Sixth President

JOHN BETTENCOURT SIMAS

(1907–1968)

Born on May 16, 1907 at Ribeira do Meio, Pico, Azores. Simas was the son of António Simas and Maria Jesus Bettencourt, both natives of Pico. He immigrated to California in 1929. Upon arrival he became employed by the Golden State Creamery in San Francisco, then later moved to Orland, California, where he stayed for a short while. He returned to the Bay Area and was employed until 1930 by Greenbrae Creamery in San Francisco. He then left to form an accounting firm. He graduated from Heald's Business College of San Francisco on December 6, 1931. He worked his way up from a dairy worker to a Public Accountant. On February 1, 1931 he married Frances Amelia who became the first pianist of U.P.E.C. John was a partner in several ventures: farming and restaurant businesses and served as President of the San Francisco Chapter of the Society of American Accountants, and as Financial Secretary of Cabrillo Civic Club No. 1 (founded on January 29, 1934 in San Francisco).

On November 20, 1937 he joined U.P.E.C. Council No. 30, San Francisco, which merged with Council No. 15. He was elected Inside Guard in 1947, Master of Ceremonies in 1948, Vice-President in 1949 and President in 1950. He presided at the U.P.E.C. Convention held in Bakersfield in 1951. During his administration he initiated 371 new members. U.P.E.C. assets at the time amounted to $2,142,441. He served on the Board of Directors in 1951, 1952, 1955 and 1956. He died on May 7, 1968 and was laid to rest at Holy Cross Cemetery in San Francisco, California.

MANUEL DA ROSA FURTADO

(1896—1981)

Born on January 1, 1896 at Salão, Faial, Azores. He is the son of António da Rosa Furtado and Maria Filomena da Glória, both natives of Faial Islands. He immigrated to California in 1914 and went to work for his brother, Jose da Rosa, in Stevinson. In 1917 he became a partner with his brother Jose, then sold his business in 1918. In 1920 he settled in Tracy with a large dairy that has been operating ever since. He served as chairman of the Dairy Department of San Joaquin County for seven years and director of the Valley Stock Marketing Association from 1930 to 1945. He was also president of the Byron-Bethany Irrigation District, member of the Milk Control Board (1936-1964) and trustee for the Lummersville (San Joaquin County) Elementary School District (1941-1949).

He has been married since 1920 to Olympia Machado Victorino, a native of Angustias, Faial, Azores, and has two sons and three daughters: Manuel Furtado, Antonio, Evelina (Costa), Eduina (Serventi) and Leodina Furtado.

He joined U.P.E.C. Council No. 137, Tracy on April 30, 1919 and was elected Marshal in 1948, Master of Ceremonies in 1949, Vice-President in 1950 and President in 1951. He presided at the U.P.E.C. Convention held in Tracy in 1952. During his term of office he initiated 592 new members and organized Council No. 173, Escalon. He was elected to the Board of Directors in October 1952 and served until February 14, 1953. He then resigned to take the Presidency again, this time for only eight months. He presided on his second term at the Convention held in Monterey, and initiated 479 new members. Assets of the society during this period were $2,183,925 in 1952 and $2,243,428 in 1953, and membership numbered 8,718. He was elected to the Board of Directors in October 1953 and served until October 1954.

He died on February 1, 1981 and was buried at the Tracy Public Cemetery, Tracy, California.

JOÃO FERREIRA NUNES

Born on January 14, 1906 at Terra do Pão, São Caetano, Pico, Azores. Nunes is the son of António Ferreira Nunes and Maria José, both natives of Pico Island. He immigrated to the United States aboard the *Britania,* Faber Line, landing in Providence, Rhode Island on February 15, 1926. He came to California and worked for his brother António from 1926 through 1927. A few years later he formed a partnership with his brother Manuel who operated a dairy, and in 1930 Nunes moved to Patterson. There he operated his own dairy until 1936 when he sold his business to go into diversified farming. He bought a 222 acre farm with his son in the partnership for three years. On November 4, 1929 he married Miss Emilia, a native of Cedros, Faial, Azores. From this marriage he had a son and a daughter: John F. Junes Jr. and Helen Jean (Smith).

He is a Past President of the Americanization Committee, member of the Farm Bureau, State Chamber of Commerce, Advisory Board for the Sacred Heart Church, Patterson, California and of the Patterson Water District for 24 years, five of which he served as chairman of its Board of Directors.

He joined U.P.E.C. Council No. 108, Crows Landing, on September 25, 1927 and transferred in 1941 to Council No. 130 in Patterson. He was elected Vice-President in 1952 and President in 1953. John presided at the U.P.E.C. Convention held in Modesto in 1954. During his term of office he initiated 517 new members in the organization which at the time had a total membership of 9,715. He served on the Board of Directors of U.P.E.C. in 1954, 1955 and 1959 through 1962.

MANUEL IGNACIO MENDONÇA
(Manuel E. Mendonca)

(1905—1985)

Born on April 11, 1905 at Rua da Matriz, Corvo, Azores. Mendonca is the son of João Ignacio Mendonca and Rosa Branca Avelar, both natives of Corvo Island. He immigrated to the United States aboard the *Britania,* Faber Line Steamship Company, landing in Providence, Rhode Island in 1922. He came to Merced and, as his first job drove mules for Crocker-Hoffman Farming until 1926. A few years later he went into business for himself and engaged in diversified farming. In 1948 he worked as a Field Representative for the Gene Mondo and Jack Melon Buying and Shipping Company, a job he held for one year in Merced, California. From 1928 through 1963 he operated a dairy off Trindade Road in Merced. He served on the Human Relations Committee of Merced in 1966. In 1926 he married Angelina Bessie, a native of Merced.

He joined U.P.E.C. Council No. 29, Merced, on December 14, 1924. Mendonça was elected Outside Guard in 1950, Inside Guard in 1951, Master of Ceremonies in 1952, Vice-President in 1953 and President in 1955. During his administration he initiated 644 new members and presided at the U.P.E.C. Convention held in Sacramento in 1955. At that time assets of the society amounted to $2,470,531 with a membership of 10,124. He was elected to the Board of Directors from 1955 through 1966, 1970 through 1974 and 1976.

He died on February 23, 1985 and was buried at the Calvary Cemetery in Merced, California.

Sixtieth President

VICENTE FRANCISCO AZEVEDO

(1894–1970)

Born on February 23, 1894 at Piedade, Pico, Azores. Azevedo was the son of Manuel Francisco Azevedo and Joaquina Candida Vicente. He was also known as Vicente Francisco Nunes and Vicente de Azevedo Nunes. He immigrated to California in 1911 and was first employed on a farm in Rio Vista. Later he was employed by the Public Works Department of that city and retired in 1955. He married Filomena Leal on June 30, 1919 and was the father of Ernestina and Vicente Azevedo. He visited his homeland several times and was noted for his love for Piedade, his birthplace, where he helped several projects for the betterment of his fellow compatriots.

He joined U.P.E.C. Council No. 47, Rio Vista, on September 16, 1911 and was elected Marshal in 1952, Master of Ceremonies in 1953, Vice-President in 1954 and President in 1955. During his term of office he initiated 672 new members. U.P.E.C.'s total membership at the time was 10,867 with assets amounting to $2,535,023. He presided at the U.P.E.C. Convention held in San Jose in 1956. In 1960 he was again elected to the presidency. During his second term he initiated 363 new members. U.P.E.C.'s total membership had reached 11,284 with assets amounting to $2,898,019. He was elected to the Board of Directors in 1948 through 1951, 1956, 1957 and 1961. In his second term he presided at the U.P.E.C. Convention held in Oakland in 1961. He died on November 19, 1970 in Rio Vista, California.

MIGUEL BORBA AZEVEDO

(1888—1966)

    Born on April 16, 1888 at Norte Grande, São Jorge, Azores. Borba was the son of Manuel J. Azevedo and Bárbara Ermelinda Bettencourt. He immigrated to California in 1905 where he worked in a dairy for a few years. Later he bought his own ranch which he operated until his retirement in 1942. He married Maria A. Simas, a native of Pico, Azores, on February 4, 1918. He had two children: Ernest and Julia (Pedersen). He served as director of the First National Bank in Crows Landing, California, director of the First Western Bank of Newman, California and director of the Portuguese-American Creamery.

    He joined U.P.E.C. Council No. 68, Newman, on December 16, 1906 and later transferred to Council No. 108, Crows Landing. He was elected Second Vice-President in 1955 and President in 1956. During his term of office there were 543 new members initiated in the organization which at the time had a membership of 11,239 and owned assets totalling $2,622,569. He presided at the U.P.E.C. Convention held in Monterey in 1957. He was elected to the Board of Directors in 1933 through 1936, 1938 through 1942, 1944 through 1946 and 1957 through 1960. He died on August 27, 1966 in Salida and was buried at the Hills Ferry Cemetery in Crows Landing, California.

SAMUEL MACHADO LINO

(1895—1977)

    Born on March 10, 1895 at Ribeirinha, Pico, Azores. Lino was the son of Manuel Machado Lino and Rosa da Conceição Alvernaz, both natives of Ribeirinha. After attending school in his home village he went to work on a farm owned by his parents. In June 1915 he immigrated to Sacramento, California, where he worked as a dairyman for six months. In 1917 he went to work on a rolling mill of the Southern Pacific Railway shop in the State Capitol for two years, then returned to dairy work in Holt Station. Later he purchased a farm of his own in Varona. In 1923 he sold his dairy business and went to work for the City of Stockton for a year, and in 1927 opened a service station after having tried the poultry business. Early in 1928 he moved to Sausalito to work for the Nunes Brothers. One of the brothers, Manuel I. Nunes, was his brother-in-law. He stayed with them for nearly eight years then went into contracting on his own. In September, 1939 he obtained employment with the Navy Yard at Mare Island and retired in 1957. He married Catarina Mello, a native of Santo Amaro, Pico, Azores on March 27, 1921. From this marriage he had four children: Manuel, George Pedro, Beatriz (MacMurray), and Laura (Hendricks).

He joined U.P.E.C. Council No. 126, Holt on August 10, 1919 and later transferred to Council No. 24, Stockton, then in March 1929 moved to Council No. 14, Sausalito. He was elected Vice-President in 1956 and President in 1957. During his term of office there were 455 new members initiated in the U.P.E.C. whose membership at the time was 10,651 with assets totalling $2,690,469. He presided at the U.P.E.C. Convention held in Arcata in 1958. He served on the Board of Directors in 1958 and 1959. He died on January 21, 1977.

Sixty-Third President

EDWARD CLEMENT MASSA

(1907—1989)

Born on May 7, 1907 at Hayward, California. Massa is the son of Manuel Maria Nascimento Massa, a native of Freixe de Espada a Cinta, Portugal, and Camilla Cotta of Terceira, Azores. He attended Hayward Grammar School (1916), Hayward Union High School (1922) and Saint Mary's College, receiving his A.B. Degree in 1929. He also attended the University of Notre Dame, receiving a Juris Doctor Degree in 1933. He taught Commercial Law, English and Political Science for several years.

In 1935 he opened an insurance office and later became a Realtor and Developer. He married Grace Francis Tomley, a native of Wrexham, Wales, on September 28, 1935. From this marriage he had two children: Michael Edward and Valerie Camille. He served as Vice-President of the Hayward Chamber of Commerce, President of the Hayward Merchants Association, First President of the Downtown Property Owners Association, Chairman for fifteen years of the Infantile Paralysis Committee of Hayward, former director of the Hanna Center (Boystown of the West) and President of the Hayward Sister City, Inc. A notable speaker and lecturer, fluent in Portuguese and English, in his university years he was the Editor-in-Chief of the *Notre Dame Lawyer*.

He joined U.P.E.C. Council No. 3, Hayward on August 6, 1933. He was elected Master of Ceremonies in 1956, Second Vice-President in 1957 and President in 1958. During his term of office there were 295 new members admitted in the order whose membership at the time was 10,654 with assets totalling $2,771,670. He presided at the U.P.E.C. Convention held in Turlock in 1959. He served on the Board of Directors from 1971 through 1975.

He died on June 4, 1989 and was buried at the Holy Sepulchre Cemetery in Hayward, California.

FRANCISCO MACHADO LINHARES

(1895—1977)

Born on April 18, 1895 at Cinco Ribeiras, Terceira, Azores. Linhares was the son of Jose Machado Linhares and Maria da Conceicao Ferreira, both natives of Terceira. He immigrated to the United States in 1912 aboard the SS *Adriatic,* landing at Ellis Island in New York. From there he continued to California where he worked in a dairy in Elmhurst for four months driving stock on foot through what is known today as Foothill Boulevard. Hen went to Turlock where he worked for nearly four years, then returned to San Leandro where he obtained employment with Phillips Dairy. In the latter part of 1918 he returned to Turlock to form a partnership with his two brothers, Antonio and Bento Linhares. He held this partnership until 1942, when he dissolved it and went into the dairy business on his own until his retirement in 1961.

On July 21, 1919 he married Miss Marguerite Fernandes, daughter of Mr. and Mrs. Joseph Fernandes, and a native of Flores Island, Azores. Mrs. Fernandes' father, Joseph, the eldest son of Manuel F. Fernandes, who had married Miss Mary Piver, immigrated to California and worked on a mining claim in Osborne, Placer County. He later moved to Alameda County and went into dairying in Fruitvale. Miss Mary L.A. Piver, a native of Providence, Rhode Island, came to Alameda County in 1891 when she was five years old with her parents, John and Margaret (Hart) Piver. Her father had been a Portuguese sailor and came from Flores to the United States and served in the Civil War as a sailor. Her mother was a native of Liverpool, England. Margaret Linhares was a granddaughter of the Piver family (Piver is anglicized for Paiva) who were pioneer settlers of Alameda County. The Linhares' had one son, William Joseph. He was a recipient of an award from the Turlock Irrigation District for decorations during the Golden Jubilee in that city in 1937.

He joined U.P.E.C. Council No. 75, Turlock, on September 29, 1928. He was elected First Vice-President in 1960 and President in 1961. During his term of office there were 446 new members initiated. U.P.E.C. membership and assets at the time were 11,244 and $3,072,556. He presided at the U.P.E.C. Convention held in Sacramento in 1962. He was elected to the Board of Directors in 1962, 1965 and 1966. He died on April 26, 1977 and was buried at Turlock Memorial Park.

ANTONE EDWARD BRAGA

(1901—1988)

Born on September 5, 1901 in San Leandro, California. Braga is the son of António Joaquim Braga, a native of Santo Espirito, Santa Maria, Azores and Maria Aurora Braga, a native of Flamengos, Faial, Azores. He attended St. Mary's Convent on Davis Street, San Leandro 1907 and Lincoln Schools. He has been engaged in diversified agriculture all his life. He built the Braga Shopping Center in the Irvington District, located in Fremont, in 1956. He farmed in Alameda County, until a few years ago when he sold his land to General Motors, where they build an assembly plant in Fremont. Braga acquired large holdings of agricultural land in Dixon, California, where he subsequently settled. He is a Past President of the Holy Name Society of Mission San Jose, Past President of the Warm Springs Chamber of Commerce during 1948 and 1949, served as Fire Commissioner for that city from 1953 through 1957, was charter member of the Fremont Chamber of Commerce and has served on several committees that have brought together the communities of Irvington, Warm Springs, Mission San Jose, Hiles and Centerville into one city known today as Fremont, in Alameda County. He married Miss Mary Elizabeth Bettencourt, a native of Palo Alto, California, on June 8, 1925. They had one son, Alton Edward.

He joined U.P.E.C. Council No. 1, San Leandro, on August 1, 1936. He was elected Second Vice-President in 1960, First Vice-President in 1961 and President in 1962. During his term of office he initiated 348 new members. Total membership at the time numbered 11,256 with assets amounting to $3,179,062. He presided at the 1963 U.P.E.C. Convention held jointly with S.P.R.S.I. in San Diego. Braga was elected to the Board of Directors in 1954 through 1959 and 1963 through 1969. He died on July 8, 1988 and was buried at the Dixon Cemetery in Dixon, California.

MANUEL NEVES

1904—1972)

Born on December 22, 1904 at Ribeirinha, Pico, Azores. Neves was the son of Luduvico Ignacio Neves and Mariana Matilde, both natives of Pico Island. He immigrated to California in 1921. He attended Sutter High School in Sacramento. In 1926 he went to work for the Swift Meat Packing Company until 1944 when he left to form a partnership with Manuel Cabral in a grocery store located on "S" Street. In later years he opened another market, Freeport Manor, also in Sacramento. In 1965 he dissolved the partnership and retired. He married Elsie Leandro, a native of Rio

Vista, California, on June 20, 1929. He was the father of Joyce Margaret (Henry).

He joined U.P.E.C. Council No. 40, Sacramento, on February 9, 1926 (later this council merged with No. 11). He was elected Outside Guard in 1943, Vice-President in 1962 and President in 1963. During his term of office there were 340 new members initiated and total membership of the society was 11,274, assets amounted to $3,260,357. He presided at the U.P.E.C. Convention held in Sacramento in 1964. He was elected to the Board of Directors in 1964 and served until his death on February 28, 1972.

Sixty-Seventh President

MANUEL BARCELLOS SILVA

(1900—1982)

Born on July 9, 1900 at Santa Luzia, Angra do Heroismo, Terceira, Azores. He is the son of Joao Maria Pereira da Silva and Angelina Corvelo Barcellos, both natives of Angra. He attended elementary school in the city of his birth and continued his studies at Angra High School. He immigrated to California in March 1920 and then worked on a farm in Stockton. From there he moved to Lincoln where he stayed for a few months.

In 1921 he obtained a job at the machine shop of the Southern Pacific Railroad in Sacramento where he remained for one year. In 1922 he went to work for the California Sash and Door Company on 16th Street in Oakland. Eleven years later he quit to go to work for Hazel-Atlas Glass Company until 1942 when he went to work at Moore Dry Dock Shipyard in West Oakland. In 1954 he went to work for the Tracy Defense Depot and retired in 1964.

He married Miss Anna Maria Cardoso, a native of Sacramento, on September 23, 1922. He had two sons from this marriage: Eugene Earl, an Assistant Fire Chief at the Army Depot in Sacramento and Wilbert Arthur, a supervisor for Pacific Telephone Company. Later he married Mary Cardoso.

He served as Supreme President in 1949-1950 of the I.S.M.M., Irmandade de Santa Maria Madalena.

He first joined U.P.E.C. Council No. 13, West Oakland, on February 14, 1924 and on August 5, 1947 he became affiliated with U.P.E.C. Council No. 25, Oakland. He was elected Inside Guard in 1958, Marshal in 1959, Master of Ceremonies in 1960, Third Vice-President in 1961, Second Vice-President in 1962, Vice-President in 1963 and President in 1964. During his term of office there were 318 members initiated. U.P.E.C. membership at the time was 11,097 with assets of $3,338,038. He presided at the U.P.E.C. Convention held in San Leandro-Oakland in 1965.

He died on April 9, 1982 and was buried in Sacramento, California.

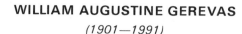

WILLIAM AUGUSTINE GEREVAS

(1901—1991)

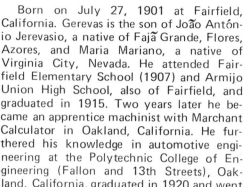

Born on July 27, 1901 at Fairfield, California. Gerevas is the son of João António Jerevasio, a native of Fajã Grande, Flores, Azores, and Maria Mariano, a native of Virginia City, Nevada. He attended Fairfield Elementary School (1907) and Armijo Union High School, also of Fairfield, and graduated in 1915. Two years later he became an apprentice machinist with Marchant Calculator in Oakland, California. He furthered his knowledge in automotive engineering at the Polytechnic College of Engineering (Fallon and 13th Streets), Oakland, California, graduated in 1920 and went to work for Magnavox. In 1930 he left this company to go to Graham Manufacturing Company in Newark where he remained until 1941. He then went to work for Friden, Inc. in San Leandro as a tool and die maker. Five years later he went to work for the City of Oakland as an instrument maker for the Electrical Department and retired in 1968. He is married to Miss Eva Evelyn Carvalho (Oaks) of Oakland and has two daughters: Elaine (Sa) and Marlene (Ciarfaglio).

He joined U.P.E.C. Council No. 56, Oakland, on May 8, 1918. He was elected Outside Guard in 1957, Inside Guard in 1958, Master of Ceremonies in 1959, Third Vice-President in 1960, Second Vice-President from 1961 through 1963, Vice-President in 1964 and President in 1965. During his term of office there were 466 new members initiated in the society and membership was 11,152 with assets of $3,415,411. He presided at the U.P.E.C. Convention held in Modesto in 1966. He was elected to the Board in 1966 and 1967, appointed to fill the vacancy left by Director Frank Souza in 1968, re-elected in 1969 and served through 1974.

He died on November 4, 1991 and was buried at the Holy Sepulchre Cemetery in Hayward, California.

JOSEPH COSTA FAGUNDES

Born on January 27, 1909 in Arcata, California. Fagundes is the son of Manuel Sousa Fagundes and Elvira Costa, both natives of Terceira, Azores. He attended Bayside Grammar School (1915) in Arcata, Patterson Elementary School (1916) and in 1919 went to the Azores with his parents. There he continued his studies at Angra do Heroismo High School. In 1929 he returned to the United States aboard the SS *Roma,* landed in Providence, Rhode Island, and continued his journey to California.

He went to work in a dairy in Patterson until 1933 when he moved to Arcata to work as an order clerk for the Hammond Lumber Co. (a firm subsequently sold to

Georgia Pacific in 1956). On April 10, 1934 he married Mary Borges, a native of Arcata, and of Azorean parentage. From this marriage there were four children: Rosemary, Josephine, Elvira (Judy) and Manuel Fagundes. Joe at one time played for the Lusitania Soccer Team in Terceira, Azores, and in California for the Samoa Olympics (1933-1936).

He joined U.P.E.C. Council No. 115, Arcata on June 19, 1938. He was elected Outside Guard in 1958, Inside Guard in 1959, Marshal in 1960, Master of Ceremonies in 1961 and 1962, Third Vice-President in 1963, Second Vice-President in 1964, Vice-President in 1965 and President in 1966. During his term of office there were 516 new members initiated in the society. Total membership was 11,216 with assets amounting to $3,531.325. He presided at the U.P.E.C. Convention held in Long Beach, California in 1967 and was elected to the Board of Directors from 1967 through 1970 and 1971 through 1976.

Seventieth President

WILLIAM GIER

(1897—1975)

Born on December 18, 1897 at Pleasanton, California. Gier was the son of Joe Gier (Aguiar), a native of Porto Formoso, São Miguel, and Ana Pacheco, a native of Vila Franca do Campo, São Miguel, Azores. He attended Pleasanton Grammar School, Tegner School in Turlock, California, and Irwin High School, from which he graduated in 1915.

Three years after his graduation he went to Lougheed, Alberta, Canada to farm 160 acres of corn, but lost his entire crop in the middle of the summer of 1919. He abandoned farming and went to work in the construction of grain elevators and as a gardner on an Indian reservation in Calgary. In 1920 he became an employee of the Canadian National Railway in the construction of railway bridges which linked Calgary and Edmonton. After leading an interesting life in the Canadian prairies he returned to Turlock to work as a grocery clerk for Stones Market. He opened a grocery store, Giers Market, at the corner of 7th and "H" Streets, Modesto, in 1930, after having worked for O.E. Johnson Market for eight years. He sold his business in 1947 and retired.

He married Miss Gertrude Bispo, a native of Alamo (Contra Costa County), California, on May 8, 1921. From this marriage there was one daughter, Mary Jane (Scheuber). He served on the School Board of Education in Ceres, California.

He joined U.P.E.C. Council No. 116, Hughson, on September 9, 1922, transferred to Council No. 52, Modeston in 1937 and returned to Council No. 116 in June, 1941. He was elected Third Vice-President in 1964, Second Vice-President in 1965, Vice-President in 1966 and President in 1967. During his term of office there were 340 new members initiated in the U.P.E.C. Total membership was 11,006 and the society had assets of $3,623.372. He presided at the U.P.E.C. Convention held in Santa Maria in 1968. Gier was elected to the Board of Directors in 1960 and served through 1962 and again in 1968. He died on September 23, 1975.

JOE SILVA JR.

(1905—1990)

Born on March 6, 1905 at Ribeirinha, Faial, Azores. Silva is the son of Jose Furtado da Silva, a native of Bandeiras, Pico Island, and Maria Leonor da Silveira, a native of Santa Luzia, Pico, Azores. He attended elementary school in his home town and immigrated a few years later to the United States aboard the SS *Cedric.* He arrived in Boston, Mass. on March 29, 1917. He came to California and went to Nipomo where he continued his schooling at Cuyama. In 1919 he went to Bataravia, California, where he worked with Union Sugar Company as an operator of a steam plow, until 1928 when he went to work for the Rosemary Farms in Santa Maria. In 1942 he went to work as a mechanic for the Hancock College of Aeronautics, Santa Maria Airport. A year later he opened a bar called El Patio at 200 N. Broadway Street, which he sold in 1950 and became maintenance man at the Santa Maria Union High School.

One of his thrills in life happened in 1943 when he flew (solo) a P-19 Fairchild after he had received instructions from Langenheim, a teacher at Santa Maria Airport.

He married Miss Antoinette Catherine Duarte, of Somis, California on April 26, 1930. From this marriage there were three sons. Still living are William A. and Douglas Silva.

He joined U.P.E.C. Council No. 171 on December 22, 1938 and transferred a year later to Council No. 66, Santa Maria, California. He was elected Outside Guard in 1960, Inside Guard in 1961-62, Marshal in 1963, Master of Ceremonies in 1964, Third Vice-President in 1965, Second Vice-President in 1966, First Vice-President in 1967 and President in 1968. During his term of office there were 525 new members initiated and assets were $3,717,784. Total membership was 10,869. Silva presided over the U.P.E.C. Convention held in Stockton, California in 1969. He served on the Board of Directors from 1969 to 1970.

He died on November 10, 1990 and was buried at the Santa Maria Cemetery , Santa Maria, California.

LEWIS CORREIA

(1916—1978)

Born on August 19, 1916 in New Bedford, Mass. Correia was the son of Anibal Correia, of Cape of Good Hope, South Africa and Maria Celestina Nunes of Funchal, Madeira Island, Portugal. In 1919 he went to Madeira with his parents, then returned to the United States around 1936. A year later he came to Oakland, California and worked as a Paint Contractor until 1958 when he began work at the Physical Plant, University of California, Medical Center in San Francisco.

In 1939 he presided over a California Committee organized to raise funds to assist flood victims in Camara de Lobos, Island of Madeira. For 20 years he took an active part in the Portuguese Drama Club of Oakland, a group organized to promote Portuguese legitimate theater in California. During World War II he served in the U.S. Navy from 1943-1945. He is married to Aurelia Correia, a native of New Bedford, Mass., daughter of Albert Correa, a well known Portuguese-American newspaper man. From this marriage there were three children: Louise, Sylvia and Lewis Correia Jr.

He joined U.P.E.C. Council No. 63 on December 15, 1939. Correia was elected Outside Guard in 1961 and 1962, Inside Guard in 1963, Marshal in 1964, Master of Ceremonies in 1965, Third Vice-President in 1966, Second Vice-President in 1967, First Vice-President in 1968 and President in 1969. During his term of office there were 405 new members initiated in the society whose assets amounted to $3,881,224. Total membership was 10,737. He presided at the U.P.E.C. Convention held, jointly with S.P.R.S.I., in Eureka. He served on the Board of Directors from 1970 through 1971.

He died on November 26, 1978.

JOÃO HERBERTO ALVES

Born on March 20, 1920 in Santa Cruz das Ribeiras, Pico, Azores. Alves is the son of Manuel Francisco Alves and Maria Nazare Pimentel, both natives of Santa Cruz, das Ribeiras, Pico. He attended elementary school in his own home village in Pico and moved in 1936 to Terceira, Azores where he attended Madeira Pinto Industrial and Trade School. In 1940 he joined the Portuguese Army and went to Lisbon to attend the Sergeant Class.

In 1957 he immigrated to Canada, in the fourth movement of immigrants from Portugal to that country. While in Canada he was employed by the Canadian National Railway. In 1961 he immigrated to California, joining his sister, Mrs. (Nazareth) Manuel Rosa, of San Diego. A few months later he came to the Bay Area and settled in San Leandro. He went to work for Millar Upholstery Company, later joined the truck division of International Harvester. He married Miss Maria Eduarda da Encarnação Carvalho Valério, a native of Ponta Delgada, San Miguel, Azores on September 6, 1947. From this marriage they had four children: Herbert Manuel, Maria de Deus, Tereza de Fátima and Eduardo Luis.

He joined U.P.E.C. Council No. 1 on August 8, 1961. He was elected Outside Guard in 1963, Inside Guard in 1964, Marshal in 1965, Master of Ceremonies in 1966, Third Vice-President in 1967, Second Vice-President in 1968, First Vice-President in 1969 and President in 1970. He presided at the U.P.E.C. Convention held in Modesto in 1971. During his term of office there were 470 mem-members initiated and membership at the time was 10,816 with assets amounting to $4,014,321. He served on the Board of Directors from 1971 through 1976, 1978, 1979, and 1987.

Seventy-Fourth President

JOSEPH MACHADO FARIA

Born on June 7, 1924, in Porto Judeu, Terceira, Azores. Faria is the son of José Machado Faria and Ermelinda F. Ramos, both natives of Terceira, Azores. He married Evelyn M. Faria of Ripon, California on April 6, 1947. They have two children: Gloria Jean (Nunes) and Clarence Gene Faria (now deceased).

Joseph and his parents immigrated to California in 1931. He settled around Patterson where he attended elementary and high schools. Later he moved to Modesto where he has continued to reside and engage in the dairy business.

He first was elected Supreme Outside Guard in 1954, leaving the officer's line in 1958 to rejoin again in 1966. He joined U.P.E.C. Council No. 130, Patterson, on April 7, 1940, and transferred to U.P.E.C. Council No. 52, Modesto, on June 24, 1953. He was elected Supreme President in 1971. During his term of office there were 848 new members initiated in the society. Assets were $4,089,308 and membership was 11,121. He presided at the Convention held in San Leandro-Oakland in 1972. He served on the Board of Directors in 1972 and 1977.

TONY XAVIER

Born on March 6, 1912 in Oakland, California. Xavier is the son of Matthew and Emilia Almeida Xavier, both natives of Santa Cruz, Flores, Azores. He married Marie (Garcia) of Feteira, Faial, Azores in 1946. He has a daughter, Sandra Braun. Tony attended Lincoln Grammar School, Lockwood Junior High and McClymonds High Schools, all in Oakland, California. He serves as secretary of the Holy Ghost Association of Alvarado Street since 1952.

He joined U.P.E.C. Council No. 55, San Leandro, on December 24, 1963 and was elected Council Secretary shortly thereafter. He was first nominated to the Supreme Council line of officers on September 1, 1965. He was elected Supreme President in 1972. During his term of office there were 657 new members initiated. Assets were $4,239,705 and membership was 11,219. He presided at the U.P.E.C. Convention held in Bakersfield in 1973 and served on the Board of Directors from 1973-1978 and from 1980-1986.

MANUEL FURTADO SIMAS

Born on September 22, 1902 in Santo Amaro, Pico, Azores. Simas is the son of Jose A. Furtado Simas and Jacinta do Carmo Simas, both natives of Santo Amaro, Azores. He married Isabel G. of New Bedford, Massachusetts in 1929. He has two sons, Manuel and Richard, and a daughter, Elsie.

He immigrated to the United States in 1920, settling in California. He first worked for Joe Perry on a farm in Lodi and two years later went into the Dairy Business on his own in Manteca, California where he has spent all his life. He was a Director of the South San Joaquin Irrigation District and served as its Chairman in 1957-58.

He first joined U.P.E.C. Council No. 164, Ripon, in 1925 and later transferred his membership to U.P.E.C. Council No. 148, Manteca. Simas was elected first Vice-President in 1972 and President in 1973. During his term of office there were 532 new members initiated. Assets were $4,332,881, and membership was 11,010. He presided at the U.P.E.C. Convention held in Anaheim in 1974. He served on the Board of Directors from 1967 to 1972 and from 1974 to 1979.

ANTÓNIO PEREIRA NEVES

Born on July 6, 1920 in Faial, Azores. Neves is the son of Manuel P. Neves of Pico, Azores and Maria S. Neves of Newport, Rhode Island. He married Maria C. Neves of Terceira, Azores in July, 1946. He has a son, António. He immigrated to California in 1959. While in the Azores he was employed by a Commercial Firm. He was a professional soccer player for the Faial Sport Club for nearly 20 years.

He first joined U.P.E.C. Council No. 43, Paramount, on June 12, 1963. Later the Council Charter was moved to Chino, and Tony transferred to Council No. 167. He was elected Supreme Outside Guard in 1967 and Supreme President in 1974. During his term of office there were 781 new members initiated. Assets were $4,420,140, and membership was 11,222. He presided at the U.P.E.C. Convention held in San Jose, California in 1975 and has served on the Board of Directors from 1975 to 1979.

GEORGE ANTHONY AZEVEDO
(1913—1984)

Born on September 13, 1913 in Patterson, California. Azevedo is the son of Manuel A. Azevedo of Pico, Azores and Maria Candida Azevedo of Terceira, Azores. He married June P. of Nebraska on August 3, 1941. He has three daughters and one son: Karen Lou (Fresquez), Frances Lou Azevedo, Georgena (Jorgensen) and George A. Azevedo Jr.

George worked on his father's ranch until the depression when his father lost the ranch. At the age of 12 he had a job hauling milk and, for several years later he was employed as a milker on the Allen Ranch in Modesto, California.

In December, 1941, he moved to Richmond, California where he became a Master Welding Instructor for the State of California, after having worked for the Kaiser Shipyards. In 1942 he became involved in the restaurant business and opened his first restaurant in Point Richmond. He continued his welding instructing and at the same time operated four restaurants, two of them located in San Pablo.

He is affiliated with the San Pablo Chamber of Commerce Board of Directors, City of San Pablo Redevelopment as Chairman, Historical Society, San Pablo Salesian's Boy's Club as Past President and member of the Board of Directors and Past Captain of the Contra Costa County Sheriff's Posse. In 1967 he was elected

Man of the Year for San Pablo.

He first joined U.P.E.C. Council No. 130 on March 20, 1949 then transferred his membership to Council No. 27, San Pablo, in 1966. During his term of office he initiated 813 new members. Assets were $4,550,724 and membership was 11,396. He presided at the U.P.E.C. Convention held in Merced in 1976. He served on the Board of Directors from 1976 through 1979.

He died on October 3, 1984 and was entombed at the St. Joseph's Mausoleum in San Francisco, California.

Seventy-Ninth President

STEVE MACHADO

Born on May 7, 1948 in Merced, California. Machado is the son of Elmer Machado of Merced, California and Sylvia Machado of Los Banos, California. Steve attended McSwain Elementary School, Atwater High School and Fresno State College. He is presently a field representative for Ferry Morse Seed Company. He married Robbin Tomlin on April 15, 1978.

Steve joined U.P.E.C. Council No. 29, Merced, on January 21, 1949. He was elected Inside Guard in 1970 and Supreme President in 1976. During his term of office there were 722 new members initiated in the society. Assets were $4,598,170 and membership was 11,818. He presided at the U.P.E.C. Convention held in Modesto in 1977. He served on the Board of Directors from 1977 through 1981.

Eightieth President

VICTOR GOMES

Born on October 16, 1918 in Lemoore, California. Gomes is the son of John Silveira Gomes and Maria Oliveira, both of Fajã dos Vimes, São Jorge, Azores. Victor graduated from Tracy High School and has dedicated his life to diversified farming around Modesto, California. He is Honorary Member of the Westport Fire Department. He served in the U.S. Armed Forces (Infantry, 7th Division) and received three battle stars for campaigns in the Aleutians, Okinawa and the Philippine Islands during World War II. He married Miss Mary C. Silva, of Tracy, California on May 18, 1948. He had five children from this marriage: Robert, Ronald, Mary Lorraine (Reynolds), Jim and Jerry.

He joined U.P.E.C. Council No. 52, Modesto, on September 4, 1970. He was elected Outside Guard in 1971 and Supreme President in 1977. During his term of office there 603 new members initiated. He served on the Board of Directors from 1978 through 1982. He presided at the Convention held in Claremont.

Eighty-First Supreme President

MARY (MATHIAS) COSTA

Born on June 27, 1918 in Terceira, Azores. She is the daughter of Paulo Cardozo and Frances Cardozo, both of Terceira. She came to California with her parents in 1920 and attended school in Clearwater, California.

On September 18, 1935 she married António Mathias. From this marriage there was one son, António M. Mathias, Jr. She was very active in church affairs, and received a citation from Pope Pius XII for her diligent work in raising funds to pay for the new church in Artesia, California.

She joined U.P.E.C. Council No. 167, Artesia, on May 14, 1968 and transferred to Council No. 43, Chino, in 1971. She was elected Supreme Inside Guard in 1972. Thereafter she was elected to all chairs in the hierarchy of the Supreme Council, step by step. She was elected Supreme President in 1978 during the Convention held in Claremont. She became the first woman to be elected President. She served on the Board of Directors from 1979 through 1982.

Mary Mathias being invested with the regalia of the presidency by Stephen Machado, Installing Officer — Convention, Claremont, 1978.

JOHN GONSALVES VIEIRA

Eighty-Second Supreme President

Born on March 20, 1918 in Lowell Massachusetts. He is the son of Augusto José Vieira of Sitio da Ribeira, Santa Cruz, Madeira and of Joana Gonsalves, also of the same village.

He came to California after having spent thirteen years in his parents native homeland, where he attended public schools as well as the seminary of Funchal, Madeira.

He arrived in California in 1937 after a short stay at New Bedford, Massachusetts. Once in Oakland, he took on all kinds of jobs, from factory worker at Ford Motor Company to salesman at Jackson Furniture Company. In the evenings he attended the Merritt Business School. Later, he attended the University of California at Berkeley, where he received a Bachelor's Degree in Social Sciences.

In 1955 he went to work for the Alameda County Social and Welfare Department, and two years later joined the same department in Contra Costa County where he has been employed as a social worker ever since.

In 1965 he took part in the International Public Assistance Conference held in Victoria, British Columbia, Canada, representing his department.

He married Alice Machado of Newman, California, on June 16, 1952. They have two sons: Ronald and John David.

Ronald Spearheaded the organization of the U.P.E.C. State Youth Council and became its first president in 1976.

John Vieira joined U.P.E.C. Council No. 1-San Leandro on January 3, 1963 and was elected Supreme Outside Guard in 1972 and Supreme President in 1979 during the Covention held in San Diego, California.

During his term of office U.P.E.C. celebrated its first centennial, and festivities on August 1, 1980 in San Leandro, California.

Honored guests at the Centennial Celebration of the U.P.E.C. included (from left) Dr. João Bosco Mota Amaral, President of the Regional Government of the Azores; His Excellency The Cardinal of Boston, Humberto Medeiros; The Honorable John Hall Themido, Ambassador of Portugal in Washington D.C.; and Mrs. Themido.

Eighty-Third Supreme President

EDWARD C. COSTA

Born in Providence, R.I. to Antonio and Maria Costa, natives of the Azores Islands.

He attended Clawson School and McClymonds High School in Oakland. He worked for General Motors for 35 years, eleven of which in management. He was President of the Brookfield Village Association for five years and Captain of the Auxiliary Police for 18 years. He was a Commander of the Reserve Police, Hayward, California.

He joined the U.P.E.C. in 1929 and was elected Supreme Outside Guard in 1973 and Supreme President in 1980.

He was married to Evelyn Thelma Silva of Sausalito, California and they had one son, Robert. Later he married Mary Mathias Costa, who served the U.P.E.C. as the Eighty-First Supreme President.

During his term of office there were 627 new members initiated. He presided at the Convention held in Anaheim, California in 1981. The assets of the Society at the time were $5,675,318.00.

He served on the Board of Directors from 1981 through 1983.

Eighty-Fourth Supreme President

HELIO T. SOUSA

Born in Rio de Janeiro, Brazil, July 16, 1922, to Jose Sousa Antao and Herminia Sousa, natives Sao Bartolomeu, Island of Terceira, Azores, where he was raised with his parents and attended elementary school.

He arrived in California in June 1949 and went to work for a dairy for 16 years. He was employed by the ABC School District for 23 years until his retirement in 1985.

He joined U.P.E.C. Council No. 167, Artesia in 1949 and was elected Supreme Outside Guard in 1974.

Helio is a member of various Portuguese fraternal societies. He married Francisca Jesus Ferreira of Sao Bartolomeu, terceira, Azores. They have a son Elliott Leo and a daughter Mary Ann.

He was elected Supreme President in 1981. During his term of office he initiated 540 new members.

He presided at the Convention held in Bakersfield, California in 1982.

He served on the Board of Directors from 1982 through 1987.

Eighty-Fifth Supreme President

JOHN J. MACHADO

Born in Bakersfield, California on November 20, 1923. Son of John J. Machado, a native of Topo, Sao Jorge, Azores and of Beatrice Caetano, of Sao Caetano, Pico, Azores.

He served in the Armed Forces during World War II; in the Infantry Branch in combat in the South Pacific. He received his combat badge in the Philippines and went to the occupation of Japan. He was honorably discharged as a Staff Sergeant, attched to the military government procurement division.

He joined the U.P.E.C. on August 11, 1947 and was elected Supreme Outside Guard in 1975, immediately after having served on the Board of Directors for five consecutive years.

John, a mechanic of gasoline and diesel engines worked as a shop manager for 25 years for a Bakersfield concern.

John is married to Lucy Arregui of Bakersfield. They have a daughter Shirley Ann Ariztia and a son John L. Machado.

He was elected Supreme President in 1982. During his term of office they initiated 662 new members. He presided at the U.P.E.C. Convention held in Merced in 1983. The assets of the organization at the time were $6,360,770.00 with a membership of 12,186 members.

He served on the Board of Directors from 1983 through 1988.

Eighty-Sixth Supreme President

HUBERT J. TRINDADE

Born on November 21, 1919 in Merced, California. The last born and 10th child of Jose Maria Trindade who was from the Island of Flores, Azores and Mary A. Trindade a native daughter of Mariposa County, California, of Portuguese desent.

Hubert is a graduate of Merced High School. He was a dairy farmer for 20 years. When ill health befell him in 1958, he was forced to terminate his dairy and farm operation.

In 1963, he was elected Assessor Collector for the Merced Irrigation District, in which capacity he served for 19 years. He retired in May of 1982.

Hubert is the father of two daughters, Monica Jennings and Carol Bango. He married Evelyn Carvalho Palermo in 1988.

He joined the U.P.E.C. Council No. 29, Merced in 1935 and was elected Supreme President in 1983. During his term of office he initiated 653 new members and presided at the Convention held in Stockton, California in 1984.

He served on the Board of Directors from 1984 through 1986.

Eighty-Seventh Supreme President

GEORGE L. TEIXEIRA

(1927—1986)

Born in Newman on June 11, 1927. He was the son of Manuel Teixeira, Sao Jorge, Azores and Lidia Teixeira, Terceira, Azores. After his tour of duty in the Army, he went into the Dairy business. He sold his dairy in 1962. After several years as an area supervisor for a firm from Fresno, he went to work for the U.P.E.C. as a Director of Public Relations, a position he held until 1979, when he resigned due to health reasons.

He was a member of the 3rd and 4th Degree Knights of Columbus for 28 years. He also served as Secretary of the local Festa Do Divino Espirito Santo for 22 years and was awarded an Honorary Life Membership in the Board of Directors. He joined U.P.E.C. Co. No. 68, Newman on March 25, 1969. He was elected to the Board of Directors in 1972, through 1974, and Supreme President in 1984.

During his term of office there were 564 new members initiated. He presided at the Convention held in Ontario, CA in 1985. The assets of the organization were $7,441,033. with a membership of 12,086.

He was married to Rose Dias, he had three sons: Gilbert, Norman and Donald.

He died on February 28, 1986 and was buried at the Hills Ferry Cemetery in Newman, California.

Eighty-Eighth Supreme President

ADELINO SANTOS

Born in Lowell, Massachusetts on September 16, 1923. He is the son of Claudio D. Santos from Madeira Island and Mariana Borges Martins from Terceira, Azores. He came to Imperial Valley, CA at the age of two.

In July 1940 he moved to Artesia. He joined U.P.E.C. Co. No. 167, Artesia in 1950, shortly thereafter he became its Secretary until 1961 when he moved to Chino, to become Secretary of Council No. 43, Chino, an office he has held ever since.

He was employed by the Chino Unified School District since February 1966 until his retirement in 1991.

He served as President of Ontario Toastmaster No. 192 (1963), President of Chino D.E.S. Festa (1974) and as its Secretary for 14 years. President of the California School Emp. Assoc. Chapter No. 102 (1980).

He married Gilberta Souza and has five children: Linda, James, Rosemary, Mark and Lori.

He was elected Outside Guard on September 6, 1978 and Supreme President in 1985. During his tenure, there were 433 new members initiated. He presided at the Convention held in Visalia in 1986.

He served on the Board of Directors from 1986 to present.

MANUEL R. MEDEIROS

Born on September 16, 1935 in Salao, Faial, Azores. He is the son of Joe G. Medeiros and Maria R. Medeiros.

He served in the Portuguese Navy for four years. While in the Navy he visited England, Angola, Mozambique, Goa, Damao and Diu in India.

He is married to Mary R. Medeiros and they have a son, Manuel Medeiros, Jr.

He came to the U.S. in 1959 and worked on a dairy farm for several years until 1967 when he bought his own dairy business in Tulare, California.

He is a member of U.P.E.C. Council No. 94 of Tulare since May 10, 1979. He is also former President of Tulare Angrense Soccer Club and Past President of St. Anthony Celebration of Pismo Beach, California.

He was elected Supreme President in 1986. During his term of office, there were 567 new members initiated. He presided at the Convention held in Turlock, California in 1987. The assets of the Society at the time were $8,917,866.28 with a membership of 12,248.

He served on the Board of Directors from 1987 to present.

MARY I. PEREIRA

Born in Los Banos, California she is the daughter of Joe Tosta and Georgina (Rocha) Tosta, both of Terceira, Azores. She is married to Frank A. Pereira and they have two sons, Richard and Lawrence.

She graduated from Los Banos High School. She was a Vice-President/Account-Executive for the American Savings and Loan Association, Turlock Branch.

She is a member of U.P.E.C. Council No. 75 of Turlock since April 27, 1980. She served on the U.P.E.C. Board of Directors until 1984 and from 1988 through 1991.

In 1987 she was elected Supreme President and became the second woman to hold the office. During her term of office there were 610 new members initiated. She presided at the Convention held in Merced in 1988.

She served on the Board of Directors from 1981 through 1983 and 1988 through 1991.

Ninety-First Supreme President

GEORGE E. CORVELO

Born in Merced, California and is the son Caetano Rodrigues Corvelo and Maria Avelar Corvelo, both natives of Fajazinha, Flores, Azores. He married the former Connie Nunes.

He graduated from Our Lady of Mercy High School in Merced and attended Merced College, receiving an Associate Arts Degree. Presently he is engaged in diversified farming.

He is a member of U.P.E.C. Council No. 29, Merced since January 27, 1955. George was elected Supreme President in 1988.

During his term in office, there were 652 new members initiated. He presided at the Convention held in Pleasanton, California in 1989. The assets of the Society at the time reached $11,099,849.23 with a total membership of 12,368 members.

He served on the Board of Directors from 1989 through present.

Ninety-Second Supreme President

ILIDIO C. PEREIRA

Born in Funchal, Madeira, on October 20, 1933. He is the son of Joao Rafael Pereira and of Maria Antónia M. Pereira, both of Funchal, Madeira.

He graduated from Escola Industrial e Comercial do Funchal in 1950. He served in the Portuguese Armed Forces, class of 1954, in Tavira, as a "Miliciano Sargeant". For 13 years he managed embroidery factories in the cities of Funchal, Ponta Delgada and Angra do Heroismo. He came to the United States on April 24, 1969, and settled in San Leandro, where he worked for Caterpillar Tractor, as a Staff Accountant for about 16 years. He became a citizen of the United States of America on January 7, 1975, in San Francisco. On December of 1975, he graduated from Chabot College with a degree in Accounting. Currently, he is Accounting Manager for Harbor Bay Integrated Digistal Services, a communications company in Alameda, California. He served as President of the League of Portuguese Fraternal Societies in 1988.

He joined U.P.E.C. in 1971, and was elected Supreme President in 1989. During his term of office there were 612 new members initiated. He presided at the Convention held in San Jose, California in 1990. The assets of the Society had grown to $12,258,636.62 with a membership of 12,416.

He served on the Board of Directors from 1990 to present.

Ninety-Third Supreme President

JOE C. ROSA

Born in Cedros, Faial, Azores on February 29, 1940. He is the son of Jose Correia Da Rosa and of Maria Santos Rosa, both of Cedros, Faial, Azores.

Jose came to California in 1963. He attended San Jose High School and San Jose City College. He was a carpenter before he became both an insurance agent and a realtor, professions he has exercised for the last 20 years.

His civic activities include among others, President of the Five Wounds Catholic School and President of the Santa Clara Sporting Club.

He is married to the former Filomena Freitas and they have four children: Dena, Zelia, Marian and Cindy.

He joined U.P.E.C. Council No. 32, San Jose on October 20, 1977 and was elected Supreme President in 1990. During his term of office there were 595 new members initiated. He presided at the Convention held in Stockton, California in 1991.

He became outright Board Member after his presidency.

Ninety-Fourth Supreme President

JOE P. ROSA

Born in Salao, Faial, Azores on December 12, 1940. He is the son of Jose Pinheiro Rosa and Felismina Simas Rosa, both natives of Faial, Azores.

Joe came to California in 1960. Upon his arrival he worked for a dairy in Tracy and later moved to Manteca where he established himself as a welder.

He is married to Rose Alves Rosa of Santa Barbara, Terceira, Azores and they have three children: Lucy, Mary Ann and David.

He joined U.P.E.C. Council No. 148, Manteca on March 13, 1979 and was elected Supreme President in 1991. He presided at the Convention held in Anaheim, California.

First Medical Examiner

ANDREW JOSEPH DEAN, M.D.

(1858–1904)

Born in 1858 at Co. Kerry, Ireland. Dean was the son of John Dean and Johanna Dean, both natives of Ireland. A graduate of a school of medicine in Philadelphia, he practiced medicine at an office located in the Gates Drug Store, Castro Street, Hayward. He later moved his office to San Leandro. He was never married.

He joined U.P.E.C. Council No. 3, Hayward, on July 3, 1887 and served as Medical Examiner for the Supreme Council of U.P.E.C. from 1890 through 1893 and again in 1896. He died on October 26, 1904 and was buried at St. Joseph's Cemetery in Hayward, California.

Second Medical Examiner

JOSÉ DE SOUSA BETTENCOURT, M.D.

(1851–1931)

Born in 1851 at Ponta Delgada, São Miguel, Azores. Son of António de Sousa Bettencourt and Rosa Joaquina, both natives of São Miguel. His parents wanted him to become a priest, so he attended High School for two years and enrolled in the English College where he studied languages, including French.

At the age of 15 he became aware of his true vocation, which was far from the priesthood so strongly desired by his parents. He dreamed of a country where he could develop to the best of his talents, and immigrated to the United States. He remained in Boston for nine years where he labored in several factories to earn a few dollars for his support. In his spare time he taught guitar and viola and wrote songs to make extra money which he sold to fellow immigrants. He enrolled at Harvard University in Massachusetts where he studied medicine for two years. In 1875 he came to California on a vacation. Attracted by the climate of the State, he moved permanently and continued his studies at Cooper College (now Stanford University) from which he graduated in 1877.

He was known as a person eager to learn in order to broaden his knowledge. He studied law at the University of California in 1885. After graduation from the law school he decided that he preferred medicine. He began to practice this profession at an office located at the Donohoe Building, 1170 Market Street in San Francisco. For a while he also taught medicine at the San Francisco Medical School until this institution closed as a result of the 1906 earthquake. Two days after this catastrophe he was named Vice-Consul of Portugal in San Francisco, a position he carried out with great dedication, facing a multitude of problems. Following his appointment, the Consulate had been engulfed by the fire which followed the earthquake.

He was selected to be part of the jury over Food Exhibits at the Universal

227

Exposition held in Saint Louis, Missouri in 1904. On November 29, 1907 he was decorated by the Portuguese Government with Military Order of Christ.

He served several fraternal organizations as Medical Examiner. He also presided over the Vasco da Gama Grove, Order of Druids. For thirty years he was the official correspondent for the Geographic Society of Lisbon. He married Gertrude E. who died in May 1893 and is buried in the San Francisco Masonic Cemetery.

He joined U.P.E.C. Council No. 7, Oakland, on September 21, 1891. He served as Medical Examiner of the U.P.E.C. from October 1891 through October 1893.

He died on December 4, 1931 and was buried on December 7 in Oakland.

Dr. J. de S. BETTENCOURT
MEDICO, CIRURGIÃO E PARTEIRO,

ESCRIPTORIO E RESIDENCIA,

No. 310 Rua Kearny,

San Francisco, Cal.

Consultas das 9 ás 10 da manha; das 12 ás 2
da tarde e das 7 ás 8 da noite

(*Progresso Californiense*, June 18, 1885)

Third Medical Examiner

JOÃO SÉRGIO ALVARES CABRAL, M.D.

Born on the Island of San Miguel, Azores. Dr. Cabral was the son of João Alvares Cabral and Rita Adelaide Alves Guerra, of Faial, Azores. He immigrated to California settling first around San Luis Obispo, where he acted as Vice-Consul of Portugal by appointment in March of 1893 of His Majesty the King of Portugal. Later he moved to San Francisco, California, where he attended Hahnemann College and received a degree in Doctor of Medicine in August of 1895.

He began his practice in Oakland with offices at 470 13th Street. Later he moved to 626 13th Street (corner of Grove Street, Oakland). Prior to his death he kept his office at his own residence at 534 15th Street, Oakland, where he used to give free consultations to the poor every Monday and Thursday of the week from 1:30 P.M. to 2:30 P.M. A special consultation price was offered to the Portuguese. One dollar would cover the office consultation and medicine to remedy the ailment of each patient.

He was married to Luisa Machado Soares, a native of the Island of Pico, Azores. From this marriage he had two daughters, Graça and Noémia. Neither daughter married and they moved to Lisbon, Portugal.

In May of 1897 he moved to Centerville, California. He served as the Editor-in-Chief of *A Pátria,* a Portuguese newspaper published in Oakland, with J.M. Rosa as administrator. On July 14, 1898 he was elected Medical Examiner for the Order of the Foresters of America, Mission San Jose Branch. In 1901 he served on the Finance Committee of the I.D.E.S. and from 1904 through 1909 as its Medical Examiner.

He joined U.P.E.C. Council No. 13 on June 28, 1896, and transferred his membership to Council No. 5 in Centerville on March 25, 1900. He was elected to the Office of Medical Examiner of the U.P.E.C. in October 1896, and served through October 1901.

His talent as a poet was known throughout the Portuguese community at the time. Many of his poems were published in the *União Portuguesa,* a newspaper published in San Francisco. He died on March 1, 1909 in Centerville.

Dr. J. S. Alvares Cabral,

MEDICO e CIRURGIÃO.

Consultorio e Residencia: 534, 15th. St. Oakland.

[Proximo do City noll]

Horas de Consulta

Em todos os dias uteis das 9 e meia ás 11 da manhã, e das 2 ás 3 e meia, e das 7 ás 7 e meia da tarde.

Consultas gratis para os pobres, todas as segundas e quintas-feiras da uma e meia ás duas e meia da tarde.

Preço geral da consulta, remedio incluido, para os portuguezes, no consultorio— 1 dollar.

Fourth Medical Examiner

JOSÉ LEAL DE AZEVEDO, M.D.

(1874—1938)

Born on September 8, 1874 at Faial, Azores. Dr. Azevedo was the son of Joaquin Leal Azevedo and Rosalia Baldeia, both of Faial. Around 1853 his father, Joaquin, came to California and worked in the mining fields of northern California. A few years later he returned to the Azores, where he married. In 1888 he returned to California to buy farmland in Freeport. Later, in partnership with his cousin, he established the Eagle Winery at Sacramento, which they operated for thirty-seven years.

Young Joseph came with his father, went to public schools, and Saint Mary's College in 1895 after which he studied medicine. A student of the College of Physicians and Surgeons of San Francisco, (Cooper's College) he graduated in 1901, and began his practice in Sacramento, where he remained for two years. He then moved to Oakland where he spent the rest of his life.

He married Amalia B. Glória in July, 1889 in Oakland (Miss Amália was the sister of Father Guilherme S. Glória.) From this marriage he had six children: Dr. Joseph L. Azevedo, Alfred, Alice, Maria and Amália (Borba).

He organized the Institute of Health at the corner of 8th and West Streets in Oakland, complete with X-rays and surgery rooms. He also served at the hospital Santo António, and was a member of the Medical Corps of Providence Hospital (26th and Broadway, Oakland, California) for a number of years. He was a director of the Prudential Mortgage Securities, a company based in Oakland, composed mostly of Portuguese: Joaquim L. Silveira, President; Virgil G. Carpogno, Vice-President; Anthony Sousa, Secretary-Treasurer; Jesse H. Woods; William Sousa and

Antonio A. Rogers of San Leandro. The company's head office was located on the 15th floor of the Tribune Tower, Oakland.

Dr. Joseph L. Azevedo served as Medical Examiner for the S.P.R.S.I. and I.D.E.S. He joined U.P.E.C. Council No. 13, West Oakland, on July 26, 1900, and served as Medical Examiner for the Supreme Council of U.P.E.C. from October 1901 until his death on December 18, 1938. He was buried at the Holy Sepulchre Cemetery in Hayward, California.

Fifth Medical Examiner

CARLOS FERNANDES, M.D.

(1893–1977)

Born on December 22, 1893 at Madalena do Mar. Madeira Island. Dr. Fernandes was the son of Rufino Fernandes and Helena de Freitas, both of Madalena do Mar. He attended Central High School of Funchal and Catholic College of Lisbon. He studied law for three years at the University of Lisbon and attended Sorbonne University of Paris, France for three and one half years. He received his Doctor of Medicine Degree from the University of Lisbon in 1921.

He immigrated to California in 1924 aboard the *Danty* and went to work for the University of California at Stanford, where he was in charge of Etiology and Hereditary Cancer for about four years. Later he became President and Chief Surgeon at St. John's Hospital (Dr. Andrew Morton's Hospital) where he practiced medicine for 14 years.

In 1921, while he was in Lisbon, he owned and edited the *Economista Portugues,* a monthly publication directed by Dr. Querim de Jesús. He was a charter member of the Pan American Medical Association of San Francisco and served as director of the International Bank of Commerce. He was assistant editor for seven years of the *Compend of Medicine and Surgery,* published in San Francisco by a group of doctors. He was appointed Consul of Portugal in the City of Oakland, and his credentials were accepted by President Calvin Coolidge on October 3, 1924. He also served as Consul General of Brasil in San Francisco.

He was first married to Martha Dutton of San Francisco. From this marriage they had a daughter, Louise (Silva). Later he married Stella Sviseck of Abardene, Washington.

He was decorated with the *Ordem do Cruzeiro do Sul,* one of the highest decorations of Brasil. This honor was given to him as a result of his personal assistance given to Mrs. Getulio Vargas, wife of the President of Brasil who had become seriously ill during his visit to the Golden Gate International Exposition at Treasure Island, California, in 1939. He was also decorated with the *Cross of Christ* from the Portuguese Government.

At one time he owned the Marconi Telegraph Station, Marshall, on Tamales Bay consisting of a 32 room hotel initially used as quarters for the telegraph personnel, a warehouse and several other structures on 42 acres. The Marconi Buildings were constructed in 1913 and 1914 and used until 1929 as part of a Trans-Pacific Telegraph System. In 1964 Dr. Carlos Fernandes sold his famous site to the Synanon Foundation.

He served as Medical Examiner of the A.P.U.M.E.C. (Associação Protectora União Madeirense do Estado da California), and of the S.P.R.S.I.

He joined U.P.E.C. Council No. 63 on December 1, 1914 and was elected Medical Examiner of the Supreme Council of U.P.E.C. on October 1939 and served until October 1952. He never became a U.S. citizen.

He died on August 1, 1977.

SAINT JOHN'S HOSPITAL

Sixth Medical Examiner

LUIZ JULIO MADEIRA, M.D.

Born on December 19, 1916 in Reigada, Portugal. Dr. Madeira is the son of Jose Augusto Madeira, a native of Figueira de Castelo Rodrigo, Beira, Portugal and Candida Augusta Julio, also of Reigada. After graduating from Guarda High School, he went to the University of Coimbra, Portugal, receiving his Doctorate in Medicine in 1942. While in Coimbra he formed part of the University Orchestra and toured most of Continental Portugal and Spain.

After graduation he became a resident-surgeon at the Civil Hospital in Lisbon. He practiced medicine in Paco d'Arcos, Portugal from 1943, when he accepted the position of doctor-in-charge of medical care to the Portuguese Cod Fishing Fleet aboard the hospital ship *Gil Eanes,* which rendered medical assistance to fishermen on the banks of Newfoundland.

He came to the United States in 1948 aboard *SS Santa Cruz.* He was a clinical affiliate in medicine at the University of California Medical Center, San Francisco after being an intern at the St. Joseph's Hospital in Tacoma, Washington.

He married Miss Berta Ormond Avila, a native of Oakland, California on February 1, 1948. From this marriage they had a son, Luiz Avila Madeira. Dr. Madeira serves as Medical Examiner for the S.P.R.S.I. and U.P.P.E.C. His memberships include the Commonwealth Club of California, the American Academy of General Practice, the Diabetes Association (President) and the Board of Industrial Physicians of California. He was on the staff of several hospitals: Peralta, Providence, Samuel Merritt, Herrick and Children's. He was awarded a fellowship in Chest Diseases by Alameda County TB and Health Association. He discontinued his medical practice to become a Medical Consultant for the Department of Health, State of California, Health and Welfare Agency.

He joined U.P.E.C. Council No. 25 on May 12, 1952. In 1975 he transferred to Council No. 1, San Leandro. He was elected Medical Examiner of the U.P.E.C. in October 1952.

Certificado de Membro Honorario
DA
U.P.E.C.
1880
U.C.P.

O CONSELHO SUPREMO
DA

União Portugueza do Estado da California

Tendo na devida consideração os merecimentos pessoais de

e, particularmente, os serviços que tem prestado e, especialmente, os que pode vir a prestar á UNIÃO PORTUGUÊZA DO ESTADO DA CALIFORNIA, concedeu-lhe admissão como

MEMBRO HONORARIO

no Conselho_____, No._____da referida UNIÃO PORTUGUÊZA DO ESTADO DA CALIFORNIA, situado em_____

Condado de_____, Estado da California, com os direitos e previlégios especiais e restritos que pela Constituição dos Conselhos Subordinados da dita UNIÃO PORTUGUÊZA DO ESTADO DA CALIFORNIA são concedidos aos Membros Honorários desta sociedade.

    Este Certificado é emitido com a expressa condição de que o dito socio, emquanto fôr membro honorário da dita União, se conformará em tudo com as leis, regulamentos e determinações da mesma, quer agora em fôrça, quer para o futuro adoptadas. Este certificado é, ainda e especialmente, sujeito ao Artigo IV da referida Constituição dos Conselhos Subordinados da U. P. E. C., em todas as suas Secções e em todos os seus parágrafos ou numeros.

    Pelo que ordenou o supradito CONSELHO SUPREMO DA UNIÃO PORTUGUÊZA DO ESTADO DA CALIFORNIA que este Certificado de Membro Honorario fosse passado e assinado pelos seus Presidente e Secretário Supremos, sob o sêlo do mesmo Conselho Supremo, no dia_____de_____de 191____, em San Leandro, Cal.

SÊLO

Presidente Supremo

Visto,_____

Secretario Supremo

Nos Abaixo Assinados, Presidente e Secretario do Conselho No._____assinámos este Certificado e apômos-lhe o sêlo dêste Conselho, ratificando a sua validação, no dia_____de_____de 191____

SÊLO

Presidente

Visto,_____

Secretario

HONORARY MEMBERS
OF THE
SUPREME COUNCIL OF U.P.E.C.

First Honorary Member

EUCLIDES GOULART DA COSTA

Da Costa was born in Horta, Faial, Azores, and was one of the few Consuls of Portugal who took an active part in the life of the Portuguese community. He served as Consul in the late 1890s. He left the U.S. to return to San Francisco as Consul of Portugal in 1924 and served until 1927. Later he was sent to the Republic of Cuba and from there to the Ministry of Foreign Affairs. He returned to Boston and in 1939 was transferred to San Francisco, California. He did extensive research work which he published in 1928 in Lisbon, Portugal, on the discovery of California by João Rodrigues Cabrilho. He was conferred title of Honorary Member in 1924.

Second Honorary Member

JOHN MUSSO

Born in Italy, Musso became Co-Director of the U.P.E.C. Band, rendering inumerous services to the musical group, which for over half a century was a very important publicity media for the organization. He was a former member of the Royal Italian Band. He was conferred title of Honorary Member in 1926.

Third Honorary Member

FRANCISCO P. ARAGÃO E. COSTA

Born on February 10, 1889, Costa first joined the Portuguese Diplomatic Corps on January 21, 1916. In 1927 he came to the U.S.A. to be in charge of Portugal's Consulate in New York, and on December 27 of that year was appointed Consul of Portugal in San Francisco, a position he held until his death on June 6, 1936.

He was conferred title of Honorary Member in 1929.

Fourth Honorary Member

DR. ANTÓNIO DE FREITAS PIMENTEL

Born at Fazenda das Lajes, Flores and a graduate of the University of Lisbon (Medicine Doctorate-1929). He practiced medicine in Faial beginning in 1930. He was Mayor of Horta, Faial from 1945 to 1953 and Governor of the district of Horta from 1953 to 1973. He became well known during the volcanic eruption of Capelinhos in 1957 for his assistance to the victims of the 13-month disaster which destroyed part of the villages of Capelo, Praia do Norte, Norte Pequeno and Ribeira Funda. He is responsible for the reconstruction of those villages which had 1,600 houses, of which 600 were brand new. Most houses were the property of immigrants who came to California in subsequent years.

He was decorated by the Portuguese Government several times. He visited California in May of 1960 and was conferred the title of Honorary Member during a banquet held in his honor in Oakland, California.

DR. MARIA F.P.D. PIMENTEL

Dr. Pimentel was born in Vila de Aljustrel, Beja, Portugal, and was a graduate of the University of Lisbon (Medicine Doctorate-1929). She married Dr. António de Freitas Pimentel in 1930 and settled in Faial where she practiced medicine through 1975, the year of her death.

In 1958 she was appointed delegate of the Institute of Family Assistance in the district of Horta, Faial. She founded the Children's Home and received two decorations from the Government of Portugal for her benevolent work. She accompanied her husband on his visit to California in May of .1960, at which time she was given the title of Honorary Member of the Supreme Council of U.P.E.C.

JOSÉ LUIZ TRIGUEIROS DE ARAGÃO

Aragão was born on November 8, 1920 in Castelo Branco, Portugal. He first joined the Portuguese Diplomatic Corps in 1946, and was placed in Portugal's Embassy of Rio de Janeiro, Brasil. In February 1956 he was appointed to Portugal's Embassy in Brussels, from there he went to Athens, Greece. On October 14, 1961 he was named Consul General of Portugal in San Francisco, California, a position he held until late 1964. He was conferred title of Honorary Member in 1962.

NUMIDICO BESSONE

Bessone was born in Lagoa, San Miguel, Azores, on August 12, 1913. After graduation in Ponta Delgada he was admitted to the Superior School of Fine Arts in Lisbon in 1932. He concluded his studies and as a thesis presented his notable work, the statue of *St. Michael, the Archangel* which stands in front of Ponta Delgada's City Hall in the Azores.

In 1939 he participated in esthetic missions promoted by the Academy of Fine arts of Lisbon in Leiria, Santarem and Viseu, for which he received the National Prize in sculpture. In 1957 he went to Italy to complete his course in sculpture in the Academy of Fine Arts of Rome. While in Rome, he received a scholarship from the Italian government to study the art of Medallia. He has exhibited his art works in various parts of the world: Rome, London, Vienna and Paris.

He is also represented in the National Museum of Contemporary Art of Lisbon, in other museums of Portugal and foreign countries.

Bessone, whose complete name is Numidico Bessone Borges de Medeiros Amorim, is the sculptor of the Monument to the Portuguese Immigrant, which now stands in Root Park, San Leandro, California. He was conferred title of Honorary Member in 1964.

VASCO VIEIRA GARIN

Garin was born in Lisbon, Portugal on June 23, 1907. He graduated from the University of Lisbon with a degree in Economics and Finance in 1929. He entered the Ministry of Foreign Affairs as a career diplomat in 1931.

He was First Secretary and later Counsellor and *Charge d'Affaires* at the Embassy of Portugal in Washington, D.C. from 1941 to 1946. He was appointed Chief of the Bureau of Political Affairs at the Ministry of Foreign Affairs in Lisbon in 1946 and Consul General of Portugal in Montreal, P.Q., Canada in 1947. After serving in the Diplomatic Corps in Asia, he was appointed Ambassador of Portugal to Canada in 1956, at the same time that he was the permanent representative of Portugal to the United Nations.

In 1964 he became Ambassador of Portugal to the United States and served until July, 1971. He was the first Ambassador of Portugal ever to visit San Leandro, California (during Portuguese Immigrant Week festivities in 1969).

He was conferred title of Honorary Member in 1967.

ANTÓNIO LEAL DA COSTA LOBO

Lobo was born in Coimbra, Portugal on May 22, 1932. He received a law degree from the University of Coimbra. He was a member of the Delegation to Conference of Tangiers in 1956, Secretary of the Portuguese Delegation to the International Court of Haia (Portugal versus India), and *Charges d'Affaires* of Portugal in Havana, Cuba from 1961 to 1963. He was appointed Consul General of Portugal in San Francisco, California from October 1966 through October 1970.

He was conferred title of Honorary Member in 1970.

DR. ANTÓNIO DUARTE NOGUEIRA

Born in 1937 in Frutal, Minas Gerais, Brasil, Nogueira is a graduate of the Faculty of Medicine, Ribeirao Preto, state of Sao Paulo in 1962. He is the author of several books on municipal administration. In 1968 he was elected Mayor of Ribeirao Preto, Brasil, Sister City of San Leandro, California, and headed a delegation of twenty community leaders to attend San Leandro's centennial celebrations in 1972. He was conferred title of Honorary Member in 1972.

Eleventh Honorary Member

DINIS A. PIMENTEL DA SILVA

Born in San José, Ponta Delgada, São Miguel, Azores, Silva is a graduate of the University of Lisbon. He served in the Geographic Institute from 1947 to 1961, the year in which he was made head of the delegation of that institute in the Azores. He was elected to the city council from 1966 to 1970 and appointed Mayor of Ponta Delgada, sister city of San Leandro, in 1970 to 1974. He was conferred the title of Honorary Member in 1972 during the centennial celebrations of San Leandro.

Twelfth Honorary Member

ANTÓNIO PINTO MACHADO

Born in Póvoa de Varzim, Portugal, Machado is a graduate in law from the University of Coimbra. He joined the Diplomatic Corps on June 1, 1955. He was Consul of Portugal in Recife, Brasil, Secretary to the Embassy of Portugal in Haia, Netherlands and *Charges d'Affaires*, Beirut, Lebanon and Manila, Philippines. After missions in Cuba and Bolivia he was appointed Consul General of Portugal in San Francisco, California on October 1, 1976. He promoted cultural programs accessible to the Portuguese community of Northern California and was conferred the title of Honorary Member in June, 1978.

Supreme Directors Walter Nicolau, Jr. and Joe I. Silva presenting Congressman Tony Coelho with certificate of Honorary membership in the Supreme Council of U.P.E.C.

Thirteenth Honorary Member

HON. TONY COELHO

Born in Los Banos, California on June 15, 1942.

He majored in Political Science at Loyola University in Los Angeles, California. He graduated in 1964 with a Bachelor of Arts Degree.

In 1965 Coelho joined the Staff of the U.S. Representative B.F. Sisk, whom he succeeded in 1978 when he was elected to Congree to represent the 15th Congressional District of California, a position he resigned in June 1989.

He is married to Phyllis (Butler) and they have two daughters, Kristin and Nicole.

To date, Coelho is the only Portuguese-American to represent California in the U.S. Congress.

He was conferred the Title of Honorary Member in March 1987.

Fourteenth Honorary Member

HON JOÃO BOSCO MOTA AMARAL

Born in Ponta Delgada, São Miguel, Azores on April 15, 1943. He is a law graduate from the University of Lisbon, Portugal. In 1966 he received a Master Degree in Social and Political Science, graduating with high honors.

He was the Editor-in-Chief of the magazine "Rumo" of Lisbon.

He was elected to the National Assembly of the Republic of Portugal in 1969. In 1974 he and other distinguished statesmen founded the Popular Democratic Party, The Majority National Party known today as PSD.

He was a staunch advocate of autonomy for the Azores region. He was elected to the Portuguese Congress on April 25, 1976, a position he has been re-elected by popular vote ever since. On September 8, 1976, he suspended his activities in Congress in order to preside over the Azores Regional Government. He is a frequent guest of the Azorean Communities of the United States.

He was conferred the Title of Honorary Member in July 1989 during one of his many visits to California.

THE CAUSA PORTUGUESA AWARD

In 1970 the Board of Directors of the society established an award to be presented to any individual who contributed to the good name and welfare of the Portuguese people in California.

The award became known as the Causa Portuguesa. Its symbol was designed by Sculptor Numidico Bessone and made of bronze by the Portuguese Mint in Lisbon.

The following people were given the award:

1970 — Hon. Jack D. Maltester, Mayor of San Leandro
1972 — Hon. Joe Gonsalves, California State Assemblyman
1973 — Edward C. Massa, Chairman, Portuguese Immigrant Week Committee
1974 — Lawrence Oliver, Tuna Industry Pioneer
1975 — William Lockyer, California State Assemblyman
1976 — Wesley McClure, San Leandro City Manager
1977 — Mary Giglitto, President of the Cabrillo Festival Committee
1979 — Tony Xavier, Community Leader
1980 — Manuel S. Mancebo, Industrialist
1981 — Dr. Eduardo Mayone Dias, University Professor
1982 — Frank S. Mendonsa, Community Leader
1983 — Mos. Manuel V. Alvernaz, Church Leader
1984 — Dr. Ramiro Dutra, University Professor
1986 — Tony Coelho, Member of the U.S. Congress
1987 — Dr. Donald Warrin, University Professor
1988 — Dr. Luiz J. Madeira, Medicine Doctor
1989 — John A. Teixeira, Community Leader
1990 — Rev. Richard A. Mangini, Church Leader
1991 — Robert Gilbert, Industrialist

First Supreme Secretary

LÚCIO JOSÉ MARTINHO

Lucio Jose Martinho, better known as Louis J. Martin, was born in Hawaii. He was the son of a family of whalers from the island of Flores, Azores, who settled in these Pacific Islands. He came to San Leandro in his teens where he resided for over fifty years.

A pioneer resident, Louis was a well-known figure, not only among the Portuguese, but also among San Leandrans in general. He served the people of this city in several capacities: City Marshal, City Clerk and City Councilman (Trustee). He was a very obliging, congenial and respected citizen who had also served as Director of the San Leandro State Bank. He was one of the founders of the San Leandro Lodge of Odd Fellows, under whose auspices his funeral services were conducted on December 31, 1917 at the I.O.O.F. Hall in that city.

He was married to Mary B. Martin and had six children: George J., Fred A., Louis J., John B., Helen B. and Marguerite C. Martin. Three children: John, Helen and Marguerite predeceased Martin. He lived on Washington Avenue, San Leandro.

He joined U.P.E.C. Council No. 1 on June 6, 1884, and became U.P.E.C.'s first Supreme Secretary in 1887, serving without interruption until 1914.

Third Supreme Secretary

MANUEL ELIAS AMARAL

Amaral was born on June 8, 1896 in Conceicão, Angra do Heroismo, island of Terceira, Azores. He was the son of Manuel Elias Amaral of Ponta Carça, São Miguel and Maria Adelina Bettencourt of São Jorge, Azores. He attended the Institute Insular Angrense in 1901 and Liceu Nacional de Angra in 1907. In 1912 he joined the Merchant Marine, working aboard SS Funchal until 1914 when he enlisted in the Portuguese Army. He left the Azores aboard the Canopic of the White Star Line, and arrived in Boston on October 10, 1919. From there he came to Watsonville, California.

In 1920 he went to work for the Carnation processing plant of Gustine. In 1924 he moved to Tulare where he was employed by the Noia's Market, until the middle of 1925 when he moved to Oakland to work as a clerk for the Souza Bros. Grocery.

He was elected Supreme Secretary in October, 1943 and served through December 1948, and as Assistant Secretary-Treasurer from January 1949 through March 1953.

He joined U.P.E.C. Council No. 40, Sacramento and later he rejoined Council No. 102, Melrose and transferred to Council No. 25, Oakland, on March 5, 1935.

He was married to Maria José Moniz, a native of Angra do Heroismo, Terceira. From this marriage there were two children: Roberto and Fernanda.

In 1970 he married the former Maria Reis Fagundes of Terceira.

Fifth Secretary

CARLOS ALMEIDA

Born on February 15, 1933 in Ponta Delgada, San Miguel, Azores. He is the son of António Da Costa Almeida and of Maria Constantina Cordeiro Soares de Albergaria Pimentel Almeida.

In September 1951 he joined the Department of Emigration in P. Delgada, processing passports for emigrants leaving the Azores for different parts of the world. In 1956 he emigrated to Montreal, P.Q., Canada to work for the Canadian National Railway as a Personnel Manager and later promoted to Inspector-(Auditor) out of the Toronto office. In 1957 he went to London and Lisbon to negotiate a contract for 1,500 laborers to work for the C.N.R. and Canadian Pacific Railway of Canada, recruiting them from the Azores. In December 1958 he moved to California, settling in San Leandro after a short stay in Modesto. He joined the office staff of the U.P.E.C. on March 16, 1959 and became Secretary-Treasurer in October of the same year at the Convention held in Turlock, CA, a position he holds ever since.

He was active in Civic Affairs in San Leandro, serving as President of the Historical-Cultural Commission (1973), President of the Library Board of Trustees (1974), San Leandro Downtown Redevelopment Committee (1964-1978), Alameda County Social Services Commission (1976), Director of the San Leandro Chamber of Commerce (three years), President of the Sister City Committee (1961), President of Alameda County Cabrillo Civic Club (1966), President of the League Portuguese Fraternal Societies (1981), President of the Calfiornia Fraternal Congress, which includes 41 fraternal societies (1987); Coordinator for the project of the Monument

Supreme Secty-Treasurer, Carlos Almeida greeted at the White House by President Jimmy Carter.

to the Portuguese Immigrant in Root Park, San Leandro, Director and Founder of the J.A. Freitas Library and of the U.P.E.C. Cultural Center. He was personally invited to the White House by three Presidents (Lyndon Johnson, Jimmy Carter and Ronald Reagan). He was honored as Young Man of the Year by the City of San Leandro J.C. (1964), Outstanding Immigrant of Portugal, International Institute of East Bay (1970) and decorated by the Portuguese Government, with the Order of Prince Henry (1980).

He is married to the former Maria Fernanda Oliveira, a native of Pico, Azores. He has two daughters, Deborah Molonson and Patty Louise Smart.

(For Second Supreme Secretary-Treasurer, see Supreme Presidents' Biographies: Manuel Fraga (Secretary, 1914-43); and for Fourth Secretary, Frank S. Roderick (Secretary, 1949-53.)

LÚCIO DA SILVA GONSALVES

(1864—1936)

Gonsalves was born in Peniche, Portugal on February 3, 1864. He became an officer in the Portuguese Army, a member of the movement which instituted the Republic in Portugal. He took part in a conspiracy to overthrow the Monarchy, which took place in Oporto in 1889. Later, he was forced to leave the country and seek refuge in France where he continued his studies. From there he went to Italy where he took up music and opera singing. He acted in the most important theaters in Europe. He left Europe to go to Brasil, where he changed his name to Mario Bettencourt da Camara in order to conceal his association with the revolutionary movement in Portugal. While in Brasil he suffered from yellow fever, which prevented him from singing. As a result, he abandoned his opera singers company of Rio de Janeiro, Brasil, to join the group that did preliminary work in the Panama Canal.

In 1892 he immigrated to San Francisco, California. His first job was as a reporter for the *Uniao Portuguesa.*

In May 1895 Camara organized the Portuguese Bicycle Club of San Francisco. On July 6, 1895 he published *A Chronica,* a bi-weekly newspaper (later monthly), printed in San Francisco. This publication was critical of the behavior of some of the Portuguese community leaders, including Father Guilherme S. Glória who, at the time, was director of *O Amigos Dos Católicos.*

In the *A Chronica,* Camara defended the good name of the Portuguese, showing his national pride when the *San Francisco Chronicle* (November 14, 1895) remarked about the methods employed by the Portuguese in getting their lands in Africa, and the *San Francisco Daily Report* accused the Portuguese immigrants in scandals connected with Lane, Meyer and Ratz of San Francisco, in an issue of promiscuity and prostitution of young girls. A libel statement tended to belittle the Portuguese community of San Francisco, at the time highly discriminated against. Camara begged the editor to clarify to its readers that none of the girls in question were Portuguese. The editor refused. On December 20, 1895, Camara answered both papers with his famous article entitled "A Lesson in History to some of the San Franciscan Journalists," which he distributed freely among the population of San Francisco and Oakland. *A Chronica* also served to show Camara's apathy towards the Monarchy regime of Portugal. It had a short life and ended on September, 1890 after publishing only 14 issues.

His influence was felt after he and 11 others, including Manuel F.M. Trigueiro, organized U.P.E.C. Council No. 15 of San Francisco on June 24, 1894. He named this council after Prince Henry The Navigator. (Camara later transferred to Council No. 30, Corte Real, of San Francisco.) However, at the time of his death he was affiliated with Council No. 19 of San Rafael.

Mário's first appearance before U.P.E.C. membership was made in October, 1895 when U.P.E.C. held its convention in Sacramento. He was present as a delegate. Soon his qualities of leadership were recognized. John G. Mattos Jr., then Supreme President of U.P.E.C., appointed young Mário to revise the Constitution of the U.P.E.C. in that year he was elected Supreme Director and also appointed to write the minutes of the convention, aided by Francisco I. Lemos. From then on he was entrusted with this work alone, seeing at all times that a complete transcript of the minutes, reports and important documents were placed in book form for future consultation. His command of the Portuguese language was reflected in every page of the several volumes of minutes (ACTAS), still in existence in the J.A. Freitas Library, and in the many articles he wrote in the various newspapers of the time.

In 1898 Camara introduced the first issue of the *U.P.E.C. Bulletin,* the official publication of the Society. It contained four pages, size 9x12, and had a circulation of 2,500 copies at the cost of $18.30 per month.

In 1900 he submitted a design for the U.P.E.C. banner which was subsequently approved by the delegation to the convention held in San Jose, California. Camara's banner design remained unchanged until 1964, when the delegation recognized the need for a change to conform to the Portuguese colors of the Republic, red and green.

In December, 1905, he organized the U.P.E.C. Band, a group of musicians he directed and led throughout the years all over the State of California. The band's first appearance took place in October, 1906 at the convention in Salinas, California.

On February 10, 1910 the Board of Directors unanimously elected Mario Bettencourt Camara to the position of Assistant Secretary of the Supreme Council, a position he held with great distinction until his death.

Partially blind, Camara committed suicide at Chris Borba Undertaker's Parlor located then at 510 E. 14th Street, Oakland. It was noon on February 12, 1936. Lying on a shelf in the lavatory where he had shot himself, were ten letters addressed, some of them stamped. One was to his wife Katherine, and another to his nephew, Jose da Silva Gonsalves of Brasil, his only two relatives. The other letters were to the Chief of Police and Coroner of Oakland, A.J. Ansen; Band Director, Manuel Medeiros, Manuel Fraga, Supreme Secretary of U.P.E.C; Gerald Bispo; Albert Moura, owners of the undertaking parlor; and one to Guilherme S. Gloria, then a layman. Camara's funeral was the largest ever held among the Portuguese community in California. It took place on the afternoon of Saturday, February 15, 1936. Thousands accompanied him to his last resting place, the Evergreen Cemetery. Mrs. Gladys Keller carried the baton of the once distinguished musician, writer, and most dynamic leader the Portuguese in California ever knew.

A Chronica

Revista Critica da Sociedade Portugueza dos Estados Unidos

PERIODICO MENSAL.

Director e Proprietario M. Bettencourt da Camara.

N°. 7	Assignaturas -Para os ESTADOS UNIDOS : **12** numeros **$ 1.00** ; **6** numeros **50 cents**; **3** numeros **25 cents** Para o extrangeiro: **12** numeros **$ 1,25** ; **6** numeros **$ 0,75**. **Annuncios 10 cents** a linha. Desconto nos repetidos e a largo prazo. Toda a correspondencia para **M. Bettencourt da Camara, P. O. Box 2567, San Francisco, Cal.**	**ANNO I.**

SAN FRANCISCO, CAL. 20 DE DEZEMBRO DE 1895.

Entered at the San Francisco Post Office as Second Class Matter.

A
LESSON IN HISTORY
TO SOME OF THE
San Franciscan Journalists
IN AN
OPEN LETTER
TO THE
PEOPLE OF CALIFORNIA
BY
A Portuguese Journalist

EARS OF THE EDITOR OF THE "SAN FRANCISCO CHRONICLE" PULLED, AND A THRASHING TO THE REPORTERS OF THE "SAN FRANCISCO DAILY REPORT".

(Translated from the Portuguese)
—

"Thou shalt see Love of Land that neer shall own
lust of vile lucre; soaring towards th' Eternal :
For 't is no light ambition to be known
th' acclaimèd herald of my nest paternal."

CAMOENS, LUSIAD, CANTO I, VERSE X.

As some news-papers of this city have lately frequently published outrageous comments referring to Portugal and Portuguese people, I think it is my strict duty to come to-day before the citizens of California to reply to the extremely brutal attacks inflicted by certain journalists of San Francisco on my glorious country.

In Europe, where the way to settle this kind of affair is different, I should already have corrected some of those journalists who have exposed their ignorance of the very briliant pages of History, so prodigally illustrated by the famous deeds and wonderful heroism of the Portuguese; but in this country, where the law imposes its *veto* on such a custom as is tolerated in Europe, we must merely apply to the only resourse we may use in overthrowing the gratuitous libels employed by some pygmies of the San Francisco Press in order to detract from the glories of my country, as well as the bravery and virtues of the Portuguese. This resource is the field of the Press, whence I now direct to the Californian people the present protest, quite plain in form though very solemn in substance.

For a long time I tried without success to discover the origin of such unwonted attacks, when a Providential casuality enlightened me.

On the 14th of last month I found in the editorial section of the *San Francisco Chronicle* of that very day the following paragraph :

"It is unusual for the Portuguese in Africa to achieve any victory by force of arms. They gained their territorial possessions mainly by barter, and when given a mile they took a league. In this way their claims to territory are large, but the British have robbed them of considerable of this ill-gotten land. We now hear that the Portuguese have actually whipped the natives in East Africa in a square fight. It must be a relief to any soldiers among them to exchange glass beads for bullets."

On the same day the *San Francisco Daily Report* giving an account of the abject crime committed by some sexagenary rascals, who used to glut their beastly lasciviousness upon miserable children, in the *pious* intention to attain a culminating point in information, printed this insidious fiction, bred in the detestable and imaginary mind of its low reporter :

"Six more little girls who were regular visitors at Lane's place were examined at the Receiving Hospital this morning and, all told, more than 70 chil-

246

dren have been taken into that den. These girls, ranging in age from 9 to 13, came from the homes of people of the poorest class; many of them are Portuguese, and if the officers of the society are not mistaken, some of the mothers have voluntarily taken their little girls to the place and accepted pay for their degradation. It is said by the officers that money has been promised to some of these unnatural parents if they will suppress testimony against the defendants.''

The mystery was unveiled.

Those two statements made by the *Chronicle* and the *Report* put an end to my lucubrations, as they revealed the origin of the frequent insults heaped upon Portugal and the Portuguese. This origin, as I will try to demonstrate, must have proceeded from the deep ignorance and masterly charlatanism of the Editor of the *Chronicle* as well as from the reporters' gleaners of falsehoods.

Let us consider each of the two statements.

According to the *Chronicle* editorial paragraph, we may deduce :

That it is not our custom to achieve any victory by force of arms in our African possessions;

That we have obtained by barter the African colonies now and long since under our control;

That our territories taken from the Kaffirs by stratagem have been largely increased by unfair means, as *we take a league when given a mile*;

That, due to such proceedings, we have obtained a great deal of territory, but the British, in accordance with the old adage in which the Nation's wisdom states that "a thief gets indulgence for one hundred years when he steals from another thief," have robbed us of the greater part of those **ill-gotten lands;**

That, said *most wise* Editor was greatly surprised at the hearing of a recent victory won by our forces against the natives of East Africa in a square fight;

And, finally, that it must have been a fair satisfaction to any of our soldiers (*not to all..three or four*) to exchange their usual work of trading in glass beads for that of bullet distributers.

This distorted picture of Portugal and Portuguese shows evidently the gross ignorance which characterizes the Editor of the *Chronicle*.

It is quite natural and comprehensible, even for a journalist who conceals his ignorance, to know nothing about any Nation or People whose history is confined within its boundary; but it is astonishing to the highest degree that a journalist or anybody with an elementary education, should be ignorant of the past of Portugal and its people's wonderful achievements.

Well; such is the case with the Editor of the *Chronicle*. He is a great ignoramus, and more than that— a charlatain, because he dares to make improper statements about a subject totally unknown to him; and even more, to disparage a country which is worthy of all homage and respect from civilized nations.

The Editor of the *Chronicle* delineating us as a people of poltroons and rascals, basely slanders the Portuguese Nation, and brings shame upon the sacred

ashes of the great and heroic Captains of land and sea who have been the first

"by hunger broken and storm's hate,
    and curst by novel climes and seas unknown ''

to plant in the four parts of the world the Tree of Civilization; the Editor of the *Chronicle* trying to expose our brave soldiers to the derision of the ignorant multitude, stabbed the representatives of those invincible legions of warriors who astonished the world with the heroism of

"............War's own prodigies,
  In Africk regions and Orient Seas.''

Very well ! Now I have in view to pull such a silly journalist's ears, and give him a brief lesson in Universal History (referring to my country) and thus fulfil at same time two of the "Seven Spiritual Works of Mercy" which command "To instruct the ignorant and correct offenders.''

A parenthesis :

It not being my intention to here make a sketch of the origin of the Portuguese nationality, as I have but little space, besides the unfitness of the place, I think it necessary to give an elucidation indispensable to the readers of light erudition as the Editor of the *Chronicle*; and it is that : our forefathers were the **Lusitans,** the first inhabitants of the Lusitania, whose history—like that of the Spaniards—is shrouded in the mists of the past.

It was from that Lusitania, one of the three primitive Roman provinces of the Spanish Peninsula, that in the eleventh century the kingdom of Portugal arose, and soon after inaugurated the epoch of conquests and marvellous discoveries, which, in the phrase of August Comte, mark the commencement of the Occidental civilization.

So, those who are instructed up to the standard measure as the Editor of the *Chronicle*, may ascertain that glorious Portugal is neither a rib of glorious Spain nor the brave Portuguese inherit their bravery from the undauted Spaniards.

Although we profess the deepest admiration for the great kingdom of Spain and for the highly remarkable deeds of its illustrious people, yet we are led to destroy the false theory that mixes together Spain and Portugal, Spaniards and Portuguese.

Suum cuique!

So, listen to me, Mr. Editor.

"So shalt thou judge which were the higher station
King of the world or Lord of such a nation.''

A hundred and sixty one years before Christ, the Praetor of Lusitania, then a Roman province, was Servius-Sulpicius Galba, who, vexed by the bravery of the Lusitanians, perfidiously ordered the massacre of 30,000 of them. One of the surviving Lusitanians by name Viriato, stimulating his fellow countrymen's patriotism, succeede in inciting them to revolt against Rome, defeating in succession the Praetors C. Vetilius, C. Plautuis, Claudius Unimanus and C. Nigidius Figulus, and finally forcing Fabius Servilianus to capitulate and sign a treaty of peace between the Roman people and the Lusitan Viriato.

So that, twenty two centuries ago the humble Lusitanian soldiers triumphantly entered the Temple, according to history consecrated to the victorious armies, carrying as a trophy the documents of the capitulation of the famous and powerful Roman army.

And yet, notwithstanding all this happened so long ago, the intelligence has not reached the *wise* Editor of the *Chronicle*.

Let us pass in silence over some other brilliant victorious achievements of the Lusitanians in old times, even the victories won by them over Annuis and A. Barca, the latter being entirely defeated after having reduced to submission for nine years all the South and West parts of the Peninsula, in a glorious campaign.

Let us also pass in silence over that long period of encroachments for ten centuries threatening to extinguish the Lusitan race, to consider the original constitution of the Portuguese nationality.

It was in 1139 that Lusitania, then—by force of the circumstances—incorporated with the kingdom of Leon, assumed its autonomy, taking the name of Portugal from the main place of Lusitania —*Portus Calle*—after the memorable battles of *San Mamede* and *Ourique*, in the last of which Don Affonso Henriques took the title of king of Portugal. In 1147, the Moors, subdued at Santarem and Lisbon, ceded successively the principal cities of Alemtejo to the Portuguese, who inflicted on them uninterruped defeats.

Affonso Henriques died in 1185, and his successors proceeded with the work of expelling the Moors from the Alemtejo and Algarves, in which finally succeeded Affonso III in 1250, taking then the title of king of Portugal and Algarves, which to day the Portuguese monarch still holds.

In 1212 the Portuguese took a very remarkable part in the battle of *Navas de Tolosa* by the assistance afforded to the Castilians against Mohammed, who attempted the subjugation of Castile, and in 1340 it was the Portuguese interference at the celebrated battle of "Salado" that gave the Castilians the victory over the Moors.

In 1385 Portugal was invaded by an army of 30.000 men with the king of Castile in front, and 5.000 Portuguese fought against them the celebrated battle of "Aljubarrota," in which the Castilians were completely routed. Such a tremendous defeat caused so much grief to the king of Castile that he dressed himself in mourning to display his intense sorrow, not for the loss of the battle, he said, but for the shame of having been so disastrously defeated by such a small army.

According to the tradition, it was in that battle that a baker-woman named Maria Brites d'Almeida, killed seven Spaniards with her baker's peel, and so she has been remembered by posterity ever since under the surname of *Aljubarrota baker-woman* (Padeira de Aljubarrota).

(This case of Portuguese heroism is to warn the Editor of the *Chronicle*, if he may happen to face any female descendent of that heroine possibly living in California).

After the peace with Castile was signed, as the Moors did not venture to invade Portugal, the Portuguese resolved to attack them. A maritime expedition was then organised, which, sailing from Lisbon on the 15th of July 1415, through some events, anchored at Ceuta (Morroco) on August, 12, of the same year. Early next day when the troops began to land, the Moors opposed them with desperate resistance and engaged in a tremendous fight, which ended the same day by the victory of the Portuguese and the conquest of Ceuta.

Then began the sequence of the glorious conquests, wonderful voyages and discoveries of the Portuguese, that I propose to relate succinctly and chronologically—in order not to bother the readers.

1418—João Gonçalves Zarco and Tristão Vaz Teixeira, in north latitude 33°, and west longitude 18° 39', discover an island (one of the Madeira group) which they name *Porto Santo*.

1419—The same navigators discover the island of *Madeira*.

———Bartholomeu Perestrello colonizes the island of Porto Santo.

1431-32—Gonçalo Velho Cabral discovers the island of *Santa Maria* (Azores).

1434—Gil Eaunes sails past *Cape Bojador*, and thereby puts an end to the dreadful legend of the *Tenebrous Ocean* (Mar Tenebroso).

1436—Gonçalves Baldaya discovers the *Rio do Oiro* (Gold River).

1441—Nuno Tristão sails as far as *Cape Blanco*.

1444—Gonçalves Velho discovers the island of *S. Miguel* (Azores).

1445—João Vaz Corte Real discovers the *Island of Jesus Christ* or *Terceira* (Azores).

———Domingos Dias sails down along the Coast to latitude 14° 43' north and longitude 19° 35' west, and rounds *Cape Verde*, to wihch he gives its present name.

———Barbacim sails as far as the *Gambia*.

———The discoveries of *Angra de Gonçalo Cintra* and of the *Senegal* also take place.

1446—A voyage of exploration as far as the *Rio Grande* is successfully carried out.

———Discoveries of *Rio de Nuno* and *Rio Tabile*.

1449—Foundation of the fortress of *Arguim*.

———Discovery of the island of *S. Jorge, Graciosa, Pico* and *Fayal* (Azores).

1452—Discovery of the islands of *Flores* and *Corvo* (Azores—Western Islands).

1458—Conquest of *Alcacer-Ceguier*, in Mauritania.

1460—Diogo Gomes and Cadamosto discover the islands of *Maio, S. Thiago* and *Fogo* (Cape Verde Archipelago).

———Portugal mourns the loss of the great *Infante Dom Henriques*, the enterprising, the daring navigator and explorer, the founder of the first astronomical and nautical school at Sagres, the promoter of the famous voyages and discoveries of the Portuguese.

1461—Pedro de Cintra continues the discoveries beyond the *Rio Grande*, going as far as *Cape Mesurado*.

1469—Discovery of *Resgate d'Oiro* or *Mina*, and of the *Cape of Santa Catharina*.

——Lopo Gonçalves discovers the *Cape of Lopo Gonçalves*.

1470—João de Santarem and Pedro de Escobar discover *St. Thomas, Annabon* and *Prince's* islands,

1471—Conguest of *Arzilla* and *Tauger* in Mauritania (Morocco) and the discovery of the islands of *Coriscos*.

- ——In the same year Santarem and Escobar explore the *Costa da Mina* or *Gold Coast*.

1472—Fernando Pò discovers the island of *Formosa*, since known as *Fernando Pò*.

1481—Building of the *Castle of St. Jorge da Mina* and the permanent settlement of the Portuguese in that region.

1484—Diogo Cam discovers the *River Zaire* and the Kingdom of the Congo, extending his voyage 200 leagues south of that river.

1486—João Affonso de Aveiro explores the territory of *Benim* in Guinea.

——The great navigator BARTHOLOMEU DIAS, for the first time known in history, reaches the Cape of Good Hope. He sails out to the Ponta do Padrão and gives the name of *Cabo das Tormentas* (Cape of the Torments) o the newly discovered Cape. In this discovtery, the greatest of modern times, Bartholomeu Dias actually accomplished work which opened the way to India.

1487—Bartholomeu Dias, bringing to the world the very important news of his discovery, arrives at Lisbon.

——João Prestes da Covilhã and Affonso de Payva undertake an expedition by land to the Indias.

1491—Founding of first Christian Church in the Congo Kingdom.

1497—On the 8th of July, the immortal VASCO DA GAMA, leaves Lisbon on his famous voyage to India. He rounds the Cape of Good Hope on the 22th of November, and discovers the Natal Coast on December 25.

1498—On the 10th of January, on his way to India, he discovers the Rio do Cobre and the Terra da Boa Gente, and some days after the Rio dos Bons Signaes (Quilimane) and on the 2th of March the island of Mozambique, following this with the discovery of Mombassa and Melinde.

1498—On the 20th day of May Vasco da Gama casts anchor near Calicut opening to Occidental civilization the portals of the enchanted Orient.

1499—Vasco da Gama leaves India, casting anchor in the port of Lisbon on August 29, having stopped in Malabar, Angedive and Zanzibar.

1500—Pedro Alvares Cabral, at the head of a second expedition to the Indias, avails himself of the opportunity to salute the Occident, takes a south-westerly course from Lisbon and discovers the *Terras de Santa Cruz*, Coast of Brazil.

——Gaspar Corte Real discovers Labrador and sails along that Coast between 57° and 77, west longitude, and 52° and 62, north lat.

1501—João da Nova discovers the island of *Ascension*.

1502—First exploring voyage to Brazil.

——Second voyage of Vasco da Gama to India, in which he discovers the kingdom of *Quilôa* (Oriental Africa) and which he submits to the dominion of Portugal.

——Discovery of the island of *St. Helena* by João da Nova.

1503—Second voyage of exploration to Brazil.

1505—Fortification of several islands and cities in India under Portuguese dominion.

——Dom Lourenço d'Almeida discovers *Ceylon*.

——Tristão da Cunha discovers the island to which he gives is own name.

1506—Almeida da Cunha discovers the island of *St. Lawrence* (Madagascar).

——Affonso de Albuquerque sails up to the straits of the Arabian Gulf.

1507—Dom Lourenço de Almeida discovers the island of Maldives.

——Duarte de Mello establishes the first Christian Church and the first hospital in Mozambique.

——Tristão da Cunha subdues the people of Ajam and takes and rebuilds the fortress of Socotrà.

——The renowned Albuquerque explores the coast of Arabia and Persia, and conquers *Ormuz*.

1508-9—Diogo Lopes de Sequeira undertakes the exploration of Madagascar, discovers *Malacca* and subdues Pedir and Pacèm in the island of Sumatra.

1510-15—AFFONSO DE ALBUQUERQUE lays the foundation of the great Portuguese Empire in the Orient.

1511—Conquest of Malacca, Goa and Molucas.

1513—Taking of Camaram in the Persian Gulf.

——Discovery of the island of Reunion.

1516—Duarte Coelho discovers Cochin-China.

1517—Thomé Pires lands in China.

——Jorge Mascarenhas discovers Riou-Kiou (Liew Islands).

——Conquest of *Azamor* and Almedina, in Mauritania.

1519—FERNANDO DE MAGALHAES, a Portuguese navigator in the Spanish service, starts on his famous voyage of the first circumnavigation of the globe, rounds Cape St. John and Cape Horn, and discovers the Estreito de Magalhães (Strait of Magelan).

1525—Gomes de Siqueira discovers an island to which he gives his own name and which at present is known to be New Holland, Australia.

1529—Belchior de Souza Tavares explores the rivers *Tigris* and *Euphrates*.

1530—A fortress is built at Diu.

1534—Colonization of Brazil.

1535—Diogo Botelho Pereira makes a voyage from Diu (India) to Lisbon accompanied by 5 Portuguese sailors and 2 slaves, in a small pinnace 11 feet in length, 6 in width and 2½ in depth.

1536—A seminary for the education of children and the propagation of Christianity is founded in the Molucas, by Antonio Galvão.

1538—Memorable siege of Diu and heroic defense of its garrison under the command of Antonio da Silveira.

249

1540—Foundation of the College of S. Thiago in Cranganor for the education of the children of the converted heathen.

1541—D. Estevam da Gama sails up the Arabian Gulf as far as Suez.

1541—Seminario da Santa Fé, for the education of christians and heathen, is founded at Goa.

1542—Discovery of Zipango or Japan by Antonio da Motta, Francisco Zeimotto and Antonio Peixoto.

——João Rodrigues Cabrilho, a Portuguese navigator in the service of Spain, discovers California, entering on the 27th of September a bay which he names San Miguel, on the shore of this bay, a short time after, was founded the first town in California, named San Diego.

——*Lourenço Marques* discovers, in Oriental Africa, the bay and river which took his name (Delagoa Bay).

1546—Second siege of Diu, gallantly defended by D. João de Mascarenhas, and terminated by a brilliant victory by D. JOAO DE CASTRO.

1549—Settlement of the city of San Salvador, Bahia, Brazil.

1550-51—Foundation of two seminaries, in Salcete do Norte and Punicale, (India).

1551—Capture of Geilolo, capital of the island of the same name in the Molucas.

1556—Gaspar da Cruz, a Portuguese missionary in China succeeds in converting to Christianity a great number of the natives.

1557—The Portuguese drive the pirates from the Chinese coast, for which they have ceded to them the peninsula of *Macau*.

1559—Capture of the city of Damão and the island of Manar.

1569—Expedition to Monomotapà, Zambesi.

——D. LUIZ D'ATHAYDE suppresses a tremendous conspiracy of the people of India against Portuguese domination.

1575—The kingdom of Angola is founded by Paulo Dias de Novaes.

1582—Capture of the island of Labua (Malucas group).

1583—The king of Chale becomes a vassal of Portugal.

1587—Foundation of the fortress of Mascate.

——Dom Paulo de Lima enters Malacca triumphantly.

1590—Capture of Candy, Capital of Ceylon.

1603—Voyage of Bento de Goes to Grão-Catayo.

1606—Dom Manuel Pereira Forjaz, first attempts the opening of a route from the kingdom of Angola to Mozambique by land.

1606-7—Nicolau Orta comes from Goa to Portugal by land.

1609—Conquest of the Island of Sundiva.

1613—Exploration of the Island of St. Lourenço or Madagascar.

1619-20—Subjugation of the king of Dondo in the interior of Angola.

1624—Father Antonio de Andrade penetrates into the interior of Li-Zang or Tibet (China) and founds a christian mission in its capital.

1648—Expulsion of the Dutch from the kingdom of Angola.

1660—Celebrated voyage of a Portuguese navigator from Japan to Lisbon by way of the Arctic. (1)

1668—Ayres de Saldanha undertakes opening a route by land between Angola and the Sena.

1722—Sovereignty of Portugal on the island of S. Lourenço.

·1725—Friendly relations between China and Portugal established.

1783—Vicente Ferreira Pires travels in the kingdom of Dahomé.

1798—Francisco Jose de Lacerda e Almeida starts on a trip towards the opposite Occidental coast through the interior of Africa, and reaches the land of Cazembe, about half way across, where he dies.

1807-10—Two Portuguese expeditions start from Loanda, Angola, across the Dark Continent and successfully reach Mozambique.

The total number of vessels employed by Portugal in these voyages is not precisely known. It is known though, that after the discovery of the Cape of Good Hope, 1497, until 1612 the number of vessels that sailed from Lisbon for the discoveries in the Indian and Pacific Oceans was 806, 425 of which made the round trip, 285 were left in India, 66 were wrecked, 20 put back to port, 6 were burned in the high seas and 4 were captured by the enemy.

Calculating the average to be 175 men for each ship including sailors and marines, we have it that during that period of 115 years, Portugal had engaged in the discoveries on the East coast of Africa and the Indian and Pacific Oceans, 141,050 men, of which 13,270 found a watery grave, or were victims of storms, of fire, of battle axes of the pirates, or assagais of the savages.

Here is, in a very condensed form, the gigantic work of Portugal and the Portuguese in Africa, in Asia, in America and in Oceania, exemplified by the titanic strife waged and kept it up to the present day, not only with aborigenes of the conquered countries, but also with the Europeans who, following the maritime route discovered by us, have attempted by all means to snatch from us the product of our super-human efforts.

In modern times, without mentioning the famous deed of the Restoration of the Independence of Portugal (1640), our army and navy always maintained in Europe the most brilliant tradition of their heroism. See the renowned victories won in the memorable battles of *Montijo* (1644) against the powerful and intrepid Spanish army; and of the *Linhas d'Elvas* (1659), of *Amexial* (1663), and of *Montes Claros* (1665), those also against Spain, then confederated with France. In 1704 the Portuguese army, soon after the declaration of war against Portugal by the King of Spain, Philippe V, invaded that country and compelled the surrender of those fortresses that opposed its march, triumphantly entered Madrid, where, on the 2nd of July, it proclaimed the archduke Charles of Austria, king of Spain, under the title of Charles III. In 1717 a Portuguese fleet at

---

(1)—See Mr. de Buache, *Parallèle des fleuves*, History and Memoirs of the Royal Academy of Sciences of Paris, 1753.

the earnest request of Pope Clement XI, went to meet a formidable Turkish armada composed of fifty vessels, which was preparing to attack Venice and Corfu, and destroyed it, thus preventing those two republics and Italy from being subjugated by the barbarians.

Then follows the Peninsular war, where the Portuguese and the English fought together against the legions of Napoleon in the following memorable engagements won by the Anglo-Luso army:

Battles—*Roliça* and *Vimeiro*, 1808; *Corunha* and *Talavera*, 1809; *Bussaco*, 1810; *Fuentes de Honor, Albueira* and *Fuente Grinaldi*, 1811; *Salamanca*, 1812; *Victoria*, *Pyreneus*, *Nivelle* and *Nive*, 1813; *Ortez* and *Toulouse* in 1814. Assaults—*Ciudad Rodrigo* and *Badajoz*, 1812, and *San Sebastian*, 1813.

The bravery of our soldiers in these engagements with the armies of the ambitious, blood-thirsty and tyrannic Napoleon is honorably written in the diaries of the British generals Arthur Wellsley (Duke of Wellington), Dalrymple and Hill, and the French generals Junot, Massena and Soult.

In summing, up to conclude this brief extract from the history of my country, allow me this transcription from "The Story of Portugal" by the most illustrious English historian Sir H. Morse Stephens (p. 2):

"The extraordinary vigour shown by the inhabitants of this small corner of Europe during the latter half of the fifteenth and first half of the sixteenth centuries is most remarkable. Not only were Portuguese navigators the first to creep down the west coast of Africa in small boats, in which modern sailors would hardly like to cross the English Channel, but they dared to double the Cape of Good Hope, and to sail across the Indian Ocean to India and Ceylon. Thence they ventured round the point of Singapore, and established themselves at Macao, from which centre they explored the coasts of China and Japan. In the other direction, to the west, they crossed the Atlantic and discovered and colonized Brazil. Lisbon became the storehouse and centre of distribution for the products of the East, and attained to a height of wealth and luxury unrivalled since the days of ancient Rome. The history of the Portuguese "conquistadores" in India for the first hundred yers after the discovery of the route round the Cape of Good Hope is one long romance; the vastness of their designs, the grandeur of their exploits, and the nobility of character of their great captains, combine to make a story of surpassing interest. And when it is remembered that the soldiers and the sailors of these great discoverers and conquerors were inhabitants of the smallest country in Europe, their success seems the more extraordinary, and the interest in the story of the nation whihc trained the Portuguese heroes becomes the more absorbing."

"This is my happy land, my home, my pride"

These are my ancestors!

These are my countrymen, this is my nationality, and I feel proud of such an admirable past. Yes, Mr. Editor of the *Chronicle!*

This is the people, who for many centuries continually fighting in the four parts of the World, you say are not in the habit of achieving victories by force of arms! This is the people, who for many centuries holding in spite of all kinds of sacrifices, their African colonies acquired by the double right of discovery and conquest, you insinuate have gotten their possessions by barter—especially!

This is the people, Mr. Editor of the *Chronicle*, who by the dishonest and perfidious agreement of great Nations were forcibly dispolied of the most part of their immense colonial empire in Africa, Asia and Oceania, that you accuse of getting lands in Africa by villainous proceedings—TAKING A LEAGUE WHEN GIVEN A MILE!

This is the people, Mr. Editor of the *Chronicle*, who crossing long since the dark continent by sea and land fighting with fury against the natives of West Africa in order to hold their own rule and promote the civilization of those savage beings, that you state to possess *ill gotten lands!*

This is the people, Mr. Editor of the *Chronicle*, who holding for so many centuries heroic struggles on the extensive grounds of the North, East, South and West coast of Africa, that on account of a comparatively unimportant victory lately won over the Vatuas, arouses in you such strange surprise!...

This is the people, Mr. Editor of the *Chronicle*, whose fearless armies of land and sea, thousand times victorious in wonderful engagements, you as a *learned silly* dare to scoff, unmannerly trying to draw upon them the resounding laughter of rogues, the low mockery of the miserable scum, and perhaps the raillery or individuals of moderate culture and good feeling!...

So, Mr. Editor of the *Chronicle*, it remains exuberantly demonstrated that your ignorance is as dense as your journalistic conscience is light. You presumed to be an erudite man, and have given the evidence of knowing nothing. You tried to display your humours, and have been ridiculous.

To be sure, you are not a Mark Twain.

The way to thoroughly know a Nation and be able to write about it is to read its history before writing, and that you have not done.

Before closing, as I have given you a severe lesson, allow me to give you also some amicable advice—although I have no reasons to be your friend : You have mistaken your profession; journalism is not your vocation. With your talents and abilities, perhaps you would make an excellent shoemaker.

Nevertheless, if you insist in writing for the public, you must recommence your education from the begining, as it is quite evident that the money your parents spent in your school training was entirely lost; and you ought to learn to revere respectable things.

Furthermore : When the *Chronicle* prints such statements as that which furnished the theme for the present rebuke, the money gotten from its subscribers or buyers is much more **ILL-GOTTEN** than our lands in Africa.

Now the *San Francisco Daily Report.*

From the insipid prose of the article of that evening paper, which we have above reproduced, one would naturally conclude that of the 70 unfortunate little girls thrown upon the road of vice many were Portuguese, some of them having been voluntarily delivered to the vultures, by their own unnatural mothers, for pecuniary remuneration.

The *Report* did not allude to any other nationality. This circumstance is to be particularly noticed—only the Portuguese deserved the base and affronting insinuation with which they were discriminated by that paper.

Certainly, no nationality can collectively answer for the wrong doings of any of its members individually.

Therefore, none of the disgrace the little victims involved in this horrible case brought upon themselves and their parents, by their innocent participation in crime, reflects upon their nationality. This is as far as the children are concerned.

As to the mothers the case differs, and is by far worse in every respect. Since the statement was made that many of the children, involved in this scandal, were Portuguese, and no other nationality was mentioned, it was evident that the mothers who had so shamelessly sold their little daughters must also have been of the same nationality. This is what the *Report* would have its readers to believe. And, though there was not a bit of truth in the malicious statement, it certainly created an impression in the public mind that we—the Portuguese in general—were a people of extremely low morals.

Fortunately, though, to the credit of every citizen of San Francisco, of other nationalities as well as ours, the infamous acts of degradation attributed by the *Report* to these wretched mothers was nothing but a *blague* of the worst kind, condemnable in many respects, since it was ascertained that none of those afflicted mothers received any of the niggardly sums proffered for the degradation of their children—degradation for which the old licentious fiends often paid the fabulous price of 5 cents !

But—and the question is of great importance to us—in the number of children mentioned as having frequented those dens of depravity not a single one of them was of Portuguese descent, as was proven, and published in a protest addressed to the newspapers of this city, and by them kindly published (with the exception of the *Chronicle*) on the 19th of last month.

And supposing some of them were the children of Portuguese parents, would it be right for the *Report* to allude to our nation to the exclusion of all others nationalities ?

Would not this fact in itself constitute an offensive exception and arouse the indignation of every respectable person ?

The statement was entirely unfounded and was really a malicious and insulting insinuation of the *Report*, directed at not only the Portuguese mothers

resident in San Francisco, but all of that nationality in general, and which only those of low corrupted morals and entirely devoid of feeling and decency would fail to indignantly protest against and resent.

The *Report*, in that horrible and disgraceful case of Lane, Meyer and Ratz, made of the Portuguese name, a selection which exceeded the limits of the highest indignity, usurping the depths of an extreme abjection, not only with the false declaration that some of the children were of Portuguese birth, but also with prominent exclusiveness, that, the degradation of those children, had been transacted by their own mothers !...

The reader of those vile, insidious calumnies, not knowing the Portuguese society of California, would undoubtedly be possessed of a repulsive feeling against every member of this honorable community. Only the *Report* caused such feelings, neither the children nor their mothers so basely calumniated, but the authors of such base calumnies.

*

By the aforesaid protest, the Californians know already that not one of the children was Portuguese, but I fear, with reasonable foundation, that the public opinion would remain very unfavorable to this people, especially if established under that great principle of *no effect without cause*, judging the *cause* from precedents that can justify those *effects*.

Nothing has ever happened before. The precedents of the Portuguese Colony do not authorize such a shameful and outrageous opinion. On the contrary, if you look at the annals of crimes committed in California, you do not see the name of one Portuguese associated with those horrible crimes that blacken the Courts of this State. You may find, though, one or two exceptions, among those who use intoxicating liquors to excess, and that is all. Among the 10,000 vagrants who infest the villages and the cities of this State, you•do not find one Portuguese. In the Registers of the Police of California, you will find hundreds of names of highwaymen, thieves and robbers, and only that of one Portuguese who stole a few jewels from his Mistress. The credit of the Portuguese people is highly appreciated by the merchants with whom they transact business in California, and, when you look into their private life, you must say that the Portuguese society is worthy of exemple. The cases of divorce, between a Portuguese husband and wife are very rare, as also they are rare between a Portuguese husband and a wife of different nationality.

The conjugal life of a Portuguese, give an opportunity for observant study. His home is like a sanctuary, of which he is the pastor.

You may see him sometimes deprived of the confort and necessaries of life, but not his wife, whom he always provides with ample means, even if at great sacrifice. No people more than the Portuguese maintain the uncorrupted tradition of the old love. The Portuguese wife, thus dominated by her husband, can not be but a true, loving help-mate becoming the must devoted partner of his life, and the kindest of mothers.

Therefore no degradation can be germinated in a dulcified ambient like this, except by aberration, which takes place only by executing the command of the fatal law of exceptions. Fortunately, I am proud to say, such aberrations are very rare.

In support of my assertions I could give extracts from the works of the best Moralists, and the most eminent Thinkers of different epochs and nationalities; but, as I intend to be as short as possible, I will only say that from the Universal Statistics of depravity, among the cultured societies of the world, Portugal figures in the last place, with her sister the Republic of Brazil.

In California, notwithstanding, the scurrilous insinuation of the *Report*, facts speak for themselves. In San Francisco, and in the principal cities of this State, where depravity is tolerated, and where vice thrives in a brutal and free way, how many unhappy Portuguese woman do you find there, trading their chastity and purity?

Not one!

Do you hear this, *gentlemen* of the *Report?*

In those degraded houses which you call *dives,* where its visitors debase the body and soul by paying 5 cents for a class of beer, and were licentiousness is freely indulged in, how many Portuguese women do you meet there among the thousands of other perverted women, to whom the lack of courage and failure of a moral education for the hard fight of an honorable life, made them bargain honesty and honor for the easy and infamous life they live?

None, gentlemen of the *Report,* calumniators, libelers, none at all !

Among the great number of those unhappy women, wrapped in miserable rags, having impressed in their faces the excess of vice and the repulsive trace of infamy, staggering upon the threshold of the tavern, or lying insensible upon the side-walks of the streets, how many Portuguese women do you meet there?

None, none at all, charlatans of the *Report! !*

Among those groups of unconscious and irresponsible children, walking the streets of San Francisco at all hours, negligently intrusted by their own mothers to the venture of the fate which sometimes leads them to the road of a Lane's house, how many Portuguese children can you find there?

None, reporters of the *Report!*

We ask our readers to compare the honorable precedents of the Portuguese Colony with the erroneus judgment of the scribbers of the *Report,* charging such a heinous accusation without any foundation or cause, perhaps with the *justified* circumstance that those children were of the poorest class.

Every one with the exception of the *illustrious* staff of the *Report,* knows that there are no milionaires among the Portuguese of California, but—in compensation—you will not find one Portuguese beggar upon the streets of San Francisco, extending the hand like thousands of others to the public charity.

The reporters of the *Report*—with that unfounded impeachment only gave us a plain proof of their most profound ignorance, and of their great charlatanism.

*

Now it remains evidently demonstrated that the Editor of the *Chronicle* is one of the silliest creatures on earth, as the reporters of the *Report* are a flock of fancy-fellows.

With such leaders as these, it is not in the least surprising if many of the California people, hold an opinion which is not exactly gratifying to us.

The Portuguese of this State do not at all deserve a severe judgment, as they are sober and good workers, respecting the laws of the country they have chosen for their struggle for life, and the women are honest and respectable, though it may seem strange to the ignorant reporters of the *Report.*

In conclusion :

If in this world the right man should always occupy the right place, the Editor of the *Chronicl* should give up journalism and go to a shoe factory.

As for the others, the reporters of the *Report,* they are of no account to inform the public through the news-papers, all that they ought to do is to sell them on the streets.

———

The only remains for me to thank these so-called journalists for the opportunity they have given me to furnish the present explanation to the public.

BETTENCOURT DA CAMARA.

Portuguese Bicycle Club

Damos hoje o emblema do nosso Club de bicyclistas, desenhado segundo o plano de Bettencourt da Camara, redactor d'esta folha, e que foi escolhido pelos fundadores da nova Sociedade.

O emblema que hoje inserimos deu-o o nosso estimado collega *The San Francisco Call* d'esta cidade, cuja extremada amabilidade e gentileza da cessão agradecemos reconhecidos em nome do Club, ao qual aquelle collega offereceu o cliché, um bello trabalho das suas importantes officinas.

GUILHERME SILVEIRA DA GLÓRIA

Without question one of the most illustrious figures in the Portuguese-American community was Guilherme Silveira da Glória. Born on July 6, 1863 in Candelaria, Pico Island, Azores. He was the son of Manuel Silveira da Glória and Isabel Marianna da Gloria. The youngest of 17 brothers, at the age of 11, he completed his elementary education in his home town and continued his studies in Latin, French and English with a well-known tutor, Manuel de Brum Ataide, for the next five years.

When he reached the age of sixteen, he decided to study for the priesthood and, since his island could not provide him with either a seminary or secondary education teachers, he had to move to Horta, Faial, a thirty-minute voyage by motor boat from Madalena, Pico.

While in Horta, he prepared for the enrollment in the seminary of Angra, Terceira, Azores, where he was admitted in 1880. While in Angra he became acquainted with Manuel Francisco Fernandes, then a student for the priesthood, who had already spent some time in California and who related the spiritual conditions facing Portuguese immigrants in the golden state. This prompted Gloria to address a letter to Bishop O'Connell asking to be accepted at Mission San Jose Seminary in California to conclude his studies, and follow Father Fernandes' suggestion to be able to assist his compatriots, who were coming in large numbers, throughout California.

A favorable reply from California reached Guilherme. After obtaining permission to emigrate he left the Azores in the company of his sisters, Isabel and Ana. Once in the golden state, he entered St. Thomas Seminary in Mission San Jose, from which, four weeks later he was ordained and said his first mass on July 28, 1885.

He later was credited with building St. Joseph's Church in West Oakland, a Portuguese National Church, which was demolished in the late 1960s to allow for Acorn Project, a low-income housing complex.

Portuguese immigrants throughout the state were arriving in increasing numbers and priests were becoming scarce. As a result of this situation Father Glória, as he was then known, traveled California in Missionary work. He became pastor for the parish of San Leandro which at the time also included the areas of San Lorenzo, Hayward and Redwood Canyon.

In 1889, Paris was the stage for the World Exposition, becoming the center of attraction for everyone, including Father Glória. Upon his return to California from the fair he stopped in the Azores to renew acquaintances of his younger days and to bring back to California his sister Maria Josefina Glória Dias (she later became the mother-in-law of Dr. José Leal Azevedo, a physician of Oakland, California), and nephew John de Glória, and nieces Isabel Luis Mendonça, Amália (Mrs. José Leal Azevedo) and Maria Josephina Gloria (Ex-President of S.P.R.S.I. and founder of the Biblioteca Camões).

In 1895 he was named pastor of San Pablo and was later transferred to St. Joseph's parish in West Oakland to fill the vacancy created by the death of Father Manuel Francisco Fernandes, on April 25, 1896, where he remained approximately two and a half years.

To his own satisfaction, but to the disappointment of his family and preceptors, his course of life was changed when he fell in love and abandoned the priesthood to marry Miss Ana Beatriz Collins, a native of Santa Ana, California and daughter of Andrew Collins, one of the early miners in the state.

From this marriage there was one child, Wm. James Gloria, a brilliant young attorney, in 1923 graduate of Hastings College of San Francisco. He was admitted to the California State Bar and entered private practice which he continued with marked success; he won national recognition in six criminal trials, including the sensational Rosetta Baker murder case. He was also the Chief Counsel in defense of an indicted Chinese, Leu Fook. William James Glória died at age 39 on January 29, 1937, two weeks after his mother's death on January 14, 1937.

Guilherme, since early age, showed his great talent in poetry. Verses were written and published in his younger years in Azorean newspapers such as *O Picoense* of Pico and in the Católico of Terceira, Azores. While in the seminary at Angra he received the Literary Award from Bishop Don João Maria Pereira de Amaral e Pimentel.

In California, his poems appeared in usch early newspapers as *Progresso Californiense, União Portuguesa* and *O Amigo dos Católicos.* In 1894, he became part owner of the *Amigos dos Católicos,* with Francisco Ignacio Lemos, then a prominent attorney of Hayward, and Manuel S. Quaresma.

This newspaper appeared first on May 26, 1888 in Irvington under the ownership of two catholic priests, Fathers Manuel Francisco Fernandes and João Francisco Tavares, who later sold it to Lemos. Guilherme S. Glória was the editor-in-chief until 1896. While in that position, he was a subject of polemics and controversies, at times very vicious, between his paper and Mário Bettencourt da Camara. Later, Glória was replaced by Joaquim Borges de Menezes, a recent arrival from New Bedford, Massachusetts, who continued the publication until June 6, 1896.

A man of letters, and considered one of the very few intellectuals the Portuguese community of California has ever had, Glória initiated, in Sacramento on October 1, 1900, the publication of a weekly newspaper he named *A Liberdade* (Liberty). In 1920, the publication offices were moved to Oakland, where they remained until 1937 when the paper was suspended as a result of Glória's shock from the sudden deaths of his wife and son.

A Liberdade at one time became a daily, the only Portuguese newspaper in California to do so.

In 1935 Guilherme S. Glória published *Poesias,* an outstanding book of eighty-four poems in addition to the epic poem, "Cabrillo" in six cantos and two hundred thirty-eight *estancias.* In 1940 he published *Harpejos,* his last collection of poems. In them he exalted, once more, his pride of being Portuguese.

During his life he translated from the English and French several novels, one of which was Florence, in four volumes of beautiful Portuguese.

Guilherme joined U.P.E.C. Council No. 1, San Leandro, on October 7, 1888. He and Francisco Ignacio Lemos were two great friends, and were responsible for the U.P.E.C. Hymn as it is known and sung today.

Guilherme Silveira Glória, a few among the many, died on January 18, 1943, and was buried at the Holy Sepulchre Cemetery in Hayward, California.

MANUEL COSTA MEDEIROS

(1890–1966)

Born on May 10, 1890 in Ponta Delgada, San Miguel, Azores. Medeiros was the son of José Costa Medeiros, native of Nordeste, São Miguel, and Rosa Amelia Conceição Sousa, also of Nordeste, São Miguel.

Manuel Immigrated to California in 1903 coming to Oakland to work for the cotton mill, known at the time as "The Portuguese College" since most newly arrived immigrants in East Oakland went to work in the mill until they learned some English and could move to better paying trades. From the cotton mill Manuel went to work for the California Sash & Door Company located in West Oakland, until 1910. He then moved to San Francisco and worked for the sugar refinery. Seven years later he sought employment with Southern Pacific Railway, a job he held for a few months when he resigned to join the Fire Department of Oakland, a job he held until his retirement in 1955.

Manuel was married to Virginia Rogers, a native of Honolulu, Hawaii. From this marriage there were two sons, Walter and Melvin.

He joined U.P.E.C. Council No. 7, Oakland, on March 18, 1906.

He had an inclination for music and pursued his vocation playing in U.P.E.C. Band from 1905, and later in the Firemen and Police Band of the city of Oakland, which he had led since 1930.

However, his activities were confined mostly to U.P.E.C., at first as a bass player under the direction of Mario Bettencourt da Camara, organizer of the Uniform Band, later named U.P.E.C. Band. Manuel became assistant director of the U.P.E.C. Band in 1926 and ten years later became director until March 28, 1966, the time he resigned due to his poor health. Later in 1967, the band was disbanded by the Board of Directors as most os its musicians were then incorporated in what was known as the San Leandro Municipal Band, for a few years under the leadership of Manuel's late son, Walter Medeiros.

The U.P.E.C. Band was once conducted by John Phillip Sousa, a great musician of Portuguese descent, when he came to San Francisco to visit the Panama-Pacific Exposition, in 1915.

Manuel died on June 20, 1966 and was buried at the Holy Sepulchre Cemetery in Hayward, California, on June 23, 1966.

Manuel C. Medeiros (front in white cap) marches U.P.E.C. Band in their last parade through East 14th Street in downtown San Leandro in 1961.

U.P.E.C. Band playing concert at auditorium in Bakersfield, 1951.

Appendices

MEMBERS WHO SERVED IN THE SUPREME COUNCIL
(Other than President, Secretary and Medical Examiner)

Council No.	Name	Year Elected
3	Amaral, M.A. do	1889 (FC) — 1887-88-89-90-91-1894 (D) — 1898 (FC)
1	Andrade Jr., M.J.	1894 (D)
13	Andrade, William A. de	1950 (FC)
29	Apolinario, James	1988 (OG)
5	Augusto, Custódio J.	1904 (M)
7	Avelar, Alberto C.	1923 (D) — 1924 (D)
29	Avelar, Jess	1954 (FC) — 1955 (OG) — 1956 (M) — 1957 (MC)
1	Avellar, Manuel M.	1889-1891 (T) — 1889 (FC) — 1893-95-97 (D)
52	Ávila, Arnaldo	1986 (OG)
63	Ávila, F.M.	1911 (D)
63	Ávila, Frank L.	1933 (FC)
29	Ávila, J.B.	1902 (OG)
5	Azevedo Jr., C.J.	1905 (MC)
47	Azevedo, João	1949 (OG) — 1950 (IG) — 1951 (M)
15	Baptista, José	1899-1900 (D)
39	Bairos, J.J.	1906 (M)
1	Barbeiro, J.I.	1905-06 (D)
1	Barradas Jr., F.C.	1887 (D) — 1889 (FC) — 1890 (G) — 1892 (MC)
1	Barreiro, Jonine	1988-91 (D)
6	Bettencourt, António M.	1889 (D)
3	Bernardo, José	1898 (MC)
5	Bernardo, Manuel J.	1944 (D)
68	Borba, Frank R.	1926-27-28-29-37 (D)
32	Borges, Domingos T.	1949-50 (D) — 1951 vc (D) — 1953-54 (D)
5	Brandão, J.F.	1899 First IG — 1900 (M)
66	Brass, John	1913 (D)
66	Braz, António V.	1932 (FC)
42	Brazil, A.T.	1901 (OG)
1	Bulcão, Manuel Silveira	1887-1888 (T) — 1890-92-93 (D)
24	Camesão, George	1983-86 (D)
97	Charamuga, Neves	1974-78 (D)
69	Codina, António E.	1965-66-67-72-75-76-78 (D)
3	Costa, Eddie C.	1973 (OG) — 1974 (IG) — 1975 (M) — 1976 (MC) — 1977 (3rd VP) — 1978 (2nd VP
1	Carvalheira, Felicissimo	1985 (OG)
8	Caetano, Francisco	1892 (M) — 1893 (MC) — 1894 (MC) — 1900 (D)
15	Camara, Mário B.	1895 (D)
169	Carvalho, Frank	1953-54-55-56-57-58-59-60 (D)
110	Castello, M.V.	1922 (OG) — 1923 (IG) — 1924 (M) — 1928 (D)

68	Caton, William A.	1949-50-51 (D)
22	Clemente, J.V.	1903 (OG)
22	Clemente, Joe M.	1929 (FC)
42	Coelho, F.S.	1946 (D)
32	Coelho, Joseph L.	1956 (OG)
11	Dias, J.P.	1954 and 1964 (OG) — 1955 and 1965 (OG) — 1955 and 1966 (M) — 1967 (MC) — 1968 (3rd VP) — 1969 (2nd VP)
11	Dias, F.R.	1954 and 1964 (OG) — 1955
75	Dias, João	1980 (OG) — 1983 (MC)
5	Diavila, Serino C.	1896 (D)
115	Dutra, João C.	1923 (OG)
103	Dutra, Joseph F.	1972 (D)
82	Encarnação, R.A.F.	1908 (OG) — 1909 (IG)
164	Enos, A.F.	1943 (FC) — 1945 (OG) — 1946 (IG) — 1947 (MC) — 1948 (VP) — 1953 (D)
23	Enos, J.I.	1908 (IG)
11	Enos, Manuel I.	1901 (MC)
115	Fagundes, Lucindo	1976 (D)
38	Feliciano, Manuel	1917 (FC)
75	Fernandes, J.C.	1921 (OG) — 1922-23 (D)
1	Ferreira, L.A.	1888 (D)
7	Fialho, F.G.	1889 (G)
158	Frade, António J.	1961-71 (D)
115	Fraga, Daniel	1986-91 (D)
15	Freitas, F.L.	1907-08 (FC)
2	Freitas, M.T.	1887 (FC) — 1888-89 (D) — 1891 (MC) — 1900-01 (D) — 1902-03 (FC)
55	Frias, A.J.	1906 (OG) — 1907 (OG)
69	Frizado, Manuel Mata	1963-64 (D)
32	Furtado, Joseph A.	1961-70 (D)
74	Garcia, F.S.	1941-42-43 (D)
25	Glória, John J. de	1925-26 (D)
3	Gomes, José F.	1902 (IG) — 1903-04 (FC)
80	Gonsalves, L.	1912-13 (D)
63	Gonsalves, Louis	1920-21-22 (FC)
63	Goularte, Carlos P.	1914 (IG) — 1915 (M) — 1916 (MC) — 1921 (D)
37	Gulart, John	1959-68 (D)
7	Henas, Manuel	1890 (FC)
14	Ignácio, M.T.	1940 (D)
100	Jacinto, John A.	1945 (D)
5	Jorge, José F.	1891 (D)
25	Joseph, J.S.	1909 (FC)
116	Lawrence, Anthony	1954 (MC) — 1955 (VP)
102	Lawrence, George L.	1924-25 (FC)
32	Lawrence (Lourenco), José	1900 (OG)
4	Leal, F.A.	1911 (OG)
7	Lemos, A.J.	1905 (M) — 1906 (MC) — 1911 (FC)
172	Lewis, Clarence	1948-49 (FC) — 1950 (M) — 1952-54-55 (D)

42	Lewis, E.R.	1924 (OG) — 1925 (IG)
42	Lewis, Manuel R.	1926 (M)
25	Lewis, Nestor	1930-31 (FC) — 1926 (M)
73	Lima, A.A.	1910 (IG)
8	Lima, Fernando I.	1989 (OG)
11	Lima, Frank Costa	1896 (G) — 1897 (MC)
94	Lisboa, Domingos	1947-48 (D)
12	Lopes, Albert J.	1931 (FC) — 1933-34-35 (D)
13	Lopes, Dr. J.C.	1933-34-35-36-37-38 (D)
119	Lopes, Manuel R.	1941-42 (FC) — 1944 (OG) — 1945 (IG) — 1946 (M)
43	Lourencio, Carlos	1983-85 (D)
1	Lucio, António	1892 (G) — 1893-98 (T) — 1901 (D)
172	Luis Jr., Luis	1951 (FC)
40	Luiz, António S.	1927-28-31-36 (D)
148	Machado, Frank	1979-82 (D)
65	Machado, Frank A.	1920-21 (D)
115	Machado, Joe	1970 (OG) — 1971 (IG)
95	Machado, John	1969-74 (D)—1975 (IG)—1976 (OG)—1977 (M)—1978 (MC)
12	Machado, M.S.	1912 (IG)
103	Machado, M.T.	1942-43-44-45 (D)
95	Machado, Victor	1948 (D) — 1950 vc (D) — 1951 c (D) — 1952-53 (D)
56	Manha, Andrew G.	1951-52-53-54-55-56-57 (FC)
4	Mariante, G.F.	1890 (D)
30	Martinho, A.S.	1898 (M)
94	Martins, Teotónio I.	1928 (OG) — 1929 (IG) — 1930 (M)
25	Mathews, F.J.	1901 (FC) — 1909 (OG) — 1911 (M) — 1912 (MC)
7	Medeiros, Manuel C.	1958 (MC) — 1959 (3rd VP)
137	Medeiros, Mary	1988 (IG)
4	Mello, Manuel	1887 (D)
1	Mendonça, J.B.	1893-1908-10 (D)
75	Miguel, Joseph P.	1959 (OG)
31	Mitchell, Manuel	1899 (1st OG) — 1900 (IG) — 1904 (MC) — 1907 (FC) — 1916 (D)
25	Monteiro, A. Garcia	1919-20-21-26 (FC)
13	Moura, Alberto	1929-30-31 (D) — 1932 (Sec D)
32	Neto, Arthur Gonsalves	1956-57-58-60 (D)
8	Neves, José	1894 (M) — 1895-96 (M) — 1898 (D)
52	Nicolau, Jr., Walter	1984-88 (D) — 1991 (OG)
14	Nunes, A.I.	1942-43-44-45 (D)
40	Nunes, António I.	1920 (OG) — 1921 (IG) — 1922 (M) — 1924 (MC)
52	Nunes, Ernest	1977 (OG) — 1978 (IG)
60	Oliveira, António	1947-53 (D)
167	Oliveira, Matheus	1943-44 (D)
69	Oliver, Lawrence	1939-40-41 (D)
68	Pedro, Luis C.	1935 (D)
68	Pedro, M.J.	1945 (FC) — 1947 (M)

5	Peixoto, F.A.	1893 (M)
11	Pereira, António V.	1895 (MC)
12	Perry, J.D.	1905 (OG) — 1906 (IG) — 1907 (M)
3	Perry, Serafim	1957 (IG) — 1958 (3rd VP) — 1959 (2nd VP)
94	Picanso, Manuel F.	1949-50-51 (D)
16	Pinto, Manuel C.	1955 (3rd VP) — 1956 (2nd VP) — 1957 (1st VP)
8	Quaresma, M.B.	1893 (G)
90	Quaresma, M.S.	1913 (OG) — 1915 (D)
32	Romano, Evarist	1987-89 (D)
15	Raphael, J.I.	1905 (D)
13	Renas, José T.	1901 (M) — 1905-06-07 (D)
32	Rodrigues, A.V.	1909-1925 (D)
15	Rodrigues, Francisco Daniel	1900-02 (FC)
7	Rodrigues, J.C.	1890-96 (D)
69	Rosa, Cristiano da	1981 (OG)
7	Rosa, José Maria da	1889 (FC) — 1890 (M) — 1891-93 (T) — 1898 (FC) — 1899-1900 (FC)
32	Rose, Carl F.	1943 (FC) — 1944-45-46-47 (D)
167	Santos, Adelino	1952 (FC) — 1978 (OG)
1	Santos, F.F.	1899 (M) — 1890-1900-05-06-07-10 (D)
21	Santos, João V.	1918 (OG) — 1919 (IG)
2	Santos, José Joaquim	1889 (D)
30	Serpa, M.C.	1905 (IG)
70	Silva, Enos N.	1946 (FC)
25	Silva, Frank R.	1948 (OG) — 1949 (IG)
102	Silva, Herculano G. da	1939 (OG) — 1940 (IG) — 1941 (M) — 1942 (MC)
74	Silva, Joe I.	1981-91 (D)
15	Silva, J.J.	1906 (D)
14	Silva, J.V.	1908-09-10-11-12 (D)
99	Silva, João M.	1922-23-24 (D)
23	Silva, Louis A.	1957 (3rd VP) — 1958 (2nd VP) — 1959 (1st VP) — 1962-63-64-65-74-75 (D)
1	Silva, M.A. da	1946-47-48-49-50 (FC)
5	Silva, M.F.	1894 (D)
11	Silva, Manuel P.	1963 (MC)
15	Simas, Frances	1961- (Pianist)
12	Soares, A.P.	1903 (IG)
100	Soares, Anthony J.	1948 (IG) — 1949 (M) — 1950 (D)
130	Soares, John M.	1932-33-34-35-36-37-38-39-40-41-42 (FC)
100	Soares, M.M.	1947 (OG)
37	Soares, Manuel	1953 (OG)
3	Smith, José	1887 (D) — 1894 (G)
1	Smith, W.D.	1888 (D)
8	Soito, Edward E.	1935 (FC)

137	Sousa, Alfred	1952 (OG) — 1953 (IG) — 1954 (M) — 1955 (MC) — 1956 (3rd VP)
95	Sousa, Frank E.	1951 (OG) — 1952 (IG) — 1953 (M) — 1954-55-56 (D) — 1957-68-77-81 (D)
163	Sousa Helio	1974 (OG) — 1975 (IG) — 1976 (M) — 1977 (MC) — 1978 (3rd VP)
24	Souza, Manuel B.	1969 (OG) — 1970 (3rd VP) — 1971 (2nd VP)
75	Souza, Manuel S.	1953 (FC)
116	Souza, Robert	1960 (IG) — 1961 (M) — 1962 (M)
32	Swayze, Everett	1976-80 (D) — 1982-86
68	Teixeira, George L.	1972-74 (D)
55	Thomas, A.B.	1904 (OG)
29	Trindade, Hubert	1976 (OG) — 1977 (IG)
116	Vargas, Edwin J.	1986-91 (D)
73	Viery, Wilfred O.	1981 (D)
17	Vargas, Joseph	1990 (OG)
11	Valim, LArry	1979-80 (D)
75	Vieira, Manuel	1987 (OG)
19	Vieira, Manuel M.	1904 (IG)

D	—	Director	VP	—	Vice President
FC	—	Finance Committee	2nd VP	—	2nd Vice President
G	—	Guard	3rd VP	—	3rd Vice President
IG	—	Inside Guard	c	—	Chairman of Board
M	—	Marshal	sec	—	Secretary of Board
MC	—	Master of Ceremonies	vcb	—	Vice Chairman of Board
OG	—	Outside Guard	T	—	Treasurer

U.P.E.C. SUBORDINATE COUNCILS

Council No.	Name	City	Date Organized	President	No. Charter Members
1	San Leandro	San Leandro	Aug. 1, 1880	A. Fonte	30
2	Hollister	Hollister	Oct. 27, 1883	A. Fonte	21
3	São João	Hayward	Jun. 24, 1885	A. Fonte	20
4	Santo Antonio de Pádua	Petaluma	Sep. 26, 1886	A. Fonte	21
5	Amor da Pátria	Centerville	Aug. 12, 1888	A. Fonte	31
6	Luiz de Camões	Mendocino	Feb. 3, 1889	A. Fonte	33
7	Flor da União	E. Oakland	Sep. 29, 1889	A. Fonte	34
8	Serpa Pinto	Pleasanton	Aug. 24, 1890	A. Fonte	30
9	Milpitas	Milpitas	Nov. 23, 1890	A. Fonte	22
10	Amor do Próximo	Mission San Jose	Jul. 12, 1891	A. Fonte	17
11	Aurora	Sacramento	Aug. 23, 1891	A. Fonte	14
12	Watsonville	Watsonville	Apr. 3, 1892	A. Fonte	25
13	W. Oakland	W. Oakland	Jan. 29, 1893	A. Fonte	15
14	Marques de Pombal	Sausalito	Sep. 27, 1893	A. Fonte	14

Council No.	Name	City	Date Organized	President	No. Charter Members
15	Infante D. Henrique	San Francisco	Jun. 24, 1894	J. Pimentel	12
16	António Fonte	Alvarado	Mar. 31, 1895	J.G. Mattos	34
17	Half Moon Bay	Half Moon Bay	Jul. 27, 1895	J.G. Mattos	13
18	Flor da Patria	Benicia	Sep. 21, 1895	J.G. Mattos	12
19	Amor da União	San Rafael	May 10, 1896	J.G. Mattos	11
20	Mousinho de Albuquerque	Concord	Jun. 21, 1896	J.G. Mattos	11
21	Fé Esperança e Caridade	Selma	Sep. 5, 1896	J. Mattos	11
22	Protecção	Hanford	Sep. 6, 1896	J. Mattos	10
23	Fraternidade	Fresno	Sep. 8, 1896	J. Mattos	12
24	Fernão de Magalhaes	Stockton	Nov. 1, 1896	F.I. Lemos	12
25	Oakland	Oakland	Dec. 27, 1896	F.I. Lemos	26
26	Pinole	Pinole	Jan. 10, 1897	F.I. Lemos	25
27	San Pablo	San Pablo	Jan. 10, 1897	F.I. Lemos	14
28	Santa Clara	Santa Clara	Mar. 1, 1897	F.I. Lemos	12
29	Merced	Merced	May 30, 1897	F.I. Lemos	20
30	Corte Real	San Francisco	May 21, 1897	F.I. Lemos	20
31	Santa Cruz	Santa Cruz	Oct. 31, 1897	A. Cunha	24
32	San Jose	San Jose	Nov. 21, 1897	A. Cunha	32
33	Danville	Danville	Jan. 16, 1898	A. Cunha	13
34	Gloria da União	Yreka	Mar. 10, 1898	A. Cunha	34
35	Pescadero	Pescadero	Apr. 17, 1898	A. Cunha	15
36	Amor Açoreano	Freeport	Jul. 3, 1898	A. Cunha	21
37	Monterey	Monterey	Sep. 11, 1898	A. Cunha	21
38	Sebastopol	Sebastopol	Apr. 23, 1899	V. Braga	11
39	Salinas	Salinas	May 14, 1899	V. Braga	14
40	Sacramento	Sacramento	Aug. 6, 1899	V. Braga	31
41	Ashland	Ashland	Feb. 4, 1900	A.J. Pinheiro	18
42	San Luiz	San Luis Obispo	Feb. 11, 1900	A.J. Pinheiro	21
43	Don Carlos	Hynes (Wilmington)	Mar. 21, 1900	A.J. Pinheiro	14
44	Ventura	Somis (Oxnard)	Mar. 22, 1900	A.J. Pinheiro	19
45	Rainha D. Amélia	Novato	Apr. 1, 1900	A. Pinheiro	41
46	Dona Maria Pia	Mt. View	Apr. 8, 1900	A. Pinheiro	13
47	Flor do Rio	Rio Vista	Apr. 22, 1900	A. Pinheiro	23
48	Cabrilho	Fairfield	May 26, 1900	A. Pinheiro	18
49	Flor Açoreana	San Mateo	Jul. 1, 1900	A. Pinheiro	11
50	Sonora	Sonora	Aug. 5, 1900	A. Pinheiro	11
51	Prosperidade	Antioch	Nov. 18, 1900	J. Valadao	12
52	Harmonia	Modesto	Nov. 25, 1900	J. Valadao	13
53	Amisade	Valona	Dec. 9, 1900	J. Valadao	13
54	Seculo Vinte	Newark	Jan. 20, 1901	J. Valadao	17
55	California	San Leandro	Feb. 24, 1901	J. Valadao	22
56	Liberdade	Oakland	May 5, 1901	J. Valadao	22
57	Madera	Madera	Nov. 24, 1901	F. Cunha	18
58	Brio da União	Newcastle	Nov. 28, 1901	F. Cunha	17
59	Progresso	Guadalupe	Dec. 7, 1901	F. Cunha	12
60	Colombo	Cayucos	Dec. 7, 1901	F. Cunha	16
61	Decoto	Decoto	Jul. 22, 1902	F. Cunha	22
62	Gilroy	Gilroy	Jul. 20, 1902	F. Cunha	14
63	Luz da União	Oakland	Jul. 27, 1902	F. Cunha	25
64	José Pimentel	Chico	Sep. 26, 1902	F. Cunha	20
65	Palo Alto	Mt. View	May 22, 1903	A. Martins	12
66	Santa Maria	Santa Maria	May 30, 1903	A. Martins	10
67	Agua Caliente	Warm Springs	Jun. 21, 1903	A. Martins	14
68	West Side	Newman	Jul. 6, 1903	A. Martins	12
69	Point Loma	Point Loma	Jan. 13, 1904	J. Woods	15
70	San Juan Bautista	San Juan Bautista	May 10, 1904	J. Woods	12

Council No.	Name	City	Date Organized	President	No. Charter Members
71	Livermore	Livermore	May 15, 1904	J. Woods	10
72	Vacaville	Vacaville	Feb. 12, 1905	M. Fraga	12
73	Flor da Palma	Vallejo	Feb. 12, 1905	M. Fraga	14
74	San Pedro	Los Banos	Aug. 12, 1905	M. Fraga	11
75	Boa Esperanca	Turlock	Sep. 9, 1905	M. Fraga	12
76	Lincoln	Lincoln	Dec. 1, 1905	L. Enos	15
77	São Jorge	Castroville	Sep. 23, 1906	L. Enos	15
78	Açores	Atwater	Feb. 16, 1907	J. Mendonca	14
79	Irvington	Irvington	May 5, 1907	J. Mendonca	18
80	Flor de Mendocino	Fort Bragg	Jul. 1, 1907	J. Mendonca	12
81	Santa Cruz	Santa Cruz (Felton)	Sep. 21, 1907	J. Mendonca	29
82	Portugal	W. Oakland	Nov. 17, 1907	A. Sarmento	20
83	America	Oakley	Nov. 24, 1907	A. Sarmento	12
84	Primeiro de Dezembro	S. San Francisco	Dec. 1, 1907	A. Sarmento	15
85	Independente	Greenview	Jun. 27, 1908	A. Sarmento	14
86	Rodeo	Rodeo	Jul. 15, 1908	A. Sarmento	14
87	Vasco da Gama	Elmhurst	Jan. 24, 1909	J. Pereira	15
88	Alum Rock	E. San Jose	Apr. 25, 1909	J. Pereira	11
89	Folsom	Folsom	Sep. 26, 1909	J. Pereira	16
90	São Gabriel	Arroyo Grande	Jun. 6, 1910	J. Pereira	11
91	Lisboa	Lemoore	Sep. 29, 1910	J. Pereira	16
92	Alhambra	Martinez	Oct. 9, 1910	J. Pereira	13
93	Napa	Napa	Nov. 1, 1910	J. Jorge	13
94	Republica	Tulare	Nov. 13, 1910	J. Jorge	10
95	Bakersfield	Bakersfield	Nov. 20, 1910	J. Jorge	13
96	Red Bluff	Red Bluff	Dec. 18, 1911	J. Jorge	10
97	Teófilo Braga	Ryde	Mar. 19, 1911	J. Jorge	13
98	Point Reyes	Point Reyes	May 21, 1911	J. Jorge	22
99	San Joaquim	Gustine	Jun. 22, 1911	J. Jorge	17
100	Redlands	Redlands	Jul. 19, 1911	J. Jorge	10
101	W. Berkeley	W. Berkeley	Aug. 10, 1911	J. Jorge	16
102	Melrose	Melrose	Sep. 9, 1911	J. Jorge	18
103	Flor do Condado de Butte	Gridley	Sep. 16, 1911	J. Jorge	26
104	São Miguel Arcanjo	Tomales	Oct. 8, 1911	J. Jorge	19
105	Terceira	Hanford	Apr. 7, 1912	A. Wilson	68
106	Flor de San Ramon	Walnut Creek	Jun. 29, 1912	A. Wilson	26
107	Paz e Progresso	Yuba City	Jul. 7, 1912	A. Wilson	11
108	Washington	Crows Landing	Aug. 2, 1912	A. Wilson	22
109	Pajaro Valley	Watsonville	Nov. 3, 1912	G. Pereira	12
110	Visalia	Visalia	Nov. 11, 1912	G. Pereira	14
111	San Gregorio	San Gregorio	Dec. 1, 1912	G. Pereira	14
112	Paz e Harmonia	Edna	Jan. 5, 1912	G. Pereira	10
113	Santa Rosa	Santa Rosa	Jan. 12, 1913	G. Pereira	11
114	Ferndale	Ferndale	Feb. 13, 1913	G. Pereira	22
115	Arcata	Arcata	Mar. 2, 1913	G. Pereira	15
116	Flor de Hughson	Hughson	Jun. 1, 1913	G. Pereira	14
117	Tipton	Tipton	Sep. 23, 1913	G. Pereira	14
118	Princeton	Princeton	Oct. 23, 1913	J. Pimentel	14
119	Flor de Riverdale	Riverdale	Nov. 1, 1913	J. Pimentel	10
120	Aurora	Livingston	Nov. 8, 1913	J. Pimentel	14
121	Salida	Modesto	Dec. 7, 1913	J. Pimentel	11
122	San Francisco	Richmond	Feb. 8, 1914	J. Pimentel	11
123	Imperial	Brawley	Mar. 28, 1914	J. Pimentel	12
124	Mill Valley	Mill Valley	Jun. 16, 1914	J. Pimentel	12
125	Lompoc	Lompoc	Oct. 1, 1914	J. Pimentel	11
126	Holt	Holt	Oct. 17, 1914	A. Homen	21
127	Sunnyvale	Sunnyvale	Oct. 18, 1914	A. Homen	16

Council No.	Name	City	Date Organized	President	No. Charter Members
128	Dixon	Dixon	Nov. 1, 1914	A. Homen	15
129	Orland	Orland	Nov. 5, 1914	A. Homen	16
130	Patterson	Patterson	Nov. 7, 1914	A. Homen	15
131	Praia da Victoria	San Rafael	Nov. 8, 1914	A. Homen	13
132	Paulo da Gama	Isleton	Nov. 15, 1914	A. Homen	24
133	Colusa	Colusa	Nov. 20, 1914	A. Homen	16
134	Silva	Niles	Nov. 29, 1914	A. Homen	17
135	Lisbon	Clarksburg	Dec. 6, 1914	A. Homen	17
136	Flor de Ceres	Ceres	Dec. 29, 1914	A. Homen	13
137	Flor de Tracy	Tracy	Dec. 31, 1914	A. Homen	14
138	Flor Unida	Santa Clara	Feb. 7, 1915	A. Homen	26
139	Flor de Dos Palos	Dos Palos	Mar. 9, 1915	A. Homen	12
140	Val de Snelling	Snelling	May 28, 1915	A. Homen	12
141	Flor de Oliveira	Oroville	Jul. 1, 1915	A. Homen	13
142	Los Alamos	Los Alamos	Jul, 1, 1915	A. Homen	18
143	Santa Barbara	Santa Barbara	Aug. 5, 1915	A. Homen	11
144	Flor de Nord	Nord	Aug. 18, 1915	A. Homen	10
145	Bernardino Machado	Wayne	Aug. 30, 1915	A. Homen	10
146	San Buena Ventura	Ventura	Sep. 9, 1915	A. Homen	13
147	Campbell	Campbell	Sep. 25, 1915	A. Homen	10
148	Manteca	Manteca	Oct. 2, 1915	A. Homen	11
149	Oceano	Oceano	Jan. 2, 1916	M. Azevedo	14
150	(no record of ever being organized)				
151	Eureka	Eureka	Apr. 20, 1916	M. Azevedo	15
152	Fowler	Fowler	May 19, 1916	M. Azevedo	10
153	Cinco de Outubro	Sacramento	Sep. 25, 1916	M. Azevedo	18
154	Angra do Heroismo	Volta	Jan. 25, 1917	J. Avelar	15
155	Nevada	Reno, Nev.	Feb. 24, 1917	J. Avelar	25
156	Mocidade	Riverside	Apr. 19, 1917	J. Avelar	14
157	Lovelock	Lovelock, Nev.	Jun. 10, 1917	J. Avelar	29
158	Yerington	Yerington, Nev.	Jun. 12, 1917	J. Avelar	25
159	Aliado	Stratford	Oct. 25, 1917	J. Dutra	19
160	Pixley	Pixley	Nov. 18, 1917	J. Dutra	10
161	Tranquility	Tranquility	Dec. 1, 1917	J. Dutra	12
162	Flor de Hardwick	Hardwick	Jan. 2, 1918	J. Dutra	13
163	João Dutra	Goshen	Sep. 6, 1918	J. Dutra	11
164	Ripon	Ripon	Jan. 8, 1920	F. Silveira	21
165	Contra Costa	Byron	Oct. 6, 1920	F. Silveira	13
166	Paz e Harmonia	French Camp	Jul. 25, 1927	T. Lopes	28
167	Dr. Oliveira Salazar	Artesia	Jun. 1, 1934	F. Freitas	11
168	Sage	Fallon, Nev.	Sep. 8, 1935	R. Rosa	11
169	Dos Palos	Dos Palos	Jan. 24, 1937	J.T. Lopes	20
170	Quatro de Julho	Snelling	Jul. 3, 1938	M. Alves	27
171	Homen (União e Protecção)	King City	Dec. 22, 1938	A. Ignacio	20
172	Victória	Orland	Oct. 4, 1945	M. Pereira	20
173	Escalon	Escalon	Dec. 8, 1951	M. Furtado	50

FAMILY NAMES OF
EARLY PORTUGUESE IMMIGRANTS IN CALIFORNIA

Abrantes
Abrão
Abreu
Affonso
Agostinho
Agrela
Aguiar
Aires
Albergaria
Alegre
Alexandre
Almada
Almeida
Alvares
Alvernaz
Alves
Amaral
Amarante
Amarelo
Amaro
Ambrósio
Ambrózio
Anacleto
Andrade
Andre
Angeja
Angelo
Aniceto
Anselmo
Apolinário
Aragão
Aranjo
Araujo
Areia
Areias
Armas
Arriaga
Arruda
Ataide
Augusto
Aveia
Aveiro
Avelar
  (Avellar)
Avila
Ázera
Azevedo
Azinheira

Baeta
Baião
Baios
Baptista

Barbeiro
Barbosa
  (Barboza)
Barcelos
  (Barcellos)
Barradas
Barrao
Barreira
Barreiro
Barreto
Barroca
Barros
Bastos
Bebereia
Belchior
Beirao
Belem
Belo
Benevides
Benjamin
Bento
Bernardo
Bertão
Bertoldo
Bettencourt
  (Bettencut)
Bezerra
  (Beserra)
Biscaia
Bispo
Boim
Bonito
Borba
Borges
Borreco
Botelho
Braga
Branco
Brandão
Brás
Brasil
Braz
Brazil
Breves
Brindeiro
Brioso
  (Briozo)
Brito
Brum
Bulcão

Cabeceiras
Cabelleira

Cabos
Cabral
Caetano
Calcado
Caldeira
Calisto
  (Calistra)
Camacho
Camara
Camilo
  (Camillo)
Campos
Canáda
Canario
Candeias
Candelaria
Canhoto
Caniço
Capela
Capinha
Cardadeiro
Cardoso
  (Cardozo)
Carlos
Carmo
Carolo
Carrancho
Carreiro
Carvalho
Carvão
Casaca
Casemiro
Casqueiro
Castanho
Castelo
  (Castello)
Castro
Catarina
Cedros
Cezar
Charamuga
Chaves
Chibante
Cipriano
  (Cepriano)
  (Seppriano)
Chrysostomo
Clemente
Clementino
Coderniz
  (Cordeniz)
  (Codorniz)
Codinha

Coelho
Comacho
Conde
Constantino
Cordeiro
Corrêa
Correia
Corvello
Corvelo
Costa
Cotta
Coucello
Coutinho
Couto
Craveiro
Cravinho
Crespo
Cristiano
Cristo
Cruz
Cunha
Custodio

Damão
Damas
Damasco
Damião
Dana
Daniel
Davide
Deus
Dias
Diávila
Dinis
  (Deniz)
Domingos
Domingues
Duarte
Dutra
Enos
Escala
Escobar
Esperanca
Espinolá
Estevão
Esteves
Estrela
Eustacio
  (Estácio)
Evangelho

Fagundes
Fantazia

Faria
Farias
Farinha
Faustino
Fayal
Feijão
Feliciano
Felix
Fellipe
Fernandes
Ferreira
Ferro
Fevereiro
Fialho
Figueira
Figueiredo
Flores
Focha
Fonseca
Fonte
Fontes
Fortuna
Fortunato
Frade
Fraga
Frago
Fragueiro
Franco
Francisco
Fragoso
 (Fragozo)
Frederico
Freire
Freitas
Frias
Frizado
Frontella
Furtado
Gabriel
Galante
Galego
Galera
Galeria
Galvão
Gama
Garcia
Gaspar
Gerevásio
Gil
Glória
Godim
Godinho
Gomes
Gonçalves
Gonsalves
Gordo

Gouveia
Graca
Grégorio
Grillo
Guardanapo
Guerra
Guido
Guilherme
Gularte
 (Goulart)
 (Gulart)

Henriques
Homem
Horta

Ignácio
Inocencio
Isidoro

Jacinto
Jardim
Jaime
Janeiro
Jeronimo
 (Jeronymo)
Jesus
Joaquim
 (Joaquin)
Jordão
Jorge
Junqueiro

Labandeira
Lacerda
Laranjeira
Laranjo
Laureano
Lázaro
Leal
 (Lial)
Leandro
Lebão
 (Libão)
Leite
Lemos
Leonardo
Levinho
Lima
Limão
Lindo
Linhares
Lino
Lira
Lisboa
Lobão

Lobo
Lopes
Loureiro
Lourenço
Louro
Lucas
Lucido
Lucindo
Lucio
Luiz
 (Luis)
Luz

Macedo
Machado
Maciel
Madeira
Madruga
Magalhães
Maldonado
Malta
Mancebo
Manhã
Manteiga
Marcellino
Marcos
Maria
Mariante
Mariero
Marteniano
Martinho
Martins
Marques
Massa
Mateus
 (Matheus)
Matias
Matos
 (Mattos)
 (Mattas)
Medeiros
Medina
Meirelles
Melo
 (Mello)
Mendes
Mendonça
Mendonsa
Menezes
Mesquita
Miguel
Miranda
Moitozo
Moleiro
Moniz
Monte

Monteiro
Morais
 (Moraes)
Morango
Moreira
Moreno
Morgado
Mota
 (Motta)
 (Matta)
Moutinho

Narciso
Nascimento
Neto
 (Netto)
Neves
Nicolau
Nobrega
Nordeste
Noia
 (Noya)
Novo
Nunes

Oliveira
Olympio
Ormonde
Ornellas

Pacheco
Paine
Pais
 (Paes)
Paiva
Paixao
Palacio
Palma
Palmeira
Pamplona
Panasco
Panarra
Pardal
Parreira
Passos
Pastor
Pasqual
 (Paschoal)
Patricio
Paula
Paulino
Paulo
Pavao
Paz
Pedras

Pedreira
(Pedreiro)
Pedro
Pedroso
(Pedrozo)
Peixoto
(Peichoto)
Penacho
Pena
Perdigao
Peregrino
Pereira
Pestana
Picanco
Piloto
Pimentel
Pinheiro
Pinho
Pinto
Pio
Pires
Pitta
Pombo
Ponte
Porto
Portugal

Quadros
Quaresma
Quental
(Quintal)

Rafael
Rainha
Ramalho
Ramos
Raposo
(Raposa)
Raulino
Real
Rebelo
Regallo
Rego
Reis
Relvas
Renas
Renda
Rezendes
(Resendes)
(Rezende)
Ribeiro
(Ribeira)
(Rebeiro)
Ricardo
Rico

Rita
(Pitta)
Rocha
Rodrigues
Rogério
(Rodgers)
Rolão
Romeiro
Roque
Russo

Sá
Sabino
Saca
Sales
(Salles)
(Sallas)
Salgueiro
Salomão
Salsa
Salvador
Santana
Santos
Saraiva
Sardinha
Sarmento
Saudades
(Soudades)
Saude
Sebastião
Segredo
Sena
(Senna)
Sequeira
Serpa
Serra
Serrão
Silva
Silveira
Silvestre
Simão
Simas
Simões
Soares
Soito
(Souto)
Solares
Sousa
(Souza)
Sózinho
Surreição

Tavares
Taveira
Teicheira
Teixeira

Teles
(Telles)
Terra
Teves
Tiago
Toledo
Tomaz
(Tomás)
Tomé
Torres
Tortas
Toste
Trigueiro
Trindade
Tristão
Tromas
Trombas
Trovão

Valadão
(Valladão)
Vale
(Valle)
Valentim
Valencio
Valente
Vales
Valim
Valleiro
Vargas
Vasconcellos
Vaz
Velho
Veloso
Venta
Ventura
Verde
Verissimo
Vicente
Victor
Victorino
Vida
Vidal
Viegas
Vieira
Vigario
Vilaes
Vital
Viveiros

Xavier

Zacarias

ANGLICIZED CALIFORNIA PORTUGUESE FAMILY NAMES

Aguir	for Aguiar	Brown	Brum
Alameda	Almeida	Brun	Brum
Alexander	Alexandre	Buran	Beirão
Almeda	Almeida	Burgess	Borges
Alvernez	Alvernaz	Caldero	for Caldeira
Alvas	Alves	Cambra	Camara
Ambrose	Ambrózio	Camello	Camilo
Andrada	Andrade	Camp	Campos
Andrew	André	Cantal	Quental
Andrews	Andrade	Cardoza	Cardoso
Aragon	Aragão	Carero	Carreiro
Arauz	Araujo	Carrier	Carreiro
Arude	Arruda	Carriere	Carreiro
Athayede	Ataide	Casemero	Casimiro
August	Augusto	Catania	Caetano
Augustina	Agostinho	Caton	Caetano
Ayres	Aires	Catten	Caetano
Azevada	Azevedo	Catrina	Catarina
		Catrino	Catarina
Bairos	for Barros	Chambers	Camara
Barber	Barbeiro	Clay	Barros
Barbera	Barbeiro	Clement	Clemente
Barbour	Barbeiro	Codeglio	Cordeiro
Barcelles	Barcelos	Codina	Codinha
Barcels	Barcelos	Coit	Couto
Barrios	Barros	Coite	Couto
Barret	Barreto	Constant	Constantino
Barry	Barros	Conti	Conde
Bean	Feijão	Corea	Correia
Benavidez	Benevides	Corey	Correia
Benevedes	Benevides	Corria	Correia
Benito	Bonito	Corry	Correia
Bennet	Bonito	Covarelli	Carvalho
Bennet	Bernardo	Crews	Cruz
Bennitt	Bonito	Cross	Cruz
Berberia	Bebereia	Curry	Correia
Bernal	Bernardo		
Bernard	Bernardo	Dambrosio	for de Ambrósio
Berne	Bernardo	Damera	de Amaral
Bertain	Bertão	Damin	Damião
Berry	Morango	Damos	Dâmaso
Bodge	Borges	Daniels	Daniel
Bordges	Borges	Daveiro	de Aveiro
Borge	Borges	Davilla	de Avila
Botela	Botelho	Days	Dias
Bothello	Botelho	Deas	Dias
Bothelo	Botelho	Debrum	de Brum
Brabosam	Barbosa	Decost	da Costa
Brager	Braga	Delima	de Lima
Bragg	Braga	Demello	de Melo
Brandon	Brandão	Dennis	Deniz
Brass	Brás	Diaz	Dias
Braze	Brás	Dimenco	Domingues
Brooks	Ribeiro	Domings	Domingues

Dondrado		de Andrade
Eanos	for	Enos
Emery		Amaral
Enes		Enos
Ennes		Enos
Ennis		Enos
Escubar		Escobar
Espingula		Espinola
Espindola		Espinola
Espindula		Espinola
Estevo		Esteves
Facha	for	Focha
Farres		Ferro
Feles		Félix
Felis		Félix
Feliso		Félix
Fellow		Fialho
Fellows		Félix
Fereria		Ferreira
Ferris		Ferreira
Ferry		Ferreira
Fields		Campos
Fields		Fialho
Figeroid		Figueiredo
Figueredo		Figueiredo
Foster		Faustino
Fragouzo		Fragoso
Francis		Francisco
Frates		Freitas
Fratis		Freitas
Fratus		Freitas
Frazer		Freitas
Gallant	for	Galante
Gaspari		Gaspar
Gasper		Gaspar
George		Jorge
Gerevas		Gerevásio
Gier		Aguiar
Gill		Gil
Geravazo		Gerevásio
Gouvea		Gouveia
Govea		Gouveia
Grace		Graça
Gracia		Garcia
Green		Verde
Hall	for	Sales
Henas		Ignacio
Hendrick		Henriques
Hendricks		Henriques
Henry		Henriques
Hill		Monte
Hines		Enos

Holmes		Homem
Homen		Homem
Hope		Esperanca
Jacinth	for	Jacinto
Jacintho		Jacinto
James		Jaime
Jaques		Joaquim
Jardine		Jardim
Jarvis		Gerevásio
Jerome		Jerónimo
Jess		Jacinto
Joaquin		Joaquim
Joeking		Joaquim
Jordan		Jordão
Kardoza	for	Cardoso
Katen		Caetano
Katon		Caetano
Katten		Caetano
King		Reis
Kuite		Couto
Lamb	for	Cordeiro
Laurence		Lourenco
Lawrence		Lourenco
Lazarus		Lazaro
Lema		Lima
Lenard		Leonardo
Levada		de Oliveira
Levin		Levinho
Lewis		Luiz
Light		Luz
Limas		Lima
Limon		Lima
Linn		Lino
Lisbon		Lisboa
Lorentz		Lourenco
Louis		Luis
Lucido		Lucindo
Lunardi		Leonardo
Madruegh	for	Madruga
Magellan		Magalhães
Manhan		Manhã
Maral		Amaral
Marcial		Maciel
Marciel		Maciel
Markes		Marques
Marks		Marques
Mateas		Matias
Mathias		Matias
Matoza		Moitoso
Matteri		Medeiros
McCiel		Maciel

Meadows	Medeiros	Perry	Pereira
Mederios	Medeiros	Peters	Pedro
Medero	Medeiros	Phillips	Filipe
Medrows	Medeiros	Pidgeon	Pombo
Meli	Melo	Pimental	Pimentel
Mell	Melo	Pine	Pinheiro
Mellow	Melo	Piver	Paiva
Mendoes	Mendes	Prara	Pereira
Menze	Mendes		
Meyers	Maio	Quail for Coelho	
Miller	Melo		
Millhouse	Azinheira	Rames for Ramos	
Moitoz	Moitoso	Raphael	Rafael
Monez	Moniz	Rapoza	Raposo
Montero	Monteiro	Raymus	Ramos
Monize	Moniz	Reposa	Raposo
Moones	Moniz	Reyes	Reis
Moore	Moura	Richards	Ricardo
Morris	Morais	Rivers	Ribeiro
Morton	Martinho	Roach	Rocha
Motoza	Moitoso	Roche	Rocha
Munice	Moniz	Roderick	Rodrigues
Muniz	Moniz	Rodgers	Rogerio
Munoz	Moniz	Rodrick	Rodrigues
Mure	Moura	Rogers	Rogério
		Rose	Rosa
Nevas for Neves			
Nevis	Neves	Sands for Areias	
Nobriga	Nóbrega	Sappers	Serpa
Norager	Nóbrega	Scares	Sequeira
Norberg	Nóbrega	Seamas	Simas
Noyer	Noia	Sears	Soares
Nursmith	Nascimento	Secara	Sequeira
		Semas	Simas
Oak for Carvalho		Shephered	Pastor
Oakes	Carvalho	Senram	Serrão
Oaktree	Carvalho	Sequira	Sequeira
Oates	Aveia	Silvay	Silveira
Olive	Oliveira	Silver	Silva
Oliveaira	Oliveira	Silveria	Silveira
Oliver	Oliveira	Silvey	Silva
Ormond	Ormonde	Silvia	Silva
		Simmons	Simões
Pachao for Paixão		Simon	Simao
Paine	Pena	Simons	Simas
Paiz	Pais	Sims	Simas
Palacioz	Palacio	Smith	Ferreira
Pareira	Pereira	Snow	Neves
Pariera	Pereira	Solomone	Salomão
Pashotte	Peixoto	Springs	Fontes
Passus	Passos	Stanton	Eustacio
Patrick	Patricio	Star	Estrela
Pavon	Pavão	Statua	Eustacio
Peacock	Pavão	Stevens	Esteves
Peary	Pereira	Steves	Esteves
Perreira	Pereira	Stone	Pedras-Pedreira

Stuve		Esteves	Valadon	for	Valadão
Suares		Soares	Valentine		Valentim
Supriano		Cipriano	Valine		Valim
Swartz		Soares	Vargen		Vargas
Swears		Soares	Vass		Vaz
Sylva		Silva	Vera		Vieira
Sylvia		Silva	Viator		Vieira
			Videll		Vidal
Tacheira	for	Teixeira	Vierra		Vieira
Tacherra		Teixeira	Viery		Vieira
Tash		Teixeira	Vincent		Vicente
Tavare		Tavares			
Taveres		Tavares	Wedge	for	Cunha
Tavis		Tavares	White		Alves
Teichera		Teixeira	Williams		Guilherme
Terry		Terra	Wolf		Lobo
Texeira		Teixeira	Wood		Madeira
Texiera		Teixeira	Woods		Madeira
Thomas		Tomaz			
Tosta		Toste	Young	for	Novo
Tosti		Toste			
Towers		Torres	Xaviel		Xavier
Travis		Tavares			
Travers		Tavares			
Trigeiro		Trigueiro			
Trinidad		Trindade			

Bibliography

BIBLIOGRAPHY

The following is a bibliography of the most important sources of information consulted for use in the preparation of this work.

PRIMARY SOURCES

A.P.P.B. — Membership Register — Conselho Açoreano No. 5-San Leandro, 1870 (J.A. Freitas Library collection)

Actas (Minutes) — Supreme Council of U.P.E.C. (from 1887 through 1947) The "Actas" were printed and kept in book form. They contain all minutes for Boards, Committees and Conventions. Most officers reports, amendments, resolutions and communications from city officials, newspapers and Portuguese community organizations. From 1948 through 1978, reports were mimeographed and some typed and are kept in the archives of the society — U.P.E.C. Home Office, San Leandro, California.

Andrade, Manuel Silveira de — Origem da Primeira Sociedade Portuguesa na California (Original manuscript kept in the J.A. Freitas Library, San Leandro.) The true remarks of a whaling voyage from the North Atlantic to the North Pacific Ocean, around Cape Horn in 1859, on board the Bark Pacific (396 tons) of New Bedford. (Original manuscript kept by daughter Maria G. Vargas — a copy is in the J.A. Freitas Library.)

Constituição — Irmandade Portuguesa do Estado da California — Oakland — 1881 — Tribune Press, Oakland, 1878.

Constituição Leis e Regulamentos d'Ordem — União Portuguesa do Estado da California — Oakland — 1881.

Dixon, Earl L. — The Portuguese in California During the 1880's and the 1890's — unpublished thesis — San Jose State College — 1965.

Original Minutes — U.P.E.C. Council No. 1 (1880-1886)

Portuguese in Hawaii — A paper by Edgar C. Knowlton — University of Hawaii — 1960.

Portuguese in Hawaii (The) — A resource Guide — Ethnic Research and Resource Center — Honolulu, Hawaii — 1973.

U.P.E.C. Council No. 1 — San Leandro — Membership Register (1880-1978)

U.P.E.C. Death Claim Register (1880-1978)

SECONDARY BOOKS

Angeles, Historic Record Co. of Los — History of Contra Costa County, 1926.

Bannick, Christian John — Portuguese Immigration to the United States, Its Distribution and Status — E. and R. Research — San Francisco — 1917.

Bernard, William S. — American Immigration Policy, A Reappraisal — Kennikat Press, N.Y.

Birmingham, Stephen — The Grandees (America's Sephardic Elite) Harper and Row Publ., N.Y., 1971.

Bromwell, William J. — History of Immigration to the Unites States — Redfield, N.Y., 1856.

Brown, John Brow — Portuguese in California — The University of California, 1944.

Bryans, Robin — The Azores — Faber and Faber — London — 1963.

Byington, Lewis Francis — The History of San Francisco — S.J. Larke Co., 1931.

Cardozo, Manoel da Silveira — The Portuguese in America — Oceana Publications, N.Y., 1976.

Case, Howard D. — The Story of Hawaii
Clarke, S.J. (The) Publishing Company — History of Alameda County — Chicago, 1928.
  — History of Kings County
  — Past and Present of Alameda County
Costa, Francisco Carreiro da — Para a História da Emigração do Distrito de Ponta Delgada — Edição do Autor 1972.
  — Acores, Olisipo — Lisboa, 1967.
Davis, Ellis A. — Commercial Encyclopedia of the Pacific Southwest — Berkeley, 1911.
Day, A. Grove — Hawaii and its People — Meredith Press, N.Y.
Freitas, J.F. — Portuguese-Hawaiian Memories — Honolulu, 1930.
Fructuoso, Gaspar — Saudades da Terra — Instituto Cultural de Ponta Delgada — San Miguel, Azores.
Fuchs, Lawrence H. — Hawaii Pono: A Social History — Harcourt Inc., N.Y.
Greaves, Manuel — Aventuras de Baleeiros Horta, Faial, Azores 1950.
  — Historias que me Contaram Horta, Azores, 1948.
Halley, ·William — The Centennial Yearbook of Alameda County — Oakland, California, 1876.
Jones, Maldwyn Allen — American Immigration — The University of Chicago Press, 1960.
Kinnard, Lawrence — History of San Francisco Bay Region — Lewis Historical Publishing Co., N.Y., 1966.
Lafler, Henry Anderson — Alameda County, The Ideal Place for Your California Home — Board of Supervisors — 1915.
Lang, Herbert O. — History of Tuolumne County — San Francisco — 1882.
Lewis Publishing Co. (The) — Illustrated History of San Joaquim County — Chicago 1890.
  — The Bay of San Francisco — Chicago, 1882.
Lima, Gervásio de — A Pátria Açoreana Editora Açoreana, Angra, Açores, 1928.
Lima, Marcelino — Anais do Municipio da Horta — Oficinas Gráficas Minerva — Famalição, 1943.
Lind, Andrew W. — Hawaii's People — University of Hawaii — Honolulu, 1967.
London, Jack — The Valley of the Moon — Grosset and Dunlap — N.Y., 1916.
Lopes, Norberto — Emigrantes Sociedade de Geografia de Lisboa 1964.
Maia, Francisco de A.M.F. e — Capitães dos Donatários (1439-1766) Lisboa — 1972
  — History of San Miguel, Azores.
Moore, Elliot — History of Stanislaus County — San Francisco, California, 1881.
Norbeck, Edward — Pineapple Town — Hawaii — University of California Press, Berkeley, 1959.
Novotny, Ann — Strangers at the Door — Bantam Pathfinder — New York, 1974.
Outcalt, John — History of Merced County — Historic Record Company — Los Angeles, 1925.
Palmer, Albert W. — The Human Side of Hawaii — The Pilgrim Press — Boston, 1924.
Pap, Leo — Portuguese-American Speech — King's Crown Press — Columbia University, N.Y., 1949.
Potter, Norris W. — Hawaii, Our Island State.
Quinn, J.M. — History of Monterey and San Benito Counties — Historic Record Co. L.A., 1910.
  — History of Stanislaus County
  — History of the State of California
  — History of the State of California and Biographical Record of the San Joaquin Valley — The Chapman Publishing Co. — Chicago 1905.

— History of the State of California and Biographical Record of Santa Cruz, San Benito, Monterey and San Luis Obispo Counties The Chapman Publishing Co. — Chicago, 1903.

Sawyer, Eugene T. — History of Santa Clara County Historic Record — Los Angeles 1922.

Serrão, Joel — Emigração Portuguesa — Livros Horizonte — Lisboa, Portugal.

Shaffer, Harry E. — A Garden Grows in Eden — The Centennial Story of San Leandro — City of San Leandro, 1972.

Siddall, John William — Men of Hawaii — Honolulu Star — Bulletin, 1921.

Silva Jr., João — Azoreans in America and Americans in the Azores — Portuguese-American Federation — Bristol, R.I., 1968.

Silveira, João Augusto da — Anais do Municipio de Lajes das Flores — Camara Municipal de Lajes — 1969.

Stevens, John L. — Picturesque Hawaii — Hubbard Publishing Co. — Philadelphia, Pa., 1894.

Stuart, Reginald R. — San Leandro — A History — First Methodist Church, 1951.

Todd, Frank Morton — The Story of the Exposition — G.O. Putman's Sons — New York, 1921.

UNESCO — The Positive Contribution by Immigrants — United Nations — Printed in France, 1955.

Valim, John C. — Historia da I.D.E.S. — Oakland.

Vandercook, John W. — King Cane, The Story of Sugar in Hawaii — Harper and Bros. — New York, 1939.

Vaz, August S. — The Portuguese in California — I.D.E.S. — Supreme Council — Oakland, 1965.

Veer, Daisy Williamson de — The Story of Rancho Santo Antonio — Oakland, 1924.

Venables, Bernard — Baleia! Baleia! Whale Hunters of the Azores — A.A. Knopf — N.Y., 1969.

Wood, M.M. — History of Alameda County — Oakland, California, 1883.

Wyndette, Olive — Islands of Destiny, A History of Hawaii — Charles Tuttle G. Vermont.

NEWSPAPERS AND PERIODICALS

American Statistical Association — The Portuguese Population in the United States — Article by Frederick L. Hoffman.

Arauto (O) — Oakland, California (1905-1917) Bancroft Library Collection — University of California at Berkeley, California (listed under Jornal de Noticias — Alameda — Microfilm)

Atwater Signal — (Atwater, California)

Boletim da U.P.E.C. — (1895-1966)

Bulletin of the Associated Milk Producers — San Francisco, 1923.

California Historical Society Quarterly — The Portuguese in California — Article by Federick G. Bohme.

Carnation (The) — Oconomowoc, Wisconsin — December 1930.

Cherry City News — (San Leandro, August 1925)

Chronica (A) — Monthly publication by Mário Bettencourt Camara — San Francisco — (1895-1896)

Colónia Portuguesa (A)

Daily Review (The) — Hayward, California — An Informal History of California — Series of articles by John Sandoval.

Fraternal Monitor (The) — October 1968.

Imparcial (O) — Sacramento, California (April 1914)

Independent Journal — San Rafael, California (May 25, 1974)

Jornal Portugues — Oakland, California (1932-1978) Microfilm collection — Bancroft Library — University of California at Berkeley.

Liberdade (A) — Sacramento, California (March 1915)

Lusitanian (The) — Oakland, California, 1936-1949 (Incomplete)

Luso-Americano (O) — Newark, N.J.

Merced-Sun-Star (The) — Merced, California (July 1947)

Morning News (The) — San Leandro, California

Newcomers in the United States — Paper presented by Herbert Bienstock — American Immigration and Citizenship — N.Y., 1976.

Novato Advance — (August 30, 1961)

Nuhou — The Hawaii News — Honolulu — 1873 — Bancroft Library, University of California at Berkeley — Microfilm collection.

Out West — Portuguese Colonies in California — Article by Emily Yates Mowry

Pioneers of Los Angeles County — In the Days of '49 — Article by J.M. Guinn.

Portugália — Oakland, California (March 1932)

Portuguese Experience in the United States (The) — Double Melt or Minority Group? — Francis M. Rogers — University of Harvard.

Portuguese Times (The) — New Bedford, Mass. (1976)

Progresso Californiense (O) — Published in San Francisco, California (1885) — Microfilm collection of J.A. Freitas Library.

Reporter (The) — Immigration — Quotas vs. Quality — Article by Paul Duke and Stanley Meisler — Jan. 14, 1965.

Revista Portuguesa — Hayward, California (1914-1920), J.A. Freitas Library (Incomplete)

San Francisco Chronicle — October 6, 1915

San Leandro Reporter — May 17, 1870 — March 2, 1951 — Microfilm S.L. Library collection.

San Leandro Standard — August 13, 1914.

San Luis Obispo Telegram Tribune — January 1946.

Sociology and Social Research — Portuguese Assimilation in Hawaii and California — Article by Gerald A. Estep, Student — University of Southern California.

União Portuguesa (A) — Oakland, California (1892-1899 and 1909-1942) (Incomplete) J.A. Freitas Library collection — U.P.E.C. Cultural Center — San Leandro, California.

U.P.E.C. Life — 1967-1978.

U.S. Congress — Senate Report of the U.S. Immigration Commission, Vol. 24, Part II — Immigrant Farmers in the Western States — Portuguese Farmers About San Leandro, California (1911).

Vallejo Evening News — January 1931.

Voz de Portugal — Hayward, California (1960-1978)

Voz Portuguesa — San Francisco, California (Mar.-Jul. 1887).

INDEX

Abandoned Property Act, 134
Advertising, 72
Afonso, João, 136
Africa, 2, 4, 128, 133
Aguiar, Gilberto Lopes, 115
Alaska, 5
Algarve, 1
Almeida, Carlos, 85, 112, 115, 116, 120, 135, 243
Almeida, Gregorio António, 40
Alves, Gil, 112
Alves, João Herbert, 214
Alves, Leopoldina C.R. 108, 181, 193
Alves, Manuel V., 126, 193
Amaral, João Bosco M. (Dr.), 136, 240
Amaral, Manuel Alexandre, 40
Amaral, Manuel E., 242
American Creamery, 94, 146
American Red Cross, 63, 64
American Trust Co., 146, 147
Amigo Dos Católicos (O), 159, 244, 256
Anaheim, 216
Andrade, Manuel S., 8, 10, 25, 26, 27, 33, 56
Anglo-Saxon, 1
Angola, 2
A.P.U.M.E.C., 109, 125, 137, 142
Aragão, José Luiz T. (Dr.), 117, 236
Arauto (O), 71, 83, 90, 94, 97, 101, 159
Arcata, 181, 207
Armstrong, Bishop Robert J., 103
Artesia, 133
Assessment, 52, 53
Associação Portuguesa de Beneficiencia da California, (A.P.P.B.), 25, 26, 109, 137, 139, 142, 160, 177
Associação Protectiva, 25, 26
Associated Milk Producers, 146, 160, 174
Atwater, 71, 174
Avelar, José C., 176
Avila, Arthur V., 125, 183, 201
Avila, Celeste Santos, 71
Avila, João Bettencourt, 174
Azevedo, George A., 217
Azevedo, José Leal (Dr.), 71, 229, 264

Azevedo, Lionel Soares, 125
Azevedo, Manuel G., 175
Azevedo, Miguel Borba, 206
Azevedo, Vicente F., 205
Azores, 1, 2, 4, 6, 10, 12, 13, 14, 15, 19, 20, 21, 24, 61, 64, 77, 130
Azores Mercantile Co., 144

Bakersfield, 202, 216
Band, 50, 76, 90, 112, 257
Bank of America, 159, 165, 174
Bank of Centerville, 160
Bank of Hayward, 160
Bank of Italy, 159
Bank of Novato, 146
Bank of Redwood City, 146
Bank of San Rafael, 146
Baptista, João, 26
Barradas, F.C. (Sr.), 40
Barroca, António, 108, 125
Bay Bridge, 103
Benicia, 60, 143, 161
Bessone, Numidico, 112, 116, 237, 241
Bettencourt, José Sousa (Dr.), 87, 94, 131, 227
Bettencourt, Manuel Jesse (Judge), 117, 120, 122
Bianchi, João de (Dr.), 107
Biblioteca Camões, 255
Bi-lingual Classes, 133
Borges, João, 60, 143
Borman, Louis, 33
Boston, 25
Botelho, Viscount of, (see Gago Medeiros)
Braga, Antone E., 115, 209
Braga, Victorino José, 33
Braga, Victorino T., 27, 33, 42, 161
Brás and Silva Monuments, 115
Brasil, 4, 133
Brava, 5
Brazil, John M., 71, 136
Brée, Álvaro de, 106
Bulcão, N.S., 40
Bullentin, 57, 68

Cabral, João Sérgio Alvares (Dr.), 143, 228
Cabral, Manuel, 115, 139, 197, 209

Cabral, Sacadura, 101
Cabrilho, João Rodrigues, 14, 106,
    128, 166, 234
Cabrilho Monument, 106, 125
Cabrillo Civic Club, 107, 115, 202
Caetano, Juan, 14
Camara, Mário Bettencourt, 68, 76,
    78, 90, 94, 97, 100, 130, 131,
    244, 256, 257 (See Consalves,
    Lucio da Silva)
Canada, 4, 19, 20
Canavarro, A. de Sousa, 15, 16
Cape Verde, 4, 5, 7, 12, 21, 64
Capelinhos, 13, 67, 235
Cardoso, Joseph J., 103, 188
Cardoz, Vincent, 26, 170
Cardozo, M.J., 33
Carnation Corp., 147
Carregadores Açoreanos, 115
Carter, Henry A.P., 15
Casas, J.B. de las, 131
Castilho, António F., 40, 73
Castle Garden, 12
Catholic, 73, 137
Causa Portuguesa Award, 241
Centerville, 36, 44, 90
Cerejeira, Gonçalves (Cardinal), 60,
    103
Challenge Creameries, 199
Chamarrita, 147
Charity Fund, 57, 60
Chicken Lane, 26
Chico, 130, 193
China, 17, 94
Chinese, 14, 15, 17
Chronica (A), 68, 246
Claremont, 218
Class Plans, 52, 53
Clube Recreativo Portugues, 135
Coates, Barrett N., 54
Coelho, João Joaquim, 40
Colónia Portuguesa (A), 71, 182, 183
Columbano, 100
Columbus, Christopher, 1, 14
Convention, 50
Cook, James, 14
Cordon, António Christiano, 25
Correa, Albert, 135, 214
Correia, Francisco E., 26
Correia, Lewis, 214
Corvo, 1, 67

Corvelo, George E., 225
Costa. Edward C., 221
Costa, Euclides Goulart da, 64, 135,
    234
Costa, Francisco Carreiro (Dr.), 136
Costa, Francisco P. Aragão E., 235
Costa, Frank S., 181
Council No. 1 San Leandro, 80, 85,
    100, 131, 136
Coutinho, Gago, 101
Crescent City, 26
Cunha, António F., 26, 87, 160
Cunha, Edward A., 161
Cunha, Firmino J., 63, 76, 137, 143,
    164, 168
Cunha, Manuel F., 26

Dabney, John Pomeroy, 6
Dabney, Samuel, 7
Dairying, 109
Damino, António, 26
Danish Creamery, 199
Darigold Milk Co. Ltd., 179
Daryglen Creameries Ltd., 179, 183
Day of Portugal, 112
Dean, Andrew J., 33, 221
Death Claims, 55
Decoration, 153
Dias, Eduardo Mayone (Dr.), 133
Duarte, Ignácio Costa (Dr.), 87, 90
Duffy, Gordon W., 120
Dutch, 14
Dutra, João, 176, 195
Dutra, José Ignacio, 33
Dutra, William, 13, 27

Ellis Island, 12, 13
Emblem, 42
England, 2, 12
Enos, A.J., 40
Enos, Louis Alfred, 167
Enos, M.M., 144, 163
Eureka, 214
Fagundes, Joseph C., 211
Faial, 1, 5, 6, 7, 8, 10, 13, 15, 57, 61,
    66, 67, 112
Fallon, 36
Fall River, Mass., 21
Faria, J.B. de (Dr.), 130, 131
Faria, José M., 215
Fernandes, Carlos (Dr.), 230

Fernandes, Manuel Francisco (Father), 73, 159, 255
Ferreira, Leanço A., 25, 26, 33, 36
Ferreira, Simão Lopes (Dr.), 94, 97
Ferro, António, 106, 135
Figueiredo, V.L., 94
Fishing, 109, 144
Flemish, 1
Flores, 1, 5, 8, 10, 25
Fonseca, Adelaide D., 90
Fonte, António, 10, 27, 30, 33, 40, 76, 83, 87, 137, 155, 157, 166
Fonte, António (School), 130
Frade, António J., 115
Fraga, Manuel, 94, 166
Freemasons, (see Masons)
Freitas, Francisco A., 190
Freitas, J. Batalha de, 94
Freitas, Joseph A., 56, 85, 115, 116, 128, 136, 181
Freitas, Lucindo, 185
Freitas, Manuel, 40
Freitas, Manuel A., 194
Freitas, Manuel T., 40, 90, 101, 129, 144
Freitas Parkway, 146
French, 1, 93
Fresno, 170
Frizado, Manuel M., 115
Furtado, Joseph A., 115
Furtado, Manuel R., 200, 203

Galli, Joseph (Father), 103
Garcia, Valentim M., 198
Garin, Vasco Vieira (Dr.), 117, 122, 231
Gaspar, Manuel, 183
General Fund, 55
Gerevas, William A., 211
Germany, 15
Gier, William, 212
Giglitto, Mary, 241
Glória, Guilherme Silveira, 40, 71, 73, 131, 135, 229, 244, 255
Glória, John J., 60
Glória, Maria J., 94, 131, 255
Glória, Maria Josefina, 135, 255
Golden Gate Bridge, 104
Godfrey, Arthur, 18
Golden Gate Exposition, 103, 125, 127, 180

Golden Gate Exposition Description 109, 110
Gold Rush, 4, 12
Gomes, Victor, 218
Gonçalves, Arthur, 85
Gonsalves, Joe A. (Assemblyman), 120, 241
Gonsalves, Julia, 131
Gonsalves, Lucio da Silva, (see Camara, Mário B.)
Graciosa, 1
Guard, 44
Gulart, John, 115
Gulbenkian Foundation, 136
Hanford, 60, 165, 191
Hawaii, 4, 7, 14, 17
Hayward, 25, 29, 36, 44, 133, 156
Henriques, Jordão M., 125
Herscher, Joseph, 33
Hillebrand, William, 15
Hollister, 40, 44, 156, 187
Holy Ghost, 147
Home Office, 80
Homen, A.J., 101, 174
Homen, Maria, 103
Honolulu, 9, 15, 16
Honorary Membership, 234
Horta, 1, 6
Hospital, 57, 137
Hospital, Saint Anthony, 58, 163
Hurtere, José De, 1
Hymn, 73

I.D.E.S., 72, 78, 87, 100, 107, 125, 131, 137, 142
Ignacio, Angelo Ramos, 107, 193
Illiteracy, 13, 131
Imparcial (O), 94, 183
Independence Day, 87
Independent Order of Portuguese Patriots, 27
India, 2, 4, 128
Insolvency, 53
Insurance Programs, 54
Irmandade Portuguesa do Estado da California, 30
Italians, 24
Jackson Street, 26, 101
Japanese, 15, 17
Jews, 4, 24
Johnson Act, 13

Johnson, Hiram W., 97
Johnson, Lyndon B., 13
Joint Conventions, 108
Jorge, José C., 103, 129, 133, 139
Jornal Portugues, 71, 107, 115, 183
Juvenile Class, 196

Kalakua, King, 15
Kanaka, 9, 14, 17
Kardoza, Vincent, (see Cardoz,
    Vincent)
Kennedy, John F., 13, 148
King Carlos, 87, 148
King, Mike, 79

Lage, Fausto (Dr.), 135
Lavrador Portugues (O), 183
Lawrence, Helen, 177
Lawrence, José Carlos Jorge, 171
Lazarus, Francis J., 187
League of Portuguese Societies, 107,
    125, 137
Legal Reserve Plans, 54
Leite, Joaquim Rodrigues da S.
    (Dr.), 131
Lemos, Albert, 115, 183
Lemos, Francisco Ignácio de, 40, 73,
    80, 94, 102, 103, 129, 130, 137,
    146, 159, 168, 183, 256

Liberdade (A), 256
Library, 135
Liga Portuguesa-Americana, 128
Liliuokalani, Princess, 16
Linguiça, 17, 147
Linhares, Francisco M., 208
Lino, Samuel M., 206
Lisbon, 2, 94, 95, 102, 116
Literacy Test, 12
Lobo, António Leal da Costa, 238
Lockyer, William (Assemblyman),
    134, 241
London, Jack, 32
Long Beach, 212
Lopes, Joaquim C. (Dr.), 108, 125,
    133
Lopes, Joseph Thomas, 192
Lopez, Thomas F., 124, 139, 184
Los Banos, 146, 195
Louisiana, 12, 15
Lovelock, 64
Lucio, António, 25, 26

Lunas, 16
Luque, John (Captain), 67, 182
Luso-American Education
    Foundation, 112
Luso-American Fraternal Federation,
    128

Macau, 4
Machado, António Pinto, **239**
Machado, John J., **222**
Machado, Steve, 218
Madeira, 4, 12, 15, 17, 21, 24, 142
Madeira, Luiz Julio (Dr.), **232**
Magellan, Ferdinand, 14
Maltester, Jack D., 71, 86, 112, 117,
    241
Mancebo, J., 67
Manha, Andrew, 139
Marce, Jean Batiste Martin, 33
Mariante, Guilherme F., 40
Marques, Anthony, 107, 141
Marshal, 44
Martinho, Henrique R., 25
Martinho, José L., (see Martins,
    Lucio José)
Martins, Anna C., 90, 130
Martins, António Maria, 130, 165
Martins, Henrique Rocha, 25
Martins, Lucindo J., 71, 80
Martins, Lucio José, 33, 40, **242**
Masons, 40, 73, 157, 184
Massa, Edward C., 85, 117, 207, **241**
Mathias, Mary, 219
Mattos, António R., 94, 108, 125
Mattos, John Garcia de (Jr.), 40, 80,
    83, 90, 93, 94, 101, 130, 137,
    143, 158, 168
Maui, 9
McClure, Wesley, **241**
Medeiros, Manuel C., 79, **257**
Medical Examiners, 220
Medeiros, José H. Gago Da Camara,
    115
Medina, Manuel Oliveira, 144
Meireles, D. António, 135
Mello, Angelo Ignacio de, 33
Medeiros, Manuel R., **224**
Mendes, Aristides do Sousa, 72
Mendocino, 44
Mendonça, Adelaide, 131
Mendonça, J.B., 83, 144

Mendonça, J.P., 94
Mendonça, José Pereira, 167
Mendonça, Manuel E., 115, 204
Mendonsa, Francisco, Santos, 200
Menezes, Joaquim B., 71, 128, 130,
169, 256
Mercantile Trust Co., 144, 146
Merced, 164, 174, 183, 202, 218
Merced Bank, 174
Mergers, 137
Mitchell, Frank (Jr.), 123, 180
Mitchell, M., 44
Mitty, John J., (Rev.), 107
Modesto, 176, 294, 211, 215, 218
Monjardino, Alvaro, 136
Monterey, 36, 106, 206
Montreal, P.Q., 19
Monument-Portuguese Immigrant,
112, 182, 237
Moors, 1
Morton, Henry R., 25, 26
Moura, Alberto, 103, 131, 183
Mozambique, 2
Musso, John, 234

Nevada, 36
Neves, António P., 217
Neves, Manuel, 117, 197, 209
New Bedford, 6, 7, 8, 9, 21
Newman, 146
New York, 12, 115
New York World's Fair, 106
Nogueira, António Duarte (Dr.), 238
Noia, António Francisco, 29
Novato, 144
Nunes, John F., 142, 204
Nunes, Manuel, 18

Oakland, 17, 31, 44, 57, 156, 174,
177, 185, 192, 194, 196, 201
Ohio, 63
Oliver, Lawrence, 144, 241
Ontario (Canada), 19
Orchard Avenue, 17
Ordem Independente Patriotas
Portugueses, 27

Panama, 12, 109
Panama-Pacific Exposition, 93, 147,
257
Password, 44

Pátria, A, 168, 228
Patriotism, 101
Peary, Hal, 117
Peixoto, Joaquim, 25
Peixoto, Manuel, 25
Pereira, Guilherme F., 94
Pereira, Guilherme Francisco, 173
Pereira, Ilidio, 225
Pereira, João, 61, 170, 192
Pereira, José Vargas, 87, 170
Pereira, Manuel, 139, 199
Pereira, Mary I., 224
Perry, Jason, 15
Perry, Manuel John, 170, 192
Perry, Tillie, 120
Petaluma, 36, 44, 156, 171
Pico, 1
Pimentel, António de Freitas (Dr.),
229
Pimentel, Francisco, 25, 36, 40
Pimentel, George, 117
Pimentel, J.J., 71, 173
Pimentel, John V., 142
Pimentel, José, 25, 29, 33, 40, 42, 61,
157
Pimentel, Mae S., 108, 125
Pimentel, Maria F.P.D. (Dra.), 235,
236
Pine, Frank E., 103
Pinheiro, António José, 162, 186
Pleasanton, 44, 158
Portuguese-American Bank, 57, 90,
94, 129, 144, 146, 163
Portuguese-American Civic Club, 107
Portuguese-American Creamery, 206
Portuguese Chamber of Commerce,
129
Portuguese Day, 107, 125, 180
Portuguese Discoveries, 248, 250
Portuguese Immigrant Week, 120, 237
Portuguese Language, 128, 130, 131
Portuguese Pavilion, 101
Portuguese Red Cross, 63, 64
Portuguese Restaurants, 144
Portuguese School, 131
Priests, 68
Prince Henry, 112
Progresso Californiense, 36, 68, 73

Quaresma, Manuel B., 71, 256
Quebec, 19

Quota, 13

R.A.B.A.M.I., 94, 142
Radio, 71, 125
Railroads, 19, 20, 97
Ralph, James (Jr.), 97
Raulino, António, 179
Reagan, Ronald (Governor), 120, 134
Reis, Manuel, 125
Reporter (O), 83
Reserve Fund, 55
Ribeiro, Candido (Rev.), 97
Rio de Janeiro, 101
Ritual, 40, 42
Roberts, Josephine, 86
Roderick, Frank, 103, 139, 185
Rodrigues, Leopoldina C., (See
    Alves)
Rogers, António, 10, 80, 165, 252
Rogers, Francis M., 136
Rogers, Maria A.C., 112, 115
Romans, 1
Root Park, 114, 120, 122
Rosa, Francisco H., 191
Rosa, Joe C., 226
Rosa, Joe P., 226
Rosa, Manuel G., 144
Rosa, Manuel Martins, 29
Russian, 5, 9

Sacramento, 71, 158, 168, 178, 192,
    197, 202, 205, 208, 210
Saint Anthony, 101
Saint Joseph's Church, 90, 255
Saint Joseph's Hall, 30
Saint Mark, 1
Saint Thomas, 7
Salinas, 167
San Diego, 7, 36, 106, 144, 200, 209,
    220
San Domingo, 7
Sandwich, Earl of, 14
San Francisco, 10, 26, 36, 66, 73, 87,
    158
San Gabriel, 87
San Joaquin Valley, 21
San Jorge, 1, 67, 128
San Jose, 57, 112, 162, 182, 198, 199,
    205, 217

San Leandro, 10, 17, 25, 30, 31, 44,
    54, 73, 122, 133, 156, 160,
    187, 191, 210, 215, 220
San Leandro City Library, 135
San Leandro Municipal Band, 79, 257
San Lorenzo, 29, 123
San Luis Obispo, 164, 181
San Miguel, 1, 15, 16, 17, 19, 61, 64,
    142
San Rafael, 46, 144, 166
Santa Cruz, 161, 175, 190
Santa Maria (Azores), 1
Santa Maria (California), 173, 182,
    184, 188, 212
Santa Rosa, 57
Santos, Adelino, 223
Sarmento, António Augusto, 168
Satan, 73
Sausalito, 46
Savings and Loan Association, 143
Scholarships, 134
Scotch, 15, 16
Sephardin, 5
Sena, Jorge de, 133
Serrão, Joaquim (Rev.), 40, 73
S.E.S. 109, 125, 137
Sicily, 61
Sick Benefit Fund, 56
Silva, Anthony J., 103, 188
Silva, Dinis A. Pimentel da, 239
Silva, Joe (Jr.), 213
Silva, John, 115
Silva, Louis A., 115
Silva, Manuel B., 120, 210
Silva, Manuel Pedro Ribeiro da (Dr.),
    86
Silveira, Alberto C., 201
Silveira, Fernando (Fred) A., 196
Silveira, Francisco Monteiro, 178
Silveira, Joaquim A., 94, 97, 129, 144
    146, 164, 229
Silveira, Joe, 25
Silveira, José Chrysostomo da, 177
Silveira, Pedro L.C., 159
Simas, António, 139
Simas, John B., 202
Simas, Manuel Furtado, 216
Simas, Mary, 109
Sister City, 238, 239
Smith, José, 40
Smith's Hall, 27

Soares, Manuel S., 102, 107, 125, 179
Sociedade União Nacional, (see
    U.N.L.I.S.)
Soito, José, 25
Sonora, 174
Sousa, Alfredo M. de (Rev.), 107
Sousa, Arthur S., 195
Sousa, Helio T., 221
Sousa, Carlos, 71
Sousa, John Phillip, 77, 257
Souza, Arnaldo C.R., 125
Spain, 14, 31, 87
Spanish, 1, 14
Spreckels, 17
S.P.R.S.I., 60, 103, 107, 125, 137,
    139, 165, 200, 209, 214
Stanley, Tames, 33
State Assembly, 159
Stichini, Ilda, 109
Stockton, 166, 177, 185, 213
Stone, Manuel, 17, 68, 168
Supreme President's (Biographies),
    155-219
Sweet Potato Growers Association,
    169, 173

Taro Root, 15
Tavares, João Francisco (Father), 159,
    256
Teixeira, António C., 72
Teixeira, George L., 223
Telles, José Maria, 30, 33
Terceira, 1, 61, 64, 67, 135
Terra Linda, 146
Themido, Hall, 136
Timor, 17
Toronto, Ontario, 19
Toza, Alfonso José, 25
Tracy, 203
Treasure Island, 103, 109
Trigueiros, Manuel F.M., 17, 68, 128
Trindade, Hubert J., 222
Trinidad, 7
Tulare, 199
Turlock, 102, 179, 194, 207

Ukelele, 17
União Portuguesa, 17, 57, 68, 128
Uniform Rank, 76
U.N.L.I.S., 128, 142, 164
U.P.C.E.C., 107, 125, 139
U.P.E.C. Bank, 143
U.P.E.C. Cultural Center, 135
U.P.E.C. Day, 123
U.P.P.E.C., 100, 107, 125

Valim, John Cunha, 94, 97, 108
    125, 128, 130, 131
Valladão, João, 163
Vallejo, 171, 189
Vancouver, 20
Vargas, António, 33
Vasco da Gama, 87
Vasconcelos, J. Mota, 112, 119
Vermont Marble Co., 115
Vicente, António Maria, 68
Victorino, António, 33
Vieira, Francisco Rodrigues, 30
Vieira, João, 25, 163
Vieira, John G., 220
Vieira, Louis Leslie, 201
Visalia, 180
Viscount of Alte, 90, 101
Voz de Portugal, 71, 115
Voz Portuguesa, 68

Warm Springs, 29
Warren, Earl, (Chief Justice), 148
Watsonville, 40, 157, 168, 172
Wells Fargo Bank, 85
Western Islands (see Azores)
Whale, 6, 7, 10
Williams, Francisco, 25, 26
Wilson, Anthony, 172
Wilson, Woodrow, 12, 64
Women, 56
Woods, Jesse Henry, 165, 229

Xavier, Tony, 216